W9-AQK-078

Children's Literature Review

volume 1

Children's Literature Review

Excerpts from Reviews, Criticism, and Commentary on Books for Children and Young People

Ann Block
Carolyn Riley
Editors

Gale Research Company
Book Tower
Detroit, Michigan 48226

Ann Block and Carolyn Riley, *Editors*
Phyllis Carmel Mendelson, *Managing Editor*
Susan Johnson and Gerard J. Senick, *Assistant Editors*
Karen M. Hilker, *Editorial Assistant*
Bernadette Meier, *Research Assistant*

Elizabeth Cheslock, *Permissions Manager*
L.E. Wisniewski, *Permissions Assistant*

Arthur Chartow, *Cover Design*

Library of Congress Catalog Card Number 75-34953
ISBN 0-8103-0077-X

Preface

As publishers of the established reference series *Something about the Author, Contemporary Authors, Contemporary Literary Criticism,* and *Book Review Index*—all reference tools for schools and libraries—we recognize a need for a digest of comment concerning children's literature. Accordingly, we would like to offer a new reference series, entitled *Children's Literature Review,* in which excerpts of recent reviews of both fiction and nonfiction for children and young people are arranged in a useful collection for teachers, librarians, and researchers in this field.

Children's Literature Review presents significant passages from current published criticism of both contemporary and older works for children. Most of the content of *CLR* is devoted to reviews and criticism of the works of today's authors. Current criticism of the works of authors of an earlier period is excerpted for *CLR*, however, if it is directed to a contemporary audience.

Therefore, no arbitrary time limits are applied to the selection of authors for *CLR*. Rather, the criterion for selection of materials is, "Will today's student, teacher, or critic find this pertinent to today's needs?"

As serious students of children's literature know, the very nature of criticism in this field is now being debated widely and fervently. As a result, the criticism of children's literature is itself an emerging discipline. One of the most valuable aspects of the new series is that, by bringing together *all kinds* of critical approaches, *CLR* enables students to evaluate the debate itself.

Each semiannual volume of *CLR* will present criticism of about forty authors and will include excerpts from more than forty-five books and various issues of about thirty-five periodicals. Each excerpt is fully identified for the convenience of readers who may wish to consult the entire chapter, article, or review excerpted.

A short paragraph preceding each author-listing identifies the author by nationality, principal genre, and, where appropriate, major awards received. Also in this section, cross-references are made to *Contemporary Authors* and *Something about the Author*—two of Gale's established bio-bibliographical reference series.

Children's Literature Review listings consist of three parts: general commentary, which deals with whole canons or major themes; excerpts pertaining to individual titles, arranged chronologically under those titles; and locator or index citations for material which, although not excerpted for *CLR*, might be of interest to students or researchers.

Three cumulative indexes will appear in each volume of *Children's Literature Review*. In addition to the author and critic indexes familiar to users of *Contemporary Literary Criticism, CLR* will include a title index listing in alphabetical order all works used in the text as subheadings for critical excerpts concerning those particular titles.

CLR Is An On-Going Series

Since *Children's Literature Review* is to be a multi-volume work of indefinite but considerable size, neither this volume nor any *one* subsequent volume should be judged apart from the concept that a single volume is but a part of a larger and more comprehensive whole. Readers may wonder, for instance, why Lewis Carroll and Elizabeth Coatsworth were omitted. Both of these important writers and many others—Herbert Zim, John Rowe Townsend, and Laura Ingalls Wilder—will be included in volume 2; Edward Ardizzone, David Macauley, E. Nesbit, and Isaac Asimov are scheduled for volume 3, and so on.

If readers wish to suggest authors they would like to have covered in coming volumes, or if they have other suggestions or comments, they are cordially invited to write the editor.

A

AIKEN, Joan 1924-

Daughter of the American poet Conrad Aiken, Englishwoman Joan Aiken writes short stories and thrillers for both adults and children. She won the 1969 Guardian Award for Children's Fiction for *The Whispering Mountain* and the 1971 Edgar Allan Poe Award for *Night Fall*. (See also *Contemporary Authors*, Vols. 9-12, rev. ed., and *Something About the Author*, Vol. 2.)

GENERAL COMMENTARY

Joan Aiken's books *The Wolves of Willoughby Chase* (1963), *Black Hearts in Battersea* (1964), and *Nightbirds on Nantucket* (1966) are exciting or funny—depending on whether a child or adult is reading them. They are takeoffs on nineteenth century melodrama, consistent in every detail. Events move with great speed, people are either very good or very wicked . . . and the storytelling is so matter of fact that even such preposterous sights as the pink whale of the third book seem, for the moment, real.

Ruth Hill Viguers, in A Critical History of Children's Literature, *revised edition, by Cornelia Meigs, Anne Thaxter Eaton, Elizabeth Nesbitt, and Ruth Hill Viguers, edited by Cornelia Meigs (copyright © 1969 by The Macmillan Co.), Macmillan, 1969, p. 473.*

Miss Aiken has . . . several Dickensian qualities. . . . Like Dickens, she loves to work with a crowded canvas and can always find room for more figures, more detail, more action. Like him, she can evoke the physical presence of places and people; like his, though on a slighter scale, her more successful characters can be basically 'flat' and yet memorable, vivid, larger than life. And where she has the time or inclination to use more than her few quick strokes she can produce portraits of impressive power.

John Rowe Townsend, in his A Sense of Story: Essays on Contemporary Writers for Children *(copyright © 1971 by John Rowe Townsend; reprinted by permission of J. B. Lippincott Company), Lippincott, 1971, p. 20.*

Aiken's *The Wolves of Willoughby Chase* tells a Gothic tale that drips with Victorian sentimentality and drama. In *Nightbirds on Nantucket* and *Black Hearts in Battersea* she displays a Dickensian relish for names that indicate character, and a sense of the ludicrous that results in such situations as a pink whale obligingly towing a trans-Atlantic cannon. *Smoke from Cromwell's Time and Other Stories* is a good collection of short stories on fanciful themes, and *The Whispering Mountain* is a broad burlesque of the fanciful adventure story.

May Hill Arbuthnot and Zena Sutherland, in their Children and Books, *4th edition (copyright © 1947, 1957, 1964, 1972 by Scott, Foresman and Co.), Scott, Foresman, 1972, p. 246.*

Unlike [Leon] Garfield [Joan Aiken] writes a direct, forceful prose with which she bulldozes the reader into acquiescence in her improbabilities.

For reasons which cannot readily be understood Miss Aiken has chosen to write about a might-have-been past. It is the Nineteenth Century and the reign of King James III. The Stuarts do not reign undisturbed: a ruthless underground movement favours the Hanoverian cause and works for the restoration of the Young Pretender Prince George. The Industrial Revolution has passed England by and the country is mostly rural and feudal. Wolves roam the woods and even come into London in hard winters. Neo-Jacobean England is more dangerous and less dull than the reality of history.

Miss Aiken moves in higher social circles than Garfield; one of her most important and genial characters is the Duke of Battersea. . . . There is a gay informality about the Batterseas which contrasts with the dour sobriety of the Hanoverians. . . . But the stories are not all of high life. Simon, the hero of *The Wolves of Willoughby Chase* (1964) and *Black Hearts in Battersea* (1965), may turn out to be the missing heir, but mostly he is the poor honest boy who makes good, while almost the most memorable and endearing of the characters is Dido, a dirty infant of the Bankside slums, as lacking in principles as in personal hygiene, whose courage is beyond all question. Miss Aiken has a keen ear for dialogue. She catches Dido's forthright cockney neatly. . . .

Gratitude for Joan Aiken's high spirits and the gusto of her story-telling may make the reader value her rather beyond her worth. These are precious qualities, but they are not enough. What Miss Aiken lacks most grievously is self-discipline. Her stories gallop recklessly in all directions at once with never a touch of rein from the author. Grand yarns, they are too casual, even perhaps too full of self-mockery to be taken entirely seriously.

Marcus Crouch, in his The Nesbit Tradition: The Children's Novel in England 1945-1970 *(© Marcus Crouch 1972), Ernest Benn, 1972, p. 39.*

ARABEL'S RAVEN (1974)

[*Arabel's Raven* is a] deliberately farfetched uproar about the consequences of Mortimer the raven's coming home one night with the taxi-driving father of little Arabel Jones. . . . There is enough clutching for hilarity here that some of this is bound to be funny, but the family's indulgence of the tiresome bird is hard to credit and their distraction is too often just mechanically madcap.

Kirkus Reviews *(copyright © 1974 The Kirkus Service, Inc.), May 1, 1974, p. 478.*

No one but the author of *The Wolves of Willoughby Chase* could create such a mélange of inventions, sustain such a pace, and give such vigor to the telling [of *Arabel's Raven*]. . . . Throughout the book, the nonsense rolls on with undiminished hilarity.

Virginia Haviland, in The Horn Book Magazine *(copyright © 1974 by The Horn Book, Inc., Boston), June, 1974, p. 278.*

A situation comedy with high potential is weakened by overextension: despite the flair with which Joan Aiken handles caricature and word play, there is so much of both [in *Arabel's Raven*] as to slow the action. Some of the humor will be less evident to American than to British children, but for all children there are oblique references that may not be perceived, primarily those malapropisms in dialogue that have latent content. The story line isn't continuous, but there's plenty of incidental action. . . . The characterization is broadly comic, the dialogue pithy and colloquial, but both seem overdone.

Zena Sutherland, in Bulletin of the Center for Children's Books *(© 1974 by the University of Chicago; all rights reserved), September, 1974, p. 1.*

ARMITAGE, ARMITAGE, FLY AWAY HOME (1968)

If an inventive author jotted ideas (for eccentrics, spirits and sorcerers, settings, situations) on index cards and dealt them out indiscriminately into ten piles, the result might resemble *Armitage:* only the presence of Harriet and Mark and their parents ties the stories together and only the expectation of the unexpected binds them internally. . . . There's no point, no consecutive plot, no conclusion. [*Armitage, Armitage, Fly Away Home* is a] shaggy ghost story.

Kirkus Service *(copyright © 1968 The Kirkus Service, Inc.), June 1, 1968, p. 603.*

Each chapter [in *Armitage, Armitage, Fly Away Home*] stands as a complete short story and each satirizes the elements of the various fantasy forms from Greek myth to sci-fi. This in no way reduces the ability of the ever so Britishly unflappable Armitage menage to amuse children who have avoided reading fantasy—the author's comic sense is that sure.

Lillian N. Gerhardt, in School Library Journal *(reprinted from the September, 1968, issue of* School Library Journal, *published by R. R. Bowker Co., a Xerox company; copyright © 1968 by Xerox Corporation), September, 1968, p. 130.*

Although [*Armitage, Armitage, Fly Away Home*] lacks the sustained interest of [Joan Aiken's] previous books, since it is distinctly episodic, the story has the same felicitous combination of humor, fantasy, and a breezy acceptance of the ridiculous.

Zena Sutherland, in Bulletin of the Center for Children's Books, *(copyright 1968 by the University of Chicago; all rights reserved), September, 1968, p. 1.*

The episodes [in *Armitage, Armitage, Fly Away Home*] are only vaguely connected. . . . All sorts of bizarre characters flit in and out of the stories. . . . The book lacks the continuity and the skillful plot structure of the author's earlier ones; but the fantastic, high-spirited concoction, well seasoned with humor, is written with unmistakable conviction.

Ethel L. Heins, in The Horn Book Magazine *(copyright © 1968 by The Horn Book, Inc., Boston), October, 1968, pp. 558-59.*

BLACK HEARTS IN BATTERSEA (1964)

[In *Black Hearts in Battersea*] Miss Aiken's villains do nothing halfway. They deprive one character of his dukedom and cheerfully plan to blow up everyone in a castle in order to prevent the discovery of their villainy.

The author manages to keep us laughing at the incredibly overdrawn characters and situations while she holds us in suspense over the outcome. [This is a] wild yarn, not to be put down once it is started, sure to give enjoyment to those over 11, as well as some younger.

Margaret Sherwood Libby, in Book Week *(©* The Washington Post*), November 22, 1964, p. 20.*

Simon, the orphan from Gloober's Poor Farm who rescued the two little girls in *The Wolves of Willoughby Chase*, is the hero of [*Black Hearts in Battersea,*] an entrancing sequel which takes place near the beginning of the nineteenth century. . . . One wonderfully extravagant adventure follows another in this fast-paced tale of intrigue and mystery which abounds with colorful, often deliciously overdrawn characters and with humor.

The Booklist and Subscription Books Bulletin *(© 1965 by the American Library Association), January 1, 1965, p. 432.*

***THE CUCKOO TREE* (1971)**

Joan Aiken [is] acknowledged mistress of the impossible-probable. Take as your first premise that the Hanoverian accession never happened and the course of English history continues superbly the same yet different. . . . *The Cuckoo Tree* is a sequel to *Night Birds on Nantucket*, bringing Dido back from America to involvement with the "Gentlemen" and some other very havey-cavey goings-on in darkest Sussex. Less serious than Miss Aiken's last, powerful novel, *The Whispering Mountain*, it is nevertheless a matter of heart as well as hilarity as the heroine labours with dogged practicality to set things to rights.

The Times Literary Supplement *(© Times Newspapers Ltd., 1971), July 2, 1971, p. 774.*

Fortunately, much of this story is the mixture as before, rollicking, superbly witty entertainment, full of surprises and reversals, with the reappearance of old friends like that sensible young Cockney Dido Twite with her inimitable turn of dialect, and (too late in the tale for their admirers) Owen Hughes and Simon, now Duke of Battersea. The sheer inventiveness is a delight. . . . There are new departures in the extra-sensory link between the triplets, and the spinechilling evil of the wizened Tante Sannie, with her voodoo magic from the West Indies, and her filthy traditional English ally, in another category from the comic villainy of earlier books. There is a deepening of the fantasy, without loss of humour, which is even more satisfying.

The Junior Bookshelf, *August, 1971, p. 229.*

The Cuckoo Tree has all the robust, self-assured vigour of the earlier volumes of [Dido Twite's] adventures [*Black Hearts in Battersea* and *The Whispering Mountain*] and it proceeds (as its own Dr. Subito might put it) accelerando to a presto prestissimo conclusion. . . . Joan Aiken's prodigal invention as a creator of characters, her now entirely acceptable vocabulary of roguery, her feeling for the outrageously comic are held in balance through most of the book and only in the climax at St. Paul's does the pace of events lead to a slightly disturbing raucousness of tone. And in the concluding chapter the loose-ends of the story are tied up with a dexterity whose swiftness is almost too precipitate.

The illustrations by Pat Marriott once again add measurably to the total effect of Joan Aiken's style. While events and verbal exchanges may proceed at a cracking pace, these beautifully-executed pen-drawings do much to reinforce the sense of mystery and romance that is also a vital feature of the book. The moonlight plotting of Fitz-Pickwick, Mr. Twite playing his hoboy on a tombstone are masterly examples of the illustrator's art and one regrets only that some of the full-page drawings are not as carefully placed in the text as they might have been.

Brian W. Alderson, in Children's Book Review *(© 1971 by Five Owls Press Ltd.), October, 1971, p. 159.*

This tale of hugger-mugger and "havey-cavey" is such a crazy-quilt of history, ordinary British and cockney humor, that one is fair exhausted by the final pages. . . .

No elementary-school student (and few Young Adults) will wade through such dialogue as: "I like puppetries but I jalouse they arena whit I'd wish tae watch the nicht afore I crownit."

Croopus! How much of this noob-shotten wilderness is there atween hie and Turpentine Sunday?

Mrs. John G. Gray, in Best Sellers *(copyright 1971, by the University of Scranton), November 15, 1971, p. 386.*

[*The Cuckoo Tree* is the] fourth in a unique line of fantasized history books that began with *The Wolves of Willoughby Chase*. . . . Dido Twite is back—in command of a series of outrageous circumstances which surround a Hanoverian plot to roll St. Paul's Cathedral into the Thames during the coronation of the new King, Richard IV. . . . A fantastic number of characters and twists of plot keep the story running at breakneck speed, with Dido always in sight and resourceful. [Joan Aiken] brings off the all-but-impossible.

Virginia Haviland, in The Horn Book Magazine *(copyright © 1971 by The Horn Book, Inc., Boston), December, 1971, p. 609.*

The precocious Dido Twite of *Nightbirds on Nantucket* reappears as the doughty heroine of an adventure story overpopulated with bizarre and villainous characters and improbably enlivened by the reunion of a long-separated pair of twins. . . . Nonsensical lampooning of period adventure stories is Aiken's forte, but in [*The Cuckoo Tree*] the plethora of characters and plots and coincidence and period palaver and thieves' cant get out of hand. Too bad, because there are some moments of high comedy.

Zena Sutherland, in Bulletin of the Center for Children's Books *(© 1972 by the University of Chicago; all rights reserved), February, 1972, p. 85.*

[*The Cuckoo Tree* is] another delightfully preposterous historical fantasy [by Joan Aiken]. . . . For readers who can surmount the heavy but colorful dialect this is a highly entertaining story with a large cast of fascinating characters, extravagant adventure, and rapid-fire action.

The Booklist *(© by the American Library Association), February 1, 1972, p. 465.*

OTHER CITATIONS

Publishers' Weekly, *October 18, 1971, p. 50.*

***DIED ON A RAINY SUNDAY* (1972)**

The ambience [in *Died on a Rainy Sunday*] is one of proper British horror, but younger readers may find it hard to empathize with Jane's maternal guilt over leaving her children to go back to work (and her resultant passivity) and seasoned mystery fans will know that it would have been good husbandry to send Myfanwy packing the day she broke the Spode teapot.

Kirkus Reviews *(copyright © 1972 The Kirkus Service, Inc.), February 15, 1972, p. 201.*

Joan Aiken's triumph [in creating suspense stories] is simply that she does it so much better than most other practitioners. In [*Died on a Rainy Sunday*], there is the added attraction of an intelligent, self-questioning heroine, rather than the ninny so often encountered in Modern Gothic.

Don't get the impression that the book is more than it claims to be: it lacks the scope and intricacy of the author's historical fantasies, such as "The Cuckoo Tree." This time round, Miss Aiken has given us a simon-pure chiller, delicious to the end.

Georgess McHargue, in The New York Times Book Review *(© 1972 by The New York Times Company; reprinted by permission), July 23, 1972, p. 8.*

The story [*Died on a Rainy Sunday*] builds with mounting suspense through increasingly ominous incidents, culminating in murder and fraught with danger to Jane and her child. Constructed adroitly and written with skill, this is a taut and convincing mystery story.

Zena Sutherland, in Bulletin of the Center for Children's Books *(© 1973 by the University of Chicago; all rights reserved), April, 1973, p. 117.*

THE GREEN FLASH AND OTHER TALES OF HORROR, SUSPENSE, AND FANTASY (1972)

In the fourteen stories chosen for [*The Green Flash and Other Tales of Horror, Suspense, and Fantasy*, Joan Aiken] combines the luxuriance of invention found in her freewheeling, full-length extravaganzas with the restrained, focused art of the short story. . . . The title story is a tour de force, its last sentence ending the book like a sudden crack of lightning. Although the stories were produced over a twenty-five-year period, the writing is amazingly consistent—almost Saki-like in its clarity and preciseness of image. . . . Brief but crucial sketches provide flashes of insight into a great variety of characterizations. . . .

Ethel L. Heins, in The Horn Book Magazine *(copyright © 1972 by The Horn Book, Inc., Boston), February, 1972, pp. 54-5.*

THE KINGDOM AND THE CAVE (1974)

If Joan Aiken chooses to indulge in a Hobbity/Prydainy pastiche one might expect her to have something more than imitation in mind. But though the route from kingdom to cave and back again must be judged a comic success, Aiken hardly extends—and only now and again hints at parody of—the familiar themes and cast. . . . Whether one takes [the kingdom of] Astalon at face value or reads [*The Kingdom and the Cave*] for the witty asides that are buried here and there . . ., this is an enjoyable if not ground-breaking expedition.

Kirkus Reviews *(copyright © 1974 The Kirkus Service, Inc.), February 1, 1974, p. 108.*

[*The Kingdom and the Cave*] is full of the delightful improbabilities and impossibilities one has come to expect from [Joan Aiken]. . . . [The] anthropomorphism of the animal characters is refreshingly original. . . . The swiftly moving story-telling style is laced with humorous turns and puns; and the author's skill in the use of onomatopoeia rises to absolute genius in characterizing a flock of rooks: "'We'll find her okay,' said the leader . . . and the others echoed, 'Okay, okay, okay,' rising about Michael until the air was full of cawing and flapping."

Paul Heins, in The Horn Book Magazine *(copyright © 1974 by The Horn Book, Inc., Boston), April, 1974, pp. 146-47.*

Things began going wrong at the Royal Palace of Astalon, and in this fast-paced, entertaining fantasy-adventure Mickle the court cat and crown prince Michael race against time to set them right. . . . A herbal concoction that induces invisibility, a magic wand, and Michael's ability to speak with animals provide neat twists in the hero's fortunes and continuously recharge the story.

The Booklist *(© American Library Association 1974), April 1, 1974, pp. 871-72.*

OTHER CITATIONS

Publishers' Weekly, *March 4, 1974, p. 75.*

MIDNIGHT IS A PLACE (1974)

The story of [Lucas' and Anna-Marie's] struggle to survive in a hostile town presents a horrifying but realistic picture of the fate of destitute orphans during an era when child labor was exploited to the fullest. There is an abundance of action, suspense and melodrama in this long and complicated story, and although the ending is suspiciously like a fairy tale, the atmosphere is skillfully maintained and there is never a dull moment.

Sarah Law Kennerly, in School Library Journal *(reprinted from the May, 1974, issue of* School Library Journal, *published by R. R. Bowker Co., a Xerox company; copyright © 1974 by Xerox Corporation), May, 1974, p. 68.*

[In *Midnight Is a Place*] Joan Aiken follows all the conventions of Dickensian fiction with just a little extra to satisfy jaded contemporary tastes. . . . It must be admitted that Ms. Aiken's staging of the human comedy . . . owes a lot to her literary predecessors and, perhaps, more to the modern reader's need to approach innocence with tongue in cheek. But it works beautifully on more than one level, and Midnight Court earns its place in the landscape of humorous fiction.

Kirkus Reviews *(copyright © 1974 The Kirkus Service, Inc.), May 1, 1974, p. 488.*

Aiken's literary forebear here is Dickens, and she does a good job with him. [*Midnight Is a Place*] is consistent and convincing. The scenes in the carpet factory are horrifying but ring vividly of truth. The finding of family and fortune at the end ring truer than they might, and I won't give away the mystery, save to say that music and kindness and coziness are involved.

Marian Engel, in The New York Times Book Review *(© 1974 by The New York Times Company; reprinted by permission), May 5, 1974, p. 18.*

The air of brooding mystery that hangs over the opening of

Miss Aiken's [*Midnight Is a Place*] pervades much of its sinuous progress. As with most of her more ambitious stories, the plots and counter-plots are impossible to summarise and the cheerfulness with which she piles up bizarre event upon bizarre event makes her one of the most exhilerating of our contemporary children's authors. Who else could give us so credible a carpet factory while patently disregarding any need for it to resemble a real carpet factory? Who else could persuade us so completely that the major hazard for the muckrakers in Blastburn's sewage system is a hoard of wild hogs?

At every point in the novel where details of event and character are paramount, Miss Aiken is triumphant and for a good half of the book one gets the feeling that this is going to be the major work that has so far eluded her. Once again though—as with *The Whispering Mountain* and *The Cuckoo Tree*—she cannot drive her ramshackle story to a persuasive conclusion and it finally rocks to a shaky halt with, on the one hand, a wholly unnecessary venture into melodrama and, on the other, an all-too-hasty tying up of loose ends. If only she had had the courage to make her long book even longer so that its ramifying plots could have had more room to work themselves out naturally, or if only she had had the self-discipline to tighten the structure of the whole thing (at cost certainly of some of the baroque ornamentation) then the reader might have found a novel whose parts added up to a most impressive work.

Brian W. Alderson, in Children's Book Review *(© 1974 Five Owls Press Ltd.), Summer, 1974, pp. 60-1.*

Joan Aiken returns here to the town of Blastburn, so vividly sketched by night in *The Wolves of Willoughby Chase*. [*Midnight is a Place*] shows the distance she has come since that delightfully fantastic melodrama. Though the comic grotesque of the James III novels has a brief fling in the larger-than-life villainy of Sir Randolph Grimsby . . . and his minions, for the most part the fantasy is grim and terrifying, and used in the service of a novel type of historical fiction. Instead of writing fictionalised biography, or recreating a period with only brief appearances of genuine historical figures, Joan Aiken has distilled the essence of the Industrial Revolution, factories, foundries, mills, collieries and more, into a single locality, which in its streets epitomises nineteenth-century city slums. Woven into the romantic adventures of the children . . . are authentic details of workers' lives in places like Murgatroyd's Carpet Manufactory: the terrible machinery accidents, the short expectation of life, unforgettably symbolised by the little procession from factory gate to cemetery. . . . As an imaginative re-creation of the horrors of child-exploitation, the book is most successful, yet, at the same time, the many threads are audaciously entwined with the familiar Aiken gusto into an absorbing, unified entertainment.

The Junior Bookshelf, *August, 1974, p. 218.*

With her customary vivacity and inventiveness, [Joan Aiken] has created another novel steeped in nineteenth-century literary traditions and devices. The lugubrious and ramshackle mansion, the filthy town with its carpet factory employing exploited workers and child labor, the labyrinthine sewer under the North Sea community suggest similar *mise en scènes* in the Brontës, Mrs. Gaskell, Dickens, and Victor Hugo; but the melodrama, which manages to avoid even a hint of sentimentality, never flags as it goes from incident to incident and reaches a happy ending. . . . [In *Midnight Is a Place*] the power of the narrative and the variety of grotesque and humorous characters . . . carry the reader along.

Paul Heins, in The Horn Book Magazine *(copyright © 1974 by The Horn Book, Inc., Boston), August, 1974, p. 383.*

While the basic plot [of *Midnight Is a Place*] is patterned, Aiken weaves about it a marvelously intricate and convincing story that has both the romance and an awareness of a need for social reform that are Dickensian. Her style, however, is her own, rich and distinctive, and the story of the struggles of Lucas and Anna-Marie after a fire razes Midnight Court and they are forced to work in the factories and sewers of the town enables her to bring in some marvelously villainous characters and to use the period argot she handles so deftly.

Zena Sutherland, in Bulletin of the Center for Children's Books *(© 1974 by the University of Chicago; all rights reserved), July-August, 1974, p. 169.*

OTHER CITATIONS

Publishers' Weekly, *March 4, 1974, p. 74.*

The Booklist, *May 15, 1974, pp. 1034-35.*

THE MOONCUSSER'S DAUGHTER (1974)

This rich, spoofy, pseudo-sinister farce is what Joan Aiken must have been practicing for with *Winterthing*. What happens is a sort of Tempest-in-a-lighthouse, the keeper being an insistently repentant former ship-wrecker who also keeps a monster named Caliban (victim of the *Miranda* wreck) trapped in a bottle in the cave below. . . . [The characters] all connect and interact with choreographed precision through an increasingly tangled web of desperation and ludicrous deceit—and all to the tune of . . . burlesquing songs. . . . [*The Mooncusser's Daughter*] might well be such stuff as grand performances are made on.

Kirkus Reviews *(copyright © 1974 The Kirkus Service, Inc.), January 1, 1974, p. 10.*

[With *The Mooncusser's Daughter*, Joan Aiken] has created a play with music which touches on themes of initiation, death, repentance, and forgiveness. Set in a lighthouse, the story centers around the hunt for a book "which holds all answers" and which is guarded by a sea monster. Staging is extremely flexible, giving the director much leeway in the areas of special effect lighting and make-up. Because of the complex themes and character personalities, this play will be of most use in upper elementary school collections.

Jill S. Weekley, in School Library Journal *(reprinted from the February, 1974, issue of* School Library Journal, *published by R. R. Bowker Co., a Xerox company; copyright © 1974 by Xerox Corporation), February, 1974, p. 58.*

Joan Aiken has a flair, and the nonsensical pastiche [of *The Mooncusser's Daughter*] has some broadly comic scenes, along with some parodies of Shakespeare's songs that are very funny for those who recognize them.

Zena Sutherland, in Bulletin of the Center for Children's Books *(© 1974 by the University of Chicago; all rights reserved), March, 1974, p. 105.*

[*The Mooncusser's Daughter* is a] fast-moving two-act play full of snappy dialog and adventure. The plot echoes elements of Shakespeare's *The Tempest*. . . . The parade of outlandish characters and the weave of fantasy and reality will appeal to children, although staging the play seems to require extensive set designing and possibly complicated lighting effects.

The Booklist *(© American Library Association 1974), April 15, 1974, p. 935.*

OTHER CITATIONS

The Times Literary Supplement, *June 15, 1973, p. 681.*

***A NECKLACE OF RAINDROPS* (1969)**

Joan Aiken is well known for her riotous historical fantasies and for her original short stories on fairy tale themes. [*A Necklace of Raindrops and Other Stories*] is for much younger children but has the same blend of fantasy, fun and originality. The large print will be helpful for inexperienced readers and the gaily coloured pictures will appeal to children, if sometimes rather garish for the adult. The use of repetition, the original twists to the stories and their child-like themes, combine to make an attractive collection.

The Junior Bookshelf, *December, 1968, p. 361.*

Eight original stories constructed in conventional folktale patterns form the contents of this attractive looking book. . . . Miss Aiken is an inventive writer and the stories have charm, but on the whole the tone is whimsical, and except in one or two of the tales, the incisive wit of her other works (*The Wolves of Willoughby Chase*, 1963; *Nightbirds on Nantucket*, 1966 . . .) is lacking. . . . On balance, a pleasant additional item.

Shirley Ellison, in School Library Journal *(reprinted from the January, 1970, issue of* School Library Journal, *published by R. R. Bowker Co., a Xerox company; copyright © 1970 by Xerox Corporation), January, 1970, p. 54.*

Miss Aiken has endless inventive power, an exact sense of timing, and a perfect ear; she tells her eight stories [in *A Necklace of Raindrops*] with a limpid simplicity that makes the marvellous seem natural; and she weaves into the fairy-tale structure, quite effortlessly, a railway train, a motor-car, an aeroplane and a bus—all of them, if we are to believe the artist, Jan Pienkowski, nostalgically obsolete models, already half legendary to adults and quite legendary to children.

John Rowe Townsend, in his Written for Children: An Outline of English-Language Children's Literature, *revised edition (copyright © 1965, 1974 by John Rowe Townsend; reprinted by permission of J.B. Lippincott Company), Lippincott, 1974, p. 236.*

***NIGHT FALL* (1971)**

More like [Joan Aiken's] adult thrillers rather than her spoofing nonsense and make-believe for children, this deftly built narrative is distinguished by originality and swiftness of storytelling. Some ten years are spanned, beginning with the time when Meg Frazer comes from Hollywood to live with her uncaring father in London. . . . The Abyssinian cat Hodge, her "lifelong friend, comforter of all those unhappy childish nights . . .," fills a splendid role in the story, from the bleakest days in London to the stunning climax.

Virginia Haviland, in The Horn Book Magazine *(copyright © 1971 by The Horn Book, Inc., Boston), October, 1971, p. 487.*

***NIGHTBIRDS ON NANTUCKET* (1966)**

[*Nightbirds on Nantucket* is] a whale of a lot of fun. Though more than a fraction tamer than *The Wolves of Willoughby Chase*, the humor is as broad as it was in *Black Hearts in Battersea* and the plot as thick. . . . Like whale blubber, the storyline is a mess to boil down, but it's got as much robust energy as one of the happier sea chanties.

Virginia Kirkus' Service *(copyright © 1966 Virginia Kirkus' Service, Inc.), June 1, 1966, pp. 540-41.*

[This is a] tongue-in-cheek, no-holds-barred adventure story, replete with a cheerful waif, an absent-minded sea captain and his fragile little daughter, a black-hearted villain-spy and his cruel spinster sister, a pink whale and a vaudeville stereotype comic German scientist. . . . Dripping with quaintnesses and brine and stereotypes and valor and all sorts of things that make the book a romping burlesque.

Zena Sutherland, in Bulletin of the Center for Children's Books *(copyright 1966 by the University of Chicago; all rights reserved), September, 1966, p. 1.*

A pink whale? Why not? In Joan Aiken's world anything is possible and the more unlikely the better. . . . [In "Nightbirds on Nantucket"] she now turns her wickedly winking eye on monsters of the deep and skulduggery in New England with . . . hilarious success. . . .

The story moves at a rattling pace, exciting, absurd, with no time for awkward questions as new surprises are sprung. The language is a heady mixture of English and American slang, plus whaling expressions, some incomprehensibilities by a dotty German scientist and graceful comments by a lordly parrot. Swallow whole and laugh.

Aileen Pippett, in The New York Times Book Review *(© 1966 by The New York Times Company; reprinted by permission), September 18, 1966, p. 30.*

The only trouble [with *Nightbirds on Nantucket*] is that Joan Aiken has fallen into one of the pitfalls of writing fantasy. Fantasy is never the license to be silly. The more farfetched a premise, the more scrupulously real, even persnickity, the frame of reference and details must be.

But in "Nightbirds on Nantucket" one preposterous idea often leaps to a further absurdity, and there seems an almost frantic determination never to let an idea or a character come to rest long enough to submit to scrutiny.

Mary Nash, in The Christian Science Monitor *(reprinted by permission from* The Christian Science Monitor; *© 1966 The Christian Science Publishing Society; all rights reserved), November 3, 1966, p. B6.*

[This] is a most exhilarating book, and though it is fantastic the story moves with such a swing that we can accept without hesitation such items as a nineteenth-century King James III reigning in London. . . . The story is full of excitements of all sorts, and the varied elements come together at the end in a fine satisfactory climax. . . . Altogether an invigorating book, in which the wit and the nonsense make such a sparkling fizz together that it is hard to tell one from the other.

The Times Literary Supplement *(© The Times Publishing Company, Ltd. 1966), November 24, 1966, p. 1071.*

OTHER CITATIONS

Lavinia Russ, in Publishers' Weekly, *August 1, 1966, p. 60.*

The Booklist and Subscription Books Bulletin, *September 15, 1966, p. 116.*

Elizabeth Enright, in Book Week, *October 30, 1966 (Part 2), p. 26.*

***NOT WHAT YOU EXPECTED* (1974)**

[*Not What You Expected*] is replete with the wit and whimsy that distinguish Aiken's writing for children. The tales have exaggeration, magic, sentiment, and a dry humor that at times broadens to become satirical; a few have a note of contrivance but most of them are airy and amusing.

Zena Sutherland, in Bulletin of the Center for Children's Books *(© 1975 by the University of Chicago; all rights reserved), January, 1975, p. 73.*

[Joan Aiken's] inventive talent is dazzlingly displayed in [this] collection of short stories as remarkable for their diversity of tone, plot, and subject matter as for their virtuosity of style. Indeed, one senses at times that her imagination chafes at the boundaries of form, that within many of the short tales there is a longer story waiting to be told. Yet each one works as an introduction to a unique and magic world where the extraordinary becomes ordinary and the unexpected commonplace. . . . Perhaps most characteristic of the collection is the author's ability to juxtapose sentiment and objectivity, tragedy and comedy, grandeur and simplicity without violating the integrity of the whole. A collection to savor rather than one to bolt down hastily, it offers selections for all ages and would be admirably suited for oral interpretation.

Mary M. Burns, in The Horn Book Magazine *(copyright © 1975 by The Horn Book, Inc., Boston), April, 1975, p. 151.*

OTHER CITATIONS

Judith Atwater, in School Library Journal, *January, 1975, p. 42.*

***SMOKE FROM CROMWELL'S TIME, AND OTHER STORIES* (1970)**

Joan Aiken is so at home with magic that she can afford to be disrespectful, poking fun with teasing affection at the conventional patterns of fantasy. Most of the tales [in *Smoke From Cromwell's Time*] have a wry humor, and all of them are written with a light, sure touch that is just right for the restrained fantasy of their plots.

Zena Sutherland, in Saturday Review *(copyright © 1970 by Saturday Review, Inc.; reprinted with permission), August 22, 1970, p. 53.*

[*Smoke from Cromwell's Time* consists of fourteen] well-written, well-constructed, completely original short stories which were published earlier in England. Nicely combining humor, nonsense, magic (with a twist), and occasional mystery, the tales, reminiscent of those of Eleanor Farjeon, are balanced in mood and spontaneous.

Margaret N. Coughlan, in School Library Journal *(reprinted from the September, 1970, issue of* School Library Journal, *published by R. R. Bowker Co., a Xerox company; copyright © 1970 by Xerox Corporation), September, 1970, p. 98.*

[Joan Aiken] demonstrates her versatility in an unusual gathering of short, original tales ranging in mood from the romantic to the rollicking. Although situations and structure are derived from traditional lore, many of the stories recall in tone and style the subtlety and lilt of Gilbert and Sullivan librettos. . . . [*Smoke from Cromwell's Time, and Other Stories* is a] superb collection for telling or reading aloud.

Mary M. Burns, in The Horn Book Magazine *(copyright © 1970 by The Horn Book, Inc., Boston), October, 1970, p. 476.*

Some of the tales [in *Smoke from Cromwell's Time*] have a gentle melancholy but most of them are robust and humorous, written with a practiced ease that permits a saucy variation of fairy tale formula without marring the story. Joan Aiken probably has, in her tales of magic, some of the most unusual fairy godmothers of the genre; the writing style is deft, the story lines imaginative even when they emerge from familiar patterns.

Zena Sutherland, in Bulletin of the Center for Children's Books *(© 1970 by the University of Chicago; all rights reserved), November, 1970, p. 37.*

OTHER CITATIONS

The Booklist, *October 1, 1970, p. 142.*

Silence Buck Bellows, in The Christian Science Monitor, *November 12, 1970, p. B7.*

THE WHISPERING MOUNTAIN (1969)

Tongue-in-cheek humor, lilting dialogue, clearly-defined characterizations, and a fast pace make [*The Whispering Mountain*] a rousing romp for Aiken fans. . . . A few simple black-and-white illustrations [by Frank Bozzo] are sprinkled throughout the book, and a glossary of Welsh words caps this delightful adventure.

Nancy Berkowitz, in School Library Journal *(reprinted from the December, 1969, issue of* School Library Journal, *published by R. R. Bowker Co., a Xerox company; copyright © 1969 by Xerox Corporation), December, 1969, p. 56.*

In another of her harrowing and hilarious Gothic adventures, [Joan Aiken] takes us hunting through the black hills of Wales for the fabled Golden Harp of Teirtu. . . . [*The Whispering Mountain* is an] elaborately plotted entertainment that will appeal to readers who have enjoyed the author's previous books.

Diane Farrell, in The Horn Book Magazine *(copyright © 1970 by The Horn Book, Inc., Boston), February, 1970, p. 39.*

Broad burlesque of fantasy-adventure might be cloying, but Joan Aiken has a deft touch of the ridiculous that lightens [*The Whispering Mountain,*] a book that isn't to be taken seriously for one moment. . . . The dialects are hilarious, especially the fractured Welsh, and the plot outlandish.

Zena Sutherland, in Bulletin of the Center for Children's Books *(© 1970 by the University of Chicago; all rights reserved), April, 1970, p. 123.*

[In *The Whispering Mountain*] Joan Aiken has zestfully essayed a double parody of a Welsh legend and a picaresque tale, and succeeded beyond reasonable expectation. . . . The author's sure touch enables her to dip occasionally into excesses of invented patois and broad character burlesque. The story, moreover, is richly diverse and extremely funny.

Zena Sutherland, in Saturday Review *(copyright © 1970 by Saturday Review, Inc.; reprinted with permission), April 18, 1970, p. 37.*

OTHER CITATIONS

The Booklist, *January 1, 1970, p. 563.*

WINTERTHING (1972)

Joan Aiken is of course an expert at manipulating ominous vibrations which can be expected to thrill both actors and audience. But almost the whole play [*Winterthing*] seems to be setting the scene for a hair-raising finale which Aiken then rejects in favor of Mrs. MacRoy's vague pseudo-profundities. However lulling her message might be for our time, it's a disappointment that this pastmistress of melodramatic novels has come up with so undramatic a play.

Kirkus Reviews *(copyright © 1972 The Kirkus Service, Inc.), November 15, 1972, p. 1315.*

This short, two-act play is a far-fetched blend of suspense and fantasy. . . . Despite the shallow characterizations and grim ending, the skillfully built suspense will intrigue upper elementary and junior high readers and actors. While less successful than her novels, Aiken's fans will enjoy her first play and it will also be useful where more children's drama is needed.

Marcia L. Perry, in School Library Journal *(reprinted from the December, 1972, issue of* School Library Journal, *published by R. R. Bowker Co., a Xerox company; copyright © 1972 by Xerox Corporation), December, 1972, p. 63.*

[In *Winterthing*, four] children and their peculiar old aunt-guardian come to a remote, imaginary spot—Winter Island. . . . There are some good roles, but the dialogue is uneven, and what Joan Aiken can create convincingly by exposition she cannot quite do with dialogue: the mood of mystery and fey magic just doesn't come off.

Zena Sutherland, in Bulletin of the Center for Children's Books *(© 1973 by the University of Chicago; all rights reserved), February, 1973, p. 85.*

[Joan Aiken's] great gift for writing tales of fantasy, horror, and suspense is wonderfully distilled in a two-act play written for performance by and for children. An eerie atmosphere is cast from the very opening. . . . Excitingly original, with sharp characterizations, [*Winterthing*] should be received with relish by young actors and audiences. Numerous songs [by John Sebastian Brown] appear in the play; and the music, with guitar chords, is included at the end of the book.

Ethel L. Heins, in The Horn Book Magazine *(copyright © 1973 by The Horn Book, Inc., Boston), April, 1973, p. 149.*

OTHER CITATIONS

The Booklist, *January 15, 1973, pp. 490-91.*

The Times Literary Supplement, *June 15, 1973, p. 681.*

THE WOLVES OF WILLOUGHBY CHASE (1963)

[Enjoy] "The Wolves of Willoughby Chase," with a straight face if you can. Children short on a sense of humor will be satisfied with the matter-of-fact explanations, while those who recognize its absurdities will feel fine because they are smart enough to know it is nonsense. Don't let them know it is meant to be nonsense, however. Let them take it straight, while you share Miss Aiken's evident enjoyment in concocting a good yarn.

Aileen Pippett, in The New York Times Book Review *(© 1963 by The New York Times Company; reprinted by permission), October 6, 1963, p. 42.*

[*The Wolves of Willoughby Chase* is] an extraordinary youthful melodrama that is real enough to be exciting yet has dreamlike overtones. . . . Children over 12 with a wide reading background will appreciate the combination of lively style and humorous and fantastic exaggeration. Younger ones and those whose limited vocabularies restrict them to simple family stories and mysteries should be fascinated but may feel uncertain whether or not the story is a serious dime-thriller.

Margaret Sherwood Libby, in Book Week *(© The Washington* Post*), November 10, 1963 (Part 2), p. 5.*

[This book is a] gravely delightful burlesque of the throbbing Victorian novel. Everything comes in double doses: two little heroines, two wicked witchlike women, two frail gentlewomen who come to see better health and happier days, two Good and Faithful servants. [Joan Aiken's] writing style is appropriately florid, sentimental, and melodramatic; the characters are appropriately stereotyped. . . . Needless to say, all ends happily with the assorted malevolent culprits getting their just deserts.

Zena Sutherland, in Bulletin of the Center for Children's Books *(copyright 1964 by the University of Chicago; all rights reserved), April, 1964, p. 121.*

Essentially [*The Wolves of Willoughby Chase*] is an enthralling, extravagant mystery fantasy filled with highly improbable but highly suspenseful melodrama and humor. The girls' friendship is well portrayed and there are many exciting incidents of personal courage and sacrifice. With its over-drawn characters and scenes of life in Victorian England, it is reminiscent of such Dickens novels as *Oliver Twist*.

John Gillespie and Diana Lembo, in their Introducing Books: A Guide for the Middle Grades *(copyright © 1970 by Xerox Corp.), Bowker, 1970, p. 108.*

OTHER CITATIONS

The Booklist and Subscription Books Bulletin, *November 15, 1963, p. 312.*

* * *

ALCOTT, Louisa May 1832-1888

An American novelist who pioneered in writing realistic stories for young people, Louisa May Alcott is best known as the author of *Little Women* and *Little Men*.

GENERAL COMMENTARY

Louisa May Alcott . . . attacks the false fronts and manners of people behaving conventionally and making a great show of politeness when they are actually backbiting. In Louisa May Alcott's books there is a variety of very short personal descriptions of people and very accurate conversations and detailed descriptions of people, mixed sometimes with very sentimental moralizing which children of nine or ten never hear. . . . Most of the time the child is not listening; he is waiting to see what happened.

Emily Neville, "Social Values in Children's Literature," in A Critical Approach to Children's Literature: The Thirty-first Annual Conference of the Graduate Library School August 1-3, 1966, *edited by Sara Innis Fenwick (© 1967 by The University of Chicago; all rights reserved), University of Chicago Press, 1967, p. 47.*

[The] really special characteristic of Alcott's writings is that they deal in a head-on manner with emotional problems and states of mind that adolescents are beginning to know and by which they are puzzled and therefore fascinated. . . .

Alcott's girls and boys are not very complex people; although they have more than one dimension, each dimension is clearly and unmistakably projected, and each trait is darkened or brightened by deep Victorian coloring. . . . Yet to ten- to twelve-year-olds this fictional world *does* suggest a psychological complexity which has been hitherto uncommon in their reading.

James Steel Smith, in his A Critical Approach to Children's Literature *(copyright © 1967 by McGraw-Hill, Inc.), McGraw-Hill, 1967, p. 136.*

Louisa [Alcott], beyond a doubt, got some of her easy flow of words from [*The Pilgrim's Progress*], as well as her compact method of saying much in brief. . . .

[Her] short stories came to be overshadowed by her longer books, but they had liveliness and vividness of their own and are well worth reexamining today. They tell so truly about actual living that we forget, many times, that they are a hundred years old. . . . She developed very fully the art of giving an example of the truth she wanted to convey, rather than preaching about it.

Cornelia Meigs, in The Horn Book Magazine *(copyright © 1968 by The Horn Book, Inc., Boston), October, 1968, pp. 546-48.*

Young people having good times together, understanding elders, enjoying warmth and security—both *Little Men* and *Under the Lilacs* begin by describing how a forlorn, small boy finds a home and affection—all these things appeal to young readers and have kept Louisa Alcott's books alive for generations of children. . . . In spite of differences in customs and conventions, the human quality in Miss Alcott's stories, her knowledge of young people, and her sympathy with youth have kept her books alive.

Anne Thaxter Eaton, in A Critical History of Children's Literature, *revised edition, by Cornelia Meigs, Anne Thaxter Eaton, Elizabeth Nesbitt, and Ruth Hill Viguers, edited by Cornelia Meigs (copyright © 1969 by The Macmillan Co.), Macmillan, 1969, pp. 212-13.*

GLIMPSES OF LOUISA (1968)

These stories [in "Glimpses of Louisa"] are awash with sentimentality and stuffed with conventional ideas from the mid-Victorian age. Reading them, one can only wonder afresh at the vitality which went into "Little Women," and which keeps it alive today.

Elizabeth Janeway, in The New York Times Book Review *(© 1968 by The New York Times Company; reprinted by permission), September 29, 1968, p. 46.*

[*Glimpses of Louisa* is a] selection of ten stories, originally published in various collections between the years 1871 and 1884. The period background, the old-fashioned phrases, and the recurrent extolling of poor, virtuous protagonists give the collection that distinctive flavor so dear to confirmed Alcott fans; the sturdy vitality of the characters and lively style have a durable appeal that may well attract new ones.

Zena Sutherland, in Bulletin of the Center for Children's Books *(copyright 1969 by The University of Chicago; all rights reserved), January, 1969, p. 73.*

***LITTLE WOMEN* (1868)**

[Louisa May Alcott] is, I suppose of all writers, the one whose name *means* sentimentality; and yet sentimentality is what she and her characters most dread. . . .

Whereas Meg was a commonplace of Alcott's own—or any—time, in Amy she actually showed sociological prescience. Or rather, I think, it showed despite her. Try as she would to prettify and moralize, she could not help making Amy the prototype of a model which did not become numerous in the United States until the 20th century—the peroxided girl-doll golddigger. . . .

With Beth, I admit, Alcott went altogether too far. Beth's patience, humility and gentle sunniness are a quite monstrous imposition on the rest of the family . . .; no one in the household could escape the blight of feeling unworthy which was imposed by Beth. . . .

Jo is one of the most blatantly autobiographical yet most fairly treated heroines in print. All that stands between her and Emma Woodhouse is her creator's lack of intellect. Alcott is not up to devising situations which analyze and develop, as distinct from merely illustrating her characters. . . .

As sentimentalists go, Louisa M. Alcott is of the gentler and less immoral sort . . .; on the whole, [she] prefers to wreak her revenges on her characters by making them unhappy in their moments of happiness. . . . Even here, one can morally if not esthetically justify her. It's all, so to speak, between consenting adolescents. All four girls are quite masochists enough to enjoy what she does to them.

Brigid Brophy, "A Masterpiece, and Dreadful" (1965), in Children and Literature: Views and Reviews, *edited by Virginia Haviland (copyright © 1973 Scott, Foresman and Co.), Scott, Foresman, 1973, pp. 66, 68-70.*

[One] of the things that holds [*Little Women*] together is the fact that all [the] cherished schemes [of Laurie and the March sisters] do, in actual fact, come to their desired ends but only after each person has accepted the modification and compromise that circumstances and his or her own character have made inevitable. The happy and irresponsible materialism and youthful vanity that clothe these ambitious plans are shed away and replaced by something far more valuable. It is the highest proof of Louisa Alcott's mastery of storytelling that none of us [realizes] this until we look back long after we have read the book.

Cornelia Meigs, in The Horn Book Magazine *(copyright © 1968 by The Horn Book, Inc., Boston), October, 1968, p. 532.*

[Girls have loved *Little Women*] because Jo was a rebel, with rebels for parents. Not the rebels of destruction—they never threw a brick—but rebels who looked at the world as it was, saw the poverty, the inequality, the ignorance, the fear, and said, "It isn't good enough" and went to work to change it. . . .

Brigid Brophy was wrong about *Little Women*. A girl in Russia cries over Beth's death, not because it is sentimental, but because it is brave. And a girl in India cries when Jo refuses Laurie, because she realizes suddenly that life is not going to hold a neat, happy ending for her. . . .

If [Ernest Hemingway] had read *Little Women*, he would have realized that it is not "sweetness and light," it is stalwart proof of his definition of courage: grace under pressure. . . .

[Girls] are right to love *Little Women*, every word of it, because it is a story about *good* people. . . . And if there is one hope for us in 1968, the only one, it is that the young recognize the power of goodness, and the responsibility that goodness demands of men and women of good will—the responsibility . . . to look at the world at it is—. . . and to say "It isn't good enough" and go to work to change it.

Lavinia Russ, in The Horn Book Magazine *(copyright © 1968 by the Horn Book, Inc., Boston), October, 1968, pp. 524, 526.*

[In *Little Women*, Louisa May Alcott] wrote swiftly, honestly, humorously of her family, herself, relatives and friends. . . . Sentiment and moral lessons straight out of *Pilgrim's Progress* to be sure, but no melodrama, no affectation. Louisa May Alcott just put sound, warm life and lots of it . . . into a packed book that the entranced reader could live in for a long time. . . .

The Centennial Edition of *Little Women* [Little, Brown and Co., 1968] with a new introduction by Cornelia Meigs is a handsome and substantial volume, well designed, with illustrations in color by Jessie Willcox Smith. The book does full justice to *Little Women*. . . .

James Playsted Wood, in Book World *(©* The Washington Post*), November 3, 1968, p. 34.*

[*Little Women*] is dated and sentimental and full of preaching and moralizing and some snobbery about the lower classes that is positively breathtaking in its horror. . . .

[But the] real attraction [of *Little Women* is] its heroine, Jo, and Jo is a unique creation: the one young woman in nineteenth-century fiction who maintains her individual independence, who gives up no part of her autonomy as payment for being born a woman—and who gets away with it. . . . For this Victorian moral tract, sentimental and preachy, was written by a secret rebel against the order of the world and woman's place in it, and all the girls who ever read it know it.

Elizabeth Janeway, "Meg, Jo, Beth, Amy, and Louisa" (1968), in Only Connect: Readings on Children's Literature, *edited by Sheila Egoff, G. T. Stubbs, and L. F. Ashley (© Oxford University Press [Canadian Branch], 1969), Oxford University Press, 1969, pp. 286, 288, 290.*

I must say, having just laughed and cried my way through ["Little Women," World, 1969], that the standard American edition comes as an astonishment. We Canadians read it as two books, "Little Women" and "Good Wives," and conditioned perhaps by memory I find it more successful that way. Between the original and its sequel there is a distinct break in tone and emphasis, and the parts seem better left physically separated.

Tasha Tudor's sketches have warmth and sweetness, but . . . all of Miss Tudor's girls resemble one another. . . . Besides, each of the little women looks younger than her stated age. . . .

Nora L. Magid, in The New York Times Book Review *(© 1969 by The New York Times Company; reprinted by permission), November 9, 1969 (Part 2), p. 65.*

[The] four March sisters come alive as nineteenth century New England girls leading uneventful lives but with roots that run deep into American soil. The lifelike character studies of the March sisters mirror the dilemmas, fun, and pathos of family experience. Sentimentality runs high in this classic story of American girlhood but it is in keeping with the emotional period when girls first come in contact with this book. As a family chronicle, this plotless story honestly reveals everyday happenings with accurate details that mark the account as a social history of the nineteenth century.

Constantine Georgiou, in his Children and Their Literature *(copyright © 1969 by Prentice-Hall, Inc.), Prentice-Hall, 1969, p. 338.*

[*Little Women*] is as genuine a bit of realism as we have ever had. . . . But right as all the details are, the reason that adults remember the book is the masterly characterizations of the four girls. No longer are people typed to represent Ignorance or Virtue, but here are flesh-and-blood girls, as different from each other as they could well be, full of human folly and human courage, never self-righteous, sometimes irritable but never failing in warm affection for each other. This ability to make her characters vividly alive was Louisa M. Alcott's gift to modern realism for children.

May Hill Arbuthnot and Zena Sutherland, in their Children and Books, *4th edition (copyright © 1947, 1957, 1964, 1972 by Scott, Foresman and Co.), Scott, Foresman, 1972, p. 100.*

Little Women marks not only an increased truth-to-life in domestic stories, with children seen as people rather than examples of good and bad; it also marks a relaxation of the stiff and authoritarian stereotype of family life, persisting from the still recent times when the Fifth Commandment came first and the earthly father was seen quite literally as the representative of the heavenly one. . . . This mellowing was necessary before the family story, of which *Little Women* is the first great example, could come into its own. A relationship between rulers and subjects had to be replaced by one of mutual affection. The family story could not work in an atmosphere of repression or of chilly grandeur. The key characteristic is always warmth.

John Rowe Townsend, in his Written for Children: An Outline of English Language Children's Literature, *revised edition (copyright © 1965, 1974 by John Rowe Townsend; reprinted by permission of J.B. Lippincott Company), Lippincott, 1974, pp. 79-80.*

***AN OLD-FASHIONED THANKSGIVING* (1881)**

[This] account of how one family spent their Thanksgiving has values of genuine meaning and interest. . . . The story is filled with lively, homely, good-humored details and with moments of excitement; and the true spirit of Thanksgiving has never been set forth more effectively than in this warm, embracing story of an old-fashioned celebration.

Beryl Robinson, in The Horn Book Magazine *(copyright © 1974 by the Horn Book, Inc., Boston), October, 1974, p. 153.*

[*An Old-Fashioned Thanksgiving* is an] old-fashioned story, replete with high moral tone and sentiment but tempered by homely warmth and Alcott's distinctive lawks-a-mussy humor. . . . [Holly Johnson's] illustrations [in the 1974 Lippincott edition] have authentic period details, but are otherwise pedestrian; the story has its own flowery charm and will be, perhaps, of special interest to Alcott fans and students of children's literature.

Zena Sutherland, in Bulletin of the Center for Children's Books *(© 1974 by the University of Chicago; all rights reserved), October, 1974, p. 21.*

* * *

ALEXANDER, Lloyd 1924-

Lloyd Alexander, noted as the creator of the mythical world of Prydain, is an American author who received the 1969 Newbery Medal for *The High King* and the 1971 National Book Award for *The Marvelous Misadventures of Sebastian*. (See also *Contemporary Authors*, Vols. 1-4, rev. ed., and *Something About the Author*, Vol. 3.)

***THE BLACK CAULDRON* (1965)**

The same characteristics that made [*The Book of Three*] so rich are again present [in *The Black Cauldron*]—a fine flow of words; an intricate, active plot; an admirable balance between the forces of black and white magic. . . . The sweep of the battles, the pressures of fear relieved by interludes of comedy, the blends of good and evil combine to make the kind of once-in-a-lifetime reading that will assure Prydain a permanent place in geographies of fictional territories.

Virginia Kirkus' Service, *April 1, 1965, p. 377.*

There are fierce armed battles and battles of the mind and heart [in *The Black Cauldron*] as Taran learns that true heroism depends on wisdom as well as courage. A wise and wondrous tale written in epic fashion. Though it is a sequel to the first book, it can be read independently.

The Booklist and Subscription Books Bulletin *(© 1965 by the American Library Association), September 1, 1965, p. 52.*

[*The Black Cauldron* is a] sequel to *The Book of Three*, and just as charming a fantasy. . . . There is, in these tales of the Land of Prydain, a satisfying wholeness of artistic conception, a graceful style, humor in dialogue and in characterization, and a robust sense of adventure.

Zena Sutherland, in Bulletin of the Center for Children's Books *(copyright 1966 by the University of Chicago; all rights reserved), January, 1966, p. 77.*

Continuing the chronicle of the imaginary land of Prydain, this second book in the series is somber and moving. The story of how Prince Gwydion leads the attempt to destroy the Black Cauldron, a weapon of evil powers owned by the Lord of the Land of Death, is filled with adventure, sacrifice, love, and even some light humor. . . . [This is a] wonderful fantasy.

Constantine Georgiou, in his Children and Their Literature *(copyright © 1969 by Prentice-Hall, Inc.), Prentice-Hall, 1969, p. 297.*

THE BOOK OF THREE (1964)

[*The Book of Three* is an] enchanting fantasy set in the imaginary country of Prydain and peopled with an intriguing set of characters. . . . Filled with exciting and valorous action, humor, and truth the fantasy is completely convincing and has some of the appeal of [C. S. Lewis'] Narnia books.

The Booklist and Subscription Books Bulletin *(© 1964 by the American Library Association), December 1, 1964, p. 344.*

Though Lloyd Alexander's *The Book of Three* is fantasy rather than history, it too is firmly based on knowledge—this time, of the Welsh legends of the Mabinogion. . . . [The] tone of the narrative is brisk and down-to-earth; as in T. H. White, voices of today echo in a fabulous world of dwarfs and warriors and talking creatures. It is a book to suit all who delight in *The Sword in the Stone*.

Janet Adam Smith, in The New York Review of Books *(reprinted with permission from* The New York Review of Books; *copyright © 1964 NYREV, Inc.), December 3, 1964, p. 16.*

[*The Book of Three* is a] long, complicated, imaginative, and very funny adventure tale set in an imaginary kingdom; nicely conceived and written in the genre of the folk legend, this is the story of a young Welsh hero. . . . The writing is sophisticated, and the body of lore and legend is complicated, but the originality of the idea and the humor of the dialogue should more than balance these mild drawbacks in appealing to readers.

Zena Sutherland, in Bulletin of the Center for Children's Books *(copyright 1965 by the University of Chicago; all rights reserved), July-August, 1965, p. 157.*

THE CASTLE OF LLYR (1966)

The struggles between the forces of good and evil continue [in *The Castle of Llyr*] at the terrific pace established in the first books [about Prydain]. Character and dialogue [are] handled humorously and dextrously, which sets this classic-in-the-making apart from other folklore-based fantasies.

Virginia Kirkus' Service *(copyright © 1966 Virginia Kirkus' Service, Inc.), March 15, 1966, p. 302.*

The third book about the fabulous country of Prydain lacks the heroic overtones of *The Black Cauldron* . . . but it has the same mixture of wisdom, humor, and fantastic adventures. . . . The introduction of the inept but stout-hearted Prince Rhun as a rival to Taran for the favor of Eilonwy adds a romantic note. Though this story like the earlier ones is complete in itself, it will be more rewarding to readers familiar with the other stories.

The Booklist and Subscription Books Bulletin *(© 1966 by the American Library Association), July 1, 1966, p. 1042.*

Now, in his third chronicle of Prydain, *The Castle of Llyr*, there are signs that Mr. Alexander is moving towards a mood of greater depth and seriousness. . . . [Although] the gaiety, the adventures and the heroism are still there, the characters have developed, as if in spite of themselves. . . . The climax is fierce and perilous indeed but touched with great humanity, and readers who themselves may have grown up a little since the first chronicle will not be disappointed.

The Times Literary Supplement *(© Times Newspapers Ltd., 1968), October 3, 1968, p. 1113.*

OTHER CITATIONS

Ruth Rausen, in Library Journal, *April 15, 1966, p. 2205.*

The Best of Children's Books: The University of Chicago Guide To Children's Literature 1966-1972, *edited by Zena Sutherland, University of Chicago Press, 1973, p. 6.*

THE CAT WHO WISHED TO BE A MAN (1973)

["The Cat Who Wished to Be a Man"] is filled with the kind of predictability that can result when a writer is too much in control of the developing action. . . .

Instead of a fantasy about a cat in a man's form, the story is really just another version of a country boy up against some city slickers. As such, it is beautifully written and eminently readable, but it is a concoction rather than a creation. It doesn't end so much as disappear, leaving the reader to wonder if it isn't Lloyd Alexander rather than the wizard Stephanus who has mastered sleight-of-hand.

Sidney Long, in The New York Times Book Review *(© 1973 by The New York Times*

Company; reprinted by permission), September 30, 1973, p. 10.

[In *The Cat Who Wished to Be a Man*, Lloyd Alexander] blends some of his favorite ingredients to produce a savory mixture. In the style of classical comedy he makes full use of broadly exaggerated stock characters: Pursewig, the greedy Mayor; Swaggart, the villainous Captain of the Watch; Dr. Tudbelly, the bombastic, Latin-quoting *"Medicus illustrius"*; and the comely Mistress Gillian, the innkeeper, for whom Lionel joyfully renounces his feline nature and becomes a total human being. A comic and ebullient fantasy; just right for reading aloud.

Ethel L. Heins, in The Horn Book Magazine *(copyright © 1973 by The Horn Book, Inc., Boston), October, 1973, p. 464.*

The plot [of this book] is not highly original in basic concept (innocent strength overcoming entrenched and malefic interests) save for the cat-into-man twist, but the style, the humor, the play on words, the rumbustious characters, and the pace of the action are delightful.

Zena Sutherland, in Bulletin of the Center for Children's Books *(© 1973 by the University of Chicago; all rights reserved), October, 1973, p. 21.*

Alas, poor tom-fool tom, [Lionel] falls in love with Gillian, and when he takes her and Dr. Tudbelly back to the forest, he asks Magister Stephanus to allow him to remain a man. I would send any cat of mine to the knacker before I'd let him cop out in such a nitwitted way. Apart from this quite unforgivable disappointment, I found [*The Cat Who Wished to Be a Man*] a pleasure to read, and I was grateful that the sermon against filthy lucre was not merely pious but truly sensible.

Jean Stafford, in The New Yorker *(© 1973 by The New Yorker Magazine, Inc.), December 3, 1973, pp. 205-06.*

As a man Lionel runs literally and figuratively into all the greed, selfishness and brutality he had been warned about, but he also finds friendship, kindness and love. [*The Cat Who Wished to Be a Man* is a] stylish farce that features pratfalls and broad characterizations and says some wise and witty things about the state of being human.

Amy Kellman, in Teacher *(excerpted with permission of the publisher, © 1974 by Macmillan Professional Magazines, Inc.; all rights reserved), March, 1974, p. 109.*

OTHER CITATIONS

Kirkus Reviews, *June 15, 1973, pp. 639-40.*

The Booklist, *October 1, 1973, p. 168.*

June Goodwin, in The Christian Science Monitor, *November 7, 1973, p. B5.*

COLL AND HIS WHITE PIG (1965)

The story [of *Coll and His White Pig*] precedes *The Book of Three* in the chronology of Prydain and it tells, with Alexander's blend of humor and excitement, how Coll turned farmer, how Dallben came to his farm and how Hen Wen was first carried off, before the boy Taran had arrived to guard her. It is an excellent introduction for independent readers moving toward the longer books and also stands on its own as a read aloud for younger children.

Virginia Kirkus' Service *(copyright © 1965 Virginia Kirkus' Service, Inc.), November 1, 1965, p. 1115.*

The combination of modern fantasy [by Lloyd Alexander] and distinguished multi-colored illustrations by Evaline Ness make up a handsome book. [*Coll and His White Pig* is for] the imaginative reader, perhaps the somewhat rare one, sensitive to beauty.

Arlene Mosel, in School Library Journal *(reprinted from the December, 1965, issue of* School Library Journal, *published by R. R. Bowker Co., a Xerox company; copyright © 1965 by Xerox Corporation), December, 1965, p. 68.*

[*Coll and His White Pig* is a] fanciful story based on characters from *The Book of Three* and *The Black Cauldron*. . . . The writing style is good, although [Lloyd Alexander's] elegance and subtlety are not as appropriate for younger children as they are for the upper-grade readers. [Evaline Ness'] Illustrations are absolutely lovely—design, color, imaginative detail, humor—all lovely.

Zena Sutherland, in Bulletin of the Center for Children's Books *(copyright 1966 by the University of Chicago; all rights reserved), January, 1966, p. 77.*

OTHER CITATIONS

Barbara Novak O'Doherty, in The New York Times Book Review, *November 7, 1965 (Part 2), p. 62.*

Ruth Hill Viguers, in The Horn Book Magazine, *December, 1965, p. 619.*

The Booklist and Subscription Books Bulletin, *December 15, 1965, p. 407.*

Margaret Sherwood Libby, in Book Week, *January 30, 1966, p. 17.*

THE FOUNDLING AND OTHER TALES OF PRYDAIN (1973)

["The Foundling and Other Tales of Prydain"] is not far removed from the chronicles themselves; it is as if Lloyd Alexander were reaching deep into the cauldron where first stories simmer to find a mythic underpinning for his mythic world. . . . [The] ingredients [for fantasy] are the same the world over and of necessity the same in Prydain, whose citizens struggle against the same evils as all men and are warmed by the same sun. Yet in their final form the tales are pure Alexander and true to Prydain.

Jean Fritz, in The New York Times Book Review *(© 1973 by The New York Times Company; reprinted by permission), November 4, 1973, p. 50.*

Alexander's six short fairy tales, set in Prydain before the time covered in his Newbery-winning quintet, demonstrates both the author's special talent for spinning this kind of story and the extent of his need to borrow plots and motifs on which to build. . . . [*The Foundling and Other Tales of Prydain* are all] worth another hearing as Alexander tells them, but hardly an important contribution to a mythological landscape.

Kirkus Reviews *(copyright © 1973 The Kirkus Service, Inc.), December 1, 1973, pp. 1308-09.*

Knowledge of the earlier books [about Prydain] is not necessary to appreciate the skill with which Mr. Alexander uses the short story form or to enjoy the wide range of moods and emotions. The hilarity of "The Rascal Crow," the grimness of "The Sword" and the romance of "The True Enchanter" suggest the variety and depth of [the *Foundling*] tales.

Amy Kellman, in Teacher *(excerpted with permission of the publisher, © 1974 by Macmillan Professional Magazines, Inc.; all rights reserved), March, 1974, p. 109.*

Six stories of the mythical land so beautifully conceived by Alexander are written with vivid grace and humor; some of the characters will be familiar to Prydain fans as related to major figures in the cycle. . . . Each tale stands alone, a small gem, and the humor and romance are echoed in the soft, deft black and white [Margot] Zemach drawings.

Zena Sutherland, in Bulletin of the Center for Children's Books *(© 1974 by the University of Chicago; all rights reserved), April, 1974, p. 122.*

Lloyd Alexander's *The Foundling and Other Tales of Prydain* . . . is an enjoyable enchantment, completely in the tradition of the well-wrought Welsh epic. Each story is a self-contained episode concerning persons who appear in Alexander's previous, prize-winning books about the imaginary realm of Prydain. As a first encounter with this kingdom, the stories may be too short to achieve the power that the book-length chronicles generate.

Mark Taylor, in Psychology Today *(reprinted by permission; copyright © 1974 by Ziff-Davis Publishing Company), all rights reserved), May, 1974, p. 20.*

OTHER CITATIONS

Publishers' Weekly, *January 7, 1974, p. 54.*

The Booklist, *February 1, 1974, p. 594.*

Virginia Haviland, in The Horn Book Magazine, *June, 1974, p. 278.*

THE FOUR DONKEYS (1972)

Alas, [Lloyd Alexander's] grossly-overblown saga of a tailor, baker and shoemaker who set out for a fair they never reach soon degenerates into a peevish shaggy dog story. . . . ["The Four Donkeys"] is a self-indulgent work.

Selma Lanes, in The New York Times Book Review *(© 1972 by The New York Times Company; reprinted by permission), November 5, 1972 (Part 2), p. 47.*

[*The Four Donkeys* is a] tightly-constructed, circular story by a master of the modern fanciful tale. . . . The tale is greatly enhanced by Lester Abrams' elegant, medieval-style, pen-and-watercolor illustrations accented by slyly humorous details. . . . This is a perfect read-aloud for second or third graders and is sophisticated enough to attract fourth- and fifth-grade readers.

Mary Lou McGrew, in School Library Journal *(reprinted from the December, 1972, issue of* School Library Journal, *published by R. R. Bowker Co., a Xerox company; copyright © 1972 by Xerox Corporation), December, 1972, pp. 53-4.*

An amusing fable tells of the morning that a Tailor, a Shoemaker, and a Baker—all highly individualistic characters—set out independently for the Fair, each one anticipating a profitable day. . . . But during the long and difficult haul, selfishness, irritation, and absurdity were transmuted into an awareness of each other's needs; and although they earned nothing at the fair, they were richer for the understanding and kindliness that eventually emerged from their struggles. [Lloyd Alexander's] leisurely, witty text is embellished with elaborately decorated pages in line and water-color [by Lester Abrams]. . . .

Beryl Robinson, in The Horn Book Magazine *(copyright © 1972 by The Horn Book, Inc., Boston), December, 1972, p. 591.*

[The] misadventures [of three irritable, self-centered tradesmen] bring them together, quite literally, pulling a donkey's load, and teach them to have a bit of compassion for one another. . . . A difficult vocabulary will limit [*The Four Donkeys*] to better readers, but its dry wit will appeal to a certain group of young listeners.

The Booklist *(© American Library Association 1973), February 15, 1973, p. 571.*

[*The Four Donkeys*] is a traditional tale, and is told clearly and concisely but with a zest and attention to detail which well befits this kind of story. Children will be intrigued by the characters who are described with verve and vigour, showing real human traits, and they will be stirred to think about the title of the book, to form their own opinions, and to draw their own conclusions. The illustrations [by Lester Abrams] in nineteenth-century style, are not always absolutely clear, having muted tones and treatment, but they harmonise well with the story and will give readers another facet upon which to ponder.

The Junior Bookshelf, *April, 1975, pp. 94-5.*

OTHER CITATIONS

Kirkus Reviews, *September 1, 1972, p. 1019.*

Zena Sutherland, in Bulletin of the Center for Children's Books, *March, 1973*, p. 101.

THE HIGH KING (1968)

The last may be the best—movement toward an ultimate confrontation between the forces of life and the forces of death give this final Prydain adventure a stronger frame and tighter weave than the preceding four. . . . Though an ancient "lion and thorn" contrivance saves Taran at a crucial moment, the finding of the enchanted sword and the defeat of Arawn are credible in conventional fastasy terms and exciting as well. (Echoes of Tolkien are louder than ever, reflecting some of his grimness but never approximating his terror.) The anticlimax should please both the popular philosopher and the sentimentalist. . . .

Kirkus Service *(copyright © 1968 Virginia Kirkus' Service, Inc.), March 1, 1968, p. 259.*

[In "The High King"] comes Mr. Alexander's master stroke: the revelation of Taran's true destiny, a secret so well kept, it would be a disservice to disclose it here, yet a secret so inevitable that the whole epic becomes a spiritual adventure with a new dimension. Bravo, indeed.

Jean Fritz, in The New York Times Book Review *(© 1968 by The New York Times Company; reprinted by permission), March 24, 1968, p. 38.*

More than a series of exciting adventures, [*The High King*] has the philosophical depth and overtones of great fantasy. . . . Sad as many of the events will seem, most readers will recognize the rightness of the conclusion. The characters have all advanced. The nonsense of Gurgi and Fflewddur has grown to humor. Eilonwy has developed in understanding but lost none of her quickness and spirit. Taran, whose character has at last completely evolved, finds the strength to do what he must in a land where "all enchantments shall pass away, and men unaided guide their own destiny." The heroic fantasy ends on a happy, triumphant note.

Ruth Hill Viguers, in The Horn Book Magazine *(copyright © 1968 by The Horn Book Inc., Boston), April, 1968, p. 172.*

For those who have learned to love the land of Prydain, reading this last volume in the cycle will be a bittersweet experience. All the marvelous and diverse characters appear again in the final struggle between good and evil. . . . In the affecting conclusion Taran chooses to stay and serve humanity rather than leave Prydain for the Summer Country, where there is no death. The fantasy has the depth and richness of a medieval tapestry, infinitely detailed and imaginative.

Zena Sutherland, in Saturday Review *(copyright © 1968 by Saturday Review, Inc.; reprinted with permission), April 20, 1968, p. 41.*

Filled with adventure, conflict, and magic, this fantasy, like many of its genre, deals with both philosophical ideas and practical realities. In a broader sense, [*The High King*] can be interpreted as a religious allegory—the story of good versus evil. In a personal sense, it is Everyman's tale: the desire of a boy to be a hero, the slowly acquired realization and acceptance of the nature of heroism, and the necessity for carrying out one's good intentions. Courage, comradeship, love, constructive behavior—the many values of civilized tradition are woven skillfully into a majestic theme.

John Gillespie and Diana Lembo, in their Introducing Books: A Guide for the Middle Grades *(copyright © 1970 by Xerox Corp.), Bowker, 1970, p. 238.*

OTHER CITATIONS

Lillian N. Gerhardt, in Library Journal, *February 15, 1968, p. 876.*

The Booklist and Subscription Books Bulletin, *April 1, 1968, p. 920.*

Zena Sutherland, in Bulletin of the Center for Children's Books, *May, 1968, p. 137.*

Marjorie D. Hamlin, in The Christian Science Monitor, *May 2, 1968, p. B8.*

***THE KING'S FOUNTAIN* (1971)**

The message [of "The King's Fountain"] is obvious but greatly oversimplified. Plain truth simply spoken by an honest man may convert a callous tyrant and correct a desperate situation—or it may not. Are all learned men pompous blowhards? Are all businessmen cunning cowards? Is bravery the absence of fear?

The author [Lloyd Alexander] and the artist [Ezra Jack Keats] have engaged their considerable talents in a sincere attempt to teach children about personal accountability but their elaborately contrived, didactic framework confuses the issues, dulls the impact and obscures the lesson.

Diane Farrell, in The New York Times Book Review *(© 1971 by The New York Times Company; reprinted by permission), July 25, 1971, p. 8.*

[*The King's Fountain* is a] picture book that has a Biblical quality, each double-page spread a canvas strikingly composed [by Ezra Jack Keats]. . . . [Alexander's] writing has a stately quality, some of it difficult for the audience which accepts a picture book format, but the plot is not complex and the theme is made clear: one must act when action is required, and one can demand action only of oneself.

Zena Sutherland, in Bulletin of the Center for Children's Books *(© 1971 by The University of Chicago; all rights reserved), July-August, 1971, p. 165.*

The simple story of the king who "once planned to build a magnificent fountain in his palace gardens . . ." at the cost of stopping "all water from flowing to the city below" is presented as a parable by an author who normally does his best in expansive narratives that flow through fantastic and humorous channels. The telling is casual rather than pointed, and misses the precision of a true parable. Moreover, . . . [Alexander's] intention was overwhelmed rather than served by [Ezra Jack Keats'] illustrations.

Paul Heins, in The Horn Book Magazine *(copyright © 1971 by The Horn Book, Inc., Boston), August, 1971, p. 373.*

Stunningly beautiful full-page paintings, among [Ezra Jack Keats'] finest, greatly expand this short, trenchant parable. . . . Alexander's theme—that the buck must stop with Everyman, that each person's conscience must form a continuum with constructive action—has obvious relevance for readers of any time or place.

Diane G. Stavn, in School Library Journal *(reprinted from the September, 1971, issue of* School Library Journal, *published by R. R. Bowker Co., a Xerox company; copyright © 1971 by Xerox Corporation), September, 1971, p. 147.*

***THE MARVELOUS MISADVENTURES OF SEBASTIAN* (1970)**

[This] story is a comic fantasy, successfully combining eighteenth-century briskness with romantic "moonshine." It can be read as an exciting series of adventures, of which many of the chapters end with a suspense line. Or it can be read as an allegory on the ambivalent power of beauty. Or —best of all—it can be read as the story of Sebastian's apprenticeship to life.

Paul Heins, in The Horn Book Magazine *(copyright © 1970 by The Horn Book, Inc., Boston), December, 1970, p. 628.*

[*The Marvelous Misadventures of Sebastian* is steeped] in an eighteenth century atmosphere. . . . The intricacy of plot, the humor and allusiveness of the writing, the exaggerated characterization, and the derring-do of romantic adventures are knit into a lively and elaborate tale that can be enjoyed for its action and appreciated for its subtler significance.

Zena Sutherland, in Bulletin of the Center for Children's Books *(© 1971 by the University of Chicago; all rights reserved), February, 1971, p. 85.*

OTHER CITATIONS

The Booklist, *November 15, 1970, p. 266.*

Amy Kellman, in Grade Teacher, *April, 1971, pp. 26, 28.*

THE PRYDAIN CHRONICLES: *The Book of Three; The Black Cauldron; The Castle of Llyr; Taran Wanderer; The High King*

The land of Prydain is shaped a bit like Wales. Its inhabitants have Welsh names, but the country itself . . . is fantasy in the great tradition. Created by the tension between the good and evil forces in the world, it is wonderfully impossible on the one hand and utterly true on the other. The cast of characters is large: giants, princes, dwarves, sorceresses, kings good and bad. Each one, no matter what shape he assumes or what role he plays, is real and in very human ways.

Jean Fritz, in The New York Times Book Review *(© 1966 by The New York Times Company; reprinted by permission), June 19, 1966, p. 36.*

Although in imaginative depth and inventiveness [the Prydain Chronicles] are a far cry from Tolkien's stories, they do combine in a lively manner elements from Welsh folklore with elaborately mythical adventures of odd and comical, if somewhat stilted, characters, quite to the taste of those just beyond the earliest fairy-tale age who enjoy complicated magical mixtures.

Margaret S. Libby, in Book Week *(©* The Washington Post*), August 21, 1966, p. 11.*

[Lloyd Alexander's] total creation [of the land of Prydain] is a remarkable achievement, a rich and varied tapestry of brooding evil, heroic action and great natural beauty, vividly conceived, romantic in mood yet curiously contemporary in its immediacy and fast action. Perhaps less winning has been his weakness for opéra bouffe comic relief in the form of the subsidiary characters, a number of whom are little more than tiresome running jokes. The bald appeal to juvenile risibilities is, in the end, rather too calculated, and inconsistent with the eloquence and grandeur of the best episodes.

Houston L. Maples, in Book World *(©* The Washington Post*), May 5, 1968 (Part 2), p. 22.*

Through the first three volumes of the [Prydain Chronicles], Taran develops in keeping with the classic tradition. Then, in *Taran Wanderer*, he confronts his own myth; and by the end of *The High King* the form of the hero has undergone a change, one which has been brought about by the fact that Taran is not, in the later volumes, operating within the classic mythology. . . . With the introduction of Craddoc in *Taran Wanderer*, Mr. Alexander skillfully shifts Taran from tenth- to twentieth-century mythology. . . . [This] is complete with Taran's acceptance of manhood. The rest of the Chronicles is consistent with his discovery of himself.

Marion Carr, in The Horn Book Magazine *(copyright © 1971 by The Horn Book, Inc., Boston), October, 1971, pp. 508, 511-12.*

The stories [about Prydain] are marvelously inventive, written in an ornate and sophisticated style. The pace, the strength of the characterizations, and the humor of the dialogue are sustained throughout, and each of the books has a host of vivid minor characters. It is not until the last book, however, that the muted theme of the hero, the champion of good against the forces of evil, emerges in triumphant pianoforte.

May Hill Arbuthnot and Zena Sutherland, in their Children and Books, *4th edition (copyright © 1947, 1957, 1964, 1972 by Scott, Foresman and Co.), Scott, Foresman, 1972, p. 221.*

Lloyd Alexander's Celtic romances lack the magnificence of Lewis's vision and the depth of his bathos alike. They share with the 'Narnia' books a preoccupation with the nature of evil and the necessity of sacrifice. . . . There are powerful episodes in [the Prydain Chronicles], but it is rather more important that there is also fun, a rare element which seldom manages to fight to the surface of the heroic fantasy.

Marcus Crouch, in his The Nesbit Tradition: The Children's Novel in England 1945-1970 *(© Marcus Crouch 1972), Ernest Benn, 1972, pp. 125-26.*

Lloyd Alexander's sagas of the medieval Kingdom of Prydain strongly suggest that all lives, real or magical, have an inherent order and logic. There are lessons to be learned, responsibilities to be carried out and rules to be obeyed not only within one's own family or school but even—and sometimes especially—in fairylands.

Selma G. Lanes, in her Down the Rabbit Hole: Adventures and Misadventures in the Realm of Children's Literature *(copyright © 1971 by Selma G. Lanes), Atheneum, 1972, p. 132.*

Though the whole [cycle] clearly springs out of Mabinogion country (old Welsh legendary landscapes, names and moods), with a probable glance or two at [T. H. White's] *The Sword in the Stone*, it is also a superb invention in its own right—a rich alliance of humour, terror, wit, ideas and some twangling harpstring notes. . . . [Throughout the Chronicles] the darkest occasions are always lightened by some character's semi-absurd yet undeniable commonsense.

The Times Literary Supplement *(© Times Newspapers Ltd., 1973), April 6, 1973, p. 379.*

Lloyd Alexander earns the respect due to one who has conceived and carried out a large, complex design. I cannot feel however that he has caught the true spirit either of Wales or of Welsh legend; or that he has created a satisfying epic in its own right. Part of his trouble, I think, comes from an imperfect marriage of ancient and modern. He has rejected antique language, which is right; but the proper purpose of such a rejection is to secure greater naturalness. In making his dialogue obtrusively contemporary-colloquial; in giving his hero the title of Assistant Pig-Keeper; in causing (for instance) the King of the Fair Folk to sound like a harassed, self-important, not very competent business man, Lloyd Alexander creates an atmosphere of anachronism which works against credibility.

Taran is a good hero. He is brave, loyal, well-meaning, a leader—a fit figure for identification—and at the same time he sometimes fails, is sometimes wrong, does not always think clearly enough or far ahead. And the spirited Princess Eilonwy is an attractive heroine, although to an adult reader at least her tone of voice eventually grows tiresome. The lesser characters depend too much on one or two endlessly stressed features or phrases. . . . And although admittedly in a five-volume romance you cannot build up tension steadily towards a single climax, there is too much to-ing and fro-ing, too frequent a feeling that one is not really getting anywhere. Only in the last fifty pages or so of *The High King*, I feel, does Lloyd Alexander rise close to the considerable heights at which he has aimed. There is a fine and memorable creation however—based on legend, but imbued with individual imaginative power—in the Cauldron Born, those deathless warriors who are evilly brought back to life but deprived of all that made them human.

John Rowe Townsend, in his Written for Children: An Outline of English Language Children's Literature, *revised edition (copyright © 1965, 1974 by John Rowe Townsend; reprinted by permission of J.B. Lippincott Company), Lippincott, 1974, p. 251.*

***TARAN WANDERER* (1967)**

[In *Taran Wanderer*, a] young man searches for his identity and finds that he is not what he was born but what he is becoming, that he is, in short, *himself*. . . . Taran, the Assistant Pig-Keeper of the first three Prydain books, passes through many Welsh terrors and not a few European clichés. . . . Were these commonplaces seen with fresh insight, were the narrative written in a more muscular, less self-conscious style, this version of a familiar theme might work; the identity crisis is universal and the adventure leading to its solution moves very well—but the extra elements are missing.

Kirkus Service *(copyright © 1967 Virginia Kirkus' Service, Inc.), February 15, 1967, p. 195.*

In the end [of "Taran Wanderer"], through his own experience of failure and with the help of four master craftsmen, Taran learns that the secret lies not in his parentage but within himself. Like all men, he is both strong and weak, courageous and fearful; but at the same time he is an individual, different from everyone else.

Lloyd Alexander's triumph is that while his plots follow a slashing heroic pattern, his quest is into the subtleties of manhood itself. It is rare that high excitement yields such quiet wisdom.

Jean Fritz, in The New York Times Book Review, *(© 1967 by The New York Times Company; reprinted by permission), April 9, 1967, p. 26.*

This poignant and spirited fourth chronicle of the mythical kingdom of Prydain has more depth than the earlier stories. . . . Taran Wanderer does not find the birthright he has been seeking but after experiencing shame, failure, and despair comes to realize that parentage makes little difference and that manhood is something not given but earned. The book will be most fully understood when read as a sequel to *The Castle of Llyr* . . . and the other Prydain stories.

The Booklist and Subscription Books Bulletin *(© 1967 by the American Library Association), April 15, 1967, p. 905.*

[*Taran Wanderer* is a] fourth book about the land of Prydain. . . . A bit more somber than the preceding books, this [one] is also more significant; although the theme is serious, there is no paucity of daring forays, wicked enchanters, tiny people, desperate fights, et cetera; there is, in fact, all of the color and adventure one expects in the land of fantasy.

Zena Sutherland, in Bulletin of the Center for Children's Books *(copyright 1967 by the University of Chicago; all rights reserved), May, 1967, p. 133.*

Of the four books [about Prydain, *Taran Wanderer*], it seems to me, can most quickly capture the younger reader's interest, so soon is he plunged into excitement. . . . As Taran begins seriously to examine his dreams and hopes, the story becomes more philosophical, but so deeply is the reader involved that there is no lessening of interest. Taran, who in the other books is the usual two-dimensional fairy-tale hero, in this story is more completely realized, so that the rather mature, thoughtful ending is very satisfying.

Ruth Hill Viguers, in The Horn Book Magazine *(copyright © 1967, by The Horn Book, Inc., Boston), June, 1967, p. 341.*

***THE TRUTHFUL HARP* (1967)**

The interplay of courtliness and wit is consistent throughout the tight story, making [*The Truthful Harp*] more than a preview of Prydain; it is more successful than *Coll and His White Pig* also in its pictorialization—the three-color illustrations [by Evaline Ness] are both rich designs and richly humorous. Any child who's known knighthood in flower will enjoy this amusing offshoot.

Kirkus Service *(copyright © 1967 Virginia Kirkus' Service, Inc.), October 15, 1967, p. 1268.*

An engaging character familiar to older readers of Mr. Alexander's books about the land of Prydain, the amiable Fflewddur Flam here is presented at the beginning of his career as a wandering bard. . . . [Evaline Ness'] illustrations are deft and humorous although sedate in color; the writing has humor, vitality, and a distinctive turn of phrase.

Zena Sutherland, in Bulletin of the Center for Children's Books *(copyright 1968 by The University of Chicago; all rights reserved), February, 1968, p. 89.*

OTHER CITATIONS

Publishers' Weekly, *November 20, 1967, p. 56.*

Zena Sutherland, in Saturday Review, *January 27, 1968, p. 35.*

Ethel L. Heins, in The Horn Book Magazine, *February, 1968, p. 58.*

***THE WIZARD IN THE TREE* (1975)**

[Lloyd Alexander] has spun tales rich in adventure and fantasy—stories that might be ordinary save for the imagination he brings to them. His plotting is excellent, his characters interesting, his language vivid, and it is risky to criticize him for not being other than he is. Nevertheless, ["The Wizard in the Tree"] has rather palled on me. . . .

[We] are confronted with [a] plot about an evil squire who is taking over the village for personal gain and in the process we are also confronted with an enormous 18th-century-sounding dialogue, meant to show us how villainous some villains can be. These scenes do not hold the reader's attention, and as Mallory and the Wizard come to be sought by the corrupt squire, the story takes on the odd characteristics of a Western—people galloping back and forth, shots fired, great fights, great captures.

In the end, of course, all turns out well and the grumpy wizard sets sail for neverland. The girl is left behind, much wiser for her adventures, and the only person who feels cheated is the reader. Perhaps this is because the story has been done so many times before, in various disguises, and done best by Mr. Alexander himself. If he is to continue as an artist, he must find new countries to explore.

Barbara Wersba, in The New York Times Book Review *(© 1975, The New York Times Company; reprinted by permission), May 4, 1975, p. 34.*

The dupes and villains of [*The Wizard in the Tree*] are robustly Dickensian, but there are no set characters; the writing is vigorous and the characterization sly, the plot an inventive embroidery of the battle between good and evil.

Zena Sutherland, in Bulletin of the Center for Children's Books *(© 1975 by the University of Chicago; all rights reserved), July-August, 1975, p. 173.*

When an overworked, orphaned servant girl with a firm faith in magic releases a displaced, crotchety enchanter from his centuries-long imprisonment in an oak, the impact on an eighteenth-century rural English village is at once chaotic and comic. Mallory, a determined, self-reliant female, is an apt choice as foil for acid-tongued Arbican whose wit is sharper than his wizardry. . . . Treachery is foiled; virtue—and ecology—triumph in the resolution of a picaresque entertainment which, although not vintage Lloyd Alexander, is amusing if only for the acerbic commentary of the dusty but undefeated wizard. The meticulously detailed, black-and-white illustrations [by Laszlo Kubinyi] effectively complement the story through their resemblance to eighteenth-century engravings.

Mary M. Burns, in The Horn Book Magazine *(copyright © 1975 by The Horn Book, Inc., Boston), August, 1975, pp. 377-79.*

OTHER CITATIONS

The Booklist, *April 1, 1975, p. 813.*

Kirkus Reviews, *April 15, 1975, p. 451.*

* * *

ANGLUND, Joan Walsh 1926-

A popular American author-illustrator, Joan Walsh Anglund is widely known for her drawings of noseless, mouthless children which appear in *Spring Is a New Beginning*, *Love Is a Special Way of Feeling*, and others. (See also *Contemporary Authors*, Vols. 5-8, rev. ed., and *Something About the Author*, Vol. 2.)

GENERAL COMMENTARY

Joan Walsh Anglund books for very young children are like Vitamin C: too much can't hurt you—but the human mechanism doesn't store it. . . . I'd like to register my preference for Anglund books in the squeeze-box format.

Ramona Weeks, in The New York Times Book Review *(© 1969 by The New York Times Company; reprinted by permission), November 9, 1969 (Part 2), p. 46.*

[In] Mrs. Anglund all is artful contrivance—more like an Oriental dried-flower arrangement than an English nosegay. Mrs. Anglund's fabricated children, their faces no more expressive than Parker House rolls, sit or stand like display dummies in their made-to-order environments. Certainly Mrs. Anglund's tableaux have an immediate and insinuating charm. They are cute, occasionally even droll, and it is tempting to remember our pasts in such cozy clichés. Yet, by consciously manipulating her child characters to fulfill the requirements of preconceived tableaux of childhood, Mrs. Auglund stiffens and falsifies children.

Selma G. Lanes, in her Down the Rabbit Hole: Adventures and Misadventures in the Realm of Children's Literature *(copyright © 1971 by Selma G. Lanes), Atheneum, 1972, p. 37.*

***A IS FOR ALWAYS* (1968)**

Miniature in format (slightly more than 3″ x 4″), enclosed in a slipcase, and decorated with demure, applecheeked moppets, this ABC is obviously a gift item rather than a library book. A typical Anglund product, [*A Is for Always*] will, no doubt, be requested by her considerable following. Libraries may wish to stock it in spite of shelving problems and standards for alphabet books.

Della Thomas, in School Library Journal *(reprinted from the March, 1968, issue of* School Library Journal, *published by R. R. Bowker Co., a Xerox company; copyright © 1968 by Xerox Corporation), March, 1968, p. 127.*

The charm, the idealism and precise delicacy of many of [Joan Walsh Anglund's] books catch the older eye and heart, it is said, instead of being serviceable and entertaining to the child. "A Is for Always," a small alphabet book, won't resolve the argument. It has the same, familiar Anglund-style moppets twined, draped, nestled on letters of the alphabet. The one word text for each page represents abstract virtues—"Obedient," "Patient," "Quick," etc. No adult would turn those things down.

George A. Woods, in The New York Times Book Review *(© 1968 by The New York Times Company; reprinted by permission), March 24, 1968, p. 38.*

***THE BRAVE COWBOY* (1959)**

The text describes [a small cowboy's] activities with sedate restraint, making the imaginative illustrations all the more effective. Small children can enjoy identifying with the child at play and adults can relish the intensity with which the brave cowboy lives in his dream world.

Zena Sutherland, in Bulletin of the Center for Children's Books *(published by the University of Chicago), March, 1959, p. 109.*

[*The Brave Cowboy* is a] charming small picture book in which a little two-holstered cowboy's imaginary adventures . . . are pictured in red in the midst of his everyday activities shown in black. While this technique may prove too subtle for some and the little cowboy may seem too babyish for others, many children will be completely captivated by the book, whether or not they are able to distinguish between the pretend and real worlds as pictured.

The Booklist and Subscription Books Bulletin *(© 1959 by the American Library Association), May 15, 1959, p. 512.*

OTHER CITATIONS

Virginia Kirkus' Service, *February 1, 1959, p. 85.*

***CHRISTMAS IS A TIME OF GIVING* (1961)**

Utterly charming—and in a way that will endear itself to both the small fry who are beginning to have associations with Christmas, and the grown-ups who want those traditions to be carried on. There are the pleasant material things of gifts and a tree, of making cookies and sharing in a crèche; there are the memories enjoyed as families gather. And throughout—without preaching—there is the spirit of Christmas as a "time of giving".

Virginia Kirkus' Service, *August 1, 1961, p. 665.*

[*Christmas Is a Time of Giving*] captures the spirit of Christmas, the giving, sharing, happy family celebrations, and the wonder and joy, all expressed in brief sentences and endearing red-and-green drawings of little children participating in holiday activities.

Charlotte Jackson, in The Atlantic Monthly *(copyright © 1961, by The Atlantic Monthly Company, Boston, Mass.; reprinted with permission), December, 1961, p. 123.*

Quaint drawings and brief text portray Christmas as a time of love and giving. . . . Although the book is slight and not particularly original, the pictures and the diminutive size are endearing and the spirit of Christmas is conveyed in a way that young children will understand.

The Booklist and Subscription Books Bulletin *(© 1961 by the American Library Association), December 1, 1961, pp. 228, 230.*

So Joan Walsh Anglund, author of "Love Is a Special Way of Feeling" and "A Friend Is Someone Who Likes You," again crystallizes a big idea in a very few words in her "Christmas Is a Time of Giving". . . . Some of her illustrations are fussy and over-quaint, but they are just right for such moments as "the time of wrapping gifts and making cookies."

Ellen Lewis Buell, in The New York Times Book Review *(© 1961 by The New York Times Company; reprinted by permission), December 3, 1961, p. 68.*

OTHER CITATIONS

Alice Dalgliesh, in Saturday Review, *December 16, 1961, p. 22.*

***COWBOY AND HIS FRIEND* (1961)**

[Joan Walsh Anglund's] little buckaroo, first met in "The Brave Cowboy," here has a large, imaginary bear for a pardner in everything he does. . . . Mrs. Anglund, in her exquisitely detailed black and white illustrations, has wisely drawn the bear as a friend in soft brown and with just a touch of the transparent.

George A. Woods, in The New York Times Book Review *(© 1961 by The New York*

Times Company; reprinted by permission), April 2, 1961, p. 18.

As a sequel to *The Brave Cowboy,* [*Cowboy and His Friend*] lacks that one's newness of technique, and the idea of a pretend playmate is, of course, not original; but it will be fully enjoyed because everything is beautifully preposterous, and childlike.

Virginia Haviland, in The Horn Book Magazine *(copyright, 1961, by the Horn Book, Inc., Boston), June, 1961, p. 257.*

***THE COWBOY'S CHRISTMAS* (1972)**

If you've seen the other *Cowboy* books the title alone should tell you all you need to know about [*The Cowboy's Christmas*]. . . . [The cowboy is] accompanied throughout all the coyly capitalized activities by his imaginary friend Bear, drawn in red beside the black reality. Isn't it time we stopped stuffing Mrs. Anglund's stocking?

Kirkus Reviews *(copyright © 1972 The Kirkus Service, Inc.), July 1, 1972, p. 719.*

The little cowboy is very busy, wrapping packages and doing chores, and he is very good, always cheerful, not getting into trouble anymore, etc. . . . All of his pictures are drawn in black (the usual no mouth, no nose Anglund cherub) and his imaginary friend the bear, drawn in [red], works and plays with him in each scene. The appeal of the Christmas setting is vitiated by the fact that the book really has no plot, and the repeated pattern of sweetness and light becomes tedious.

Zena Sutherland, in Bulletin of the Center for Children's Books *(© 1972 by the University of Chicago; all rights reserved), November, 1972, p. 37.*

OTHER CITATIONS

Publishers' Weekly, *July 10, 1972, p. 46.*

***COWBOY'S SECRET LIFE* (1963)**

[*Cowboy's Secret Life* is a] small book with a minimum of text, the illustrations using, as did *Brave Little Cowboy*, two colors—one picturing the real activity, the other the imagined scene. . . . Not much to it, but a child can easily see the pretending, and the drawings will beguile Anglund fans.

Zena Sutherland, in Bulletin of the Center for Children's Books *(copyright 1963 by the University of Chicago; all rights reserved), September, 1963, p. 1.*

Moppets who enjoy their own peregrinations into special, private worlds will relish the magical adventures of this brave cowboy [in *Cowboy's Secret Life*]. . . . Real and imaginary exploits [are] charmingly defined by the author-artist.

Charlotte Jackson, in The Atlantic Monthly *(copyright © 1963, by The Atlantic Monthly Company, Boston, Mass.; reprinted with permission), December, 1963, p. 170.*

OTHER CITATIONS

Gertrude B. Herman, in Library Journal, *September 15, 1963, p. 3338.*

Margaret Sherwood Libby, in Book Week, *September 22, 1963, p. 18.*

Pamela Marsh, in The Christian Science Monitor, *November 14, 1963, p. 2B.*

***A FRIEND IS SOMEONE WHO LIKES YOU* (1958)**

This tiny book, diminutively illustrated in color by the author, deals gracefully with a basic and often painful theme. For the child, learning to make friends, in a world where, just a few months ago, no one really existed but mama and papa, is a challenging task. Sweetly, unobtrusively, Joan Anglund leads the youngster into the social arena, providing him with a host of little helpers. . . . [The] old fashioned delicacy of this little book will make *A Friend Is Someone Who Likes You* a favorite companion in the nursery.

Virginia Kirkus' Service, *August 15, 1958, p. 605.*

[*A Friend Is Someone Who Likes You* is a] small book with delicate and detailed drawings and some gentle thoughts, for reading aloud to small children. . . . The proposals that a brook shows how it likes you by letting you sit quietly beside it, and the wind shows that it likes you by following you everywhere you go, seem to strain the idea.

Zena Sutherland, in Bulletin of the Center for Children's Books *(published by the University of Chicago), September, 1958, p. 2.*

Delicate drawings and poetic text define a friend in terms understandable and satisfying to the young child, though perhaps not sufficient for the literal-minded adult. An intimate, charming little book. . ., [*A Friend Is Someone Who Likes You*] is the kind many adults will take pleasure in giving to a very special child, and is likely to appeal as much to the child's mother as to the child himself.

Ruth Hill Viguers, in the Horn Book Magazine *(copyright, 1958, by the Horn Book, Inc., Boston), December, 1958, p. 461.*

OTHER CITATIONS

Laura E. Cathon, in Library Journal, *September 15, 1958, p. 2492.*

Helen Fuller, in Saturday Review, *November 1, 1958, p. 43.*

***LOVE IS A SPECIAL WAY OF FEELING* (1960)**

[*Love Is a Special Way of Feeling*] is charming. . . . Mrs. Anglund's continuing choice of abstract—and important—subjects for children is commmendable. But her tendency to ignore rather than acknowledge the ambiguities inherent in her themes, her bent toward the didactic, and her apparent inability to distinguish between the way people feel about each other and about things is unfortunate.

Irma Simington Black, in Saturday Review *(copyright © 1960 by Saturday Review, Inc.; reprinted with permission), March 19, 1960, p. 42.*

Love is defined in the young child's terms to make a perfect valentine of a little book for any time of the year. There is no variety in Mrs. Anglund's pictures of children but the gentleness and delicacy of her drawings are very appealing.

Ruth Hill Viguers, in The Horn Book Magazine *(copyright, 1960, by the Horn Book, Inc., Boston), April, 1960, p. 123.*

[This] gentle little book is one that certainly should not be forgotten. It is impossible to read its simple rhythmic text—or even to look at its pictures—without a flood of "happy feeling." Little girls should love it as much as uncles and fathers, mothers and aunts.

The Christian Science Monitor *(reprinted by permission from* The Christian Science Monitor*; © 1960, The Christian Science Publishing Society; all rights reserved), May 12, 1960, p. 6B.*

OTHER CITATIONS

Ellen Lewis Buell, in The New York Times Book Review, *January 31, 1960, p. 32.*

Laurie Dudley, in Library Journal, *March 15, 1960, p. 1299.*

The Booklist and Subscription Books Bulletin, *April 1, 1960, p. 486.*

MORNING IS A LITTLE CHILD **(1969)**

[If] your delight requires children like the very, very cute, good, sweet, and dainty mouthless marvels of Joan Walsh Anglund—then *Morning Is a Little Child* is just the book for you.

It is Mrs. Walsh's realization of angel infants in an earthly heaven, and it is pretty as a briar rose, fresh as a laundered baby-dress, and, in short, not everyone's idea of childhood. . . .

In any case, what's so wrong with daydreams? Sometimes they hint at a hidden goodness. Sometimes even the impossible ones come partly true.

Neil Millar, in The Christian Science Monitor *(reprinted by permission from* The Christian Science Monitor*; © 1969 The Christian Science Publishing Society; all rights reserved), November 6, 1969, p. B3.*

This artist's drawings of children with outsize heads and chubby featureless faces are an acquired taste. Possibly the book has been set out in this particular way in imitation of Kate Greenaway's books of verse, but the total effect is very different. There is an antiseptic air about these clean children in their neat environments and the verses they illustrate are little more than jingles, often sentimental. The opening verses set the tone, "Morning is a little child waking from a dream/, Noontime is a yellow cat licking yellow cream/ . . . "

The Junior Bookshelf, *February, 1971, p. 17.*

OTHER CITATIONS

Sada Fretz, in School Library Journal, *September, 1969, p. 98.*

SPRING IS A NEW BEGINNING **(1963)**

[*Spring Is a New Beginning* is a] small book, with a slight and lyrical text; a full page of rather sentimental drawing illustrates each few lines of text. . . . A pleasant text, but one that seems more appropriate for somewhat older children who can appreciate the mood and style of the writing.

Zena Sutherland, in Bulletin of the Center for Children's Books *(copyright 1963 by the University of Chicago; all rights reserved), March, 1963, p. 105.*

[Joan Walsh Anglund's] pattern has turned to stereotype. The phrases describing spring somehow seem more saccharine than sweet and they lack the freshness of the earlier titles. Most librarians and their library patrons have already decided whether or not they like diminutive children minus mouths and noses. The conclusion to be drawn here is that this text has nothing to offer that other existing titles about spring don't offer with more originality and spontaneity. This one is for the greeting card stores.

Patricia H. Allen, in School Library Journal, *(reprinted from the April, 1963, issue of* School Library Journal, *published by R. R. Bowker Co., a Xerox company; copyright © 1963 by Xerox Corporation), April, 1963, p. 51.*

OTHER CITATIONS

Pamela Marsh, in The Christian Science Monitor, *February 28, 1963, p. 11.*

WHAT COLOR IS LOVE? **(1966)**

The illustrations [in *What Color Is Love?*] are of the thoroughly familiar Anglund children, a style that might be called post-Hummel marzipan. . . . The skin tones employed are not distinct. There is one child shown who might be Chinese or just suffering a touch of jaundice. Two more are rather dark but considerably lighter than the average Sicilian. The total effect brings to mind the book review attributed to Abraham Lincoln: "People who like this sort of thing will find this the sort of thing they like." The market is as assured as it is for red velvet valentines bearing the word "Mother" in gold.

Virginia Kirkus' Service *(copyright © 1966 Virginia Kirkus' Service, Inc.), February 15, 1966, p. 177.*

In this little book with illustrations in [Anglund's] usual style, the message is obvious to the adult, but is it really needed for little children, most of whom have not yet learned about prejudice?

School Library Journal *(reprinted from the March, 1966, issue of* School Library Journal, *published by R. R. Bowker Co., a Xerox company; copyright © 1966 by Xerox Corporation), March, 1966, p. 221.*

[*What Color Is Love?* is a] small book with small-detail illustrations, some in black and white and some in pale pastels; both the pictures and the text are mildly sugared and innocuous. The text does have some value in the simple way it suggests that people not be judged by external characteristics. . . . The book ends with the question of the title, rather weakly.

Zena Sutherland, in Bulletin of the Center for Children's Books *(copyright 1966 by the University of Chicago; all rights reserved), July-August, 1966, p. 173.*

* * *

ARMSTRONG, William H(oward) 1914-

William Armstrong, an American author who has written articles and books on education, writes children's books which often involve Black Americans. His *Sounder* won the 1970 Newbery Medal and a 1970 Lewis Carroll Shelf Award. (See also *Contemporary Authors*, Vols. 19-20 and *Something About the Author*, Vol. 4.)

BAREFOOT IN THE GRASS (1970)

[An] initial overdose of the bucolic laced with laudanum ("Free to roam and dream, unhampered by sophisticated restraints . . .") makes [*Barefoot in the Grass*] anything but a tempting life-story. Besides, it's over before it's hardly begun, being summarized on page twelve—in the subjunctive mood that along with dropped g's and "plain stuff" in quotes sets the style. . . . Label it dry goods and fancy notions.

Kirkus Reviews *(copyright © 1970 The Kirkus Service, Inc.), November 1, 1970, p. 1203.*

[This] biography [of Grandma Moses] is weak despite the interesting subject, quite full details on her life, and a background colored by period flavor. . . . The writing is heavy with rural idiom in the dialogue, laden with flowery phrases . . . and committed to the use of quotation marks for quite ordinary words and phrases: "They gave substance and dimension to 'the stuff' of dreams and memory" or, ". . . among those who came to 'pay their last respects'."

Zena Sutherland, in Bulletin of the Center for Children's Books *(© 1971 by the University of Chicago; all rights reserved), February, 1971, p. 86.*

[*Barefoot in the Grass*] is a folksy slice of Americana and an affectionately sentimental view of [Grandma Moses] as child, hired girl, wife and mother. Eight full-color plates and both endsheets enliven the text, which substitutes for appraisal of Grandma Moses' work brief commentaries by John Canaday and Louis Bromfield. While waiting for a livelier, less moralistic treatment, young readers wanting the salient facts of the artist's life would do better to consult standard reference works than this rather tedious biography.

Priscilla Moxom, in School Library Journal *(reprinted from the March, 1971, issue of* School Library Journal, *published by R. R. Bowker Co., a Xerox company; copyright © 1971 by Xerox Corporation), March, 1971, p. 125.*

HADASSAH: ESTHER THE ORPHAN QUEEN (1972)

[*Hadassah: Esther the Orphan Queen* is a] palatable introduction to the book of Esther. In this retelling, William Armstrong captures the spirit of the orphaned Esther, who becomes a queen, and her uncle Mordecai, who rises to the rank of prime minister. . . . Passages describing the palace of Xerxes and the streets of Susa will appeal to youngsters' imaginations, and the message of faith and hope for all minorities is conveyed.

Gertrude Serata, in School Library Journal *(reprinted from the January, 1973, issue of* School Library Journal, *published by R. R. Bowker Co., a Xerox company; copyright © 1973 by Xerox Corporation), January, 1973, p. 65.*

As presented [in *Hadassah*], the tale [of Esther] is so tediously burdened with long bits of Jewish history presented as dialogue and so heavy in writing style that the romantic appeal is almost buried.

Zena Sutherland, in Bulletin of the Center for Children's Books *(© 1973 by the University of Chicago; all rights reserved), January, 1973, p. 69.*

THE MacLEOD PLACE (1972)

[*The MacLeod Place*] is a story about Good—as exemplified by the MacLeod farm's natural beauty, and the "old ways of living" which it embodies and preserves—and Evil —which is to say, the destructive trend of progress. . . . Although the characters in this book are somewhat simple, and flatly drawn, the farm itself—its sounds, its smells, its innocent excitements—becomes real and important to the reader. What finally happens to the MacLeod Place, and how Tor's heritage is passed onward to him, are themes which are tenderly handled in this ecological fable.

Maggie Scarf, in The New York Times Book Review *(© 1972 by The New York Times Company; reprinted by permission), November 5, 1972 (Part 2), pp. 2, 10.*

[In *The MacLeod Place*, Armstrong's] plain, dignified prose is well attuned to the subject, an old man at home with nature, but the point is so heavily and frequently reiterated that readers don't have a chance to make their own observations or experience their own responses. Armstrong sets his stage (introducing themes and characters and summarizing background events) in an unlikely five-page monologue that Tor addresses to his dog, and the dialogue is jarringly unnatural. . . . The episodes of family history that are worked into the conversation (some about sheltering runaway slaves seem to be included to establish the MacLeod's humanitarian credentials) as well as Tor's prophetic dream (more like a daydream) which is given inflated emphasis, simply slow down a story which moves with little enough dispatch as it is.

Kirkus Reviews *(copyright © 1972 The Kirkus Service, Inc.), November 15, 1972, p. 1311.*

This boring hymn to nature revolves around whether the federal government will build a highway through the MacLeod family farm in Virginia's Blue Ridge Mountains. . . . Mingled in the slow-moving plot are stories of past events on the farm and descriptions of the sights, sounds, and smells of rural life. The numerous nature passages will prove too much for most young readers, and the only messages in this entirely marginal offering seem to be that there's nothing to do in the city and that Mennonites make great neighbors.

Margaret A. Dorsey, in School Library Journal *(reprinted from the March, 1973, issue of* School Library Journal, *published by R. R. Bowker Co., a Xerox company; copyright © 1973 by Xerox Corporation), March, 1973, pp. 103-04.*

The strongest aspects of [*The MacLeod Place*] are in creating a vivid atmosphere and in the relationships between boy and his grandfather, but the writing style is ponderous and the plot moves slowly; the dialogue is not natural . . . and the book is weakened by such pretentious passages as, "None of the red blood of Scotch Highlanders had been leached out by the generations which separated Angus MacLeod from his sturdy forebears who had crossed the sea, penetrated the wilderness, and tamed it."

Zena Sutherland; in Bulletin of the Center for Children's Books *(© 1973 by the University of Chicago; all rights reserved), May, 1973, p. 133.*

THE MILLS OF GOD (1973)

[In *The Mills of God*] Aaron, like his nameless counterpart in "Sounder," is a character with whom young readers will identify and ache; however, he is so unremittingly good that he is a bit hard to swallow. . . .

The story moves slowly; the action is subdued and understated and somehow fails to draw the reader into it. However, Mr. Armstrong uses detail well. . . . The book comes alive during the scenes involving the dog, but the high-action moment of the story, when Aaron is threatened by the bull, is slowed almost to somnambulance by over ten pages of backflashes.

Lynn Hall, in The New York Times Book Review *(© 1973 by The New York Times Company; reprinted by permission), October 7, 1973, p. 8.*

An Appalachian story, set in the Depression Era, [*The Mills of God*] does indeed grind slowly, its minimal value in the picture it gives of the period and locale. . . . The pace of the book is plodding, with long passages of static exposition, and the characterization is superficial; since the most forceful character is Ruffner, it seems quite out of character that this domineering, tough man should commit suicide out of remorse for an action that might have only indirectly been responsible for the boy's supposed death—it is also an awkwardly abrupt ending.

Zena Sutherland, in Bulletin of the Center for Children's Books *(© 1973 by the University of Chicago; all rights reserved), December, 1973, p. 57.*

OTHER CITATIONS

Publishers' Weekly, *July 16, 1973, p. 111.*

Robert Nye, in The Christian Science Monitor, *November 7, 1973, p. B4.*

SOUNDER (1969)

[*Sounder*] journeys among lonely and vicious events of a tragic, terrifying nature. There are no lies. But I am not sure children should read this book. If so, perhaps parents should loiter nearby, ready to enforce their child's revulsion from violence so truly and so well described. . . .

The deliberate cool of its telling follows McLuhan's rule: We are urged into participation, a moral questioning and a moral wonder. When we stop reading, we want to hear the living voice, the distinctively human sound of this anonymous, black family.

June Meyer Jordan, in The New York Times Book Review *(© 1969 by The New York Times Company; reprinted by permission), October 26, 1969, p. 42.*

There is an epic quality in the deeply moving, long-ago story of cruelty, loneliness, and silent suffering. The power of the writing lies in its combination of subtlety and strength. Four characters are unforgettable: the mother, with her inscrutable fortitude and dignity; the crushed and beaten father; the indomitable boy; and the "human animal," Sounder.

Ethel L. Heins, in The Horn Book Magazine *(copyright © 1969 by The Horn Book, Inc., Boston), December, 1969, p. 673.*

[*Sounder* is a] rarely beautiful, understated novel about an impoverished black sharecropper and his family in the American South. . . . The human characters' namelessness lends them universality as oppressed people, while [William Armstrong's] authentic, detailed descriptions of their particular appearance, home, food, and hard-to-casually-brutal environment assure their individuality. . . . An utterly effective depiction of the repressive environment makes readers understand that the characters lack behavioral options: they are neither ineffectual nor cowardly, but heroic and noble; seeming passivity is really a quiet, stoical dignity. . . . An extraordinarily sensitive book, guaranteed discussions now and a long life in the memories of all readers.

Diane G. Stavn, in School Library Journal *(reprinted from the December, 1969, issue of* School Library Journal, *published by R. R. Bowker Co., a Xerox company; copyright © 1969 by Xerox Corporation), December, 1969, p. 56.*

The story of a black sharecropper's family, [*Sounder* is] written with quiet strength and taut with tragedy. . . . Grim and honest, the book has a moving, elegiac quality that is reminiscent of the stark inevitability of Greek tragedy.

Zena Sutherland, in Bulletin of the Center for Children's Books *(© 1971 by the University of Chicago; all rights reserved), February, 1971, p. 86.*

The philosophical content of [*Sounder*] moves one in such a manner that those words which spring most readily to mind —'human dignity', 'love', 'hope', and 'faith', seem inadequate. These qualities are there, but to mention them is something like describing Beethoven's Ninth as 'tuneful'.

Margot Petts, in Children's Book Review *(© 1971 by Five Owls Press Ltd.), April, 1971, p. 54.*

What the white author of *Sounder* has done to the Black characters is to diminish their role as instruments in effecting change. More important, the author has denied Black youth the privilege of having role models with which they can identify and find fulfillment. . . .

[William H. Armstrong] renders the father and boy impotent, much as William Styron portrayed the character of Nat Turner. The mother's character pales against the strong Black women history tells us about—Harriet Tubman, Sojourner Truth. When you study the Black actors in *Sounder*, you wonder how Black people could have survived social genocide since 1619.

Rae Alexander, "What is a Racist Book?," in The Black American in Books for Children: Readings in Racism, *edited by Donnarae MacCann and Gloria Woodard (copyright 1972 by Donnarae MacCann and Gloria Woodard), Scarecrow, 1972, pp. 61-2.*

[One] may question whether a superb book like *Sounder* is not also aesthetically flawed by its moral limitations—its nostalgic evocation of endurance with all hostility (except in one fantasy passage) repressed; an insensitivity which puts a man [in] jail for stealing food yet neglects to describe the economic impact of his imprisonment on his family; and its final tone of specious optimism which denies the irrevocable psychic damage to the child of the experiences so vividly evoked.

Evelyn Geller, "Aesthetics, Morality, and the Two Cultures," in The Black American in Books for Children: Readings in Racism, *edited by Donnarae MacCann and Gloria Woodard (copyright 1972 by Donnarae MacCann and Gloria Woodard), Scarecrow, 1972, p. 37.*

The style of *Sounder* is white fundamentalist; the words, imagery, and philosophy are simple, direct, and interwoven into the story are occasional religious tales offering hope of a "heavenly sanctuary." . . . The music of Sounder's family is more the "white spiritual" than "blues." Black language, a vital and historic means of communication for the creation of a story of Black people, is totally absent. . . .

Why is no one in the sharecropper's family identified by a name, except the dog, Sounder? The mother is simply "mother," the father, "father," and the youth, "boy." This would be an acceptable literary device in the hands of a Black author. For a white author to resort to it immediately raises the issue of white supremacy. Within the white world, deep-seated prejudice has long denied human individualization to the Black person. . . .

The mother in the story is the Black stereotype of the Southern Tradition. Toward her children she shows no true feeling, no true compassion—strictly a Southern interpretation of Black motherhood.

Albert V. Schwartz, "Sounder: A Black or a White Tale?," in The Black American in Books for Children: Readings in Racism, *edited by Donnarae MacCann and Gloria Woodard (copyright 1972 by Donnarae MacCann and Gloria Woodard), Scarecrow, 1972, pp. 90, 92.*

We do not need any more books like William Armstrong's *Sounder*, where a black child who watches his father destroyed by racism overcomes the horrors of childhood to attain the lofty position of being allowed to sit in the white man's kitchen and help the white man's children become intellectually stimulated.

Dorothy M. Broderick, in her Image of the Black in Children's Fiction *(copyright © 1973 by Dorothy M. Broderick), Bowker, 1973, p. 180.*

Some of the charges made against *Sounder* seem obviously misguided; the fact that the sharecropper's family are referred to as the father, the mother, the boy, rather than by name is surely not because 'within the white world, deep-seated prejudice has long denied human individualization to the black person'. It must have been the author's intention that his characters should appear universal, not tied down to a local habitation and a name. A charge of lack of authenticity is hard to evaluate; it depends on what you mean by authenticity. To me it has always seemed that truth in a novel is truth to the enduring, underlying realities of human nature; and that these enduring realities are recognizable whatever the context. It is not necessary or desirable that writer or critic be restricted to what he knows from direct experience; otherwise no man could write about women, no middle-aged person could write about old age; no one at all could write about the past. . . .

Sounder, though by no means a masterpiece, is a brief, bleak book that tells an elemental story of hardship, suffering and endurance; tells it memorably and well.

John Rowe Townsend, in his Written for Children: An Outline of English Language Children's Literature, *revised edition (copyright © 1965, 1974 by John Rowe Townsend; reprinted by permission of J.B. Lippincott Company), Lippincott, 1974, p. 275.*

OTHER CITATIONS

Zena Sutherland, in Saturday Review, *December 20, 1969, p. 30.*

***SOUR LAND* (1971)**

In *Sour Land*, beautiful descriptions of nature, seasonal

change, and the peculiar peace and understanding possible to a man who works with the soil cannot compensate for passionless characters and a lack of drama that is incredible given the potentially stirring situations. . . . Here, the elderly, otherworldly protagonist, so superior to temporal events, is too noble to be interesting, and the names given the other characters fail to concretize what are no more than Greek choral voices observing and reflecting on the evil of hatred and violence and the ultimate inviolability of the human soul.

Diane G. Stavn, in School Library Journal *(reprinted from the March, 1971, issue of* School Library Journal, *published by R. R. Bowker Co., a Xerox company; copyright © 1971 by Xerox Corporation), March, 1971, pp. 133-34.*

This book will be well received by the child who has never known a black person except in legend or myth. Unlike "Sounder," Mr. Armstrong's first book, which was painful, stunning poetry . . ., "Sour Land" is a crushing disappointment. It presents a boringly super-good black man, Moses Waters, whose main purpose in life seems to be to make himself agreeable to the Stones, the white family he sort of eases himself into. . . . [Though] he's a fine schoolteacher and speaks perfect English in a stiff, rather rhetorical style, he is easily recognizable as guess who? Uncle Remus's great grandson.

Poor, noble Moses Waters! That the battered but real presence I knew in "Sounder" should come to this; this smooth, meek, white-washed fake fit for nothing so well as Progressive Plantation magazine.

Alice Walker, in The New York Times Book Review *(© 1971 by The New York Times Company; reprinted by permission), May 9, 1971, pp. 8, 10.*

The story [of *Sour Land*], quietly told, is autobiographical in source; and, on the surface, is idyllic in its picture of country life. Despite the constant undercurrent of local disapproval of the Stone family's intimacy with Moses . . . only in the last chapter—four years after the opening of the story—do the events leading to the final violence occur. . . . [The] story, told with deep feeling, avoids indignation. . . . A sincerely idealistic and elegiac presentation of one of America's tragic dilemmas.

Paul Heins, in The Horn Book Magazine *(copyright © 1971 by The Horn Book, Inc., Boston), June, 1971, p. 285.*

Clearly meant as an indictment of prejudice and violence, [*Sour Land*] loses impact because Moses Waters is portrayed almost as a Christ figure. He knows everything, he accepts everything, he is patience and tolerance incarnate; he is not convincing. "In his eyes was a gentleness and depth of light. To look into these eyes, floating in their dark sea and filled with understanding, was to feel the presence of a secret, and of a voice crying out in deafening silence—discover me."

Zena Sutherland, in Bulletin of the Center for Children's Books *(© 1971 by the University of Chicago; all rights reserved), July-August, 1971, p. 165.*

B

BOND, (Thomas) Michael 1926-

An English author best known for his character Paddington Bear, Michael Bond writes short stories, articles, and radio and television plays as well as humorous books for children. (See also *Contemporary Authors*, Vols. 5-8, rev. ed., and *Something About the Author*, Vol. 6.)

GENERAL COMMENTARY

I thought on first meeting Paddington that he was a little too Poohish to be original. This first impression was unjust. Paddington shares with Pooh only his bearishness—and this superficially, for Pooh has sawdust under his pelt—and a certain sententiousness of speech. The humour of Paddington is largely visual; it is not what he is but what he does and how he does it that is funny. . . . [Paddington] has become a part of the folk-lore of childhood, not because he appears in a great or even a particularly good book, but because there is something in his personality which lodges permanently in the imagination.

Marcus Crouch, in his The Nesbit Tradition: The Children's Novel in England 1945-1970 *(© Marcus Crouch 1972), Ernest Benn, 1972, pp. 106-07.*

A BEAR CALLED PADDINGTON (1960)

Utter and lovable nonsense this—but somehow one reads with enchantment and credulity about Paddington and his marmalade, Paddington and the sticky cream buns, Paddington and a succession of mishaps, all in good faith. It's all very English—but then so are Alice and Mary Poppins and Peter Pan and a host of other favorites of makebelieve. Illustrated in line by Peggy Fortnum. This is the sort of book best shared in a family read aloud.

Virginia Kirkus' Service, *August 15, 1960, p. 676.*

OTHER CITATIONS

Pamela Marsh, in The Christian Science Monitor, *November 3, 1960, p. 5B.*

Virginia Haviland, in The Horn Book Magazine, *February, 1961, p. 53.*

HERE COMES THURSDAY! (1967)

[In *Here Comes Thursday!*, the mice's] view of the Grumblies, or human beings, is something like that of the Borrowers for the human beans they knew; but this make-believe lacks the literary distinction of a Borrowers fantasy and the appeal to the very young of this author's Paddington stories. Thursday's story depends upon a more sophisticated play on words and ideas. . . . The book offers fun for shared reading aloud. The ink sketches [by Daphne Rowles] amplify the humor and the liveliness.

Virginia Haviland, in The Horn Book Magazine *(copyright © 1967, by The Horn Book, Inc., Boston), December, 1967, p. 748.*

[Michael Bond] has once again demonstrated his ability to successfully balance animal and human traits, so that the animal characters are readily open to reader identification and their mundane activities are made to seem interesting. Two badly stereotyped foreigners—a mad German scientist with a Katzenjammer Kids accent and a Texas tourist cousin—intrude jarringly on the otherwise mild yet pleasant adventures of the amiable British mice. On the whole, [*Here Comes Thursday!*] seems best suited to doling out in small read-aloud portions just before bedtime.

Elinor S. Cullen, in School Library Journal *(reprinted from the March, 1968, issue of* School Library Journal, *published by R. R. Bowker Co., a Xerox company; copyright © 1968 by Xerox Corporation), March, 1968, p. 127.*

[*Here Comes Thursday!*] has the fluent style and light humor that have made [Michael Bond's] books about Paddington so popular, but it lacks the contrast between an engaging animal character and the realism of human family life that adds a pleasantly nonsensical note.

Zena Sutherland, in Bulletin of the Center for Children's Books *(copyright 1968 by the University of Chicago; all rights reserved), March, 1968, p. 106.*

OTHER CITATIONS

The Times Literary Supplement, *November 24, 1966, p. 1087.*

Kirkus Service, *October 1, 1967, p. 1204.*

The Booklist and Subscription Books Bulletin, *January 1, 1968, p. 541.*

PADDINGTON ABROAD **(1972)**

That thrifty "young English bear of quality" follows an eventful itinerary on his summer tour of France with the Browns. . . . These new adventures [in *Paddington Abroad*], which have been abroad in England for several years now, prove once again that "bears always fall on their feet"—particularly if their name is Paddington.

Kirkus Reviews *(copyright © 1972 The Kirkus Service, Inc.), November 1, 1972, p. 1238.*

Although all of [Michael Bond's] books about Paddington, the bear who lives with the Brown family in London, follow the same pattern, each has been greeted by readers with equal enthusiasm. . . . [Peggy Fortnum's] engaging drawings, the brisk pace, and the light style and humor are no less amusing here as Paddington makes elaborate preparations at home and gets into scrapes in France.

Zena Sutherland, in Bulletin of the Center for Children's Books *(© 1973 by the University of Chicago; all rights reserved), March, 1973, p. 102.*

OTHER CITATIONS

Mary M. Burns, in The Horn Book Magazine, *April, 1973, p. 160.*

PADDINGTON AT LARGE **(1963)**

Paddington Brown, young British bear, once again brings into play his special talent for trouble. For Paddington, the simplest acts—cutting grass or attending a concert—have a way of beginning in mundane fashion, rising to hilarious heights and ending with all forgiven. . . . Whether read aloud to younger children or by the children themselves, there are bound to be gales of laughter for all concerned.

Dorothy M. Broderick, in The New York Times Book Review *(© 1963 by The New York Times Company; reprinted by permission), October 6, 1963, pp. 42-3.*

As in the other Paddington books, each chapter [in *Paddington At Large*] is a separate episode, written in a calm, bland style, about an entirely improbable caper of Paddington Brown. . . . Fun to read aloud, and especially suitable for installment reading.

Zena Sutherland, in Bulletin of the Center for Children's Books *(copyright 1963 by the University of Chicago; all rights reserved), December, 1963, p. 54.*

OTHER CITATIONS

Margaret Sherwood Libby, in Book Week, *November 10, 1963 (Part 2), p. 8.*

PADDINGTON AT WORK **(1967)**

[This] sixth story about an engaging bear is just as amusing as were the preceding ones. Paddington lives with an English family, and one of the charms of the books is their bland acceptance of a bear that is all-but-human. . . . The style is breezy, the action nicely paced. Younger children are a good read-aloud audience for the episodic adventures, but the occasional word-play is a bonus for the independent reader.

Zena Sutherland, in Bulletin of the Center for Children's Books *(copyright 1968 by The University of Chicago; all rights reserved), November, 1968, p. 38.*

OTHER CITATIONS

Publishers' Weekly, *August 28, 1967, p. 277.*

PADDINGTON BEAR **(1973)**

Loyal fans of Peggy Fortnum's [drawings of] Paddington will be disappointed to see that remarkable bear plunked down in such pedestrian surroundings [in *Paddington Bear*]. . . . Bond himself has done the adaptation from the first two chapters of *A Bear Called Paddington* and, even though the changes are basically subtractions rather than outright alterations, it seems a shame to rob Paddington of some of his best lines. . . . [The] motivation for these spin-offs is no doubt primarily commercial. They look it. And anyone who cares as much for a good value as Paddington does can wait until he's old enough for the genuine article.

Kirkus Reviews *(copyright © 1973 The Kirkus Service, Inc.), September 1, 1973, p. 961.*

Bond's classic bear is poorly served in this slight and short retelling of his arrival at Paddington Station and his adoption by the Brown family. The simplified language here has lost the flavor of *A Bear Called Paddington* (. . . 1960), yet it's too difficult to qualify as easy reading. Although [Fred Banbery's] watercolor illustrations capture some of the wistful charm of Peggy Fortnum's line drawings, this is no substitute for the original Paddington. . . .

Katherine Heylman, in School Library Journal *(reprinted from the December, 1973, issue of* School Library Journal, *published by R. R. Bowker Co., a Xerox company; copyright © 1973 by Xerox Corporation), December, 1973, p. 41.*

[*Paddington Bear* brings] the adventures of that lovable bear from "darkest Peru" to a whole new audience. The text, aimed at the K-2 set, describes Paddington's delightful misadventures similar to those found in the original books for older readers. The new illustrations [by Fred Banbery] depict a totally different bear from the one created by Peggy Fortnum, but this one is just as beguiling with a character all his own.

Barbara Dill, in Wilson Library Bulletin *(copyright © 1974 by The H. W. Wilson Co.), January, 1974, p. 381.*

A picture book adaptation of the first two chapters of *A*

Bear Called Paddington pares down the incidents and eliminates the descriptive material that gave—and gives—the original Paddington stories their raffish charm. Here there is the situation, but no opportunity to develop the small Peruvian bear as a character. [Fred Banbery's] illustrations, while they resemble Peggy Fortnum's original drawings, aren't of the same calibre and charm. While this separate and simplified adaptation is an adequate story, it seems a pity not to use the original. . . .

Zena Sutherland, in Bulletin of the Center for Children's Books *(© 1974 by the University of Chicago; all rights reserved), February, 1974, p. 90.*

***PADDINGTON HELPS OUT* (1961)**

Paddington's efforts to help others, or to deal with the barrier set up by a very human British environment, are as original and entertaining as the sincere little "monster" himself. Paddington's world accepts a talking bear but does not accept his *gaucheries* in polite society; thus the inconsistency here is the *tour de force* of some very English farce.

Virginia Kirkus' Service, *July 1, 1961, p. 539.*

The mixture [in *Paddington Helps Out*] is as before and perhaps it's greedy to ask for anything else. Children who have chuckled over his earlier escapades and his endearing combination of bearishness and boyishness will welcome him back as old friend. Still, the first fresh surprise has worn off and one must hope that Paddington will not always be constricted to a formula. He's far too original for that.

Ellen Lewis Buell, in The New York Times Book Review *(© 1961 by The New York Times Company; reprinted by permission), August 27, 1961, p. 22.*

OTHER CITATIONS

Virginia Haviland, in The Horn Book Magazine, *October, 1961, p. 443.*

***PADDINGTON MARCHES ON* (1964)**

Delightful though the little bear is—and he is no less lovable [in *Paddington Marches On*] than in previous books—one has the uncomfortable feeling that Mr. Bond is now doggedly thinking up new adventures for him—that tales as well as bear are plodding on. But 6-10's will probably welcome them.

Patience M. Daltry, in The Christian Science Monitor *(reprinted by permission from* The Christian Science Monitor; *© 1965 The Christian Science Publishing Society; all rights reserved), May 6, 1965, p. 3B.*

If we didn't have the pictures to remind us that he is a bear, we might assume Paddington is a little boy. This thought unmasks the story ["Paddington Marches On"] as the uninteresting device it is.

Jerome Beatty Jr., in The New York Times Book Review *(© 1965 by The New York Times Company; reprinted by permission), May 9, 1965, p. 24.*

[This is a] fifth book about one of the most beguiling animal characters of recent years: Paddington, a bear "from darkest Peru." . . . The plots and ploys are an amusing blend of wildly improbable Laurel and Hardy situations and a bland, grave style; both the realistic (and occasionally acidulous) and the fanciful are deftly echoed in Peggy Fortnum's illustrations.

Zena Sutherland, in Bulletin of the Center for Children's Books *(copyright 1965 by the University of Chicago; all rights reserved), December, 1965, p. 58.*

***PADDINGTON TAKES THE AIR* (1971)**

On looking back through the previous eight Paddington books one is immensely impressed by the way each collection of stories comes up so fresh and full of humorous and highly original situations.

The latest collection [*Paddington Takes the Air*] is well up to standard and whether read by children or by parents to children, both are sure to end up by laughing out loud at the comical exploits of this most unusual bear. He has been compared to Pooh . . . and it is certain that he will be just as enduring in the years to come. . . . Whether having a tooth capped, attending an evening dance, or taking part in a gymkhana, when Paddington literally takes the air, every situation is exploited to the full by Michael Bond's sense of humour.

As previously, the most unusual things happen to Paddington, many of his own making, but all are plausible in the context of each story. An accolade too for Peggy Fortnum's so simple, but effective drawings which have projected the Paddington image in all the books. . . . Compulsive reading for all ages.

Eric Hudson, in Children's Book Review *(© 1971 by Five Owls Press Ltd.), February, 1971, p. 16.*

***THE TALES OF OLGA DA POLGA* (1972)**

Michael Bond's account of the vicissitudes of a guinea-pig in *The Tales of Olga da Polga* will amuse readers and listeners. The world is seen through the eyes of the cunning Olga, whose puffed-up ego is gently deflated by Noel, the worldly wise cat, by the jauntily perky hedgehog, Fangio, and by Graham, the gloomily philosophical tortoise. . . . There is a touch of Bunter and Falstaff in Olga, and as an incidental and unobtrusive bonus, readers will get some sound practical advice on how to keep a guinea-pig happy and healthy.

The Times Literary Supplement *(© Times Newspapers Ltd., 1971), October 22, 1971, p. 1333.*

Garrulous, cheeky and omnivorous, Olga da Polga squeaks through a series of adventures in her new life with a family she affectionately knows as Mr., Mrs., and Karen Sawdust. . . . [Her] observations . . . are perfectly scaled to a guinea pig's eye-view. Olga may not be destined to go as far as her fellow Peruvian Paddington, but like him she transforms childishness into virtue and child-sized scrapes into triumphs with an elan that's contagious.

Kirkus Reviews *(copyright © 1973 The Kirkus Service, Inc.), January 15, 1973, p. 60.*

[Michael Bond] has drawn another beguiling creature with a distinct personality—a guinea pig whose cleverness equals that of Paddington. . . . [*The Tales of Olga da Polga*] has far more than an average amount of charm and humor: The repartee between Olga and Noel the cat, Fangio the hedgehog, and sleepy Graham the tortoise becomes a game of oneupmanship; and there's plenty of action as well.

Virginia Haviland, in The Horn Book Magazine *(copyright © 1973 by The Horn Book, Inc., Boston), June, 1973, p. 268.*

Olga da Polga is a guinea pig with an exuberant zest for life and a penchant for inventing stories such as a romantic explanation of why guinea pigs have no tails. Although Olga expresses herself in human terms, her actions evince the innate characteristics of a guinea pig and the author's deft chronicle of her many adventures is a delightful blend of realism and fancy.

The Booklist *(© American Library Association 1973), June 15, 1973, p. 987.*

[In *The Tales of Olga da Polga*] the humor is not so much in Olga's adventures, since she is hutchbound, but in her personality. Complacently confident of her own charms and given to outrageous invention when it suits her purpose, [Olga tells her] tales . . . to other animals with such assurance that they believe her impromptu fibs readily. Not as much action here as in the Paddington stories, but the humor and vitality of [Bond's] writing make Olga and her tall tales highly amusing.

Zena Sutherland, in Bulletin of the Center for Children's Books *(© 1973 by the University of Chicago; all rights reserved), November, 1973, p. 38.*

OTHER CITATIONS

Charlotte Burton, in Library Journal, *April 15, 1973, p. 1384.*

Keo Felker Lazarus, in The Christian Science Monitor, *May 2, 1973, p. B5.*

Donald B. Reynolds, Jr., in Top of the News, *November, 1973, p. 80.*

* * *

BURTON, Hester 1913-

Hester Burton, an English author who has edited books for adults, is well-known for her historical novels for children. She received the 1963 Carnegie Medal for *Time of Trial*. (See also *Contemporary Authors*, Vols. 9-12, rev. ed.)

BEYOND THE WEIR BRIDGE (1970)

Life in England in the years immediately following the English Civil War is vividly re-created through the characterization and experiences of three young people whose childhood friendship survives separation, individual differences, and conflicting attitudes. . . . A moving love story as well as an atmospheric historical narrative, [*Beyond the Weir Bridge*] underlines the importance of tolerance and understanding in personal relationships and social actions.

The Booklist *(© by the American Library Association), November 15, 1970, p. 266.*

[In *Beyond the Weir Bridge*, Hester Burton] works on a wide canvas, interweaving her tale of romantic love with the passion of personal commitment to religious, scientific, and political ideas and beliefs. Her characters are memorable but in some respects less engrossing than the powerfully evoked life and events of the time in which they lived.

Diane Farrell, in The Horn Book Magazine *(copyright © 1970 by The Horn Book, Inc., Boston), December, 1970, p. 622.*

[*Beyond the Weir Bridge*] is the well-written story of three friends who have to decide for themselves the importance of religious beliefs, parental loyalty, patriotism and love. . . . As fiction this will certainly provide pleasure, and its historical aspects, particularly the sections on the Plague and Quaker movements, will heighten curiosity about English history.

Diane Porter, in School Library Journal *(reprinted from the September, 1971, issue of* School Library Journal, *published by R. R. Bowker Co., a Xerox company; copyright © 1971 by Xerox Corporation), September, 1971, p. 171.*

OTHER CITATIONS

Zena Sutherland, in Bulletin of the Center for Children's Books, *January, 1971, p. 71.*

CASTORS AWAY! (1963)

In *Castors Away* the sea battle is only part of Miss Burton's story of a turn-of-the-century family of four children, a widowed father, a maidservant of character and an army deserter. Trafalgar provides an effective though not a glorious climax. One wonders for some time why the deserter should have been a wheelwright's apprentice or why Edmund should be articled to a prominent surgeon, for instance, but both matters have their eventual place. The grimness, not the glory of the battle is emphasised; it is also the event that brings each member of the family out of childhood into harsh and challenging reality and with its associations, persons and events shape the pattern of their futures. *Castors Away* takes a little time to get under full sail but once fairly at sea the voyage is full of interest.

The Junior Bookshelf, *July, 1962, p. 126.*

There is real flavor here of period, as well as the excitement of romance, adventure, sea-battles, and a zest for living that makes you admire the Henchman family almost from page one. There is a warmth in the writing and a feeling for young people that is honest and real. Seventh-

and eighth-graders should love [*Castors Away!*] for its compelling storytelling and its exciting background. Highly recommended.

Clayton E. Kilpatrick, in School Library Journal, *(reprinted from the September, 1963, issue of* School Library Journal, *published by R. R. Bowker Co., a Xerox company; copyright © 1963 by Xerox Corporation), September, 1963, p. 173.*

OTHER CITATIONS

Zena Sutherland, in Bulletin of the Center for Children's Books, *June, 1963, p. 156.*

Virginia Haviland, in The Horn Book Magazine, *August, 1963, pp. 388-89.*

***THE FLOOD AT REEDSMERE* (1968)**

Overlaying the facts of this great storm [of 1953] on a fictional framework, Hestor Burton shows the shape of courage in English children and their elders. . . .

The small talk is movingly authentic as disaster links neighbor to neighbor, children to oldsters, simple folk to gentry. This powerful story, with its factual source, its accelerated climax, and its man-nature conflict is the best of documentary fiction.

Jane Manthorne, in The New York Times Book Review *(© 1968 by The New York Times Company; reprinted by permission), May 5, 1968 (Part 2), p. 14.*

[*The Flood at Reedsmere*] re-creates the catastrophe with accuracy and interprets its effects with insight. Although there is no real plot, the sequence of dramatic events subtly creates powerful suspense, while the characterizations have the clarity of individuality and truth.

Ethel L. Heins, in The Horn Book Magazine *(copyright © 1968 by The Horn Book, Inc., Boston), June, 1968, p. 322.*

[*The Flood at Reedsmere*] begins very slowly, detailing the personalities involved and the events leading up to the floods; not until the flood itself arises does the story develop suspense or convey a sense of immediacy. The events are realistically and believably portrayed, but many of the characters are lifelessly drawn. There is a good deal of humor in the telling and once they get past the slow first chapters, the action is strong enough to carry readers to the end.

Janet Hellerich, in School Library Journal *(reprinted from the September, 1968, issue of* School Library Journal, *published by R. R. Bowker Co., a Xerox company; copyright © 1968 by Xerox Corporation), September, 1968, p. 130.*

Natural disasters seldom follow the tidy construction of art, and Mrs Burton's narrative, admirably as it deals with each episode, lacks a satisfactory flow of climax and resolution. This need not be blamed entirely on the flood; her later work revealed that structure is not Mrs Burton's strong point. In this context it does not much matter. *The Great Gale* [published in the U.S. as *The Flood at Reedsmere*] is not a novel so much as a chronicle told in terms of human beings, and it bears throughout the quality of absolute authenticity.

Marcus Crouch, in his The Nesbit Tradition: The Children's Novel in England 1945-1970 *(© Marcus Crouch 1972), Ernest Benn, 1972, p. 158.*

OTHER CITATIONS

The Booklist and Subscription Books Bulletin, *June 1, 1968, p. 1138.*

***THE HENCHMANS AT HOME* (1972)**

No contemporary [of Hester Burton's] shows so understandingly, and so tenderly, the anguish of growing pains. *The Henchmans At Home* is not so much a novel as a set of linked short-stories about a family, strung out over ten years. It is also an effective study in social history, revealing the changing society of Suffolk during a decade of quiet revolution. Mrs. Burton evokes the age as skilfully as she does her principals, William, Ellen and Rob and their able, dedicated father and their convention-ridden mother. On this small canvas, she still achieves real portraits, not sketches, and the same sure touch and integrity inform the least of her characters. A gentle, humorous and moving book.

The Junior Bookshelf, *February, 1971, p. 51.*

[*The Henchmans at Home* contains an] old-fashioned family history in six self-contained episodes, the continuity supplied by the characterization of the three growing Henchmans and the certainties of their comfortable Victorian existence. . . . [Some episodes] turn out to be more interesting than they promise. . . . But it takes some sympathy with charity bazaars and amateur theatrics to get that far in each, and a willingness to identify with a bygone sensibility to appreciate the virtues of this solid slick for younger ladies.

Kirkus Reviews *(copyright © 1972 The Kirkus Service, Inc.), January 15, 1972, p. 73.*

Neither as demanding nor rewarding as Burton's historical novels, this string of stories [in *The Henchmans at Home*] is still marked by the author's skillful depiction of time and place and her ability to create real and satisfying characters.

Margaret A. Dorsey, in School Library Journal *(reprinted from the April, 1972, issue of* School Library Journal, *published by R. R. Bowker Co., a Xerox company; copyright © 1972 by Xerox Corporation), April, 1972, p. 143.*

[This is] a warm, realistic story of life in the family of a country doctor, spanning eleven years and consisting of six complete short stories. . . . Funny, serious, touching—the stories vary as the growing experiences of the three young people vary, but all contribute to the depiction of a steady growth of personality and character and of the building of family strength. Beautifully and convincingly written, the story of the trials, triumphs, and everyday experiences of the Henchmans comes to a satisfying conclusion. . . .

Beryl Robinson, in The Horn Book Magazine *(copyright © 1972 by The Horn Book, Inc., Boston), April, 1972, p. 143.*

Set in a small Suffolk town in the 1890's, [*The Henchmans at Home*] is a delightful period piece. . . . [Hester Burton's] writing has vitality and an easy flow, and the convincing period details and historical background are buttressed by the pervasiveness of Victorian attitudes and mores.

Zena Sutherland, in Bulletin of the Center for Children's Books *(© 1972 by the University of Chicago; all rights reserved), April, 1972, p. 118.*

OTHER CITATIONS

The Booklist, *April 15, 1972, pp. 721-22.*

***IN SPITE OF ALL TERROR* (1969)**

Dunkirk and the Battle of Britain come to life in the story of fifteen-year-old Liz Hawtin. . . . Although the broad events of 1939 and 1940 are presented in brief dispatch-like statements (the title of the book is a phrase taken from one of Churchill's speeches), the feeling of the wartime events are presented—as in *War and Peace*—through the eyes of a participant. . . . The major and minor characters, Cockney and Oxonian, are convincing, if typical; but Liz and Ben are well portrayed in their development toward maturity in the novel based on the author's own recollections.

Paul Heins, in The Horn Book Magazine *(copyright © 1969 by The Horn Book, Inc., Boston), August, 1969, pp. 414-15.*

In this superior historical novel, [Hester Burton] gives personal, immediate meaning to facts of war and history through very real, sympathetic characters. . . . Along with Liz, Ben and . . . the British people, American readers will live through the false war of autumn 1939, the terror, courage, and resourcefulness displayed at Dunkirk, and the beginning of the blitz. [*In Spite of All Terror* is a] really good book about the past for teen-aged girls concerned with the future.

Susanne Gilles, in School Library Journal *(reprinted from the September, 1969, issue of* School Library Journal, *published by R. R. Bowker Co., a Xerox company; copyright © 1969 by Xerox Corporation), September, 1969, p. 165.*

Mrs Burton was herself involved in the tragi-comedy of evacuation [during the Second World War], and she puts herself and her family, in the thinnest of disguises, into [*In Spite of All Terror*]; and for once the eye-witness is an expert witness with a keen sense of proportion but no Olympian attitudes. This story of a little girl who went into the country to escape the bombs glows with truth and compassion.

Marcus Crouch, in his The Nesbit Tradition: The Children's Novel in England 1945-1970 *(© Marcus Crouch 1972), Ernest Benn, 1972, p. 85.*

OTHER CITATIONS

The Times Literary Supplement, *October 3, 1968, p. 1107.*

Zena Sutherland, in Bulletin of the Center for Children's Books, *October, 1970, p. 23.*

***KATE RIDER* (1974)**

The plot is taut and the characterisation firmly handled. By concentrating upon the disruptive effect of the [English] Civil War on the lives of one family, [*Kate Rider*] avoids the meaningless stereotypes so usual in other novels of this period. At the same time the background of events is very well sketched in. An alpha, then, for this book. As ever, the illustrations by Victor Ambrus are superb.

Victor E. Newburg, in Children's Book Review *(© 1975 Five Owls Press Ltd.), Spring, 1975, p. 25.*

Hester Burton in *Kate Rider* returns to a theme—the agony of waiting at home while others fight a war—and to a period, the English Civil War—which she has written about before: these are, perhaps, her strong suit as a writer. However, this is a slightly disappointing book. A marvellously textured and loving picture of a farm being worked by too few hands emerges, and a picture of an honest rural life. Hester Burton is good at drawing portraits of likable people, but the history is curiously unintegrated with the fiction—for much of the book it arrives in gobbets by way of news bulletins, and even when the heroine is in the middle of a siege, hungry and in danger, the battle has a muted quality, as though she had gone through it dreaming. Few people read novels for the history, and so these lapses would hardly matter if the fate of the Rider family were story enough on its own; but what happens to them all, though plausible enough and sometimes touching, lacks a coherent shape. Kate, however, is charming enough to beguile the reader all the way.

Jill Paton Walsh, in The Times Literary Supplement *(© Times Newspapers Ltd., 1975), April 4, 1975, p. 369.*

***NO BEAT OF DRUM* (1967)**

Hester Burton's *No Beat of Drum*, though a moving reconstruction of village life during the Agrarian Revolution and the 1830 Labourers' Revolt, is first of all a good novel, with real people. It is not concerned with well-known figures, nor does it openly campaign against a rigid justice which regards a parish orphan's life as of less value than a pedigree mare's, though we understand the personal tragedy involved. . . .

The Times Literary Supplement *(© The Times Publishing Company Ltd. 1966), November 24, 1966, p. 1078.*

What happens to [Joe in Van Diemen's Land] as he searches for Mary and Dick, as well as his life in Hampshire and the long trip on the convict ship, make colorful and absorbing, if depressing, reading. The plot itself, however, is tiresomely conventional, in the Horatio Alger mode, and rather spoils the effect.

Taliaferro Boatwright, in Book World *(©* The Washington Post*), December 31, 1967, p. 10.*

There is, perhaps, too much incident in the plot [of *No Beat of Drum*], but the characterizations are good and the author, from a sure knowledge of the period, writes with forceful honesty of the sordid and precarious lives of the tenant farmers of southern England.

Shirley Ellison, in School Library Journal *(reprinted from the January, 1968, issue of* School Library Journal, *published by R. R. Bowker Co., a Xerox company; copyright © 1968 by Xerox Corporation), January, 1968, p. 81.*

[*No Beat of Drum*] is a fascinating and well-written historical novel of penal colony life in the 1830's. . . . Young readers will enjoy the story while learning a little known facet of English history.

Best Sellers *(copyright 1968, by the University of Scranton), January 1, 1968, pp. 391-92.*

Though the major characters [in *No Beat of Drum*] are fictional, their trials are based on historical fact. Mrs. Burton, not softening reality because her audience is young, has produced a splendid novel of outstanding power and beauty.

Robin McKown, in The New York Times Book Review *(© 1968 by The New York Times Company; reprinted by permission), February 4, 1968, p. 26.*

OTHER CITATIONS

The Booklist and Subscription Books Bulletin, *January 15, 1968, p. 590.*

Mary Silva Cosgrave, in The Horn Book Magazine, *February, 1968, pp. 68-9.*

Zena Sutherland, in Bulletin of the Center for Children's Books, *April, 1968, p. 123.*

***THE REBEL* (1972)**

Like its intelligent, demanding hero this is an uneasy, restless, vivid book—about interesting, concerned people whose lives reflect and illuminate the times they live in. In this sense *The Rebel* gave me the same sort of enjoyment as did reading Hester Burton's *Thomas* [published in the U.S. as *Beyond the Weir Bridge*]—but of the two, *Thomas* has a quality of completeness that *The Rebel* lacks. *The Rebel* seems to me too short a book to satisfy the demands of its theme; I want to know what Stephen made of his job in 'the ragged school' in Manchester and what the children made of him—and it seems to me a necessary working-out of the theme that the reader should know. Perhaps Mrs. Burton is writing a sequel?

Nina Danischewsky, in Children's Book Review *(© 1971 by Five Owls Press Ltd.), December, 1971, p. 196.*

[In *The Rebel*] Miss Burton tries to cram too much into too short a space, and should be taken to task for so doing. Children may like events to crowd in thick and fast, but one cannot expect them to swallow such an incredible succession of incidents without protest. Indeed Miss Burton does herself a disservice; she has written several absorbing and enjoyable books; it is a great pity she has not spent more thought and time on this one, so that her characters could develop with more realism and probability.

The Times Literary Supplement *(© Times Newspapers Ltd., 1971), December 3, 1971, p. 1518.*

Both Stephen's social commitment and Catherine's domesticity are tastefully accommodated [in *The Rebel*] in spite of the author's evident disposition toward the latter and the absence of any emotional grit in either character. A brisk pace and richness of language—Stephen's attempt to explain himself in French, verses from his favorite poems, the formal letters written by the family—add to this neat, well furnished historical romance.

Kirkus Reviews *(copyright © 1972 The Kirkus Service, Inc.), July 1, 1972, pp. 727-28.*

The historical details [in *The Rebel*] are vivid, the writing style vigorous, the characterization sound. The minor threads of the plot (the affairs of Stephen's sister and brother, a thwarted romance, etc.) are not as firmly meshed as they are in most of Burton's stories, but this is still superior to most historical fiction written for young people.

Zena Sutherland, in Bulletin of the Center for Children's Books *(© 1972 by the University of Chicago; all rights reserved), September, 1972, p. 3.*

Not only does [Hester Burton] plausibly re-create the ambivalence of the times [portrayed in *The Rebel*], but she also endows her characters with believable motivation as she interweaves a tranquil romantic subplot with the story of Stephen's passionate political involvement. A compelling, dramatic narrative.

Mary M. Burns, in The Horn Book Magazine *(copyright © 1972 by the Horn Book, Inc., Boston), October, 1972, pp. 466-67.*

Set in England and France during the early stages of the French Revolution, [*The Rebel* is an] average historical novel. . . . Some young readers may be confused by the shifts in focus from Stephen to his sister Catherine and bothered by the foreshadowing of important events in the story. However, the plot should hold more mature readers and Burton's ideas about politics and revolution are worthy of their attention.

Lyle H. Wignes, in School Library Journal *(reprinted from the October, 1972, issue of* School Library Journal, *published by R. R. Bowker Co., a Xerox company; copyright © 1972 by Xerox Corporation), October, 1972, pp. 116-17.*

OTHER CITATIONS

Publishers' Weekly, *July 17, 1972, p. 122.*

The Booklist, *September 15, 1972, p. 99.*

RIDERS OF THE STORM (1973)

If this story has a hero, it is Stephen Parkin whom the reader may have met already in *The Rebel*; but the book is rather the picture of a city at a certain time, Manchester in the late eighteenth century. . . . If Stephen is the only character who is neither wholly good nor wholly bad, this fact does not detract from the liveliness of the picture [of the early industrial era] which conveys more than a straight text-book could the feeling of those times. . . . Ideas rather than characters are the theme of the story, but accompanied by plenty of action to please the young reader. [Victor Ambrus] provides typical pen drawings . . . combining with the author to make yet another outstanding book.

The Junior Bookshelf, *February, 1973, p. 34.*

This stirring sequel to *The Rebel* takes Stephen Parkin to a school for poor children in Manchester, where he assists in the education of children destined for the cotton mills. . . . It hardly needs to be said that Hester Burton has done full justice to her main theme—social and constitutional reform—and has demonstrated every shade and degree of opinion in her characters without over-statement.

Margot Petts, in Children's Book Review *(© 1973 Five Owls Press Ltd.), February, 1973, p. 15.*

The soot of polluted Manchester and the suspicions aroused by a relatively timid group of social activists establish both relevance and authenticity of background [in *Riders of the Storm*]. However, young Stephen Parkin never seems to outgrow either his impulsiveness or his tendency toward self pity, and qualities that were appropriate to his *Rebel* days make him ill-fitted for the serious business of domestic politics. Rudderless.

Kirkus Reviews *(copyright © 1973 The Kirkus Service, Inc.), September 15, 1973, p. 1042.*

Stephen's ideals, frailties, and devotion to his friends are sympathetically handled [in *Riders of the Storm*]; the other characters are well portrayed, and the plot is exciting. The plight of the workers and England's social and economic ills in the late 18th and the 19th Centuries are accurately reconstructed in the story and in Ambrus' black-and-white illustrations.

Nancy Berkowitz, in School Library Journal *(reprinted from the December, 1973, issue of* School Library Journal, *published by R. R. Bowker Co., a Xerox company; copyright © 1973 by Xerox Corporation), December, 1973, p. 52.*

Well written, more tightly structured than *The Rebel*, and fast-paced, [*Riders of the Storm*] is both an exciting story and a sturdy study of corruption and mob violence in a time of political stress.

Zena Sutherland, in Bulletin of the Center for Children's Books *(© 1974 by the University of Chicago; all rights reserved), January, 1974, p. 74.*

OTHER CITATIONS

The Booklist, *November 1, 1973, p. 289.*

Beryl Robinson, in The Horn Book Magazine, *April, 1974, pp. 150-51.*

TIME OF TRIAL (1964)

[*Time of Trial* is an] absorbing story set in England in 1801, with colorful period detail, good characterization, and an evenly sustained plot development. . . . The outcome is realistic, the author avoiding trite situations both in the main theme and in the love story. The dramatic episodes are handled with restraint; the social message is handled with a quiet sympathy that is devoid of sentimentality.

Zena Sutherland, in Bulletin of the Center for Children's Books *(copyright 1964 by the University of Chicago; all rights reserved), April, 1964, p. 123.*

An incident in the struggle for social justice in England a century and a half ago plays an important part in this romantic novel. . . .

Hester Burton is completely at home in the period. This is strong, absorbing writing, arousing sympathy for the exploited and admiration for those willing to suffer for their principles.

Margaret S. Libby, in Book Week *(©* The Washington Post*), May 10, 1964, p. 16.*

When Hester Burton . . . writes a historical novel, it is not a modern romance with appliqués of research but a sound portrait of the period, presented with unobtrusive scholarship. At the same time she makes it painfully clear that human problems simply do not change.

"Time of Trial," set in England during the Napoleonic wars, is a rich and rousing piece of work, relating the attempts of Bookseller Pargeter to better the lot of London's poor. . . . Mrs. Burton's pages throb with life, color and a host of fascinating characters.

Mary Stolz, in The New York Times Book Review *(© 1964, by The New York Times Company; reprinted by permission), May 10, 1964 (Part 2), p. 8.*

The history and the sights, sounds, and smells of England in 1801 come brilliantly alive [in *Time of Trial*]. Characterizations are especially strong against authentic, well-researched backgrounds. Mrs. Burton writes with a flair for history, a feeling for people, and a fine command of words. A worthy successor to *Castors Away!*

Jeraline N. Nerney, in School Library Journal *(reprinted from the September, 1964, issue of* School Library Journal, *published by R. R. Bowker Co., a Xerox company; copyright © 1964 by Xerox Corporation), September, 1964, p. 181.*

OTHER CITATIONS

Nora E. Taylor, in The Christian Science Monitor, *May 7, 1964, p. 8B.*

Ruth Hill Viguers, in The Horn Book Magazine, *June, 1964, p. 302.*

* * *

BYARS, Betsy 1928-

Betsy Byars, an American author, received the 1971 Newbery Medal for *The Summer of the Swans*. (See also *Contemporary Authors*, Vols. 33-36 and *Something About the Author*, Vol. 1.)

THE DANCING CAMEL (1965)

Camilla's choice [in *The Dancing Camel*] teaches children the valuable lesson that the only true happiness lies in not standing out from the crowd; she lacks temper because anything approximating emotion is *verboten* in kid books and Abul is shown to be a non-villainous villain because the world is, as everyone knows, a cheerful and excellent place from which evil was long ago banished. Harold Berson's line drawings perfectly capture the spirit of Miss Byars' text: they are stiff and lifeless, too.

Richard Schickel, in Book Week *(©* The Washington Post*), October 10, 1965, p. 18.*

Even as a child I think I would have said "so what?" to "The Dancing Camel," about Camilla, who will dance for pleasure but not for profit. It offers a tidy little moral without much meat. You end up liking the tricky trader almost as much as Camilla.

Sandra Schmidt, in The Christian Science Monitor *(reprinted by permission from* The Christian Science Monitor*; © 1965 The Christian Science Publishing Society; all rights reserved), November 4, 1965, p. B4.*

OTHER CITATIONS

Virginia Kirkus' Service, *June 15, 1965, p. 573.*

Aileen O'Brien Murphy, in Library Journal, *September 15, 1965, p. 3786.*

Helen Boyle, in The Horn Book Magazine, *December, 1965, p. 624.*

THE 18TH EMERGENCY (1973)

[*The 18th Emergency*] is Byars in a lighter mood (although we never question Mouse's desperation) and her projection of the marked victim's sharpened senses, fantasies of rescue, and frantic thoughts are both funny and empathic.

Kirkus Reviews *(copyright © 1973 The Kirkus Service, Inc.), April 1, 1973, p. 382.*

Thoughtful and sensitive, "The 18th Emergency" is as serious and as real as bloody noses, bullies and tests of honor in a small boy's life. . . . For its skillful portrayal of the loneliness of fear as well as a boy's emotional battle with himself—his frantic thoughts, his fantasies of escape, his gradual awakening to the way things are as against the way he wishes they were—"The 18th Emergency" weighs in this spring as a bantam champion.

The New York Times Book Review *(© 1973 by The New York Times Company; reprinted by permission), May 6, 1973 (Part 2), p. 7.*

[In *The 18th Emergency*] Mouse is alone with his problem—and he finally goes to meet it alone. Byars registers the feelings of a scared boy with the same perception that characterized her book, *The Midnight Fox*.

The Booklist *(© American Library Association 1973), June 15, 1973, p. 988.*

The writing style [in *The 18th Emergency*] is more staccato than it is in other books by Betsy Byars, the treatment lighter, but the perceptiveness is just as sharp and the lesson (not in the least didactic in presentation) is clear: reality is more bearable than fear.

Zena Sutherland, in Bulletin of the Center for Children's Books *(© 1973 by the University of Chicago; all rights reserved), September, 1973, p. 4.*

[In *The 18th Emergency*] Betsy Byars . . . has drawn her young knight's world with delicate lines and perceptive shadings. . . . You may not agree with Benjie that violence has to be part of his solution. But he is a solid and charming character all the same.

Jennifer Farley Smith, in The Christian Science Monitor *(reprinted by permission from* The Christian Science Monitor*; © 1973 The Christian Science Publishing Society; all rights reserved), October 3, 1973, p. 10.*

OTHER CITATIONS

Publishers' Weekly, *May 7, 1973, p. 65.*

Beryl Robinson, in The Horn Book Magazine, *August, 1973, p. 378.*

Syd Hoff, in The New York Times Book Review, *August 19, 1973, p. 8.*

GO AND HUSH THE BABY (1971)

[*Go and Hush the Baby* is a] very simple, warm, casual and realistic story. . . . Mother is busy—not washing dishes, not ironing, but painting a picture—and she wants Will, who is about to go play baseball, to pacify the baby. . . . Not suitable for reading aloud to a group since the speakers are not identified, the book will be enjoyed most by the individual child (especially one with a baby brother or sister), or by a parent and a child sharing it together.

Marion Marx, in School Library Journal *(reprinted from the April, 1971, issue of* School Library Journal*, published by R. R. Bowker Co., a Xerox company; copyright © 1971 by Xerox Corporation), April, 1971, p. 92.*

[*Go and Hush the Baby*] is a nicely-observed comedy about a liberated mother, busy at her easel, who enlists her older son's help in jollying a wailing baby out of his discontent. Older siblings will appreciate the big brother's casual compliance and ultimate success.

Selma G. Lanes, in Book World *(© The* Washington Post*), May 9, 1971 (Part 2), p. 8.*

OTHER CITATIONS

The Booklist, *May 1, 1971, p. 747.*

Zena Sutherland, in Bulletin of the Center for Children's Books, *June, 1971, p. 153.*

THE GROOBER (1967)

[There] isn't much you can say about the groobers. They are totally nonsensical (with the stress on the non-); adults may be tickled by their foolish simplicity, and children who consider them simply foolish will find plenty of room to color in their own improvements.

Elinor Cullen, in School Library Journal *(reprinted from the May, 1967, issue of* School Library Journal, *published by R. R. Bowker Co., a Xerox company; copyright © 1967 by Xerox Corporation), May, 1967, p. 49.*

OTHER CITATIONS

Kirkus Service, *March 15, 1967, p. 334.*

Zena Sutherland, in Bulletin of the Center for Children's Books, *July-August, 1967, p. 166.*

THE HOUSE OF WINGS (1972)

From the beginning Sammy's first day with his Ohio grandfather is experienced not as a more or less skillfully constructed fiction but as a vibrant reality that happens as we read. . . . By the end [of *The House of Wings*] we too have come to know the touchingly but unsentimentally rendered Sammy and the marvelous old man.

Kirkus Reviews *(copyright © 1972 The Kirkus Service, Inc.), April 15, 1972, p. 477.*

[In "The House of Wings," Betsy Byars demonstrates] again her extraordinary ability to explore that primitive point of experience where man and nature confront each other. She writes out of the same tradition that has produced other enduring Newbery winners—Armstrong Sperry's "Call It Courage," for instance, and Maia Wojciechowska's "Shadow of a Bull"—but she has reversed the theme, speaking not of Man Against Nature but of Man in Need of Nature and in search of his spiritual salvation. . . .

[Thanks] to Mrs. Byars's precise understanding of cranes, owls, boys and grandfathers, we . . . are in a sense restored. Not reassured necessarily, but refreshed by this vision of man at home in his natural world.

Jean Fritz, in The New York Times Book Review *(© 1972 by The New York Times Company; reprinted by permission), April 23, 1972, p. 8.*

The House of Wings borders on acceptable adult short story writing. . . . A young boy reeling from the pain of temporary parental abandonment forges a relationship with an eccentric grandfather whom he despises. In attempting to rescue and mend a wounded crane, they come to respect each other for what they are, and as men. The story has a certain depth and life and is morally conspicuous in that the pay-off is maturity rather than "getting" something.

Julia Whedon, in Book World *(© The* Washington Post*), May 7, 1972 (Part 2), p. 11.*

Concentration adds strength to [*The House of Wings*] which is focused entirely upon the two sharply drawn human characters and which takes place within a twenty-four-hour period. In atmosphere and effect, the book is reminiscent of Wilson Gage's *Big Blue Island*. . . .

Ethel L. Heins, in The Horn Book Magazine *(copyright © 1972 by the Horn Book, Inc., Boston), August, 1972, p. 368.*

Betsy Byars seems to get away to a very slow start in *The House of Wings*. . . . [The story] is presented with meticulous honesty, but the slow, minute-by-minute detail of the action and the sparing dialogue do not make for pace or for a gripping story. Neither Sammy nor his grandfather, the crane or even the owl in the spare bedroom is a very forthcoming character, excellently though the natural history of the birds is presented, and the interaction between them all seems, to adapt the author's own description of the crane, to be awkwardly angular.

The Times Literary Supplement *(© Times Newspapers Ltd., 1973), April 6, 1973, p. 382.*

From a rather unconvincing opening [*The House of Wings*] develops into a pleasant long short-story which will appeal to wild-life lovers. . . . Mrs. Byars economically conveys the atmosphere of summer in Ohio, of the ramshackle farmstead overrun by birds, and sketches in deftly the characters of the tough old man and the equally dogged Sammy. Their developing relationship is made entirely credible. . . .

Judith Aldridge, in Children's Book Review *(© 1973 Five Owls Press Ltd.), September, 1973, pp. 111-12.*

OTHER CITATIONS

Publishers' Weekly, *April 17, 1972, p. 59.*

The Booklist, *July 15, 1972, p. 1002.*

Margaret A. Dorsey, in Library Journal, *September 15, 1972, p. 2946.*

Zena Sutherland, in Bulletin of the Center for Children's Books, *November, 1972, p. 39.*

THE MIDNIGHT FOX (1968)

Tommy is not the first hung-up juvenile hero but he is one of the best, and he remembers that summer with Aunt Millie, Uncle Fred and Hazeline with straight-from-the-(skinny)-shoulder sincerity. . . . It's not what he does . . . but how he tells it that makes him such a stand-out, and his digressions (watching an ant on Petie's sneakers, counting hand wrinkles to calculate the day he'll die) are steady, smooth and well-spaced. The laughs are most frequent in the beginning, which gets a reader's attention, and the sly, slow build-up to the final black fox episode is as firm as you could ask for.

Kirkus Service *(copyright © 1968 The Kirkus Service, Inc.), October 1, 1968, p. 1111.*

Tom is an ingratiating character, acutely conscious of the people around him and accepting their limitations with an awkward grace; his musings about Petie and their past ploys are hilarious, his concern for the black fox so much a passion that he cannot tell anyone about it. [Betsy Byars'] writing really sounds like the vocabulary and phrasing of a small boy, and the story develops with ease and pace.

Zena Sutherland, in Saturday Review *(copyright © 1968 by Saturday Review, Inc.; reprinted with permission), November 9, 1968, pp. 64-5.*

[*The Midnight Fox*] is written with quick, quiet humor and some delightful daydreaming sequences, both as convincingly the product of a nine-year-old's pen as are the more serious episodes of the main theme.

Zena Sutherland, in Bulletin of the Center for Children's Books *(copyright 1969 by The University of Chicago; all rights reserved), January, 1969, p. 74.*

What distinguishes [*The Midnight Fox*] from many others on the same theme is the simplicity and beauty of the writing and the depth of the characterization. The boy relates his imaginative introspections with wry humor. He is perceptive enough to understand that many of his problems are caused not so much by the adults in his life as by his interaction with them. His parents, Uncle Fred and Aunt Millie are given fully human dimensions.

Diane Farrell, in The Horn Book Magazine *(copyright © 1969 by The Horn Book, Inc., Boston), February, 1969, p. 52.*

[The] narrator of Betsy Byars's *The Midnight Fox* . . ., Tom, is a splendidly un-hearty hero. . . . But [he] is ready for the experience he has in the story: the perception of beauty in, and feeling for, a wild creature. . . . This is a fine book, I think. It is beautiful in glimpses, and between the glimpses it is often truly funny.

John Rowe Townsend, in his Written for Children: An Outline of English Language Children's Literature, *revised edition (copyright © 1965, 1974 by John Rowe Townsend; reprinted by permission of J.B. Lippincott Company), Lippincott, 1974, p. 279.*

OTHER CITATIONS

Jeraline Nerney, in Library Journal, *December, 1968, p. 4721.*

THE SUMMER OF THE SWANS (1970)

With increasing frequency juvenile fiction is contracting to the dimensions of a short story and the endoskeleton (dialogue, stage directions, asides to the audience) of drama—of which the climax to Sara's season of discontent is a *good* example. . . . [*The Summer of the Swans*] is a succession of clicks that connect, a sparse but acute self-possessing.

Kirkus Reviews *(copyright © 1970 The Kirkus Service, Inc.), March 15, 1970, p. 320.*

The thoughts and feelings of a young girl troubled by a sense of inner discontent which she cannot explain are tellingly portrayed in [*The Summer of the Swans*]. . . . Percipient characterization and realistic dialog heighten the impact of the low-keyed but penetrating story of human relationships and emotions.

The Booklist *(© by the American Library Association), June 15, 1970, p. 1276.*

[Seldom] are the pain of adolescence and the tragedy of mental retardation presented as sensitively and as unpretentiously as in the story of Sara and Charlie, the brain-damaged younger brother she loved so protectively. . . . [*The Summer of the Swans* is a] subtly told story, echoing the spoken and unspoken thoughts of young people.

Ethel L. Heins, in The Horn Book Magazine *(copyright © 1971 by the Horn Book, Inc., Boston), February, 1971, p. 54.*

[*The Summer of the Swans*] has a fine balance in relationships, some sharp characterization and interaction, good dialogue, and only enough action to be a foil for the perceptive development of a situation.

Zena Sutherland, in Bulletin of the Center for Children's Books *(© 1971 by the University of Chicago; all rights reserved), February, 1971, p. 87.*

OTHER CITATIONS

Pamela Marsh, in The Christian Science Monitor, *May 7, 1970, p. B6.*

Amy Kellman, in Grade Teacher, *September, 1971, p. 154.*

THE WINGED COLT OF CASA MIA (1973)

Except for the colt's wings [*The Winged Colt of Casa Mia*] is a typical realistic story—with none of the hushed wonder that usually accompanies such a fantasy element—in which the relationship between a boy and a man is intertwined with a boy's love for an animal. . . . Byars reworks the boy-man-horse formula with considerable skill but with none of the richly imagined vitality of her *House of Wings* (1972).

Kirkus Reviews *(copyright © 1973 The Kirkus Service, Inc.), October 1, 1973, pp. 1094-95.*

[*The Winged Colt of Casa Mia*] is readable and the characterization good. However, [Betsy Byars] is not at her best here: the introduction of the one fantastic element in an otherwise realistic story keeps it from jelling. It has all the familiar elements of run-of-the-mill horse tales, and even the colt's wings don't lift the book very high above the ordinary.

Elizabeth Haynes, in School Library Journal *(reprinted from the November, 1973, issue of* School Library Journal, *published by R. R. Bowker Co., a Xerox company; copyright © 1973 by Xerox Corporation), November, 1973 p. 46.*

The story [of *The Winged Colt of Casa Mia*] hurries and stumbles along like the colt itself. It has a spare, classic brevity and comes to an abrupt halt after the colt's first perfect flight. . . .

The adult reader will think of Pegasus and symbolism and will discover that it took both the painful effort of the man and the insistent love of the boy to get the clumsy creature off the ground and accomplish the miracle. . . . But a boy or girl reading this book will say, "It was really something."

Jane Langton, in The New York Times Book Review *(© 1973 by The New York Times Company; reprinted by permission), November 4, 1973, p. 42.*

Humor is inherent in the conversations between Charles and his uncle, a one-time movie stunt man whom Charles adores, and in the conversations between Uncle Coot and the angry neighbor. Charles' book learning about horses and his ineptness in dealing with things in a firsthand way provide more incongruities. The episodes are skillfully worked out and supply a splendid mixture of high drama, mystery, and often unexpected amusement—all of which are evoked in [Richard Cuffari's] wash drawings.

Virginia Haviland, in The Horn Book Magazine *(copyright © 1974 by The Horn Book, Inc., Boston), February, 1974, pp. 47-8.*

[In *The Winged Colt of Casa Mia*, the] style is smooth, the structure spare, the characterization good although not probing; the combination of realism and fantasy is believable in the context, but it somehow lacks impact—perhaps because, with two aspects of the plot, (the relationship between boy and man, and the story of the winged colt) each robs the other of drama although in a literary sense they combine well.

Zena Sutherland, in Bulletin of the Center for Children's Books *(© 1974 by the University of Chicago; all rights reserved), March, 1974, p. 108.*

[In *The Winged Colt of Casa Mia*] there seem to be two books . . . in a pretty small space: a psychological novel written from Uncle Coot's viewpoint and a fantasy seen from Charles's. Both are fine in themselves but they don't, in spirit or style, overlap. The idea of a flying colt is splendid in the context of a ten-year-old's world, but full of unnecessary complications and unanswered questions in that of an adult. So you don't quite believe or don't, at any rate, suspend disbelief.

Isabel Quigley, in Times Literary Supplement *(© Times Newspaper Ltd., 1975), April 4, 1975, p. 371.*

[*The Winged Colt of Casa Mia* is a] beautifully presented, sensitively written and unusual 'pony' story [which] presents two inherent difficulties. In place of a child narrator, there is an adult, the uncle faced with bringing up a nephew who regards him as a superman, because he has been a stunt-rider in films. . . . The growing antagonism and lack of communication, presented from the adult side, is difficult for a child reader to identify and sympathise with. Secondly, a colt with wings belongs to fantasy, while the rest of the plot is grounded in well-drawn matter of fact. So far from making the fantasy-element more acceptable, this makes the reader distractingly unsatisfied about the colt's future in this materialist world, from which the ranch is not entirely remote. At least Mary Poppins flew away on a gust of wind: the colt is still there and growing fast at the end of the story. On the human level, the man who risks his life to save the stranded colt and the boy who realises his uncle is even more important to him than the colt have come to understand each other. There is a basic improbability, however, that anyone so diffident about explaining himself to the boy should have the eloquence to tell this story so movingly.

The Junior Bookshelf, *June, 1975, p. 194.*

OTHER CITATIONS

Robert Nye, in The Christian Science Monitor, *November 7, 1973, p. B4.*

C

CAMERON, Eleanor 1912-

Eleanor Cameron is an American author who published a novel for adults, writes articles and books about children's literature, and writes science fiction, fantasy, and other fiction for children. (See also *Contemporary Authors*, Vols. 1-4, rev. ed., and *Something About the Author*, Vol. 1.)

GENERAL COMMENTARY

Miss Cameron has the knack of pointing out self-deceptions and other antics of growing up without making them appear either important or "cute." And all the while she is imparting ideas about integrity and consideration.

Patience M. Canham, in The Christian Science Monitor *(reprinted by permission from* The Christian Science Monitor; *copyright © 1971 The Christian Science Publishing Society; all rights reserved), May 6, 1971, p. B6.*

***THE BEAST WITH THE MAGICAL HORN* (1963)**

[This is a] well-told if not very original fairy tale. . . . Many children will wish Mrs. Cameron had written another modern space fantasy . . . rather than this traditional fairy tale; however, they will enjoy the excitement and humor, and parents will find it pleasant for reading aloud. The illustrations [by Beth and Joe Krush], in black and white and color, have a strong sense of outline and design.

Elizabeth Minot Graves, in The New York Times Book Review *(© 1963 by The New York Times Company; reprinted by permission), November 10, 1963 (Part 2), p. 46.*

In fairy tale style, [*The Beast with the Magical Horn* tells] the story of Alison, the poor and beautiful mountain girl who won the heart of a Prince. . . . Authentic style for the genre, but slow-moving; the story lacks both the lightness and the pace that are the best features of the author's previous books.

Zena Sutherland, in Bulletin of the Center for Children's Books *(copyright 1964 by the University of Chicago; all rights reserved), January, 1964, p. 75.*

OTHER CITATIONS

Margaret Sherwood Libby, in Book Week, *October 13, 1963, p. 17.*

The Booklist and Subscription Books Bulletin, *November 15, 1963, p. 313.*

Eloise Rue, in Library Journal, *November 15, 1963, p. 4471.*

***THE COURT OF THE STONE CHILDREN* (1973)**

Cameron's delicate time fantasy is set in a San Francisco museum furnished with the transported appointments of an old French castle. . . . Sometimes the discussions [about time] illuminate the adventure less than they weigh it down with reminders of the author's intent, and when even Nina's new landlady enters quoting a passage about existing out of time, it's hard to suspend incredulity. Nevertheless, the Gil/Nina/Domi relationship constitutes the center of an impressively executed pattern—and, incidentally, a far more ambitious use of a museum background than Claudia's detective work in Konigsburg's *Mixed-Up Files*.

Kirkus Reviews *(copyright © 1973 The Kirkus Service, Inc.), October 15, 1973, p. 1159.*

[Eleanor Cameron's style of writing in "The Court of the Stone Children"] is the kind of writing that one associates with adult novels, and indeed the author has not made a single concession to the conventions of childhood. Her story is complex, multi-layered, and while there are those who will simply find in it an expert Gothic tale, there will be others to catch the note of melancholy that pervades it from beginning to end. The poignance of objects outliving their owners, and the immutable sadness of all human existence: these are Mrs. Cameron's themes. One commends her for them and stands at a very slight distance—in admiration.

Barbara Wersba, in The New York Times Book Review *(© 1973 by The New York Times Company; reprinted by permission), November 4, 1973, p. 28.*

One of Eleanor Cameron's favorite themes—the intermingling of past, present, and future—is exposed in *The Court of the Stone Children*. . . . Although average readers may flounder in the story's intricate and constantly shifting time track, the mystical, dreamlike quality comes through and will appeal to children.

Sarah Law Kennerly, in School Library Journal *(reprinted from the December, 1973, issue of* School Library Journal, *published by R. R. Bowker Co., a Xerox company; copyright © 1973 by Xerox Corporation), December, 1973, p. 60.*

Although early portions of [*The Court of the Stone Children*] lag, the author's highly imaginative integration of such diverse elements as childhood adjustment, concepts of time, prophetic dreams, mystery, and fantasy is ultimately successful and undoubtedly thought-provoking for the special reader.

The Booklist *(© American Library Association 1974), January 1, 1974, p. 487.*

Based on the premise that time is not a linear succession of events but a circle or globe within which present, past, and future are held in everlasting equilibrium, the carefully constructed narrative [of *The Court of the Stone Children*] is sufficiently detailed to provide a satisfying conclusion; and the loving evocation of the San Francisco setting lends credibility to the events described. [This is a] gentle yet compelling story.

Mary M. Burns, in The Horn Book Magazine *(copyright © 1974 by The Horn Book, Inc., Boston), April, 1974, p. 151.*

[*The Court of the Stone Children*] gives us the meeting of two girls—lonely, sensitive Nina, who lives in the San Francisco of today, and Dominique, who lived in the France of Napoleon. This time fantasy is masterful, deftly blending the aura of a historical period with a present-day setting. The writing is accomplished and at times arresting, and the style, like a clear reflecting pool, adds a shimmer to the image within.

Mark Taylor, in Psychology Today *(reprinted by permission; copyright © 1974 by Ziff-Davis Publishing Company; all rights reserved), May, 1974, p. 20.*

OTHER CITATIONS

Ethna Sheehan, in America, *December 1, 1973, pp. 429-30.*

Zena Sutherland, in Bulletin of the Center for Children's Books, *January, 1974, p. 75.*

Publishers' Weekly, *January 7, 1974, p. 54.*

***MR. BASS' PLANETOID* (1958)**

That same audience which signed on for the earlier flight of fantasy, *Stowaway to the Mushroom Planet*, will enjoy the newest variations on that earlier theme—though readers who are unfamiliar with the first book may find [*Mr. Bass' Planetoid*] confusing. . . . Caution: If readers do not wear Special Polarizing filters they may disappear in the final chapter. Or unravel.

Virginia Kirkus' Service, *June 15, 1958, p. 415.*

Peppered with fantastic phrases, and scrambled scientific codes, this fast-paced tale is sure to enlist the interest of readers of the author's "Wonderful Mushroom Planet" and the Miss Pickerell stories by Ellen MacGregor.

Della McGregor, in Saturday Review *(copyright © 1959 by Saturday Review, Inc.; reprinted with permission), February 28, 1959, p. 36.*

OTHER CITATIONS

Albert Monheit, in Library Journal, *September 15, 1958, p. 2496.*

Margaret Warren Brown, in The Horn Book Magazine, *October, 1958, p. 381.*

***A ROOM MADE OF WINDOWS* (1971)**

This is a wonderful novel, a rare bridging of the distance between books for children and adults. It is about Julia Redfern on her way to becoming a writer, a process illuminated with many truths and insights. . . .

Julia's world is full of *people*, not shadowy types as in lesser books, and she responds to them in their complexity and uniqueness. . . .

With seeming effortlessness and no didacticism, [Eleanor Cameron] gives us a strong sense of the time and place. And as if all this were still not enough, there's the added delight of Trina Schart Hyman's faithfully detailed drawings.

Doris Orgel, in The New York Times Book Review *(© 1971 by The New York Times Company; reprinted by permission), April 25, 1971, p. 40.*

[In *A Room Made of Windows*] Eleanor Cameron writes beautifully, with awareness and insight. She weaves fascinating subplots into Julia's story. But action is not stressed. Interest and excitement grow out of inner conflicts and interplay of character. This result is a wise, strong, literate book—a delight to read.

Polly Goodwin, in Book World *(©* The Washington Post*), May 9, 1971 (Part 2), p. 5.*

Constructed with great skill, [this] story is one of human relationships among strikingly real, intense personalities. . . . The period of the book is somewhat vaguely defined; young people may not grasp the clues—often found in [Trina Schart Hyman's] soft-pencil line drawings—and sense the early 1920's. But the setting and atmosphere pervade the story. . . . Everywhere there is imagery in the telling, reminders that [Eleanor Cameron] places great importance on "evidence of the senses." And she writes with assurance and control, without hesitation, yet at a deliberately leisurely pace, allowing herself the luxury of digressions that add richness and dimensions to the story.

Ethel L. Heins, in The Horn Book Magazine *(copyright © 1971 by The Horn Book, Inc., Boston), June, 1971, pp. 290-91.*

[*A Room Made of Windows*] has several minor plots, but they are skillfully woven together in a solid and mature approach to the development of an adolescent's growing understanding. Julia, self-centered and sensitive, responds to the needs of others with increasing perception. The characters are firmly delineated, the dialogue and interrelationships deftly conceived.

Zena Sutherland, in Bulletin of the Center for Children's Books *(© 1971 by the University of Chicago; all rights reserved), June, 1971, p. 153.*

A Room Made of Windows . . . is a [very] relaxed affair, a loosely textured tale woven with many different coloured threads and a multiplicity of patterns. . . . [But] it is crammed so full that one feels as though [Eleanor Cameron] had been permitted to write only one children's book in her life and was determined to get everything in; character, culture, wisdom, music, art, literature, cats, dogs, birds. . . . Though the story is always lively, and points in many exciting directions, this widely panoramic view inevitably makes it appear superficial and the answers to everything a bit too easy. . . .

The Times Literary Supplement *(© Times Newspapers Ltd., 1972), November 3, 1972, p. 1319.*

Julia's room . . . gives her, simultaneously, a sanctuary and contact with the rest of the world. Julia needs both quite desperately. . . . She is no introspective 'Lady of Shallot' in her windowed room; meeting with others . . . is essential to her if her insatiable appetite for 'experiences' to record is to be dulled at all.

In the course of the story, Julia both 'experiences' and gains experience: learning painfully how to give in gracefully, the unwisdom of leaping to conclusions, the self-destroying nature of selfishness, and the meaning of inevitability.

Margot Petts, in Children's Book Review *(© 1973 Five Owls Press Ltd.), February, 1973, p. 12.*

OTHER CITATIONS

Publishers' Weekly, *April 12, 1971, p. 83.*

The Booklist, *May 15, 1971, p. 797.*

Mrs. John G. Gray, in Best Sellers, *May 15, 1971, p. 98.*

Marianne Hough, in Library Journal, *May 15, 1971, p. 1800.*

A SPELL IS CAST **(1964)**

[In *A Spell Is Cast*, characterization] is very good, the seaside atmosphere is described colorfully, and the possible contortions of plot are nicely avoided: there are logical explanations for all the events that seem to Cory mysterious or miraculous. The picture of Stephanie, selfish, impulsive, and generous, is sharp and vivid; she appears at the end of the book, reproaching the child she had always neglected, and just as quickly admitting her own culpability.

Zena Sutherland, in Bulletin of the Center for Children's Books *(copyright 1965 by the University of Chicago; all rights reserved), January, 1965, p. 70.*

How [Cory Winterslow] faces her problems and helps to resolve some of them is told in a hauntingly poignant presentation that pictures the fears and anxieties of a small girl unsure of her place in the adult world. There is enough of a mystery to give the story appeal; more sensitive readers will appreciate the full depths of Cory's plight.

The Booklist and Subscription Books Bulletin *(© 1965 by the American Library Association), July 1, 1965, p. 1028.*

From its opening [*A Spell is Cast*] is absorbing and real. It is creative storytelling at its best—style, plot, characterizations, atmosphere, and flavor give importance and intensity to what might have been, in less skillful hands, just another story of an appealing child longing for a home.

Ruth Hill Viguers, in A Critical History of Children's Literature, *revised edition, by Cornelia Meigs, Anne Thaxter Eaton, Elizabeth Nesbitt, and Ruth Hill Viguers, edited by Cornelia Meigs (copyright © 1969 by The Macmillan Co.), Macmillan, 1969, p. 578.*

OTHER CITATIONS

Judith Higgins, in Teacher, *May-June, 1974, p. 82.*

STOWAWAY TO THE MUSHROOM PLANET **(1956)**

With its scientific detail, with its neatly systematized new little world, and with its crafty interpretation of both the baser and finer instincts of mankind, this funny sequel to *The Wonderful Flight to the Mushroom Planet* will delight anyone who isn't like Horatio, the stowaway.

Virginia Kirkus' Service, *July 1, 1956, pp. 433-34.*

A great many eight- to ten-year-old boys will be made very happy by the sequel to "The Wonderful Flight to the Mushroom Planet." There is in [this] second book no diminishing of the expert combination of fact and fantasy, of science and wonder, of humor and imagination which made the first book so original and delightful.

Elizabeth Nesbitt, in Saturday Review *(copyright © 1956 by Saturday Review, Inc.; reprinted with permission), September 22, 1956, p. 35.*

OTHER CITATIONS

The Booklist and Subscription Books Bulletin, *September 1, 1956, p. 28.*

Elsie T. Dobbins, in Library Journal, *September 15, 1956, p. 2036.*

Virginia Haviland, in The Horn Book Magazine, *October, 1956, p. 351.*

THE TERRIBLE CHURNADRYNE **(1959)**

[In *The Terrible Churnadryne*,] Tom and Jennifer, a

brother and sister, make an easy passage between the adult world of scepticism and the world of children which admits the wonderful and awesome. . . . A vivid atmosphere permeates this book which as in the author's previous *Mushroom Planet* stories and *Mr. Bass' Planetoid* combines scientific data with skillfully administered imagination. Illustrations by Beth and Joe Krush further emphasize the charm and quaint atmosphere of the text.

Virginia Kirkus' Service, *September 15, 1959, p. 701.*

The story [of *The Terrible Churnadryne*] moves convincingly on the border between realism and fantasy; fast-paced, suspenseful writing describes the efforts of the townspeople to track and trap the churnadryne. Some of the adult characters are overdrawn, but they do contribute humor to a very readable adventure story.

Zena Sutherland, in Bulletin of the Center for Children's Books *(published by the University of Chicago), November, 1959, p. 43.*

Eleanor Cameron's adventure-thirsty fans will be completely engrossed in her exciting suspense-fantasy ["The Terrible Churnadryne"]. Although more down-to-earth than her marvelously inventive "Mushroom Planet" books, it has enough of a science-fiction twist to capture her readers' imaginations. Heightening reality through lively descriptions of the eccentric townspeople and the ever-changing ocean landscape, she achieves a matter-of-course acceptance of the extraordinary.

Alice Low, in The New York Times Book Review *(© 1959 by The New York Times Company; reprinted by permission), November 1, 1959 (Part 2), p. 48.*

[This] story skirts the edge of fantasy while it tells with humor and good characterization of events that might happen in almost any little seacoast town. For who can be sure that all such creatures as the *Elasmosaurus* are really extinct? A different kind of mystery with a great deal of atmosphere.

Ruth Hill Viguers, in The Horn Book Magazine *(copyright, 1959, by the Horn Book, Inc., Boston), December, 1959, p. 481.*

***TIME AND MR. BASS: A MUSHROOM PLANET BOOK* (1967)**

[*Time and Mr. Bass*] moves from science fiction to moral fantasy, revealing the history of the Mycetians as conflict between good and evil. . . . Boys who enjoyed the earlier [Mushroom Planet] books will take the step into stranger than science-fiction in their stride.

Kirkus Service *(copyright © 1967 Virginia Kirkus' Service, Inc.), January 15, 1967, pp. 56-7.*

The fifth book in this science fiction series [*Time and Mr. Bass*] has the moral overtones of an epic. . . . Mushroom Planet fans will welcome these strange new adventures in which the three friends journey to Tyco's ancestral home in Wales and to Basidium in their search for lost relics and hidden secrets of the past.

The Booklist and Subscription Books Bulletin *(© 1967 by the American Library Association), May 15, 1967, p. 988.*

To a fifth space fantasy involving David and Chuck and their Mycetian friend Tycho Bass, [Eleanor Cameron] has added new dimensions—a realm of magic reaching into Welsh mythology and a conflict between good and evil. . . . [In] the Welsh scenes the chilling designs of the evil Narrow Brain strengthen the impact of the book. The legendary background, drawn in part from the King Arthur story, is completely interwoven and essential to the fantasy, and the annual gathering of the eisteddfod is implicit in the scene of the Great Thronging.

Virginia Haviland, in The Horn Book Magazine *(copyright © 1967, by The Horn Book, Inc., Boston), August, 1967, pp. 460-61.*

OTHER CITATIONS

Publishers' Weekly, *February 6, 1967, p. 75.*

Dorothy Gray, in Library Journal, *March 15, 1967, p. 1314.*

***THE WONDERFUL FLIGHT TO THE MUSHROOM PLANET* (1954)**

As [David and Chuck] embark on their wonderful flight to Basilium X, the mushroom planet, all small boys are enabled to share in their extraordinary adventures through this modern fanciful tale.

The scientific inquiry of youth today will find satisfaction from the moment each reader discovers that David likes "Dr. Dolittle in the Moon" and becomes lost in his remarkable adventures. . . . In fact, a new favorite has come to challenge the popularity of the eccentric and amusing "Miss Pickerell!"

Alice Brooks McGuire, in Saturday Review *(copyright © 1954 by Saturday Review, Inc.; reprinted with permission), November 13, 1954, p. 74.*

OTHER CITATIONS

Virginia Kirkus' Bookshop Service, *July 1, 1954, p. 387.*

The Booklist, *September 15, 1954, p. 46.*

Elizabeth Johnson, in Library Journal, *September 15, 1954, p. 1663.*

* * *

CORBETT, Scott 1913-

An American author who has written more than thirty-five fantasy, mystery, science, and other fiction and nonfiction books, Scott Corbett is well known for his "Trick" series. He received the 1962 Edgar Allan Poe Award for *Cutlass Island*. (See also *Contemporary Authors*, Vols. 1-4, rev. ed., and *Something About the Author*, Vol. 2.)

***THE BASEBALL TRICK* (1965)**

This is the fifth trick . . . performed by the Fenton, Kerby, Bumps club. The trio may be good for a few more encores, but they really don't have much left up their sleeve. . . . The unexpected results of the big game are riotous—in action more than humor. The three friends, initially well-conceived, have begun to wear out their welcome.

Virginia Kirkus' Service, *May 15, 1965, p. 500.*

The mixture of realism and fantasy [in *The Baseball Trick*] is quite palatable, since the writing style is light and humorous; the passages about Waldo, the dog, are a bit heavy with whimsy.

Zena Sutherland, in Bulletin of the Center for Children's Books *(copyright 1965 by the University of Chicago; all rights reserved), September, 1965, p. 6.*

OTHER CITATIONS

Ellen Goodman, in The New York Times Book Review, *November 7, 1965 (Part 2), p. 46.*

THE BIG JOKE GAME **(1972)**

Ozzie Hinkle, who likes jokes and board games and little else, wakes up after a fall in a limbo that is one big joke game. . . . This is one of Corbett's featherweight entertainments mostly for aficionados of bad jokes; others will find Ozzie funniest when he's not trying: "Say Bub, are you *sure* this isn't Disneyland?"

Kirkus Reviews *(copyright © 1972 The Kirkus Service, Inc.), April 15, 1972, p. 477.*

[Mircea Vasiliu's lively] drawings illustrate [Scott Corbett's] fanciful story with a message: people don't enjoy someone who clowns all the time. . . . The story has plenty of action, but the plot falters due to a repetition of stress situations and a heavy application of punning humor. Ozzie's companion reveals, when his charge has learned how to control his tongue, that he is actually a guardian angel, and he leaves Ozzie to re-enter the real world as a chastened and wiser boy.

Zena Sutherland, in Bulletin of the Center for Children's Books *(© 1972 by the University of Chicago; all rights reserved), September, 1972, p. 5.*

Young Ozzie's jokes, limericks, and spoonerisms and the big game he and his guardian devil play with Ozzie's future as the stake will delight nine- through twelve-year-olds. [*The Big Joke Game*] is interesting and well conceived and makes sure-fire read-aloud material.

Marian Canoles, in School Library Journal *(reprinted from the February, 1973, issue of* School Library Journal, *published by R. R. Bowker Co., a Xerox company; copyright © 1973 by Xerox Corporation), February, 1973, p. 66.*

THE CASE OF THE GONE GOOSE **(1966)**

For the younger mystery fans, the best book of the season is, without a doubt, *The Case of the Gone Goose* by Scott Corbett. . . . How Roger goes about solving the brutal murders of Tom, Dick and Harry (Mr. Chadburn's prize geese) makes a delightfully funny detective story, neatly plotted and refreshingly different.

Sarah Law Kennerly, in School Library Journal *(reprinted from the November, 1966, issue of* School Library Journal, *published by R. R. Bowker Co., a Xerox company; copyright © 1966 by Xerox Corporation), November, 1966, p. 109.*

Younger readers will admire Roger's deductive reasonings [in *The Case of the Gone Goose*] as, accompanied by his humble assistants, Shirley, his ever-hungry, oversized twin, and Thumbs Thorndyke, his best friend, he coolly plots his investigation, sorts out evidence, and arrives at the ultimate logical solution.

Ethel L. Heins, in The Horn Book Magazine *(copyright © 1967, by The Horn Book, Inc., Boston), February, 1967, p. 65.*

OTHER CITATIONS

Virginia Kirkus' Service, *June 15, 1966, p. 576.*

THE CASE OF THE SILVER SKULL **(1974)**

The plot is adequately constructed and there is some suspense in the story, but [*The Case of the Silver Skull*] is weakened by the flatly stereotyped characterization and by a jocose style that reaches—at times—a little too hard for humor.

Zena Sutherland, in Bulletin of the Center for Children's Books *(© 1974 by the University of Chicago; all rights reserved), June, 1974, p. 155.*

OTHER CITATIONS

Kirkus Reviews, *March 1, 1974, p. 243.*

Sarah Law Kennerly, in Library Journal, *May 15, 1974, p. 1487.*

THE CAVE ABOVE DELPHI **(1965)**

The cave is a scenically located one but contains no more suspense in connection with its treasure than the usual backyard ones junior fictional detectives so frequently stumble into. . . . The book does offer the clues in advance for sleuth-it-yourselfers, but no build-up of mood for impetus. Our entrails tell us this mystery will have bored readership.

Virginia Kirkus' Service, *June 15, 1965, p. 679.*

[This is a] tersely written story—well-seasoned with humor—with a skillfully developed plot, a lively sense of place evoking twenty-five hundred years of history, and a set of distinctive major and minor characters.

Ethel L. Heins, in The Horn Book Magazine *(copyright © 1965 by The Horn Book, Inc., Boston), December, 1965, p. 631.*

OTHER CITATIONS

Lenore Glen Offord, in The New York Times Book Review, *November 7, 1965 (Part 2), p. 59.*

CUTLASS ISLAND (1962)

Although some aspects of [*Cutlass Island*] strain credulity a bit, the natural humor, the swift pace, and the ingenious use of the island's fortifications—an arsenal of antiquated Civil War weapons and a fort—in the final action recommend the book to boys.

> The Booklist and Subscription Books Bulletin *(© 1962 by the American Library Association), November 1, 1962, p. 222.*

The pace of [''Cutlass Island''] never slackens nor does the bounce and inventiveness of the true-to-life young heroes. Even though the characterizations of the grownups are superficial and the plot somewhat improbable, boys who like 150-page books with pictures, humor and plenty of excitement will find this good reading.

> *Jane Wylie, in* The New York Times Book Review *(© 1962 by The New York Times Company; reprinted by permission), December 9, 1962, p. 36.*

[*Cutlass Island*] has pace and suspense, but the ending seems overdone, and there is not an adequate explanation of the role of the criminals or the nature of their cache.

> *Zena Sutherland, in* Bulletin of the Center for Children's Books *(copyright 1963 by the University of Chicago; all rights reserved), February, 1963, p. 93.*

OTHER CITATIONS

I. Elizabeth Stafford, in Library Journal, *October 15, 1962, p. 3892.*

Charlotte Jackson, in The Atlantic Monthly, *December, 1962, p. 178.*

DANGER POINT: THE WRECK OF THE BIRKENHEAD (1962)

Careful research has obviously gone into the re-enactment of these disasters [in *Danger Point*] just as sensationalism has obviously been deleted. The result is a fine though hair-raising account for sea buffs everywhere.

> Virginia Kirkus' Service, *December 15, 1961, p. 1090.*

The best chapters of ''Danger Point'' are written in an eyewitness style that brings this distant tragedy to life. Scott Corbett has fleshed out his rather slim story with accounts of other maritime disasters. Some of these, such as the wreck of the Medusa in 1816, make grim reading but help put the Birkenhead episode in perspective.

> *Robert Berkvist, in* The New York Times Book Review *(© 1962 by The New York Times Company; reprinted by permission), March 18, 1962, p. 26.*

Written in reportorial style the dramatic narrative [of *Danger Point*] is slow in starting because of the unnecessary inclusion of several other briefly related shipwrecks introduced to underscore, by comparison, the gallant conduct aboard the *Birkenhead* which established the tradition of ''women and children first.''

> The Booklist and Subscription Books Bulletin *(© 1962 by the American Library Association), May 15, 1962, p. 654.*

OTHER CITATIONS

Julia Losinski, in Library Journal, *March 15, 1962, p. 1328.*

DEAD MAN'S LIGHT (1960)

A small boy, preferably an orphan, a lonely older man, and a New England lighthouse make up one of the sure formulas for engrossing juvenile fiction. Here, in the story of Tommy Brackett and his Uncle Cyrus, the keeper of *Dead Man's Light*, they appear suitably menaced by avaricious and cruel relatives, unscrupulous political bigwigs, and ruthless criminals. . . . Told with spirit and sympathy, this is an old fashioned story with all the ingredients to appeal to even the most space-minded youngster, a story which illustrates the timeless effectiveness of sentiment, mystery, and nostalgia.

> Virginia Kirkus' Service, *May 15, 1960, p. 384.*

Orphan boy, incredibly cruel aunt, kindly widow, bluff, heart-of-gold lighthouse keeper, obviously evil villains, secret map, mysterious grave with skeleton, fabulous diamond—in spite of such stock characters and unbelievable plot, Mr. Corbett writes good prose at such a swift pace that adventure-seeking readers, reluctant or otherwise, will probably finish the story at one gulp, enjoying every minute.

> *Margaret W. Brown, in* The Horn Book Magazine *(copyright, 1960, by the Horn Book, Inc., Boston), October, 1960, p. 403.*

OTHER CITATIONS

Inger Boye, in School Library Journal, *September, 1960, p. 62.*

Saturday Review, *November 12, 1960, p. 94.*

THE DISAPPEARING DOG TRICK (1963)

[*The Disappearing Dog Trick*] is an irresistible combination for younger boys: magic, a disappearing pet, and two boys on their own for an evening and night of cooking and sleeping out. This third story about Kerby lacks the freshness of the first, *The Lemonade Trick*, but it has a particularly fast pace and will be just as much sought and enjoyed.

> *Virginia Haviland, in* The Horn Book Magazine *(copyright © 1963, by The Horn Book, Inc., Boston), April, 1963, p. 171.*

[In *The Disappearing Dog Trick*, Kerby and Fenton] lope around town getting into one improbable caper after another, and reaching home with Waldo retrieved—just in time to put on a virtuous act when parents call to check.

Nonsense, but not overdone; what the boys do is fantasy, what they say is matter-of-fact (if obstreperous) pure boy.

Zena Sutherland, in Bulletin of the Center for Children's Books *(copyright 1963 by the University of Chicago; all rights reserved), July-August, 1963, pp. 172-73.*

The trick here is to decide whether Mr. Corbett is putting us on or not. . . . The . . . chase of Waldo and ultimate rescue by Mrs. Graymalken is not as funny as it should be and the combination of magic and everyday events does not, at least for this reviewer, quite come off. It may, however, for some 8-12's.

Marian Sorenson, in The Christian Science Monitor *(reprinted by permission from* The Christian Science Monitor; *© 1963, The Christian Science Publishing Society; all rights reserved), August 8, 1963, p. 11.*

OTHER CITATIONS

Susan Drysdale, in The New York Times Book Review, *May 12, 1963, p. 27.*

The Booklist and Subscription Books Bulletin, *June 1, 1963, p. 822.*

DR. MERLIN'S MAGIC SHOP (1973)

Although easier than Corbett's Trick books and attractively illustrated, *Dr. Merlin* . . . offers very little action and the numerous color pictures cannot save the slow-moving story. Mercer Mayer's *A Special Trick* (Dial, 1970) is scarier fare.

Carol Chatfield, in School Library Journal *(reprinted from the February, 1974, issue of* School Library Journal, *published by R. R. Bowker Co., a Xerox company; copyright © 1974 by Xerox Corporation), February, 1974, p. 51.*

[*Dr. Merlin's Magic Shop*] may have a minimal appeal to fantasy-lovers, but it is slight and contrived, unconvincing as a fantasy, and not as skilled a blend (nor as funny) as Corbett's fanciful "Trick" books.

Zena Sutherland, in Bulletin of the Center for Children's Books *(© 1974 by the University of Chicago; all rights reserved), June, 1974, p. 156.*

EVER RIDE A DINOSAUR? (1969)

In spite of [Scott Corbett's] breezy style, this suburban fantasy (concerning middle-aged milquetoast Tad, middle-aged hypochondriac Cousin Charlie, and a seven-million-year-old brontosaurus named Bronson) starts with Tad bringing out the garbage and never really gets out of the kitchen despite the slew of gimmicky supernatural effects. . . . With much better prehistoric monster fiction available (Lampman's *The Shy Stegosaurus of Indian Springs*, . . . 1962), it is doubtful that readers, including reluctant older ones, will care enough about good old Tad to make the trip with him.

Marianne Hough, in School Library Journal *(reprinted from the May, 1969, issue of* School Library Journal, *published by R. R. Bowker Co., a Xerox company; copyright © 1969 by Xerox Corporation), May, 1969, p. 97.*

"I don't know how you feel about garbage." In substance and in spirit this is a fine opening for a story that is untrammeled fantasy and happy humor.

There is too much explanation of how it all comes about, but what comes is splendid. . . . Any child who really has never met a talking dinosaur, and many of those who have, will enjoy a ride with Tad, Bronson, and Scott Corbett.

James Playsted Wood, in Book World (© The Washington Post), *May 4, 1969 (Part 2), p. 30.*

Science fantasy compounded out of humorous elements of magic makes a swiftly read tale for those who find Evelyn Lampman's *Shy Stegosaurus* . . . and Oliver Butterworth's *The Enormous Egg* . . . irresistibly amusing. . . . [Scott Corbett's] freewheeling fun [grows] more inventive as the complexities of city and museum entrance raise their hurdles. Highly acceptable nonsense.

Virginia Haviland, in The Horn Book Magazine *(copyright © 1969 by The Horn Book, Inc., Boston), August, 1969, pp. 409-10.*

OTHER CITATIONS

Zena Sutherland, in Saturday Review, *September 13, 1969, p. 37.*

Zena Sutherland, in Bulletin of the Center for Children's Books, *November, 1969, p. 41.*

THE HOME RUN TRICK (1973)

As usual Corbett puts enough spin on his latest *Trick* that kids with even a casual interest in baseball will be caught up in the first pages and held all through the briskly unorthodox game that makes up half of the story. Because the winner will have to play an unknown girls' team, both sides are trying desperately to lose without arousing the umpire's suspicion. Unfortunately Corbett cops out in the end when a third team is chosen to play the girls so that we never do see the Tomboys in action.

Kirkus Reviews *(copyright © 1973 The Kirkus Service, Inc.), March 1, 1973, p. 254.*

Although the situations are less ingenious and the humor more strained than in the earlier books of the series, the easy-to-read format, the rapid sequence of events, and the ample use of baseball jargon will insure interest [in *The Home Run Trick*]. But the weakening formula needs a new additive—or a Feat o' Magic from Mrs. Graymalkin.

Mary M. Burns, in The Horn Book Magazine *(copyright © 1973 by The Horn Book, Inc., Boston), June, 1973, p. 270.*

As usually happens in the "trick" books, an element of magic is used in pursuit of the desired result. The action [in *The Home Run Trick*] consists of the boys' ruses to achieve their goal and in the play of the decisive game. Not a strong plot, but the lively action, the humor of [Corbett's] text and [Galdone's] illustrations, the baseball sequences, and the general joie de vivre carry the story.

Zena Sutherland, in Bulletin of the Center for Children's Books *(© 1973 by the University of Chicago; all rights reserved), September, 1973, p. 5.*

THE LEMONADE TRICK **(1960)**

[*The Lemonade Trick* is a] most acceptable blend of realism and nonsense fantasy. . . . Mr. Corbett has built up . . . a [real] personality and situation for his very down-to-earth hero. The author has a happy gift of dealing humorously with both the recognizable and the fantastic to the end that little boys will chuckle through their reading as they do over Henry Huggins and Little Eddie.

Virginia Haviland, in The Horn Book Magazine *(copyright, 1960, by the Horn Book, Inc., Boston), April, 1960, p. 128.*

[*The Lemonade Trick* is a slight] but amusing tale of what happened when Kerby added two drops of a strange chemical solution to lemonade. . . . Not an outstanding book, but a good, funny story with a very likeable and well-drawn main character. Humorous illustrations in black and white by Paul Galdone. Recommended.

Laura E. Cathon, in Junior Libraries *(reprinted from the May, 1960, issue of* Junior Libraries, *published by R. R. Bowker Co., a Xerox company; copyright © 1960 by Xerox Corporation), May, 1960, p. 55.*

[Corbett's] "Trick" series, of which [*The Lemonade Trick*] is the first, is noted for its easy reading style and engaging plots. . . . Paul Galdone's humorous illustrations add good pictorial clues for the young readers. . . .

In addition to its situation humor and plot construction, both of which are suited to middle graders, [*The Lemonade Trick*] touches upon the fact that it is desirable for youngsters to learn to get along with one another. By sketching three familiar archetypes—the thinker, the doer, and the bully—the author also suggests that differences in temperaments should be understood and tolerated.

John Gillespie and Diana Lembo, in their Introducing Books: A Guide for the Middle Grades *(copyright © 1970 by Xerox Corp.), Bowker, 1970, pp. 33-6.*

OTHER CITATIONS

Virginia Kirkus' Service, *February 1, 1960, p. 90.*

The Booklist and Subscription Books Bulletin, *June 15, 1960, p. 633.*

ONE BY SEA **(1965)**

[*One by Sea* is an] adventure story set in the nineteenth century. . . . The plot is improbably melodramatic, and the story has several stereotyped characters; there is some appeal in the bits of local color and period detail, but it seems whelmed by the action.

Zena Sutherland, in Bulletin of the Center for Children's Books *(copyright 1965 by the University of Chicago; all rights reserved), June, 1965, p. 145.*

[The] chief drawback [of *One by Sea*] is that it has too many traditional characters. . . . Its plot is traditional, too: a boy's flight from his grandfather to find his father (a clipper ship captain), a flight beset by mysterious strangers who seem to thwart his every move. . . . The adventures the hero goes through are close to a boy's heart: a shipwreck, a secret tunnel, a chase in the fog. The ingredients, though familiar, are well handled, and the story moves swiftly.

Taliaferro Boatwright, in Book Week *(©* The Washington Post*), July 11, 1965, p. 16.*

OTHER CITATIONS

Marguerite Bagshaw, in Library Journal, *March 15, 1965, p. 1548.*

John M. Connole, in The New York Times Book Review, *June 20, 1965, p. 24.*

PIPPA PASSES **(1966)**

[*Pippa Passes* is a] story for girls, set in part in a summer camp; the writing style and dialogue are adequate. The book has some bits of characterization and some bits of action that compensate considerably for the pervading weakness, diffusion of plot. The story is constructed within the short span of a long day; in time and setting, therefore, it is compact indeed. Perhaps because of this the diffusion seems the more obvious. . . . [The] story has suspense and, in some of the camp scenes, humor; the relationships with adults are realistic and often are seen with perspicacity.

Zena Sutherland, in Bulletin of the Center for Children's Books *(copyright 1966 by the University of Chicago; all rights reserved), November, 1966, pp. 39-40.*

OTHER CITATIONS

Virginia Kirkus' Service, *March 15, 1966, p. 302.*

Alice Dalgliesh, in Saturday Review, *August 20, 1966, p. 37.*

THE RED ROOM RIDDLE **(1972)**

Spooky scenes, snappy dialogue, the ambience of October 31st in a year when "there was no television (and) even radio was just getting started": [*The Red Room Riddle*] is just the sort of Halloween story kids clamor for every year. . . . Skeptics . . . might be dissatisfied with the open ending, but anyone looking for a chance to suspend disbelief will be rewarded with a proficient blend of smiles and shivers.

Kirkus Reviews *(copyright © 1972 The Kirkus Service, Inc.), April 1, 1972, p. 399.*

[*The Red Room Riddle* is a] scary story, perfect for Halloween but lively reading at any time, about the adventures of two boys in a haunted house. . . . Told by Bruce with bright and sometimes funny comments, and illustrated [by Geff Gerlach] with full-page, black-and-white drawings, whose exaggerated humor supports both the scary and the funny elements, the tale is entertaining from beginning to open-ended finish.

Beryl Robinson, in The Horn Book Magazine *(copyright © 1972 by The Horn Book, Inc., Boston), June, 1972, p. 267.*

OTHER CITATIONS

Sarah Law Kennerly, in Library Journal, *May 15, 1972, p. 1928.*

***RUN FOR THE MONEY* (1973)**

Steve's imagination runs in high gear throughout this light, fast-paced mystery adventure that centers on his mission to deliver a set of valuable stamps to one Mr. Kingsley Brant. . . . The overtly simple errand activates Steve's paranoia and his crosstown journey takes on some devious and humorous twists that eventually result in his uncovering part of a missing coin collection and turning in the evil fence. [*Run for the Money* is a] nimble tale, sure to please Corbett readers.

The Booklist *(© American Library Association 1974), February 1, 1974, pp. 598-99.*

OTHER CITATIONS

Kirkus Reviews, *November 1, 1973, pp. 1199-1200.*

Publishers' Weekly, *February 11, 1974, p. 64.*

Susan L. Pickles, in Library Journal, *February 15, 1974, p. 570.*

***TREE HOUSE ISLAND* (1959)**

[*Tree House Island*] is an exciting, fast-paced mystery for teen-age boys—and girls, too, if they like a plot with plenty of daring action, thrills and danger. . . .

There's a pleasant little bonus of romance, too. Exceptionally good writing carries out a well-constructed plot.

Silence Buck Bellows, in The Christian Science Monitor *(reprinted by permission from* The Christian Science Monitor; *© 1959, The Christian Science Publishing Society; all rights reserved), May 14, 1959, p. 13.*

The setting for *Tree House Island* is a part of the New England coast with some small islands just off shore. The story is a worn one with a couple of stock villains posing as bird watchers. . . . The sea and sand holiday feeling is the nicest thing about this book. The treasure at the end of the hunt . . . lacks some of the old glamour and shine.

The Times Literary Supplement *(© The Times Publishing Company Ltd. 1959), May 29, 1959, p. xxi.*

Although not a unique mystery story [*Tree House Island*] has a well-constructed plot, considerable humor, and some lively, convincing young heroes who outwit a pair of bank robbers. . . . Tree-house spying and boating as an aid to the unraveling of the plot provide incidents for special amusement. Well above average.

Virginia Haviland, in The Horn Book Magazine *(copyright, 1959, by the Horn Book, Inc., Boston), August, 1959, p. 287.*

OTHER CITATIONS

Virginia Kirkus' Service, *January 1, 1959, p. 7.*

The Booklist and Subscription Books Bulletin, *May 15, 1959, pp. 512-13.*

Margaret Mahon, in Saturday Review, *July 18, 1959, p. 37.*

***THE TURNABOUT TRICK* (1967)**

[So] much is thrown [into *The Turnabout Trick*] that the story is overcrowded, but all these elements will appeal to boys in grades 3-5 as well as slow junior-high readers. Though it sometimes reflects an adult point of view, the humor has a crazy charm. On the whole, the boys' conversation is believable.

Patricia Alice McKenzie, in School Library Journal *(reprinted from the April, 1967, issue of* School Library Journal, *published by R. R. Bowker Co., a Xerox company; copyright © 1967 by Xerox Corporation), April, 1967, p. 68.*

Although [*The Turnabout Trick*] seems thinner and less spontaneous than the first books in the ["Trick"] series it is, nonetheless, lively and funny and because it is also easy to read may be useful with reluctant readers.

The Booklist and Subscription Books Bulletin *(© 1967 by the American Library Association), July 1, 1967, p. 1146.*

[*The Turnabout Trick* is a] sixth book about Kerby Maxwell, the boy whose acquaintance with Mrs. Graymalkin (to say nothing of his experiments with the magical chemistry set she gave him) has led to so many tricks and fanciful adventures in previous books. . . . The story has the zany, romping appeal of the other Trick books, but also has the same repetitive whimsy whenever the animals are being described.

Zena Sutherland, in Bulletin of the Center for Children's Books *(copyright 1967 by the University of Chicago; all rights reserved), September, 1967, p. 4.*

OTHER CITATIONS

Kirkus Service, *February 15, 1967, p. 198.*

Ethel L. Heins, in The Horn Book Magazine, *August, 1967, p. 469.*

***WHAT MAKES A BOAT FLOAT?* (1970)**

What makes a boat float is smartly demonstrated in two pages in the Zim and Skelly [book] *Cargo Ships* . . .; here the explanation is encyclopedic in size (taking in Archimedes' "Eureka!") and style—i.e. the terminology of physics. Also, Zim's procedure—reshaping a block of steel into a shell—makes more immediate sense that Corbett's—removing its core. . . . But [*What Makes a Boat Float?*] proceeds to consider what makes a boat *stay* afloat and so acquires added value. . . . The young look and big type belies the complexity of the explanations and the requisite grasp of abstractions; but the applications may prove useful where some groundwork has been laid.

Kirkus Reviews *(copyright © 1970 The Kirkus Service, Inc.), April 15, 1970, p. 468.*

Good drawings [by Victor Mays] help to clarify [Scott Corbett's] well-written text. [*What Makes a Boat Float?*] is good collateral reading for elementary science students as they investigate the principles mentioned. It's an interesting book for voluntary casual reading, also.

Science Books *(copyright © 1970, by the American Association for the Advancement of Science), Vol. 6, no. 2 (September, 1970), p. 160.*

OTHER CITATIONS

The Booklist, *July 1, 1970, p. 1340.*

***WHAT MAKES A LIGHT GO ON?* (1966)**

This attempt to answer fundamental questions about the nature of electricity, and the operation of common electrical devices and appliances, is replete with fundamental factual and scientific errors. A glossary in such a book is a good attribute but the one appended lacks several fundamental terms.

Science Books *(copyright © 1966 by the American Association for the Advancement of Science), Vol. 2, No. 2 (September, 1966), p. 108.*

[*What Makes a Light Go On?* is an] excellent introductory book on electricity; [Len Darwin's] illustrations are very clear, well placed, and adequately captioned. Mr. Corbett uses lucid analogies and familiar phenomena in explaining the movement within an atom, magnetic attraction and repulsion, and the nature of electricity. . . . The terminology is accurate but is never more complex than is necessary; the text includes a discussion of the necessity for caution and precaution. A combined index and glossary is appended.

Zena Sutherland, in Bulletin of the Center for Children's Books *(copyright 1966 by the University of Chicago; all rights reserved), September, 1966, p. 6.*

***WHAT MAKES A PLANE FLY?* (1967)**

With the use of a folded paper airplane, a toy balloon, and carefully executed and labeled drawings, Mr. Corbett presents a satisfactory simplified explanation of the basic principles of aerodynamics and aeronautics for children. Older students and adults lacking such a simple foundation will enjoy reading it too. While specialists in the field may consider [*What Makes a Plane Fly?*] too superficial, and point out technical inaccuracies, its contents are about all a child who has not had a basic course in physics can be expected to understand.

Science Books *(copyright © 1968 by the American Association for the Advancement of Science), Vol. 4, No. 4 (March, 1968), p. 339.*

In brief, logical steps [Scott Corbett] describes the ways in which the shape of an airplane and the design of its wings affect performance; the structural and operational control of flight deviations; the parts of an airplane, and the physical forces that affect flight.

Zena Sutherland, in Saturday Review *(copyright © 1968 by Saturday Review, Inc.; reprinted with permission), March 16, 1968, p. 39.*

OTHER CITATIONS

Zena Sutherland, in Bulletin of the Center for Children's Books, *March, 1968, p. 107.*

The New York Times Book Review, *May 5, 1968 (Part 2), p. 52.*

D

DAHL, Roald 1916-

Roald Dahl is an English short story writer and novelist who writes for both children and adults. His best known work for children is *Charlie and the Chocolate Factory*. (See also *Contemporary Authors*, Vols. 1-4, rev. ed., and *Something About the Author*, Vol. 1.)

GENERAL COMMENTARY

The fantasies of Roald Dahl have improved in style and simplicity with each of his books. *James and the Giant Peach* (1961) . . . is an inventive and elaborate story. In *Charlie and the Chocolate Factory* (1964) . . . [Dahl] uses the faults of the children as an opportunity to discourse on social behavior, but the fantastic setting, lively dialogue, and exaggeration in plot have appealed to many readers. *The Magic Finger* (1966) is simpler in structure and stronger in its message: shooting animals for sport is deplorable. . . . Less humorous than *Charlie*, this has better construction and a light, easy style.

May Hill Arbuthnot and Zena Sutherland, in their Children and Books, *4th edition (copyright © 1947, 1957, 1964, 1972 by Scott, Foresman and Co.), Scott, Foresman, 1972, p. 258.*

CHARLIE AND THE CHOCOLATE FACTORY (1964)

Not by any means an ordinary book, this is called by the publisher an "Uproarious morality tale." It is indeed a morality tale, it has some uproarious moments, and it has a good deal of common sense. It also has a few labored moments and a few belabored ideas, not so many that the book is not enjoyable, but enough to make it seem too long.

Zena Sutherland, in Bulletin of the Center for Children's Books *(copyright 1965 by the University of Chicago; all rights reserved), April, 1965, p. 115.*

[*Charlie and the Chocolate Factory* includes] some good old-fashioned moralizing . . . to make everyone feel guilty; bad children get their come-uppance in sub-Belloc fashion, though some of their vices are modern (e.g., chewing-gum and television). Poverty is, as traditionally, equated with virtue (and is presumably incorruptible by the riches awarded to it). The writing seems more frantic, attention-grabbing than in *James and the Giant Peach*. Still, it is highly enjoyable, inventive and original. [The book contains more] good verse, more good illustrations.

The Times Literary Supplement *(© Times Newspapers Ltd., 1967), December 14, 1967, p. 1225.*

Younger readers will enjoy [*Charlie and the Chocolate Factory*], with its infectious fun and outlandish episodes, while the more mature ones will discover overtones of a religious nature, as well as the moral precept of good behavior rewarded. [Roald Dahl] catalogs the misbehavior of each naughty child and its consequences in a clever rhyme that heralds each misdeed.

John Gillespie and Diana Lembo, in their Introducing Books: A Guide for the Middle Grades *(copyright © 1970 by Xerox Corp.), Bowker, 1970, p. 62.*

What I object to in [*Charlie and the Chocolate Factory*] is its phony presentation of poverty and its phony humor, which is based on punishment with overtones of sadism; its hypocrisy which is epitomized in its moral—stuck like a marshmallow in a lump of fudge—that TV is horrible and hateful and time-wasting and that children should read good books instead, when in fact the book itself is like nothing so much as one of the more specious television shows. . . .

Possibly its tastelessness, including the ugliness of [Joseph Schindelman's] illustrations, is, indeed (whether the author meant it so or not), a comment upon our age and the quality of much of our entertainment.

Eleanor Cameron, in The Horn Book Magazine *(copyright © 1972 by The Horn Book, Inc., Boston), October, 1972, p. 440.*

[The] racism [in *Charlie and the Chocolate Factory*] consists of the time-dishonored stereotypes, childishness and dependency upon whites, with which the Black characters are presented. (The Black characters are exploited as workers and dehumanized, and they are presented en masse with group characteristics only.) . . .

As workers in the factory, the Black characters are exploited. The owner clicks his fingers sharply when he wants a worker to appear. The Oompa-Loompas are made to test various kinds of candies, sometimes with unfortunate effects. . . . [The] implication is that Black characters are forever dependent upon the white boss. I believe this message comes across in a particularly strong manner, because it is not verbalized and yet the whole plot rests upon it.

Lois Kalb Bouchard, "A New Look at Old Favorites: Charlie and the Chocolate Factory," in The Black American in Books for Children: Readings in Racism, *edited by Donnarae MacCann and Gloria Woodard (copyright 1972 by Donnarae MacCann and Gloria Woodard), Scarecrow, 1972, pp. 112-15.*

I find a certain point of view (or is it the *lack* of a point of view?) felt in *Charlie and the Chocolate Factory* . . . to be extremely regrettable when it comes to Willy Wonka's unfeeling attitude toward the Oompa-Loompas, their role as conveniences and devices to be used for Wonka's purposes, their being brought over from Africa for enforced servitude, and the fact that their situation is all a part of the fun and games. . . .

The book is wish-fulfillment in caricature, and as caricature, it is removed from reality. . . . But the situation of the Oompa-Loompas *is* real; it could not be more so, and it is anything but funny.

Eleanor Cameron, in The Horn Book Magazine *(copyright © 1973 by The Horn Book, Inc., Boston), April, 1973, p. 127.*

[*Charlie and the Chocolate Factory*] is fantasy . . . [and] should not be exhorted to weigh itself down with the woes of the real world. . . . We need not spend any more time agonizing over the exploitation of the Oompa-Loompas than we do over that of the poor peasantry in fairy tales.

[The] only valid objection Mrs. Cameron raises [in her criticism of *Charlie and the Chocolate Factory*] is the one concerning the origins and characteristics of the Oompa-Loompas. . . . [This] objection has been heeded and acted upon in a new 1973 printing of the book [in which] the Oompa-Loompas are little men with long hair who come from Loompaland and bear no resemblance to any known racial group.

Ellen Chamberlain, in The Horn Book Magazine *(copyright © 1973 by The Horn Book, Inc., Boston), June, 1973, p. 227.*

[Roald Dahl presented a] black-and-white Victorian morality [in *Charlie and the Chocolate Factory*] . . . and reinforced it with a violence to equal anything by Wilhelm Busch. . . .

Mr Dahl, undeniably, is a clever and accomplished writer, the story moves at a good pace, the detail is highly inventive if not imaginative, and some of Mr Wonka's sweets have a pleasing zaniness. . . . [But] the message is . . . dubious. In Mr Dahl's world it is all right to take something given by the benevolent despot, Mr Wonka; but all wrong to take something for yourself. By implication, energy, action, is evil; to be good you have to be passive, to accept, just like Charlie.

The Times Literary Supplement *(© Times Newspapers Ltd., 1973), June 15, 1973, p. 683.*

[The] plot develops in a linear, almost picaresque fashion, in that event is added to event in the straightforward structuring of Charlie's adventures. It does not grow from qualities in the characters or from the initial situation. . . . Charlie himself is a cipher, his appeal lying in his poverty and in his politeness. He is every 'inner' adult's version of a good child 'seen but not heard'. This is particularly true in the factory, where he speaks only as a kind of chorus figure. . . . Willy Wonka himself is a larger than life 'character', loud, boisterous, loquacious. Apart from him the main interest lies in the children. . . . They all have one exaggerated dominant characteristic—(Augustus Gloop—greed; Veruca Salt—spoilt tantrums; Violet Beauregarde—gum chewing; Mike Teavee—television addiction)—all of which are common adult prejudices. They appeal to the worst in children, the cruel tendency to ostracize those who are different or odd. If they are archetypes they are those of the comic paper—physical and social misfits. (pp. 25-6)

[Willy Wonka] represents the conservative, traditional attitude of adults to children (no equality here) and Charlie in the end wins all, not because of any positive good or noble qualities, but because he is poor, quiet and polite. The language of the book is as exaggerated as the characters. All the adult's speech is peppered with italics and emphasis. This is particularly true of Willy Wonka, who has a wearisome tendency to rant in top key (this is very noticeable when reading the book aloud). Such hyperbolic words as fantastic, enormous, terrific, extremely, and colossal recur again and again throughout the book always in italics or capitals. Idiom and vocabulary are limited and repetitive. . . . Although exaggeration is of the essence of the book, there are times when it seems to me that Dahl's use of language degenerates into carelessness and even coarseness. (pp. 27-8)

The fantasy [of *Charlie*], though beyond [children's] actual experience, has much in common with familiar literary experience, fairy tales, folklore, comic strip and cautionary tale. It centres on a Chocolate Factory . . . a place that has affinities with well-known fairy castles and prince's palaces in its labyrinthine quality and the magical surprises to be encountered there. (p. 29)

The pace of *Charlie* is fast, even hectic; it is entirely unsubtle; its humour is fairly crude. . . . [The story] appeals to all . . . children, who recognize in it much that they have met before, especially its most obvious (if, to adult eyes, distorted) moral, that good triumphs over evil. (pp. 29-30)

Anne Merrick, " 'The Nightwatchmen' and 'Charlie and the Chocolate Factory' as Books to Be Read to Children," in Children's Literature in Education *(© 1975, APS Publications, Inc.; reprinted by permission of the publisher), No. 16 (Spring, 1975), pp. 21-30.*

OTHER CITATIONS

Constantine Georgiou, in his Children and Their Literature, *Prentice-Hall, 1969, p. 294.*

CHARLIE AND THE GREAT GLASS ELEVATOR (1972)

In a perfectly silly and pointlessly tasteless sequel to

Charlie and the Chocolate Factory, Mr. Willie Wonka's glass elevator goes into orbit carrying Charlie, his parents, and the bed that three of the grandparents haven't left for 20 years. . . . With humor that depends on gratuitous references to the President's pottie or the results of a very strong laxative, with the Oompa-Loompas still fetching and carrying, this has all the faults that disturbed grown-ups and none of the inspired outrageousness that attracted children to its predecessor.

Kirkus Reviews *(copyright © 1972 The Kirkus Service, Inc.), July 15, 1972, p. 802.*

["Charlie and the Great Glass Elevator" is] pretty shoddy merchandise. . . . It's almost funny, almost suspenseful, only coyly screwball. Once again [as in "Charlie and the Chocolate Factory"] the central character seems to be mysteriously missing. . . .

Lacking . . . a thematic device, "Charlie and the Great Glass Elevator" becomes just a string of random jokes and adventures held together by that enviable British glibness of style—punning and colloquial—that sounds as if it must be good, even though it's all manner, without substance. . . . Dahl's every line implicitly reassures us that nothing important is really going on here, nothing is really at stake—a reassurance reinforced, incidentally, by Joseph Schindelman's dry and distancing illustrations.

Julia Whedon, in The New York Times Book Review *(© 1972 by The New York Times Company; reprinted by permission), September 17, 1972, p. 8.*

In the course of the narrative, a weak attempt is made to redeem the Oompa-Loompas from racial obloquy by ascribing to them long golden hair in youth, and morality is paid the dubious lip service of a cautionary tale in verse about a little girl who ate too many of her grandmother's chocolate-coated laxatives. As a fantasy, the narrative is concocted and cerebral; as a funny story, [*Charlie and the Great Glass Elevator*] lacks the juices and flavors of natural and unforced humor.

Paul Heins, in The Horn Book Magazine *(copyright © 1973 by The Horn Book, Inc., Boston), April, 1973, p. 142.*

Here there is exaggeration and action and little else. Charlie, his mother and father, and his grandparents . . . encounter a space ship as the glass elevator orbits the earth, they are attacked by Creatures, they rescue some astronauts, they visit the President of the United States (depicted as a slangy fool) and the grandparents take rejuvenating medicine and so on and on. There's always an appeal to some readers in slapstick, and the sequel of any successful book will always be greeted hopefully by its fans, but this is a comedown—Oompa-Loompas and all.

Zena Sutherland, in Bulletin of the Center for Children's Books *(© 1973 by the University of Chicago; all rights reserved), September, 1973, p. 5.*

OTHER CITATIONS

Publishers' Weekly, *September 4, 1972, p. 51.*

Katherine Heylman, in Library Journal, *December 15, 1972, p. 4070.*

***FANTASTIC MR. FOX* (1970)**

In the history of the children's story, it is traditional for the fox to be depicted as the cunning enemy, the wily trickster who inevitably in the end meets with his just deserts, sometimes fatal. But in Mr. Dahl's latest offering [*Fantastic Mr. Fox*], Reynard the Hunter becomes Mr. Fox the hunted. . . . This modern fable does not have the ingenuity or the atmosphere of fantasy of *Charlie and the Chocolate Factory* or *James and the Giant Peach*. The moral would seem to be 'crime pays in the end', not the kind to be encouraged. A good-sized type is used for easy reading although some young readers will be puzzled by some of the author's choice of words, such as 'goons', 'cocky' and 'dingbat'. The text is enhanced by the many delightful drawings by Donald Chaffin.

Eric Hudson, in Children's Book Review *(© 1971 by Five Owls Press Ltd.), February, 1971, p. 17.*

[*Fantastic Mr. Fox*] has action and a sprightly style, humor with a dollop of slapstick. It does not have the imaginative quality of *Charlie and the Chocolate Factory*, but the animals are appealing, and the broad humor mitigates the acidulous portrayal of the human characters.

Zena Sutherland, in Bulletin of the Center for Children's Books *(© 1971 by the University of Chicago; all rights reserved), February, 1971, p. 89.*

Boggis, Bunce and Bean must be three of the nastiest farmers ever to appear in a children's book. Their villainy reaches new heights as they fanatically try to kill our hero, the fantastic Mr. Fox. . . . The irony of the final situation can be appreciated even by the younger children. The plot is fast-moving and suspenseful. The author uses language with verve, embroidering his descriptions of the farmers so that they become nastier in every chapter. [This is a] good book to read aloud.

Amy Kellman, in Grade Teacher *(excerpted with permission of the publisher; © 1971 by Macmillan Professional Magazines, Inc.; all rights reserved), April, 1971, p. 26.*

OTHER CITATIONS

Cherie Zarookian, in Library Journal, *March 15, 1971, p. 1106.*

Lavinia Marina Learmont, in Books and Bookmen, *March, 1974, p. 100.*

***JAMES AND THE GIANT PEACH* (1961)**

[*James and the Giant Peach*] is a broad fantasy with all the gruesome imagery of old-fashioned fairy tales and a good measure of their breathtaking delight. . . . The tricky little rhymes and songs that run through the text add a memorable touch to a "peachy" first book for children. Nancy Burkert's gentle, entrancing illustrations in full color take us visually through James' world.

Virginia Kirkus' Service, August 15, 1961, pp. 727-28.

To travel from England to America is quite an adventure for a small boy, especially if he does it in a giant peach in company with several enormous insects. Some children may find it an exciting and rambunctious fantasy. However, one thing children are not tough-minded about is losing parents suddenly, and at the beginning of this story James's parents are eaten by a large rhinoceros escaped from the zoo, "their troubles over in thirty-five seconds flat." . . . Nancy Burkert's attractive pictures, some in color, soften the story considerably.

Alice Dalgliesh, in Saturday Review *(copyright © 1962 by Saturday Review, Inc.; reprinted with permission), February 17, 1962, p. 32.*

Children's books by sophisticated adult writers are to be dreaded normally; not this one though. Downtrodden James travels land, sea and air by house-size peach accompanied by giant but amiable insects . . . crushing downtreading Aunts en route and finishing up in New York. The violence is the "Fee fi fo fum, grind your bones to make my bread" variety, much liked by children, no worse than Alice, Lear, and most fairy tales; harmless anyway. It is vivid, robust, entertaining and funny. There's some splendid verse thrown in as well and that's rare enough. Good illustrations, too.

The Times Literary Supplement *(© Times Newspapers Ltd., 1967), December 14, 1967, p. 1225.*

OTHER CITATIONS

Constantine Georgiou, in his Children and Their Literature, *Prentice-Hall, 1969, p. 294.*

THE MAGIC FINGER (1966)

[*The Magic Finger* is an] unusual and effective fanciful story, told by a girl of eight who is the dea ex machina but who participates only in the preliminary events, a weak matrix for a strong inner story. . . . The light style and the appeal of the natural dialogue are echoed by the light touch and charming, realistic details of the illustrations. . . . The story lacks the humor of the author's *Charlie and the Chocolate Factory* (. . . 1964).

Zena Sutherland, in Bulletin of the Center for Children's Books *(copyright 1965 by the University of Chicago; all rights reserved), April, 1965. p. 40.*

Though a chilly book—with its slightly eerie pictures by William Pène du Bois—*The Magic Finger* is told with a skill and tact that will stimulate fantasy. Mr. Dahl doesn't belabor the tricks and his young readers are left to get on with their own spellbinding.

Elinore Standard, in Book Week (© The Washington Post*), October 30, 1966 (Part 2), p. 16.*

[This is an] unusual book dealing with a family of duck hunters and the sense of justice that overtakes them when a little girl casts her spell on them by means of "the magic finger." Quite believable, this poetic account possesses a delightful vein of humor that runs through the heart of the story.

Constantine Georgiou, in his Children and Their Literature *(copyright © 1969 by Prentice-Hall, Inc.), Prentice-Hall, 1969, p. 294.*

OTHER CITATIONS

Lavinia Russ, in Publishers' Weekly, *August 1, 1966, p. 60.*

George A. Woods, in The New York Times Book Review, *September 4, 1966, p. 16.*

The Booklist and Subscription Books Bulletin, *October 15, 1966, p. 264.*

Virginia Haviland, in The Horn Book Magazine, *December, 1966, p. 709.*

The New York Review of Books, *December 15, 1966, p. 28.*

* * *

De ANGELI, Marguerite 1889-

Marguerite de Angeli, an American author-illustrator who won the Newbery Medal in 1950 for *The Door in the Wall*, is noted for her books dealing with people and places in Pennsylvania. (See also *Contemporary Authors*, Vols. 5-8, rev. ed., and *Something About the Author*, Vol. 1.)

GENERAL COMMENTARY

Marguerite de Angeli was . . . a pioneer in relating stories about the minority groups around her home in Philadelphia. Her stories are slight, but the warm pictures she paints, both with colors and words, of Amish, Quaker, and Pennsylvania-Dutch children are important. *Henner's Lydia* (1936), *Skippack School* (1939), *Yonie Wondernose* (1944), and *Thee, Hannah!* (1940) are all pleasant stories about interesting people.

May Hill Arbuthnot and Zena Sutherland, in their Children and Books, *4th edition (copyright © 1947, 1957, 1964, 1972 by Scott, Foresman and Co.), Scott, Foresman, 1972, pp. 440-41.*

BOOK OF NURSERY AND MOTHER GOOSE RHYMES (1954)

[*Book of Nursery and Mother Goose Rhymes* is a] beautiful new collection of nursery rhymes. An oversize book, it opens wide and flat, inviting to reader, listener, and viewer alike, to offer nearly 400 rhymes, all the old favorites and the less familiar, and over 250 lovely imaginative and decorative pictures both in full color and in black and white. The selection is varied but consistent, the pictorial interpretation flavorsome.

The Booklist, *September 1, 1954, p. 22.*

Marguerite de Angeli's *The Book of Nursery and Mother Goose Rhymes* is one of the most beautiful editions of Mother Goose available on the market today. It is a large book, ideal for children and adults to enjoy together. It contains more than 300 rhymes and jingles and almost as many lovely pictures. Some of the illustrations are full page—done in soft clear pastels. Mrs. de Angeli's children are always beautiful and graceful, but lively; the babies are truly enchanting. Detailed backgrounds and numerous decorative touches on many pages make this book an artistic experience.

Paul C. Burns and Ruth Hines, "Marguerite L. de Angeli: Faith in the Human Spirit" (1967), in Authors and Illustrators of Children's Books: Writings on Their Lives and Works, *edited by Miriam Hoffman and Eva Samuels (copyright © 1972 by Xerox Corp.), Bowker, 1972, p. 113.*

Charmingly illustrated, *Book of Nursery and Mother Goose Rhymes* includes practically every familiar Mother Goose Rhyme, verse, and melody. It is dignified and graceful, and is in possession of precisely the kind of pictures suited to interpret rather literally the mood and meanings of the text. Her pictures, especially the ones of animals and children, are so realistically drawn that no strain falls on the young child's power of inference when he is invited to look at the pictures of this spacious book while the rhymes are read aloud.

Constantine Georgiou, in his Children and Their Literature *(copyright © 1969 by Prentice-Hall, Inc.), Prentice-Hall, 1969, p. 69.*

Marguerite de Angeli's *Book of Nursery and Mother Goose Rhymes* . . . is too big for small children to handle alone, but it is fine for children and adults to look at together. The verses are not arranged in any particular order, so a nursery jingle is often followed by a ballad of sufficient substance to suit the oldest children. However, the rich offering of verses and illustrations makes this an edition to cherish and to pass on to the next generation.

May Hill Arbuthnot and Zena Sutherland, in their Children and Books, *4th edition (copyright © 1947, 1957, 1964, 1972 by Scott, Foresman and Co.), Scott, Foresman, 1972, p. 119.*

THE DOOR IN THE WALL (1949)

Warmth and love flow from [this] poignant tale of a boy crippled and haunted by fear. His triumphant victory over handicap stands out clearly in language that is appropriately tender, and matched with beautiful illustrations.

Deep spiritual values also rise to the surface of this inspiring tale of triumph over misfortune and handicap. On several occasions during the telling of the tale the friar and others speak of finding a door in the wall, which is symbolic of a solution to a problem, a way to success.

Constantine Georgiou, in his Children and Their Literature *(copyright © 1969 by Prentice-Hall, Inc.), Prentice-Hall, 1969, pp. 325-26.*

This heartwarming story [of *The Door in the Wall*] is beautifully illustrated in the author's most colorful style. The characters are less convincing than the situations, but the book is of great interest to all children, and brings special comfort to the handicapped.

May Hill Arbuthnot and Zena Sutherland, in their Children and Books, *4th edition (copyright © 1947, 1957, 1964, 1972 by Scott, Foresman and Co.), Scott, Foresman, 1972, p. 499.*

FIDDLESTRINGS (1974)

[In *Fiddlestrings*] Marguerite de Angeli's hero, eleven in 1898, has her husband Dai de Angeli's name, and her story has the air of a family memoir. . . . [Dai's] lessons and concerts and schoolboy fights in Philadelphia and his sometimes rash (and lovingly chastised) escapades with boats and guns during an Atlantic City summer are set down with fondness and fidelity, an artless style that sometimes seems merely inept, and no pretense of a plot.

Kirkus Reviews *(copyright © 1974 The Kirkus Service, Inc.), February 15, 1974, pp. 184-85.*

In this fictionalized biography De Angeli details the growing up years of her husband, Dai, who lived in Philadelphia and Atlantic City at the turn of the century. . . . Some readers will find this a pleasant bit of nostalgia, but to most it will just seem dated.

Roberta Nolan Canavan, in School Library Journal *(reprinted from the April, 1974, issue of* School Library Journal, *published by R. R. Bowker Co., a Xerox company; copyright © 1974 by Xerox Corporation), April, 1974, p. 56.*

[*Fiddlestrings*] has a happy blend of pranks, music, family affection, and period detail; the writing style is smooth. Marguerite de Angeli has a special talent for making her children convincingly of their time and, at the same time, children of any time, anywhere.

Zena Sutherland, in Bulletin of the Center for Children's Books *(© 1974 by the University of Chicago; all rights reserved), May, 1974, p. 141.*

OTHER CITATIONS

Publishers' Weekly, *March 11, 1974, p. 50.*

THE OLD TESTAMENT (1960)

A superb rendering of the text of the King James version of the Old Testament, skillfully abridged and arranged in historical sequence, by Dr. Samuel Terrien, of the Union Theological Seminary, provides the vehicle for Mrs. de Angeli's lovely pictures. . . . Through these pictures she has captured the very look and feel of the sun-drenched hills of the land of the Old Testament, with their rocky barrenness, occasional lushness under sparse water. The people, too, may well have looked as she has pictured them—though a bit more rugged and swarthy.

Virginia Kirkus' Service, *August 15, 1960, p. 690.*

Some of [Marguerite de Angeli's] pictures [in *The Old Testament*] are beautiful, others less successful, but all are full of atmosphere and there are well over one hundred and fifty of them, many full-page, and thirty-one in four colors. The inviting text pages have large well-spaced type and marginal decorations. The selection and arrangement (which gives continuity to the reading) prove that the Bible need not be retold to captivate children.

Ruth Hill Viguers, in The Horn Book Magazine *(copyright, 1961, by the Horn Book, Inc., Boston), February, 1961, p. 62.*

***TURKEY FOR CHRISTMAS* (1965)**

[*Turkey for Christmas* is a] warm family story set in the early part of the century. . . . Thirteen-year-old Bess is the central character; it is through her realization of the real meaning of Christmas that the author speaks. The story is imbued with sentiment rather than with sentimentality; the book has an appealing felicity of period detail. [This is a] revised and newly-illustrated edition of a 1944 title.

Zena Sutherland, in Bulletin of the Center for Children's Books *(copyright 1965 by the University of Chicago; all rights reserved), September, 1965, p. 6.*

* * *

DeJONG, Meindert 1906-

A Dutch-born American noted for his books about the Netherlands, Meindert DeJong received the 1955 Newbery Medal for *The Wheel on the School*, the 1962 Hans Christian Andersen Award, and the 1969 National Book Award for *Journey from Peppermint Street*. (See also *Contemporary Authors*, Vols. 15-16 and *Something About the Author*, Vol. 2.)

GENERAL COMMENTARY

To those who are cool about Mr. DeJong's work, [the] exhilarations and tremblings and throbbings of intense excitement appear excessive. To an admirer, there seem to be two answers to this charge. The first is that the excitement is an aspect of Mr. DeJong's skill as a storyteller and of his sheer high spirits as a writer. The second is that it is essentially of a degree that a child, and only a child, feels. . . . [This] tension that drives all the books is exactly the tension a child feels, immoderate and sometimes alarming. To an admirer it would seem to be one of the things that distinguish Mr. DeJong's work from nearly everything else being written for children today. His writing is close, in a way that the writing in ninety-nine out of a hundred children's books is not, to the impetuous, overbrimming quality of a child's emotions. (pp. 278-79)

And the fact is that all [the] fears and fevers and excitements that mark Mr. DeJong's books are rooted in exact and entertaining social observation. In the wide world of America Mr. DeJong has not forgotten the small world of Holland. He has a deep feeling for the life of a community, his books are full of grandparents and elders of all kinds and his children are firmly placed in a hierarchy of age. (p. 279)

One would like room to discuss, or simply to illustrate, Mr. DeJong's powers of humorous observation (his books are funny in the way that life is funny): his brilliant eye for relationships between children (for example, that, in *Shadrach*, of little Davie with his elder brother Rem, comforter and betrayer at once). One would like to say a great deal about Maurice Sendak, who has illustrated all the books and who shares his author's view of people entirely. There can be few illustrations anywhere more affectionate and enchanting—and absolutely appropriate—than those in which he draws his, and Mr. DeJong's, tiny, touching Dutch people. (pp. 279-80)

"When Once a Little Boy . . ." in The Times Literary Supplement *(© The Times Publishing Co. Ltd. 1959), December 4, 1959 (reprinted in* Children and Literature: Views and Reviews, *edited by Virginia Haviland, Scott, Foresman, 1973, pp. 277-80).*

With matchless insight, forthrightness, sensitivity, and tenderness DeJong portrays his characters' every thought and emotion as though he were actually inside the characters. The characters, each with a real but unique personality, are drawn with understanding. . . .

[DeJong's] style is uncluttered, informal and realistic. He obviously writes about things for which he has considerable respect and which he knows well. His plots are suspenseful, fast moving, and simple. The settings, incidents, and characters are portrayed in great depth. He has an adequate balance among description, dialogue and action.

Patricia Jean Cianciolo, "Meindert DeJong" (1968), in Authors and Illustrators of Children's Books: Writings on Their Lives and Works, *edited by Miriam Hoffman and Eva Samuels (copyright © 1972 by Xerox Corp.), Bowker, 1972, pp. 115, 120.*

Few Writers can see to the core of a child's emotions as Mr. DeJong does and interpret them without slipping into hypersensitivity or sentimentality. Sometimes the poetic iteration of his style verges on monotony. But not in [*The Wheel on the School* and *Far Out the Long Canal*]. Had he written nothing more than these, *The House of Sixty Fathers*, and *The Tower by the Sea*, Meindert DeJong's place in children's literature would be secure. . . .

Few writers have been able to express so movingly a child's intense love for a pet as Mr. DeJong does in a number of his animal stories, especially in *Shadrach* (1953). . . . Because he drew from his inner childhood, Mr. DeJong could give a story like *Shadrach* action and suspense to hold readers of any age.

Ruth Hill Viguers, in A Critical History of Children's Literature, *revised edition, by Cornelia Meigs, Anne Thaxter Eaton, Elizabeth Nesbitt, and Ruth Hill Viguers, edited by Cornelia Meigs (copyright © 1969 by The Macmillan Co.), Macmillan, 1969, pp. 558, 599.*

DeJong is a limited and rather old-fashioned writer whose main springs of inspiration clearly come from a childhood which itself was a good many years ago. He is an adequate technician, as you would expect of a man who has published a score of books, but not a brilliant stylist. . . . He seems to me to have two remarkable talents which justify his career and the honours he has received. One is that of achieving an extraordinary empathy with children and animals; the other is that of expressing joy. And the latter is one of the rarest gifts of all. Come and go what may, there is always room for joy.

John Rowe Townsend, in his A Sense of Story: Essays on Contemporary Writers for Children *(copyright © 1971 by John Rowe Townsend; reprinted by permission of J. B. Lippincott Company), Lippincott, 1971, p. 74.*

The Wheel on the School (1954), a tenderly told story which won the Newbery Medal, gives a remarkably detailed picture of life in a Dutch fishing village and also has unusual social values. . . . *Journey from Peppermint Street* (1968), which won the National Book Award for Children's Literature, is set in Holland in the early 1900's. Beautifully written, it . . . [has] a universality that transcends the setting. . . .

Meindert DeJong has the gift of wonder and delight. Whatever the outward action of his tales, it is the inner grace of his children and animals that moves readers, young or old.

May Hill Arbuthnot and Zena Sutherland, in their Children and Books, *4th edition (copyright © 1947, 1957, 1964, 1972 by Scott, Foresman and Co.), Scott, Foresman, 1972, pp. 443-44.*

Though he has continued to publish since then, Meindert DeJong seems to me to exemplify the latter-day-traditionalist approach which was possible and indeed natural for writers of the 1950s but which, for better or worse, began to seem out of date as the sixties advanced. In DeJong's books, children are part of a stable community maintained by the orderly succession of the generations: grandparents are wise, parents are staunch and respected, and it is the natural state of childhood to be secure and happy.

John Rowe Townsend, in his Written for Children: An Outline of English Language Children's Literature, *revised edition (copyright © 1965, 1974 by John Rowe Townsend; reprinted by permission of J.B. Lippincott Company), Lippincott, 1974, p. 276.*

THE ALMOST ALL-WHITE RABBITY CAT (1972)

["The Almost All-White Rabbity Cat"] is a restless, sentimental, confused book for readers 8 to 11 about a lonely boy who keeps finding and losing and chasing a cat over an apartment house. The story goes on like a bad dream with improbable characters dashing in and out of it. . . . Meindert DeJong has written too many distinguised books to have his reputation affected by one mistake, but surely this is a mistake.

Jean Fritz, in The New York Times Book Review *(© 1972 by The New York Times Company; reprinted by permission), April 23, 1972, p. 8.*

With the visit of a cat who can unlock doors to lonely Barney's new city apartment, this begins as one of DeJong's quiet, deliberate boy-and-pet stories which almost stand still at each step to record a child's minutest impressions. Soon, however, . . . the whole thing becomes uncharacteristically souped up and slapdash. . . . Like Barney and his parents DeJong too is more at home in the quiet countryside. His frantic city interlude, which includes an encounter with a stereotyped hippie selling a cat he doesn't own, is as unseemly as Mother's stir-crazy shenanigans.

Kirkus Reviews *(copyright © 1972 The Kirkus Service, Inc.), May 1, 1972, p. 536.*

[*The Almost All-White Rabbity Cat*] seems to say we're all children at heart and wouldn't it be great if you could get your parents to give up their cheerless, demanding adult life and regress ever backwards with you? Typically, rural life is defined as nurturing and good. Urban life is punishing and bad. . . . The language is forced—a kind of borderline babytalk—but the fantasy is suitably wicked and keeps you going. It is a giant no-no intended for children and not literal-minded reviewers and parents.

Julia Whedon, in Book World *(©* The Washington Post*), May 7, 1972 (Part 2), p. 11.*

DeJong's animal characters are always sympathetic, but the combination of a contrived plot and superficially drawn human characters [in *The Almost All-White Rabbity Cat*] is marked enough to outweigh the writing style and the affection for animals that mark a story perhaps as much anti-urban as pro-animal.

Zena Sutherland, in Bulletin of the Center for Children's Books *(© 1972 by the University of Chicago; all rights reserved), July-August, 1972, p. 167.*

[Meindert DeJong] clearly establishes personality and situation [in *The Almost All-White Rabbity Cat*]. He deals convincingly with Barney's boredom in a new apartment. . . . Barney's joy at meeting an apartment-house cat is legitimately exaggerated. The poetic and emotional description of this discovery is typical DeJong. . . . But succeeding developments are strange and weak. Rosita's trick of opening defectively hung doors is copied by Barney and even by his mother, who make discoveries that lack credibility; for behind various doors Barney and his mother discover a baby lion, a white wallaby, and a large boa constrictor.

Virginia Haviland, in The Horn Book Magazine *(copyright © 1972 by The Horn Book, Inc., Boston), August, 1972, pp. 369-70.*

This disappointing offering from a well-known author displays DeJong's usual smoothly skilled writing, but plot and characters are poorly conceived. . . . Though the plot [of *The Almost All-White Rabbity Cat*]—jerked along by the frequent escape of an animal from someone's grasp—may amuse some young readers or listeners, the story as a whole presents a questionable picture of unliberated motherhood (and childhood) and the nature of urban living.

Margaret A. Dorsey, in School Library Journal *(reprinted from the September, 1972, issue of* School Library Journal, *published by R. R. Bowker Co., a Xerox company; copyright © 1972 by Xerox Corporation), September, 1972, p. 129.*

A wry comment on modern American city life, this is also a comical day in the life of Barney. . . . The invention and style are a little strained at times, as the title shows, but all in all an amusing story, with that slightly sinister flavour that often occurs in Meindert DeJong's books.

> The Times Literary Supplement *(© Times Newspapers Ltd., 1972), December 8, 1972, p. 1489.*

OTHER CITATIONS

Publishers' Weekly, *April 17, 1972, p. 59.*

ALONG CAME A DOG **(1958)**

Mr. DeJong has written a very moving story, full of suspense. Like all his books, [*Along Came a Dog*] is distinguished for the quality of its writing and for the way in which he is able to interpret the thoughts and feelings not only of human beings but also of animals and even the members of the henyard. Mr. Sendak's drawings are so closely in sympathy with the story that it seems impossible to imagine the one without the other.

> *Jennie D. Lindquist, in* The Horn Book Magazine *(copyright, 1958, by The Horn Book, Inc., Boston), June, 1958, pp. 196-97.*

Barnyard life, realistically portrayed, is the setting for this simple story. . . . It is a poignant tale, rich in characterization and sensitively told, which moves dramatically toward an eventual happy conclusion. Mr. Sendak's drawings sustain the mood so that there is a fine blend between text and pictures.

> *Julia Jussim Brody, in* Saturday Review *(copyright © 1958 by Saturday Review, Inc.; reprinted with permission), June 28, 1958, p. 27.*

[*Along Came a Dog* is the] story of a small hen, cast out of the flock because she is crippled; of a stray dog looking for a home; and of a man who lived alone. . . . This simple theme is treated by the author with delicacy and strength, in lovely and lucid prose. The story is absorbing and poignant, and its appeal will probably be greatest to a sensitive and perceptive reader.

> *Zena Sutherland, in* Bulletin of the Center for Children's Books *(published by the University of Chicago), July-August, 1958, p. 119.*

However uneasy one may feel at heart about the handicapped hen one takes to the dog as to any animal who parodies human qualities of observation and deduction, and to the Man who talked to animals because he leads a lonely but not selfish life which in the end moves even his materialistic employer to acts of generosity and tolerance. There is evidence of great care and thought in the writing, and while the style of the book is unusually good it is more than matched by the inventiveness of the details of incident. [The] author's . . . reputation certainly will not suffer from this present offering.

> The Junior Bookshelf, *October, 1959, p. 217.*

In [*Along Came a Dog*] there are only two human characters, and they are both grown men. The world of this book is the world of the farmyard hens and the big, homeless dog who hides among them. But Mr. DeJong has not deserted children, for these animals are the children of the story, with (on the part of the dog) a child's longing for love, and (on the part of the chickens) a child's touching grotesquerie of behaviour. Not that the animals here are merely children on all fours, or with wings. They are indubitably animals, beautifully characterized. More than once in his earlier books Mr. DeJong must have reminded adult readers, in his style and especially in his sympathetic understanding of animals, of D. H. Lawrence. The thought may have been put away with an embarrassed shrug, but, though it remains an excessive thought, there is something in it: for Mr. DeJong has some of Lawrence's power to convey, by a special use of vocabulary and a special movement of his prose, the essential character of any animal. It is so here, with his hens and his preposterous, ill-fated rooster: and the effect, as in so much that Mr. DeJong does, is not only very exciting but beautiful, touching, and most warmly and eagerly alive.

> *"When Once a Little Boy . . ." in* The Times Literary Supplement *(© The Times Publishing Co. Ltd. 1959), December 4, 1959 (reprinted in* Children and Literature: Views and Reviews, *edited by Virginia Haviland, Scott, Foresman, 1973, p. 280).*

OTHER CITATIONS

Virginia Kirkus' Service, *February 15, 1958, p. 134.*

Agnes Krarup, in Library Journal, *April 15, 1958, p. 1284.*

THE EASTER CAT **(1971)**

Cat-loving little girls are legion; and they will surely be drawn to the frustrated one in the story [of *The Easter Cat*]. . . . Millicent's grown-up brothers and sister-in-law—with the help of a friendly neighbor-policeman—work out a satisfying ending to a story that is pleasing, if not profound. One cannot but wonder whether [Meindert DeJong] will yet return to the unique originality and emotional depth of many of his earlier books.

> *Ethel L. Heins, in* The Horn Book Magazine *(copyright © 1971 by The Horn Book, Inc., Boston), August, 1971, p. 382.*

For each reader whose dreams are vicariously fulfilled by [*The Easter Cat*], another may be put off by [DeJong's] preoccupation with crawly settings; save for a brief interlude in an alley, the story places Millie in the dark of an uneasy night, in the dark of a spooky cellar, in the dark of a cobwebbed secret room and in a deserted rat-infested warehouse. The gloom is lightened only a little by the tenderness and joy of the child with her pet; the author's usual felicity of style is absent, as is the sustained poignancy of his *The Last Little Cat*. . . .

> *Janet French, in* School Library Journal *(reprinted from the September, 1971, issue of* School Library Journal, *published by R. R. Bowker Co., a Xerox company; copyright © 1971 by Xerox Corporation), September, 1971, p. 159.*

[Meindert DeJong's] love of animals, and his consistent

theme of the exciting and meaningful relationships children can have with them, account for the extensive library borrowing of his books. With *The Easter Cat* we come to at least his third book about a cat, and the charm is still there. . . .

Underlying [the] situation [in this book] (which could so easily be sentimentalised) is a gentle realism: no easy answer is found, allergies don't vanish overnight. But a solution is found and hope is given and these are the relationship's deserving.

C. S. Hannabuss, in Children's Book Review *(© 1972 by Five Owls Press Ltd.), April, 1972, p. 42.*

OTHER CITATIONS

Publishers' Weekly, *April 12, 1971, pp. 82-3.*

The Booklist, *July 1, 1971, p. 907.*

Zena Sutherland, in Bulletin of the Center for Children's Books, *September, 1971, p. 4.*

***FAR OUT THE LONG CANAL* (1964)**

[*Far Out the Long Canal* is a] wonderfully evocative story, unified in construction, convincing in characterization, and universal in the concept that underlies the story line. . . . The picture of the small community, madly skating, gay and reckless with the joy of being on the ice again has the charm and the color of a canvas.

Zena Sutherland, in Bulletin of the Center for Children's Books *(copyright 1965 by the University of Chicago; all rights reserved), January, 1965, p. 72.*

Winter in a little North Sea coast village, the canals alive with flying skaters, has a familiar romantic appeal; the naturalness of the characters and the tender, humorous understanding of the intensity of a little boy's yearnings give [*Far Out the Long Canal*] depth and reality. [Nancy Grossman's] line drawings have feeling and genuine Dutch atmosphere.

Virginia Haviland, in The Horn Book Magazine *(copyright © 1965, by The Horn Book, Inc., Boston), February, 1965, p. 50.*

Intense, determined, reckless and brave, Moonta is a boy to love. . . . The account of his experiences [in *Far Out the Long Canal*] . . . is as fine a winter's tale of Holland as we have ever read (and we adored *Hans Brinker* when we were growing up). It seems almost to put skates on our feet and let us join the entire community of Wierum as it enjoys a holiday on the white, frozen canals.

Margaret S. Libby, in Book Week (© The Washington Post)*, February 28, 1965, p. 19.*

[This] story is leisurely, but only as a child's story should be, taking time to dwell duly upon incidents, experiences and objects. The excitements are the genuine, sensuous ones of childhood. At the same time . . . the social relationships are strong; and at the heart of them lies the family itself. For once at least the love between mother and child is expressed directly, warmly, and yet without emotionalism. . . .

The Times Literary Supplement *(© The Times Publishing Company Ltd. 1965), December 9, 1965, p. 1133.*

OTHER CITATIONS

The Booklist and Subscription Books Bulletin, *February 1, 1965, p. 525.*

Anne Izard, in Library Journal, *February 15, 1965, p. 958.*

***GOOD LUCK DUCK* (1950)**

Timothy's frustrating experiences with the noisy duck at the fair and his discovery of the reason for the little duck's constant squawking are told in a story that is tender and gentle despite the hurly-burly carnival background. Lively illustrations [by Marc Simont] in gay color.

The Booklist, *May 15, 1950, p. 291.*

[In *Good Luck Duck* very] little [happens] really, certainly nothing of importance, and yet one is caught up in the minutiae with which the pages are filled. The flatness and practicality of the style highlight the delicious nonsense of the story-line. . . . The deliberately simple pictures by Marc Simont complement the story and help to make a book which will delight six to eight-year-olds and may prove a welcome discovery for readers-aloud among the adults.

Gabrielle Maunder, in Children's Book Review *(© 1975 Five Owls Press Ltd.), Spring, 1975, p. 16.*

First written in 1950, . . . [*Good Luck Duck's*] story and style are simple and unsophisticated. Timothy is very much an idealised boy, entirely lacking in the brashness which we now—perhaps unfortunately—regard as realistic.

The Junior Bookshelf, *February, 1975, p. 37.*

OTHER CITATIONS

Alice M. Jordan, in The Horn Book Magazine, *May, 1950, pp. 188-89.*

Virginia Kirkus' Bookshop Service, *February 1, 1950, p. 58.*

***A HORSE CAME RUNNING* (1970)**

In the here and now U.S., a *little* boy of nine or so is a sticky proposition, and Mark's hopes and fears for his old horse Colonel and injured newcomer Creek flatten out into one long wearisome worry. . . . [The] mighty moments [in *A Horse Came Running*] . . . are diminished by being made much of. At the last Colonel dies, and Mark is assured of Creek to replace him . . . but Mark has forfeited sympathy by his sentimental pining from the start.

Kirkus Reviews *(copyright © 1970 The Kirkus Service, Inc.), April 1, 1970, p. 380.*

As in [Meindert DeJong's] previous books, the story [of *A Horse Came Running*] consists of more than mere happenings; it is made up of deeply felt experiences. Mark's birthday, his love for the two horses, and his responses to Mr. and Mrs. Sayers and to his unobtrusively understanding mother are so melded in his emotional world that the fact that neither locale nor decade is mentioned becomes immaterial. [Paul Sagsoorian's] pencil sketches suggest the vigor and the simplicity of the story.

Paul Heins, in The Horn Book Magazine *(copyright © 1970 by The Horn Book, Inc., Boston), August, 1970, p. 388.*

[*A Horse Came Running* is a] disappointing novel in which only the first two chapters have any beauty or structure. . ... Though there are some moments of real warmth, this isn't a very satisfying novel; children will benefit more from reading horse stories by W. Farley . . . or M. Henry . . ., or Kjelgaard's animal stories.

Sandra Meyer, in School Library Journal *(reprinted from the September, 1970, issue of* School Library Journal, *published by R. R. Bowker Co., a Xerox company; copyright © 1970 by Xerox Corporation), September, 1970, p. 169.*

Despite the almost embarrassing emotionalism of [Meindert De Jong's] writing and the exaggerated intensity of the boy's feelings for [his] two horses, which far outweigh his concern for his absent parents, [*A Horse Came Running*] is commendable for its vivid, involving account of the tornado and its grim and terrifying aftermath. . . .

The Booklist *(© by the American Library Association), October 15, 1970, p. 190.*

***THE HOUSE OF SIXTY FATHERS* (1956)**

[*The House of Sixty Fathers* is a] vividly realistic story of China during the early days of the Japanese invasion. . . . Once again [Meindert DeJong] has shown his ability to paint starkly realistic word pictures that give the reader the full impact of the terror, pain, hunger, and finally the joy that Tien Pao knew during his search for his family.

Bulletin of the Center for Children's Books *(published by the University of Chicago), February, 1957, p. 76.*

To many youngsters, warfare is easily glamorized, but [*The House of Sixty Fathers*] presents a starkly realistic picture of the horror and suffering caused by war. This picture is softened only by the many tender relationships described in the book, particularly those involving the boy's attitudes toward his river god and his parents. Tien Pao's incredible courage and perseverance will appeal to many young readers. The separation theme is also important, and emphasizes the strength of relationships in the novel.

John Gillespie and Diana Lembo, in their Introducing Books: A Guide for the Middle Grades *(copyright © 1970 by Xerox Corp.), Bowker, 1970, p. 194.*

OTHER CITATIONS

Jennie D. Lindquist, in The Horn Book Magazine, *December, 1956, pp. 448-49.*

The Booklist and Subscription Books Bulletin, *December 1, 1956, p. 180.*

***HURRY HOME, CANDY* (1953)**

The creativeness and artistry of [Meindert DeJong] . . . is once again evidenced in the starkly realistic, compassionate story of the odyssey of Candy, a little lost dog that becomes a stray. The aloneness, the hunger, and the fear experienced by the little whip-tailed cur in his year of wandering, and the mounting suspense as security and companionship at last seem imminent for Candy, are at times almost beyond bearing. No one who reads the book is ever again likely to feel indifferent toward stray animals.

The Booklist, *December 15, 1953, p. 172.*

[*Hurry Home, Candy* is a] shattering book, almost too painful to be borne. No writer today twists the heart as cruelly as Meindert DeJong, and he has never tested the endurance of his readers more strongly. . . . [Children] may like animals enough to be glad to share Mr. DeJong's rich knowledge of them, but . . . they may be baffled by the adult-sized subtleties. Here, in fact, is a book, like the same writer's *Shadrach*, for adults to read about children and animals rather than a book for children. The work of a master, nevertheless.

The Junior Bookshelf, *July, 1962, p. 128.*

***JOURNEY FROM PEPPERMINT STREET* (1968)**

The real miracle [in "Journey from Peppermint Street"] is the author himself who has again, as he has done so many times in the past, written a story that will be best remembered for its deep and simple tenderness. No one knows as well as Meindert DeJong how a boy loves.

Jean Fritz, in The New York Times Book Review *(© 1968 by The New York Times Company; reprinted by permission), November 3, 1968 (Part 2), p. 33.*

Unfortunately for the credibility of an otherwise simple story of small boy excitements and Dutch daily life at the turn of the century, eight-year-old Siebren's first venture away from home ends in one of those storms that rip through so many other, lesser, juvenile novels. . . . Despite some over obvious character building through sensitive Siebren, many of his moments are amusing, and there are well-drawn, occasionally irritable and eccentric adult characters as well as interesting revelations of a different country long ago to keep readers going.

Lillian N. Gerhardt, in School Library Journal *(reprinted from the December, 1968, issue of* School Library Journal, *published by R. R. Bowker Co., a Xerox company; copyright © 1968 by Xerox Corporation), December, 1968, p. 44.*

[*Journey from Peppermint Street* is beautifully] written, with vivid characterization and a compelling evocation of the excitement, the atmosphere of the dark night and the strange surroundings, and the warm comfort of achieving new horizons. The relationships between Siebren and the members of his family are particularly good; they have a universality that is compelling.

Zena Sutherland, in Bulletin of the Center for Children's Books *(copyright 1969 by the*

University of Chicago; all rights reserved), January, 1969, p. 76.

[The narrative of *Journey from Peppermint Street*] is certainly brilliant, mind-reading, and Meindert DeJong has climbed right inside Siebren's head, but more selectivity and pace would make the story easier to read. Another stumbling-block is the style of Siebren's thoughts as he talks to himself. When he sticks to plain narrative all is well, but he too often addresses himself in phrases beginning "Oh, but . . ." or "Hey!" or "Why!" and continuing with a rather studied artlessness: "Oh, it was lovely-wonderful". . . .

Style apart, the story is unusual, and gradually warms up, becoming really interesting and exciting as Siebren and his grandfather finally reach their objective.

The Times Literary Supplement *(© Times Newspapers Ltd., 1969), June 26, 1969, p. 698.*

OTHER CITATIONS

Kirkus Service, *October 1, 1968, p. 1112.*

Polly Goodwin, in Book World, *March 2, 1969, p. 15.*

***THE LAST LITTLE CAT* (1961)**

Written with tenderness and simplicity, [*The Last Little Cat* is] the story of a small homeless kitten. . . . The slow pace and low key of the writing style indicate that the book will not appeal to all children, but for those who love animals and those who can appreciate literary quality and sustained mood, this is a story of great charm.

Zena Sutherland, in Bulletin of the Center for Children's Books *(copyright 1961 by the University of Chicago; all rights reserved), November, 1961, p. 40.*

[*The Last Little Cat* presents] an account of an unusual and touching relationship between two animals. . . . In flowing rhythmic prose it sensitively and charmingly describes how the last little runt kitten born in a kennel-barn came to receive not only a welcoming home but the gift of a blind old dog. . . . Appealing sketches of a scrawny kitten and a great long-haired dog.

Virginia Haviland, in The Horn Book Magazine *(copyright, 1962, by The Horn Book, Inc., Boston), February, 1962, pp. 46-7.*

[In *The Last Little Cat* the] author has a rhythmic style, with a repetitive, almost poetic manner that savours of traditional folklore. There is a directness and a frankness too in the telling and a sense of order and design that makes a fresh and vivid impact. Occasionally the method of constant repetition becomes unbalanced, overdone and obtrusive and then the rhythm and sense of design are spoiled. For the most part, however, sympathy and close observation give clear and accurate detail. The illustrations by Jim McMullen are sharp and almost ugly at times, but emphasise the subject and the directness and pungency of the author's work.

The Junior Bookshelf, *October, 1962, p. 184.*

OTHER CITATIONS

Phyllis Fenner, in The New York Times Book Review, *November 12, 1961 (Part 2), p. 40.*

The Booklist and Subscription Books Bulletin, *November 15, 1961, p. 200.*

***THE LITTLE COW AND THE TURTLE* (1955)**

The happy story of the friendly little cow's adventures with the wild birds and animals, with hoboes, bicycling children, and a huge and ancient snapping turtle that is making its laborious way to fresh water is told with the author's usual charm, originality, drama, and suspense. Wonderful for reading aloud.

The Booklist, *November 15, 1955, p. 131.*

[*The Little Cow and the Turtle* is a] delightful tale of a little white cow who has individuality and personality (but is not personified). . . . The book is perhaps better suited to reading aloud to individual children or to groups of children than for solitary reading, for it has the kind of humor that demands to be shared. An excellent book for family use since there is much here to appeal to all ages.

Bulletin of the Center for Children's Books *(published by the University of Chicago), February, 1956, p. 67.*

OTHER CITATIONS

Jennie D. Lindquist, in The Horn Book Magazine, *October, 1955, p. 366.*

Virginia Kirkus' Service, *October 15, 1955, p. 786.*

***THE MIGHTY ONES* (1959)**

[Meindert DeJong] has taken the [Biblical] characters—the slender thread of story—and woven around them stories that are sheer imagination, translating the spirit of place and time into almost modern terms. . . . For those to whom the familiar King James' version is difficult to give to children, and who are willing to have the stories told in modern, realistic terms, [*The Mighty Ones*] may solve a real problem.

Virginia Kirkus' Service, *February 15, 1959, p. 138.*

[*The Mighty Ones* contains] the hero tales of the early Old Testament . . . retold (each with its prefacing portion of the Bible) in vivid, sometimes poetic language and, though modern in style, with the dramatic force of classic retellings of heroic legends. The success and interest of content lie in three ways: in the connected sweep of centuries of Biblical history; in the interpretation of event, from the dawn of creation to the establishment of the Israelite nation; and in the quality of moving dramatization which makes the stories newly significant. Harvey Schmidt's striking modern drawings deepen the impression of emotional fervor and power.

Virginia Haviland, in The Horn Book Magazine *(copyright, 1959, by the Horn Book, Inc., Boston), June, 1959, pp. 218, 220.*

These are no ordinary retellings of Bible stories but imaginatively conceived full reconstructions of events and perceptive character portrayals. [They are graphically] written in dynamic, modern prose which gives a sense of immediacy yet retains the spirit of the Bible. Each story is preceded by an excerpt from the Bible and the book is illustrated with strong, effective drawings [by Harvey Schmidt].

The Booklist and Subscription Books Bulletin *(© 1959 by the American Library Association), June 15, 1959, p. 576.*

***NOBODY PLAYS WITH A CABBAGE* (1962)**

All children who have ever suffered the disappointment of a dying project—especially those who have found a suitable substitute—will understand Jim's experience and appreciate its satisfying conclusion. [*Nobody Plays with a Cabbage* is truly] childlike in spirit and form.

Virginia Kirkus' Service, *March 1, 1962, p. 234.*

[*Nobody Plays with a Cabbage*] has a most satisfactory conclusion. Mr. DeJong, delighting in a world at child's-eye level, shares this delight, awakening a responsive wonder in the adult reader as well as entrancing small children with his never-flagging tale.

Pamela Marsh, in The Christian Science Monitor *(reprinted by permission from* The Christian Science Monitor; *© 1962, The Christian Science Publishing Society; all rights reserved), May 10, 1962, p. 1B.*

Meindert DeJong, one of our finest storytellers, has spun a sensitive tale of man and nature's interdependence. One wonders, however, if ["Nobody Plays with a Cabbage"] is not more a story *about* a child than for one. Pre-schooler Jim is not apt to interest third and fourth graders who will be able to read the book, and whether younger children will understand the story if it is read aloud is questionable.

Dorothy M. Broderick, in The New York Times Book Review *(© 1962 by The New York Times Company; reprinted by permission), May 13, 1962 (Part 2), p. 34.*

As in *Shadrach*, Mr. DeJong's special genius for recalling the intense anticipations of childhood has achieved something again unique, charming in style, and haunting in its emotional strength. All the little feelings between Jim and his older brother, his mother, father, and neighbor are sensitively portrayed to make [*Nobody Plays with a Cabbage*] real, suspenseful, and ultimately joyous. Free line drawings [by Tom Allen] enhance fervor and suspense.

Virginia Haviland, in The Horn Book Magazine *(copyright, 1962, by The Horn Book, Inc., Boston), June, 1962, p. 273.*

OTHER CITATIONS

Zena Sutherland, in Bulletin of the Center for Children's Books, *April, 1962, p. 123.*

The Booklist and Subscription Books Bulletin, *April 15, 1962, p. 577.*

Helen M. Brogan, in Library Journal, *May 15, 1962, p. 2022.*

***PUPPY SUMMER* (1965)**

The children's adventures are interesting, but not unusual or suspenseful. The language is often colloquial ("Man, was it dry in that potato patch") and the tone leisurely and comfortable. The strength of ["Puppy Summer"] lies in Mr. DeJong's sympathetic understanding of people and animals and his evocation of a pleasantly rural world.

Esther Hautzig, in The New York Times Book Review *(© 1966 by The New York Times Company; reprinted by permission), July 10, 1966, p. 38.*

The theme of children who must part from pets is not unusual, but Mr. DeJong's handling of the theme makes this an unusual book. . . . [*Puppy Summer* is quietly] written, with a gentle affection that permeates the story, both an affection for the puppies and a sympathetic and quite charming relationship between the children and their grandparents.

Zena Sutherland, in Bulletin of the Center for Children's Books *(copyright 1966 by the University of Chicago; all rights reserved), September, 1966, p. 7.*

Puppy Summer . . . is an enchanting account of the last few weeks of summer on a farm, even though I have some grudges. Grandma and Grandpa make a warm little world for Jon and Vestri . . .; and Mr. DeJong moves those sweet little puppies from the children's dream to their burden with skill and accuracy. . . .

[If] the grandparents had managed even a tiny indication to the children—naturally grieved by the end of summer—that there were a few enjoyable aspects to their 10-months-a-year life, it would have been a better story, and they certainly would have been better grandparents.

Maggie Rennert, in Book Week *(©* The Washington Post*), September 4, 1966, p. 15.*

OTHER CITATIONS

Virginia Kirkus' Service, *April 15, 1966, p. 423.*

The Booklist and Subscription Books Bulletin, *September 15, 1966, p. 118.*

***SHADRACH* (1953)**

As he writes more books Meindert DeJong's prose takes on more of the exciting rhythms and emotions that make it thrillingly close to life itself. In [*Shadrach*] he writes of his native Holland, a farm, and small Davie's ownership of his first pet—a black rabbit named Shadrach. . . . Deepening the story is the astute but warmly related pattern of changing family relationships as Davie matures as a person himself.

Virginia Kirkus' Bookshop Service, *March 1, 1953, p. 147.*

So sensitively is [*Shadrach*] written, it is as though the author were actually inside the boy experiencing his every emotion and feeling the love and understanding of Davie's family. The charming pen-and-ink drawings [by Maurice Sendak] are in perfect harmony with the text. Limited in appeal, probably, but will be treasured by the right child; should be on every library's Parents Shelf.

The Booklist, *May 15, 1953, p. 308.*

[This] tale of Davie and his black rabbit, Shadrach, arises directly from a child's experience and emotion. Readers feel with Davie the longing for Shadrach's arrival, the joy and worry caused by his presence. . . . The beautifully written prose gives the story dimensions and resonances akin to those in the classics treasured from generation to generation. Illustrations in black-and-white [by Maurice Sendak] have the same quality in this enchanting book, which adults will enjoy as much as their children.

Blanche Weber Shaffer, in Saturday Review *(copyright © 1953 by Saturday Review, Inc.; reprinted with permission), May 16, 1953, p. 52.*

OTHER CITATIONS

Mary Strang, in Library Journal, *April 15, 1953, p. 739.*

***THE SINGING HILL* (1962)**

Although ["The Singing Hill"] is an introspective book, needing some introduction, it has that sense of urgency which Mr. DeJong creates so well. He is just as close as ever to the emotions and perplexities of childhood. We know Ray, his father and mother, understand the family jokes and understand the intimacy they create, and even the teasing of the older brother and sister. We see them too in Maurice Sendak's illustrations which are grave without being solemn and illumined with subtle lights.

Ellen Lewis Buell, in The New York Times Book Review *(© 1962 by The New York Times Company; reprinted by permission), November 4, 1962, p. 34.*

[*The Singing Hill* is a] tender and moving story of a small boy who learns enough confidence in the world about him and courage in himself to feel not quite so small. . . . Beautifully written, with fine characterization; the action goes forward in a remarkable blend of quiet movement and vivid revelatory scenes that capture realistically the conversations of the older children, the solitary play of the youngest child, and the quality of the relationships between the child and each of his parents. [Maurice Sendak's] illustrations have a similar aura of quiet and a charm that is in complete accord with the mood of [Meindert DeJong's] writing.

Zena Sutherland, in Bulletin of the Center for Children's Books *(copyright 1962 by the University of Chicago; all rights reserved), December, 1962, p. 56.*

Writing with his customary matchless insight, sensitivity, and tenderness, [Meindert DeJong] portrays the little boy's every thought and emotion and his relationship with his family, particularly his parents. [*The Singing Hill* will] probably be enjoyed most when read aloud.

The Booklist and Subscription Books Bulletin *(© 1963 by the American Library Association), February 15, 1963, p. 494.*

***THE WHEEL ON THE SCHOOL* (1954)**

[DeJong] has written a story with perceptive characterization, gentle humor, and mounting suspense; here also are dramatic action and an objective approach to give the story a stronger appeal for children. Effective wash drawings [by Maurice Sendak].

The Booklist, *November 15, 1954, p. 137.*

[In *The Wheel on the School*, Meindert DeJong] is particularly successful in his vivid characterization of each of the six children, and in showing how their enthusiasm spreads to all the adults so that the whole village feels the tremendous importance of getting the storks to nest in Shora, and everyone plays a part in making the dream come true. Good bookmaking with illustrations [by Maurice Sendak] that belong to the story. For a boy, a girl, or for a family or schoolroom to share.

Jennie D. Lindquist, in The Horn Book Magazine *(copyrighted, 1954, by The Horn Book, Inc., Boston), December, 1954, pp. 431-32.*

In [*The Wheel on the School*] Mr. DeJong tells of an event in the lives of the people of a small Dutch fishing village. . . . [It is a] powerfully written story in which the reader finds himself as excited and concerned over the fate of the storks as are the children of the village.

Bulletin of the Center for Children's Books *(published by the University of Chicago), April, 1955, p. 67.*

Once in a while a book comes along which establishes itself in the first paragraph; there is a certainty of touch which is unmistakable. *The Wheel on the School* is of this rare company. . . . The narrative is leisurely, naive, intimate. It is about and for children, but there is no sense of writing down to the child; Mr. DeJong is talking quietly, reflectively, as if to himself, and we are privileged to overhear. It is all so spontaneous that one realises, with something of a shock, that the book conforms to all the theoretical criteria of a good children's book, in interest, narrative, style, characterisation and tone.

The Junior Bookshelf, *November, 1956, p. 271.*

Probably the most striking quality of Mr. DeJong's work is the enormous excitement he generates in all his books. This is not only quite distinctive: it is also a matter of controversy. Those who cannot admire him call it hysteria. It is there, at once, in *The Wheel on the School.* From the moment that Lina . . . reads out her composition, "Do You Know about Storks?" the excitement begins. Why do no storks nest in Shora? A passionate tension is the mood in which the children examine this question. And when they resolve that it is because the roofs are too sharp, and that they must find a cartwheel to put on the roof of their school, the excitement becomes tremendous. In the search for the wheel each of the children has his own adventure, and all the adventures explode together in a roaring climax of discovery and rescue: which takes us only halfway through the book, with another series of adventures, blown at us by one of Mr. DeJong's superb outbursts of bad weather, sweeping down upon us and whirling us towards yet another climax. The whole thing trembles with impatience and anxiety.

"When Once a Little Boy . . ." in The Times Literary Supplement *(© The Times Publishing Co. Ltd. 1959), December 4, 1959 (reprinted in* Children and Literature: Views and Reviews, *edited by Virginia Haviland, Scott, Foresman, 1973, pp. 277-78).*

[*The Wheel on the School* is] firmly anchored to the realities of life in a small community. Part of Mr de Jong's success comes from his manner; he has a most engaging throw-away style which shows how keen and exact an ear he has for the cadences of speech and with what skill he heightens them to make them acceptable on the printed page. For the rest, the great charm of *The Wheel on the School* is that it gives a complete picture of a village so small that one can get to know each house and its inhabitants intimately.

Marcus Crouch, in his The Nesbit Tradition: The Children's Novel in England 1945-1970 *(© Marcus Crouch 1972), Ernest Benn, 1972, pp. 92-3.*

* * *

Du BOIS, William (Sherman) Pène 1916-

An American author-illustrator, William Pène du Bois received the 1948 Newbery Medal for *The Twenty-One Balloons*. (See also *Contemporary Authors*, Vols. 5-8, rev. ed., and *Something About the Author*, Vol. 4.)

GENERAL COMMENTARY

An American writer expert in using the familiar as a springboard to fantastic adventures is William Pène du Bois. . . . The excursions of his imagination are governed by science and controlled by his strong love of order. . . . The humor and suspense of all of Mr. du Bois's tales owe as much to the smoothness and clarity of his style as to careful attention to every detail.

Ruth Hill Viguers, in A Critical History of Children's Literature, *revised edition, by Cornelia Meigs, Anne Thaxter Eaton, Elizabeth Nesbitt, and Ruth Hill Viguers, edited by Cornelia Meigs (copyright © 1969 by The Macmillan Co.), Macmillan, 1969, pp. 473-74.*

THE ALLIGATOR CASE (1965)

This has a very fast pulse. It is the sort of highly articulate nonsense that *Mad* magazine used to achieve in its hey-day to the delight of the more literate younger readers. . . . The alligator case is too intricate to synopsize, but it offers certain developmental values never encountered elsewhere. . . . The illustrations are marvelously funny and in full color. So is the vocabulary.

Virginia Kirkus' Service, *August 15, 1965, p. 827.*

[*The Alligator Case*] is a very funny story, solemnly told with the stock situations and tired clichés of the comics reproduced with charming innocence. The author-artist's own illustrations are lively and convincing in detail, not only true to the text but also revealing a gay appreciation of the way childish fantasy enlivens a workaday world.

Aileen Pippett, in The New York Times Book Review *(© 1965, The New York Times Company; reprinted by permission), August 29, 1965, p. 22.*

[*The Alligator Case* is a] delightful romp, delightfully illustrated. Told by a crafty and persistent Boy Detective, this is the tallish tale of three dastardly thieves who use a small-town circus as cover for their crime. . . . [Du Bois] has immense fun with plot and word-plays; it is a tribute to his skill that both retain spontaneity and humor.

Zena Sutherland, in Bulletin of the Center for Children's Books *(copyright 1965 by the University of Chicago; all rights reserved), October, 1965, p. 31.*

The narrator of this fast-paced yarn is a nameless boy detective who, a master at disguises and logical reasoning, is so alert and eager that he begins working on the Alligator Case before a crime has been committed. . . . Although this is not the best work of the author-illustrator, the story of the young hero's wild weekend and the brightly colored illustrations, both done with Du Bois' straight-faced humor, are fresh and diverting.

The Booklist and Subscription Books Bulletin *(© 1965 by the American Library Association), November 15, 1965, p. 330.*

OTHER CITATIONS

Library Journal, *September 15, 1965, p. 3788.*

Virginia Haviland, in The Horn Book Magazine, *October, 1965, p. 497.*

William Cole, in Book Week, *October 3, 1965, p. 21.*

Alice Dalgliesh, in Saturday Review, *January 22, 1966, p. 45.*

BEAR CIRCUS (1971)

With a happy unity of text and full-color pictures, Mr. du Bois, a brilliant impresario, displays his longtime love for the circus and his own flair for showmanship. The unhappy, innocent bears and the concerned kangaroos provide a perfect introduction for the circus high jinks—all described and illustrated with meticulous, leisurely detail.

Ethel L. Heins, in The Horn Book Magazine *(copyright © 1971 by The Horn Book, Inc., Boston), December, 1971, p. 601.*

OTHER CITATIONS

The Booklist, *December 15, 1971, p. 366.*

Zena Sutherland, in Bulletin of the Center for Children's Books, *January, 1972, p. 73.*

CALL ME BANDICOOT (1970)

Fourth in [du Bois'] series of books on the seven deadly sins, [*Call Me Bandicoot*] has stinginess as a leitmotif, but the imaginative embroidery of the storyteller's art almost eclipses the theme. [The story is written] with wit and sophistication and illustrated with elegance.

Zena Sutherland, in Bulletin of the Center for Children's Books *(© 1971 by the University of Chicago; all rights reserved), March, 1971, p. 105.*

OTHER CITATIONS

Kirkus Reviews, *October 1, 1970, p. 1095.*

ELISABETH THE COW GHOST (1936)

Rewritten with new illustrations, [*Elisabeth the Cow Ghost*] is a new version of Du Bois' 1936 picture book of the same title. . . . The text is disappointing, but Mr. Du Bois has a charm in his drawing that lends the story humor. For large collections that would like all of Mr. Du Bois' books.

Arlene Mosel, in School Library Journal *(reprinted from the May, 1964, issue of* School Library Journal, *published by R. R. Bowker Co., a Xerox company; copyright © 1964 by Xerox Corporation), May, 1964, p. 82.*

One of the first books by [William Pène du Bois], published by Nelson in 1936, was the story of Elisabeth, the cream-colored cow. . . . The small size—about six inches square—the brief, uncomplicated text, and the clear vigorous drawings in yellow and black admirably suited the childlike nonsense. Now the story has been completely retold and redrawn for a new generation, and the ingenuousness, which was its great charm, has been lost. The amusing, attractive new book [Viking, 1964] will probably appeal to older children [more] than the early book did; but anyone who knew the original edition is likely to regret the sophistication of this one.

Ruth Hill Viguers, in The Horn Book Magazine *(copyright © 1964, by The Horn Book, Inc., Boston), June, 1964, p. 274.*

William Pène Du Bois, with his never-failing inventiveness, gives young readers a marvelous ghostly heroine—Elisabeth the cow, pet of the Norman boy Leo. . . . [This] is a fine short tale.

The pictures (in black and white with a little tan) are rendered with the precision we expect from this artist, but are quite different in effect from any previous ones because the details of cross-hatching and dotted shadows are not reduced as finely (with the exception of a charming scene on the jacket), making some scenes eerie and confused.

Margaret Sherwood Libby, in Book Week *(© The Washington Post), August 9, 1964, p. 15.*

THE GIANT (1954)

[*The Giant* is] an entrancing tall tale, one of Du Bois' best, which achieves and maintains perfect man-to-mouse proportions throughout and attests to the unique imagination and sense of humor of this author-artist.

The Booklist, *November 1, 1954, p. 114.*

William Pène du Bois has written and illustrated a keenly imagined tale so casual in its good humor and so plausible in its improbabilities that one is carried away to a satisfying end without a moment of doubt in passing. . . . The easy charm of Mr. du Bois' telling is richly supplemented by the imaginative precision of his drawings to make [*The Giant*] a delightful book.

Maria Cimino, in Saturday Review *(copyright 1954 by Saturday Review, Inc.; reprinted with permission), November 13, 1954, p. 80.*

[*The Giant* is a] fanciful-realistic story of a young boy of giant proportions who is being hidden away in a town in middle Europe. . . . The account of how the author purportedly discovered the giant and helped to bring him out into the open is told with a straight-faced humor that lends a note of reality to the story. Du Bois's illustrations are excellent for giving an impression of the size of the giant.

Bulletin of the Center for Children's Books *(published by the University of Chicago), July, 1955, p. 98.*

OTHER CITATIONS

Jennie D. Lindquist, in The Horn Book Magazine, *December, 1954, p. 434.*

THE HARE AND THE TORTOISE & THE TORTOISE AND THE HARE/LA LIEBRE Y LA TORTUGA & LA TORTUGA Y LA LIEBRE (with Lee Po, 1972)

[*The Hare and the Tortoise & the Tortoise and the Hare* presents the] famous foot race and a turn-about sequel, each told in parallel English and Spanish texts and acted out with consummate stage presence against storybook pastel backgrounds. . . . [The] economically characterized principals and the piquant eccentricity of crabs wearing bathing suits and prim hogs in Eton collars make [the first story] a winner. The second, less satisfactory, episode is set in a shimmering, pointilistic undersea kingdom. . . . The reversal of roles (and shift of stylistic gears) in scene two may be a little abrupt, but Du Bois' ingenuity helps bridge the gap and in the realm of bilingual materials, this is a commanding performance.

Kirkus Reviews *(copyright © 1972 The Kirkus Service, Inc.), July 1, 1972, p. 720.*

[This is an] unusually attractive bilingual picture book. Alternate pages, divided to accommodate English and Spanish versions of two stories, are accompanied by [Mr. du Bois'] full-page illustrations. . . . The only drawback of the book is that the texts are backed by color washes which impede facility of reading. But the bilingual texts should be tempting to any reader with a normal curiosity. The humor of the line drawings and harmony of the watercolors are as rewarding as the stories.

Paul Heins, in The Horn Book Magazine *(copyright © 1972 by The Horn Book, Inc., Boston), October, 1972, pp. 460-61.*

[*The Hare and the Tortoise & the Tortoise and the Hare* is a] disappointing dual-language title in two parts. . . . The narrative, both in English [by William Pène du Bois] and Spanish [by Lee Po], is clumsy, poorly written and dull, and the lack of text coordination renders the book useless for language learning. For example, the text reads "laughing and choking" when "choking with laughter" is the exact translation of "ahogándose de risa." In addition, masculine pronouns are used with the feminine noun "la liebre," and there are grammatical errors, numerous misprints, one missing word and one out of sequence. While allowances can be made for obvious Anglicisms, libraries won't need this title which cannot be redeemed by [du Bois'] competent illustrations.

Daisy Kouzel, in School Library Journal *(reprinted from the November, 1972, issue of* School Library Journal, *published by R. R. Bowker Co., a Xerox company; copyright © 1972 by Xerox Corporation), November, 1972, p. 61.*

OTHER CITATIONS

Publishers' Weekly, *January 8, 1973, p. 65.*

THE HORSE IN THE CAMEL SUIT (1967)

This wordy tale of Swami Tarragon and a stolen racehorse is jammed into a period of one weekend, and it will be a lost one for a good many readers 6 to 10: they won't be able to follow the story. . . .

Still, [du Bois] has a boundless imagination, and a wry, fanciful style. His description of a carnival show is entertaining, authentic and informative. Swami, the villain, is a wild, interesting character who would be much more fun to hear from again than the hero. Let's hope he gets out of jail in time for another, easier story by Mr. du Bois.

Jerome Beatty Jr., in The New York Times Book Review *(© 1967 by The New York Times Company; reprinted by permission), September 17, 1967, p. 34.*

[*The Horse in the Camel Suit*] is for the superior reader who can handle a long, involved plot, first-person narration, and whose reading experience is equal to the word-play and cleverly turned phrases that are the hallmark of Du Bois' humor. [His] colorful drawings are characterized by the same expert technique and subtle humor as found in the text.

Jean Pretorius, in School Library Journal *(reprinted from the October, 1967, issue of* School Library Journal, *published by R. R. Bowker Co., a Xerox company; copyright © 1967 by Xerox Corporation), October, 1967, p. 178.*

[*The Horse in the Camel Suit* is to] be read, as it is written, with tongue firmly in cheek. . . . [Du Bois'] illustrations are charming and very funny; the story is very funny, rather complicated, and sophisticated in both vocabulary and humor.

Zena Sutherland, in Bulletin of the Center for Children's Books *(copyright 1968 by the University of Chicago; all rights reserved), January, 1968, p. 77.*

Once again the nimble-witted boy detective brings a group of clever rascals to justice. . . . In a brilliant and complex denouement, the experts at karate, escape, ventriloquism, and mind reading fall straight into the detective's trap. Story and pictures are tossed off with a showman's flourish; both are touched with the usual Pène du Bois sparkle and wit.

Ethel L. Heins, in The Horn Book Magazine *(copyright © 1968 by The Horn Book, Inc., Boston), April, 1968, pp. 175-76.*

OTHER CITATIONS

Publishers' Weekly, *July 31, 1967, p. 55.*

Kirkus Service, *August 1, 1967, p. 877.*

Polly Goodwin, in Book World, *September 10, 1967, p. 36.*

LAZY TOMMY PUMPKINHEAD (1966)

The perils of a power failure come home to Lazy Pumpkinhead in this slapstick sermon. . . . Lazy Tommy somehow seems to resemble Struwwelpeter, and he's not likely to get much sympathy for his sufferings. It's a pie-in-the-face put down, a disappointment from a distinguished author-illustrator.

Virginia Kirkus' Service *(copyright © 1966 Virginia Kirkus' Service, Inc.), October 15, 1966, pp. 1095-96.*

Illustrated with characteristic meticulous realism, the story [of *Lazy Tommy Pumpkinhead*] becomes a *reductio ad absurdum*, producing the kind of earthy slapstick which younger children—particularly boys—find hilariously funny.

Ethel L. Heins, in The Horn Book Magazine *(copyright © 1967, by The Horn Book, Inc., Boston), February, 1967, p. 61.*

[*Lazy Tommy Pumpkinhead* is a] nonsense story with delightful, daft illustrations; in the terrible tale of Tommy there is a not-so-subtle message about sloth, or the mechanized age, or physical fitness, or Something. It isn't likely that the reader will care. . . .

Zena Sutherland, in Bulletin of the Center for Children's Books *(copyright 1967 by the University of Chicago; all rights reserved), February, 1967, p. 87.*

OTTO AND THE MAGIC POTATOES (1970)

[*Otto and the Magic Potatoes*], longer of text and smaller of type than its predecessors, is less a picturization than a story with alternate opening picture spreads. And these amplified marvels, rather than the capricious plot entanglements and the lengthy conversations, are the main, indeed the sustaining attraction.

Kirkus Reviews *(copyright © 1970 The Kirkus Service, Inc.), March 1, 1970, p. 238.*

Broadly nonsensical and delightfully bland, the sequel to other Otto stories is no less wonderfully illustrated (architectural precision of detail combined with fanciful embellishment and imaginative humor, melting colors) but the plot development has halting moments. . . . The outcome is unexpected, mildly amusing but not particularly sequential.

Zena Sutherland, in Bulletin of the Center for Children's Books *(© 1970 by the University of Chicago; all rights reserved), December, 1970, p. 57.*

OTHER CITATIONS

The Booklist, *July 15, 1970, pp. 1406-07.*

***OTTO AT SEA* (1936)**

Otto, a giant dog, may be at sea, but he is by no means lost. . . . William Du Bois' boldly colored illustrations vividly illustrate the madcap continental atmosphere in which the unusual but always dignified Otto performs.

Virginia Kirkus' Service, *July 1, 1958, p. 452.*

Originally published in 1936, this [Viking, 1958] welcome re-issue [of *Otto at Sea*] has new and larger drawings. . . . Pictures, brilliant in the pure colors of the author's recent *Lion*, show the giant but benign Otto useful as only this author might imagine, combatting the waves and carrying out rescue operations. Ingenious fun, sure to be enjoyed by a new generation of listeners and young readers.

Virginia Haviland, in the Horn Book Magazine *(copyright, 1958, by the Horn Book, Inc., Boston), October, 1958, p. 377.*

***OTTO IN TEXAS* (1959)**

[*Otto in Texas* is a] fantasy for children who can accept the premise of a giant dog as big as a house and a series of adventures as complex as the State of Texas, where they take place. . . . [This] present-day Wild West tale seems busy, loud, and adult.

Claudia Lewis, in Saturday Review *(copyright © 1959 by Saturday Review, Inc.; reprinted with permission), December 19, 1959, p. 43.*

A straight-faced tall tale, [*Otto in Texas*] has inimitably amusing du Bois details in the text and even more in the handsome color drawings. Children may think this book funnier that *Otto at Sea*.

Virginia Haviland, in The Horn Book Magazine *(copyright, 1960, by the Horn Book, Inc., Boston), February, 1960, p. 29.*

OTHER CITATIONS

Virginia Kirkus' Service, *September 1, 1959, p. 650.*

***PETER GRAVES* (1950)**

Wider in appeal, in our opinion, than *The Twenty-One Balloons* and tops in nonsense value, this story of an elderly scientist, an inventive youngster and the anti-magnetic element—Furloy—should top the juvenile humor list. . . . [*Peter Graves* is] a wacky, hilarious yarn.

Virginia Kirkus' Bookshop Service, *September 1, 1950, pp. 518-19.*

[*Peter Graves*] is a story that all boys and girls who enjoyed "The Twenty-one Balloons" and Robert McCloskey's "Homer Price" will want for a Christmas present. The beauty of the drawings make it a treasure for art lovers. . . .

Exquisitely precise drawings of the inventions, lovely pictures of the professor's house, and a marvelous portrait sketch of the professor himself illustrate a story that is as exciting as one of the new science-fiction books and much, much more fun.

Blanche Weber Shaffer, in Saturday Review *(copyright © 1950 by Saturday Review, Inc.; reprinted with permission), November 11, 1950, pp. 48-9.*

[*Peter Graves*] is a whimsical fantasy in the American tradition of *Oz, The Phantom Tollbooth* and Walt Disney. It is a quarter-century old; an unsubtle book depending on the humorous possibilities of anti-gravity and a mad scientist, concepts which have been done to death, for its appeal. The diction is elaborate and extravagant, so marking the book out for older children, though only the less sophisticated among them. Basically, neither Peter Graves nor Houghton Furlong are interesting people, which they should be to make their improbable adventures realistic instead of just deadpan. 'The practical uses of a discovery of mine' says Houghton 'have always seemed pretty much of a bore, or at least an anticlimax'. Sometimes the writer's treatment of his material has the same effect.

Jessica Kemball-Cook, in Children's Book Review *(© 1975 Five Owls Press Ltd.), Winter, 1974-5, pp. 153-54.*

OTHER CITATIONS

Jennie D. Lindquist and Siri M. Andrews, in The Horn Book Magazine, *September, 1950, p. 375.*

***PORKO VON POPBUTTON* (1969)**

[Like] most of Mr. Du Bois' books, the story [of *Porko Von Popbutton*] is as clear in the superb draughtsmanship of the illustrations as it is in the text. . . . Mr. Du Bois vividly depicts prep school adoration of sports and amusingly describes the game with Queen Mary. Dialogue is frequently fast and funny, and readers will devour the author's color illustrations which tell the story in controlled comic exaggerated line.

Susan T. Halbreich, in School Library Journal *(reprinted from the May, 1969, issue of* School Library Journal, *published by R. R. Bowker Co., a Xerox company; copyright © 1969 by Xerox Corporation), May, 1969, p. 84.*

["Porko Von Popbutton"] is a delightful tale, dripping with fat but with no self-pity. . . . [William Pène du Bois], who supplies his own attractive illustrations, has a well-developed sense of humor, a keen appreciation of what the fat boy goes through and a style of story telling that is fresh, simple and hard-hitting.

Richard F. Shepard, in The New York Times Book Review *(© 1969 by The New York Times Company; reprinted by permission), May 4, 1969 (Part 2), p. 26.*

The illustrations [in *Porko Von Popbutton*] are expectedly handsome, the story has a fresh and lively plot, and the writing style is deliberately, blatantly breezy. While the hockey game and the school setting give color and action, it is really Porko's gluttony that is the theme of the book.

Zena Sutherland, in Saturday Review *(copyright © 1969 by Saturday Review, Inc.; reprinted with permission), July 19, 1969, p. 43.*

OTHER CITATIONS

Laura Polla Scanlon, in Commonweal, *May 23, 1969, pp. 296-97.*

Polly Goodwin, in Book World, *June 22, 1969, p. 12.*

PRETTY PRETTY PEGGY MOFFITT **(1968)**

[William Pène du Bois] has produced both a fanciful spoof on what might have happened in the childhood of the real Peggy Moffitt, the famous model for designer Rudi Gernreich—and an eye-popping show of his clothes, in illustrations that sparkle with flashes of wit and visual gimmicks. . . .

Clever and modern, this story has snap, crackle and pop, and a little of the put-on of today.

Margaret F. O'Connell, in The New York Times Book Review *(© 1968 by The New York Times Company; reprinted by permission), May 5, 1968 (Part 2), p. 47.*

[In his *Pretty Pretty Peggy Moffitt*, du Bois'] illustrations show a mod, mod child, exquisitely dressed; her cereal-bowl haircut meets her lashes (in the style of the model on whom Peggy is patterned) and her vapid expression contrasts with the wild disarray of her sprawling, falling body. Everything about the format suggests a rather young audience, but the nuances of style, the bland inanities, or the social commentary will be lost on most of that audience.

Zena Sutherland, in Bulletin of the Center for Children's Books *(copyright 1968 by The University of Chicago; all rights reserved), July-August, 1968, p. 172.*

THE TWENTY-ONE BALLOONS **(1947)**

[*The Twenty-One Balloons*] is certainly the most remarkable book for children this year. The young artist, one of the few prodigies who have preserved their talents in adult life, has written and illustrated a story of fantastic adventure which has some of the nightmare quality of Münchausen but which has a queer sanity of its own. There is in the narrative and the drawings alike a crazy logic which is reminiscent of Heath Robinson's mechanical wonders. . . .

Is it a children's book? The safest verdict is that some children, like some adults, will love its absurdity, its humour and its essential seriousness. It is certainly a very queer book, from which gleams a vein of genius. The exact description of fantastic inventions, which would undoubtedly work if anyone were crazy enough to make them, will appeal to children, as will the restrained, mannered prose, which narrates in so sober a fashion the vast improbabilities of the story.

Few books have so successfully matched story and picture. The numerous illustrations are not only most beautiful in themselves but also exact and illuminating interpretations of the story. The production is worthy of the quality of this remarkable book, in which fantasy, invention and high adventure are so happily blended.

The Junior Bookshelf, *October, 1950, pp. 130-31.*

A mixture of fantasy and science, [*The Twenty-One Balloons*] demonstrates [du Bois'] skill in combining literary style and creative imagination. . . . Reminiscent of H. G. Wells' science fiction tales, it will appeal to many beginning science fiction fans. In addition, Mr. du Bois' superb artistic craftsmanship conveys both the imaginative and scientific quality of his story in numerous and detailed drawings. . . .

These zany adventures are pure reading pleasure. The idea, however, of a novel approach to political and economic affairs, such as a restaurant-type government, is in a more serious vein and would provoke a good discussion. In addition, the technical and scientific principles are so well explained and illustrated that the reader will scarcely notice how much he has learned.

John Gillespie and Diana Lembo, in their Introducing Books: A Guide for the Middle Grades *(copyright © 1970 by Xerox Corp.), Bowker, 1970, pp. 266, 268.*

The fantasies of William Pène du Bois are as orderly and logical as mathematics, and his illustrations have the same graceful balance. . . .

[In *The Twenty-One Balloons*, Professor William Waterman Sherman] tells his story of landing on the island of Krakatoa . . . and finding its inhabitants inventors of the most amazing super-gadgets. These are described in detail and drawn meticulously. Since the island is volcanic, the people have planned a machine for escape should the volcano erupt, and of course it does. And off they go in their airy-go-round. Related with the utmost simplicity, the story piles up suspense until the explosion is a relief.

May Hill Arbuthnot and Zena Sutherland, in their Children and Books, *4th edition (copyright © 1947, 1957, 1964, 1972 by Scott, Foresman and Co.), Scott, Foresman, 1972, p. 256.*

The strange humour of *The Twenty-One Balloons* . . . derives from pairing a great natural disaster—the explosion of the island of Krakatoa—with a most elaborate and precisely described artificial society. . . . The absurdity of [the story] is intensified by its sobriety. Never once does William Pène du Bois lose his gravity; he takes himself, his invention and his audience entirely seriously. The adventures, and the marvellously detailed drawings in which the author showed how they actually happened, are in fact not funny at all, nor is the exquisitely mannered prose; it is the idea which is fundamentally and deeply comic.

Marcus Crouch, in his The Nesbit Tradition: The Children's Novel in England 1945-1970 *(© Marcus Crouch 1972), Ernest Benn, 1972, p. 105.*

F

FITZGERALD, John D(ennis) 1907-

An American author, John D. Fitzgerald is known for his stories about growing up in Utah with his brother, The Great Brain.

***BRAVE BUFFALO FIGHTER (WADITAKA TATANKA KISISOHITIKA)* (1973)**

Fitzgerald's first-person story [*Brave Buffalo Fighter*] is based on the diary of ten year-old Susan Parker who with her parents and twelve year-old brother Jerry traveled by wagon train from their comfortable home in St. Joseph, Missouri, to Fort Laramie. . . . From the start . . . there are illustrations of Jerry's courage, responsibility and general manliness—all preparation for his climactic feat and sacrifice. . . . Though much of the dialogue is stiff and repetitive, that the story is based on fact adds interest to both the details of pioneer coping and the highlights of Jerry's adventure.

Kirkus Reviews *(copyright © 1973 The Kirkus Service, Inc.), June 15, 1973, p. 642.*

***THE GREAT BRAIN* (1967)**

[*The Great Brain*] starts humorously, ends tenderly, and never drowns in nostalgia. . . . The book sees The Great Brain change into what might be The Great Heart but always manages to offer sentiment rather than sentimentality. Funny, believable, and completely enjoyable.

Elinor S. Cullen, in School Library Journal *(reprinted from the November, 1967, issue of* School Library Journal, *published by R. R. Bowker Co., a Xerox company; copyright © 1967 by Xerox Corporation), November, 1967, p. 66.*

This autobiographical yarn is spun by [the Great Brain's] brother John Dennis ("J.D."), age seven, who has a self-declared little brain but who can tell stories about himself and his family with enough tall-tale exaggeration to catch the imagination of any mischievous boy. . . . The laughter is balanced by events of sadness—the death by starvation of Abie Glassman and the contemplated suicide of a crippled boy. Life in a small Utah town at the end of the 1800s has been reconstructed through the captivating storytelling of the author of the adult book *Papa Married a Mormon*.

Helen B. Crawshaw, in The Horn Book Magazine *(copyright © 1967, by The Horn Book, Inc., Boston), December, 1967, p. 753.*

Tom, aged 10, was The Great Brain—and knew it. So did his 7-year-old brother, J. D., whose idol he was and who acts as narrator in this highly entertaining story of reminiscence set in Mormon Utah in 1896. . . .

The skill at characterization, the wit, the flavor of nostalgia that made the author's *Papa Married a Mormon* such a delight are all at work in a tale young and old should enjoy.

Polly Goodwin, in Book World (© The Washington Post*), June 9, 1968, p. 16.*

OTHER CITATIONS

Kirkus Service, *October 15, 1967, p. 1269.*

Zena Sutherland, in Saturday Review, *February 24, 1968, p. 51.*

Judith Higgins, in Grade Teacher, *October, 1971, pp. 95-6.*

***THE GREAT BRAIN AT THE ACADEMY* (1972)**

In 1897, while younger brother J.D. copes at home as described in *Me and My Little Brain* (1971), Tom Fitzgerald exercises his *Great Brain* (1967) as a seventh grader at the Jesuit run Catholic Academy. . . . Even though Tom's great brain is usually employed in the service of his "money hungry heart" (J.D.'s phrase), you've got to admire his talents, and J.D.'s mellower perspective makes a sympathetic filter.

Kirkus Reviews *(copyright © 1972 The Kirkus Service, Inc.), October 1, 1972, pp. 1143-44.*

OTHER CITATIONS

The Booklist, *March 1, 1973, p. 646.*

***THE GREAT BRAIN REFORMS* (1973)**

[The Great Brain] tops his own record for double-dealing in a fast-paced episodic narrative which ends unexpectedly, but logically, with his promise to reform. . . . And although Tom gets his well-deserved comeuppance from the knickers set, Great Brain fans will no doubt hope that his reform will be a redirection of, rather than a complete turning from, his ingenious ploys.

Mary M. Burns, in The Horn Book Magazine *(copyright © 1973 by The Horn Book, Inc., Boston), June, 1973, p. 271.*

As in earlier volumes, the Great Brain's outrageous schemes [in *The Great Brain Reforms*] are softened by truly poignant episodes, and if nothing in this book is quite as moving as the death of the old Jewish merchant in *The Great Brain* . . . it is still noteworthy on its own merits and as part of a marvelously sustained series.

Janet D. French, in School Library Journal *(reprinted from the October, 1973, issue of* School Library Journal, *published by R. R. Bowker Co., a Xerox company; copyright © 1973 by Xerox Corporation), October, 1973, pp. 114-15.*

[*The Great Brain Reforms*] is more episodic than its predecessors but still captures a lot of the fun and flavor of small-town living at the turn of the century. Tom's younger brother John, after narrating the various ways Tom defrauds one boy after another, finally engineers a way to stop the Great Brain's escalating escapades, which take a dangerous turn when several boys almost drown as a result of one of his money-making schemes.

The Booklist *(© American Library Association 1973), November 1, 1973, p. 291.*

OTHER CITATIONS

Kirkus Reviews, *April 15, 1973, p. 456.*

Zena Sutherland, in Bulletin of the Center for Children's Books, *January, 1974, p. 77.*

ME AND MY LITTLE BRAIN (1971)

[*Me and My Little Brain* is a] very satisfying sequel to *The Great Brain* (1967) and *More Adventures of the Great Brain* (1969). . . . As in the earlier books, an engaging picture of family life in Utah is presented, and J.D.'s scrapes—portrayed with equal effectiveness in the text and in Mercer Mayer's detailed pen-and-ink drawings—prove as amusing as the exploits of his brainy older brother.

Sarah M. Thrash, in School Library Journal *(reprinted from the November, 1971, issue of* School Library Journal, *published by R. R. Bowker Co., a Xerox company; copyright © 1971 by Xerox Corporation), November, 1971, p. 114.*

Lively, humorous, suspenseful, [*Me and My Little Brain*] derives much of its appeal from the author's perceptive, conversational style, which is as indicative of adolescent ambivalence as the sudden voice change. [Mercer Mayer's] full-page, pen-and-ink drawings appropriately convey the period flavor of the text.

Mary M. Burns, in The Horn Book Magazine *(copyright © 1972 by The Horn Book, Inc., Boston), April, 1972, p. 144.*

[*Me and My Little Brain*] is Tom Sawyer country—we are some miles further west and a decade or two later but the feeling's just the same. . . . Mr. Fitzgerald has humour, ingenuity and a light touch with character and situation; he also has sympathy, insight and depth.

C. E. J. Smith, in Children's Book Review *(© 1974 Five Owls Press Ltd.), Autumn, 1974, pp. 109-10.*

OTHER CITATIONS

Publishers' Weekly, *November 22, 1971, pp. 40-1.*

The Booklist, *January 15, 1972, pp. 432-33.*

Zena Sutherland, in Bulletin of the Center for Children's Books, *May, 1972, p. 139.*

MORE ADVENTURES OF THE GREAT BRAIN (1969)

A type of infant Machiavelli is given individuality in *More Adventures of the Great Brain* (a sequel to *The Great Brain*) by John D. Fitzgerald. . . . There is innocence and inoffensive cosiness in the Brain's machinations, well caught in Fritz Wegner's illustrations. We view his adventures in the mellow light of family reminiscence.

The Times Literary Supplement *(© Times Newspapers Ltd., 1972), December 8, 1972, p. 1490.*

The humour of [this book] is . . . American in tone, style and invention. The revived aromas of Bret Harte, Mark Twain, Robert Benchley, even of Thruber or Damon Runyon, it seems, are wafted in tantalising whiffs through the account of T.D.'s exploits in which cunning sometimes merges into ingenuity. . . . Strangely, all the hilarity and deviousness so effectively transposed into print are in the end submerged under a warm blanket of family solidarity, homely discipline, neighbourly tolerance and a sense of values which we used to hope had persisted beyond the year 1896.

The Junior Bookshelf, *February, 1973, p. 24.*

In less skilled hands Tom could emerge as a nauseating piece of work, but there is no fear of this: this Tom is a worthy equal of the more famous Tom Sawyer . . .; the book throbs with vitality and through it runs a genuine respect for people and the things that matter.

David L. Rees, in Children's Book Review *(© 1973 Five Owls Press Ltd.), February, 1973, p. 16.*

THE RETURN OF THE GREAT BRAIN (1974)

Having solemnly sworn before a judge and jury of his peers to mend his ways, twelve-year-old T. D. Fitzgerald, also known as the Great Brain, stars as the reformed hero in the author's latest collection of reminiscences about his boyhood in turn-of-the-century Utah. . . . [*The Return of the Great Brain* is a] fast-paced and amusing period piece, sure to please Great Brain fans.

Mary M. Burns, in The Horn Book Magazine *(copyright © 1974 by The Horn Book, Inc., Boston), June, 1974, pp. 282-83.*

* * *

FITZHUGH, Louise 1928-1974

An American author and artist, Louise Fitzhugh is best known for creating the memorable *Harriet the Spy*. (See also *Contemporary Authors*, Vols. 29-32 and *Something About the Author*, Vol. 1.)

***BANG BANG YOU'RE DEAD* (1969)**

[*Bang Bang You're Dead* is a] literary ABM that overshoots its mark. . . . The plot and characterizations have so obviously been pawned for the anti-war moral that, after seeing the first couple of pages, children will know the outcome—as good boys, the heroes are not going to ever play real war again. Fitzhugh furthers this melodrama with etchings of pie-eyed, angry young men poking at eyes, lunging at an enemy's throat, and gushing blood.

Daryl Alexander, in School Library Journal *(reprinted from the September, 1969, issue of* School Library Journal, *published by R. R. Bowker Co., a Xerox company; copyright © 1969 by Xerox Corporation), September, 1969, p. 148.*

OTHER CITATIONS

Martha Bennett King, in Book World, *July 13, 1969, p. 17.*

***HARRIET THE SPY* (1964)**

[In *Harriet the Spy*] the characterizations are marvelously shrewd; the pictures of urban life and of the power structure of the sixth-grade class are realistic. Some of Harriet's behavior is utterly reprehensible; some of her parents' treatment of her is unfortunate, but all of this is devastatingly real. The story grows, moving from an acid humor to compassion as the first image of a fractious and rather nasty girl gives way to the image of a little girl whose fierce candor and rebellious pride make it hard for her to get the love and approval she so desperately needs.

Zena Sutherland, in Bulletin of the Center for Children's Books *(copyright 1964 by the University of Chicago; all rights reserved), December, 1964, p. 53.*

The vibrant Harriet—a memorable character—is the creation of Miss Fitzhugh, an author-illustrator whose bold portraits in both words and pictures are delightful and, at times, shocking. . . .

The child's realization that people's feelings must not always be sacrificed to an individual's interpretation of truth is honestly explored. Too, the devotion that a youngster can feel for his current interest is forcefully stressed. The savagery of a child's innocent jottings about human behavior and the tenderness of the inward moments of childhood are effectively shown by the author's crisp, staccato style.

John Gillespie and Diana Lembo, in their Juniorplots: A Book Talk Manual for Teachers and Librarians *(© 1967 by the R. R. Bowker Co.), Bowker, 1967, pp. 178, 180.*

When we find a book like *Harriet the Spy* which makes a noteworthy attempt to deal with many difficult problems, we must ask, "How are they resolved?" and "Will this make it easier for a child to deal with such problems?" . . .

When a method of coping is presented, we must ask if the manner of dealing with the problem is desirable in terms of the child's well-being. Spying presents a distorted picture and so does not really satisfy the curiosity that motivates the spying. I am, therefore, not convinced that Harriet's continuing to spy at the end of this book is a very desirable solution.

Jacquelyn Sanders, "Psychological Significance of Children's Literature," in A Critical Approach to Children's Literature: The Thirty-first Annual Conference of the Graduate Library School August 1-3, 1966, *edited by Sara Innis Fenwick (© 1967 by The University of Chicago; all rights reserved), University of Chicago Press, 1967, p. 21.*

I cannot forget *Harriet the Spy* by Louise Fitzhugh because, though I do not believe for a moment that Harriet's salvation could have been worked so quickly through a single letter from a loved adult, I still recall the vivid characterization of a child, sick in her mind, and unable to communicate with superficial, socialite parents, who loses herself in spying on others to enhance her constant "making-up." . . . What Harriet wanted were her parents, and the tragedy was that they did not know how to give themselves to her, or even realize that she needed them.

Eleanor Cameron, in her The Green and Burning Tree: On the Writing and Enjoyment of Children's Books *(copyright © 1962, 1964, 1966, 1969 by Eleanor Cameron; reprinted by permission of Little, Brown and Co. in association with The Atlantic Monthly Press), Little, Brown, 1969, p. 238.*

Harriet's character is really quite consistent with the description we are given of Ole Golly's part in her upbringing. In a permissive atmosphere in which her ideas are taken seriously by her nurse, she has come to believe that all experience must be explored; at the same time she has been taught that she can and indeed must be objective in her observation of this experience. . . .

The people [Harriet] spies upon are her neighbours, her teachers, her parents, and her friends. None of them is 'real' in the sense that we could imagine such people existing in our own world. They are all exaggerations, even caricatures, yet they are real as symbols of the follies of contemporary society. Harriet's parents are presented far more realistically than most parents in modern children's books. At the beginning they ignore their parental responsibilities, but they do come to Harriet's aid when she is in trouble and so do her teachers. This runs counter to the current American trend of making adults ineffectual, which implies that children are in opposition to adults. . . .

Miss Fitzhugh's approach to life, . . . if it is to be pigeonholed, should be described as 'naturalistic' rather than 'realistic'. She introduces into children's literature a mode of fictional writing that adults have learned how to deal with adequately in their own literature but that they do not quite know what to make of in a children's book. . . . Louise Fitzhugh . . . brings a child to terms with adult life and in the process reveals its unpleasantness and dishonesty. . . .

Sheila Egoff, "Precepts and Pleasures: Changing Emphasis in the Writing and Criticism of Children's Literature" (1969), in Only Connect: Readings on Children's Literature, *edited by Sheila Egoff, G. T. Stubbs, and L. F. Ashley (© Oxford University Press [Canadian Branch], 1969), Oxford University Press, 1969, pp. 438-40.*

[*Harriet the Spy* is a] wryly told mystery for younger children about an intensely curious little child, Harriet, who keeps a secret notebook filled with honest jottings about her parents, classmates, and very close friends. . . . [Louise Fitzhugh's unpretentious] drawings accompany [her] interesting story of a nosey, brash 11-year-old spy.

Constantine Georgiou, in his Children and Their Literature *(copyright © 1969 by Prentice-Hall, Inc.), Prentice-Hall, 1969, p. 409.*

Despite . . . a heroine who seems at first merely an uninhibited all-American child—and despite the illustrations which suggest one much younger than Harriet's eleven years—[*Harriet the Spy*] is a remarkable book. Quite *when* one finds it becoming an addiction is hard to pinpoint: amid the welter of apparent realism, it takes a long time to realise the strong underlying fantasy. . . . From this reprehensible pastime [spying], Harriet gains real understanding of the nature of tragedy and happiness. It is extraordinary how deeply involved one becomes, almost against one's will, with these characters.

The Junior Bookshelf, *October, 1974, pp. 295-96.*

Harriet, in Louise Fitzhugh's *Harriet the Spy* . . ., emphatically is not the ordinary child who 'might be you'; she is a most extraordinary and disconcerting child. She lives in Manhattan, is eleven, and intends to be Harriet M. Welsch the famous writer when she grows up. After school each day she gores round her 'spy route', observing people and writing down her comments in a notebook. . . . Yet she is without malice; the truth is that she actually has the dedication, devastating honesty and ruthlessness of the artist. She faces at her own level the problems of the communicator who cannot help arousing suspicion but who still needs friends. . . . *Harriet the Spy* is one of the funniest and most original children's books of recent years. . . .

John Rowe Townsend, in his Written for Children: An Outline of English Language Children's Literature, *revised edition (copyright © 1965, 1974 by John Rowe Townsend; reprinted by permission of J.B. Lippincott Company), Lippincott, 1974, pp. 277-78.*

THE LONG SECRET (1965)

[In] this sequel [to *Harriet the Spy*], Harriet is much less of a controversial character, and sadly, she's lost lots of her sassy spriteliness. . . . *The Long Secret* is not as good, or perhaps cohesive, a story as the first one, partly because Harriet is subsidiary to her friend Beth Ellen. . . . The scene is a small town on Long Island; the writing is not nearly as seriously funny as in the original; and even though Louise Fitzhugh is still well ahead of the field, the book is not as appealing as the first.

Virginia Kirkus' Service *(copyright © 1965 The Kirkus Service, Inc.), October 1, 1965, p. 1045.*

The Long Secret brings back Harriet the spy, one of the most fatiguingly ill-mannered children imaginable, which is curious, since she seems to have the only normal parents in the book. . . .

Miss Fitzhugh is immensely talented but somewhat overpoweringly energetic in firing her ammunition. In the end one doubts that she has written a story for girls at all, but rather one for their elders, telling them how foolish and unsatisfactory their world must seem to the young.

Houston L. Maples, in Book Week (© The Washington Post) *October 31, 1965 (Part 2), pp. 20, 41.*

["The Long Secret"] is good . . . because, like ["Harriet the Spy"], it's capable of surprising even an adult reader; because it knows that girls of 12 aren't exactly women, but have most of the symptoms of womanhood, including that galloping irrationality which so markedly characterizes the sex; because it allows its children, though they are girls, to know that work one really likes to do ranks alongside love as life's great experience; because its child characters look upon a visit to Elizabeth Arden as a form of child exploitation—which it is. . . .

I admire Miss Fitzhugh for seeing what children are really like—in their behavior and their feelings—and for recognizing how little connection there usually is between the two.

Carolyn Heilbrun, in The New York Times Book Review *(© 1965 by The New York Times Company; reprinted by permission), November 21, 1965, p. 56.*

With subtlety, compassion, and her remarkable ability to see inside the minds and hearts of pre-adolescent children while portraying them from the world of the adult, Miss Fitzhugh has written a second story about Harriet and her friends. . . . The breezy, irreverent style and story line are deceptive; [*The Long Secret*] offers a sensitive and realistic description of young girls' reactions to the onset of puberty. This second book may be less of a bombshell to timid librarians and reviewers, but its impact may be more durable than that of *Harriet the Spy*.

Patricia H. Allen, in School Library Journal, *(reprinted from the December, 1965, issue of* School Library Journal, *published by R. R. Bowker Co., a Xerox company; copyright © 1965 by Xerox Corporation), December, 1965, p. 75.*

The sequel [to *Harriet the Spy*], *The Long Secret* (1965), is less intense, more sophisticated, and equally funny at times. . . . The inclusion of an evangelist family, several jaded characters of the jet set, and a wise old man make the book more cluttered and not as effective as *Harriet*, but it has two episodes that are particularly perceptive. In one, Harriet and her mother have a serious discussion of faith and religion, and in the other Harriet and her friends talk about menstruation, a long-standing taboo subject in children's books.

May Hill Arbuthnot and Zena Sutherland, in their Children and Books, *4th edition (copyright © 1947, 1957, 1964, 1972 by Scott, Foresman and Co.), Scott, Foresman, 1972, pp. 448-49.*

***NOBODY'S FAMILY IS GOING TO CHANGE* (1974)**

In [*Nobody's Family Is Going to Change*], the author examines once again some of the incongruities and ironies in the lives of middle-class children. . . . Despite the seriousness of the story, it is told with great humor; but both children lack verisimilitude. Willie's furious commitment to a professional career is difficult to accept in an otherwise ordinary, immature seven-year-old: "My life is being ruined . . . and I can't do anything about it. I have no control over it whatsoever." Even Emma, who sees herself in terms of Golda Meir, Simone de Beauvior, and Bella Abzug, would be more credible if she were a little older.

Ethel L. Heins, in The Horn Book Magazine *(copyright © 1975 by the Horn Book, Inc., Boston), April, 1975, pp. 146-47.*

* * *

FLEISCHMAN, (Albert) Sid(ney) 1920-

Noted for his humorous tall tales for children, Sid Fleischman has also written novels, mysteries, and screenplays. In 1969 he received a Lewis Carroll Shelf Award. (See also *Contemporary Authors*, Vols. 1-4, rev. ed.)

GENERAL COMMENTARY

The nearest American parallel to Leon Garfield is Sid Fleischman, whose novels also are 'period' rather than 'historical' and who writes picaresque tall tales full of entertaining roguery. Like Garfield Fleischman is fond of flamboyant, larger-than-life characters, and of mysteries of origin and identify; a recurrent Fleischman theme is the discovery of a father or father-substitute. His principal literary influence appears to be Mark Twain, but there are other echoes, too; Mrs. Daggatt's orphanage, for instance, in *Jingo Django* . . ., has a ring of Dickens about it.

John Rowe Townsend, in his Written for Children: An Outline of English Language Children's Literature, *revised edition (copyright © 1965, 1974 by John Rowe Townsend; reprinted by permission of J.B. Lippincott Company), Lippincott, 1974, p. 229.*

***BY THE GREAT HORN SPOON!* (1963)**

[Sid Fleischman is] an author with a talent for turning matter of fact situations into uproarious fun. ["By the Great Horn Spoon!"], with its offbeat characters and unusual setting, reaffirms the author's ability and with Eric von Schmidt's line drawings is all great merriment.

Dorothy M. Broderick, in The New York Times Book Review, *(© 1963 by The New York Times Company; reprinted by permission), October 6, 1963, p. 42.*

[*By the Great Horn Spoon!*] moves from one delightful scene to another aided and abetted by some wonderfully witty line drawings. And whether Mr. Fleischman is telling us how it was to round the Horn in an old steam and sailing vessel or what San Francisco and the rough mining camps were like, the reader can only rejoice in a continuously enjoyable word picture. Some of the adjectives this book deserves are adventurous, truly humorous and original.

Marian Sorenson, in The Christian Science Monitor *(reprinted by permission from* The Christian Science Monitor*; © 1963, The Christian Science Publishing Society; all rights reserved), November 14, 1963, p. 5B.*

[*By the Great Horn Spoon!* is a] story of the California Gold Rush, episodic and picaresque, with a humorous exaggeration of seedy or swashbuckling characters that compensates for the somewhat extended treatment.

Zena Sutherland, in Bulletin of the Center for Children's Books *(copyright 1964 by The University of Chicago; all rights reserved), March, 1964, p. 110.*

Sid Fleischman's *By the Great Horn Spoon!* is decidedly flippant. A mock-heroic tale of the 1849 gold-rush, it is decorated by Eric von Schmidt with the sort of scratchy drawings that seem aimed at the sophisticated reviewer rather than at the child reader. . . . This is a spirited story which contrives to surprise until the end, and is both exciting and amusing.

The Times Literary Supplement *(© The Times Publishing Company Ltd. 1965) June 17, 1965, p. 505.*

OTHER CITATIONS

Esther M. Swift, in Library Journal, *September 15, 1963, p. 3348.*

The Booklist and Subscription Books Bulletin, *October 15, 1963, p. 207.*

Margaret Sherwood Libby, in Book Week, *November 10, 1963 (Part 2), p. 14.*

Ethel L. Heins, in The Horn Book Magazine, *December, 1963, pp. 598-99.*

***CHANCY AND THE GRAND RASCAL* (1966)**

Chancy and his Uncle Will, a "coming-and-going man and a Grand Rascal," have a series of adventures that take them from the Ohio farmlands to the Great Plains in search of Chancy's brother and sisters. . . . Although the plot and characters are lively, it is the colorful language that sparks this delightfully fresh tall tale. The black-and-white drawings [by Eric von Schmidt] are as exaggerated as the story.

Amy Kellman, in School Library Journal *(reprinted from the October, 1966, issue of* School Library Journal, *published by R. R. Bowker Co., a Xerox company; copyright ©*

1966 by Xerox Corporation), October, 1966, p. 226.

[*Chancy and the Grand Rascal* is an] entirely diverting story by a master of the tall tale. . . . The fact that Chancy and Uncle Will eventually rescue Indiana from a curmudgeon and take her to Abilene, to be reunited with the two younger children, is of less importance than the fact that Uncle Will and Chancy have a series of wonderfully improbable adventures.

Zena Sutherland, in Bulletin of the Center for Children's Books *(copyright 1966 by the University of Chicago; all rights reserved), November, 1966, p. 41.*

For all readers who adore braggadocio and consider Paul Bunyan and Pecos Bill the apogee of American humor, "Chancy and the Grand Rascal" is a godsend. A perfect blend of one part quest story and two parts tall tale, it is one of the finest and funniest juvenile books to be written in a long while. . . . This is recommended reading for all who love to laugh.

Jane Yolen, in The New York Times Book Review *(© 1966 by The New York Times Company; reprinted by permission), November 6, 1966 (Part 2), pp. 40, 42.*

The background [of *Chancy and the Grand Rascal*] is achieved with meticulous authenticity and unobtrusive naturalness. . . . Sid Fleischman's historical sense is excellent, his handling of detail immensely skilful and assured, and the book's humorous passages, amid all the adventure and violence, are funny without contrivance or cruelty. Is it then grudging to complain that Chancy remains not *quite* warm and appealing enough, and that Uncle Will embodies rather too easily all the American pioneer virtues—is too much of a walking *deus ex machina* in every scrape?

The Times Literary Supplement *(© Times Newspaper Ltd., 1967), November 30, 1967, p. 1145.*

OTHER CITATIONS

Virginia Kirkus' Service, *July 1, 1966, p. 625.*

The Booklist and Subscription Books Bulletin, *September 15, 1966, p. 119.*

***THE GHOST IN THE NOONDAY SUN* (1965)**

[This] true pirate yarn [is] spun out in fine style by [Sid Fleischman]. . . . The ending is a bit soft—the villains all meet their due simply, going down in the briny—but the incidents along the way are all carried out in skull-and-cross-bones fashion. Good adventurous seafare for boys.

Virginia Kirkus' Service, *March 1, 1965, p. 245.*

[*The Ghost in the Noonday Sun* is a] pirate story in which the standard ingredients of shanghaied boy, villainous captain, and buried treasure are handled with a deft touch and a fine sense of humor. . . . Delightful escape reading, told with gusto and a nice ear for flavorful language.

Sarah Law Kennerly, in School Library Journal, *(reprinted from the September, 1965, issue of* School Library Journal, *published by R. R. Bowker Co., a Xerox company; copyright © 1965 by Xerox Corporation), September, 1965, p. 152.*

[*The Ghost in the Noonday Sun* is a] rollicking yarn of pirates and buried treasure. . . . The intrepid Oliver learns a bit about seafaring and a lot about pirates, and proves that a sharp mind is better than a ghostly gift when it comes to finding buried treasure. A goodly combination of adventure and humor.

The Booklist and Subscription Books Bulletin *(© 1965 by The American Library Association), September 1, 1965, pp. 54-5.*

OTHER CITATIONS

Virginia Haviland, in The Horn Book Magazine, *October, 1965, p. 490.*

***JINGO DJANGO* (1971)**

Refined larceny and slapdash adventure comprise the greater part of [*Jingo Django*]. . . . Jingo is in the best independent tradition of Jaimie Macpheeters and Huck Finn, while Mr. Peacock-Hemlock-Jones is a more fully developed version of the Grand Rascal from *Chancy and the Grand Rascal*. And while not always Bible-Belt blest, the "good guys" are always decent and fairly gallant; the villains are all thoroughgoing rotters; and the story is a vitally told, just-plain-fun tale to read. The broadly farcical caricaturing of [Eric von Schmidt's] line drawings perfectly complements the burlesque mood of [Sid Fleischman's] story.

Sheryl B. Andrews, in The Horn Book Magazine *(copyright © 1971 by The Horn Book, Inc., Boston), August, 1971, p. 383.*

Not so much a fiction as a stringing together of events, ideas, characterizations and stylistic devices in imitation of a fiction, Sid Fleischman's "Jingo Django" is slickly produced, ultimately inadequate. . . .

[No incident] fulfills any necessity more important than the necessity of sticking in so much of adventure, of friends, of foilable enemies. . . . Strangely enough the book gets worse as it goes along—as it is crammed more and more full of events that become increasingly schematic, more fantastic but less imaginative.

Roger Greenspun, in The New York Times Book Review *(© 1971 by The New York Times Company; reprinted by permission), October 17, 1971, p. 8.*

[Jingo Hawk and Mr. Peacock-Hemlock-Jones] proceed [on their treasure hunt] in near-Münchausen style by coach, flat-bottomed boat and caravan. But there is much more than mere Münchausen in this story, for as they travel an ever-growing warmth of feeling goes along with them. Convincingly understated, but all the stronger for that, it resolves itself into one of the most satisfactory father and son reunions of all time.

The Times Literary Supplement *(© Times Newspapers Ltd., 1971), December 3, 1971, p. 1509.*

OTHER CITATIONS

The Booklist, *July 15, 1971, p. 954.*

***McBROOM TELLS THE TRUTH* (1966)**

[*McBroom Tells the Truth* is a] romping and delightful tall tale, written in a blandly ingenuous style, and illustrated with [Kurt Werth's] lively and humorous drawings. . . . Entertaining to read aloud, [this is] a tale that should be enjoyed by young listeners and by readers from middle grades through middle age.

Zena Sutherland, in Bulletin of the Center for Children's Books *(copyright 1966 by the University of Chicago; all rights reserved), April, 1966, p. 129.*

OTHER CITATIONS

Lavinia Russ, in Publishers' Weekly, *January 10, 1966, p. 89.*

Jeanne B. Hardendorff, in Library Journal, *January 15, 1966, p. 424.*

The Booklist and Subscription Books Bulletin, *March 1, 1966, pp. 662, 664.*

***McBROOM'S GHOST* (1971)**

Capable of mimicking anyone and everything from Josh himself to John Philip Sousa's marching band, [*McBroom's Ghost*] appeared, disappeared, and reappeared in a fashion calculated to upset the most stolid of families. How the McBrooms finally exorcised their mischievous guest is told in a clutch of colorful incidents, narrated by Josh in the tongue-in-cheek tradition of tall-tale humor. Exaggerated descriptions . . . make this book a rollicking piece of drollery for telling or reading aloud. [Robert Frankenberg's] cartoon-like illustrations add to the fun.

Mary M. Burns, in The Horn Book Magazine *(copyright © 1971 by The Horn Book, Inc., Boston), December, 1971, p. 605.*

OTHER CITATIONS

Publishers' Weekly, *September 6, 1971, p. 51.*

Elaine T. McDonald, in Library Journal, *October 15, 1971, p. 3458.*

The Booklist, *November 15, 1971, p. 291.*

Zena Sutherland, in Bulletin of the Center for Children's Books, *February, 1972, p. 90.*

***McBROOM'S ZOO* (1972)**

You'd think that McBroom's truth-stretching tongue would have tuckered itself out by now but the fact is his yarns are as "eternal clever" as ever. . . . The young-'uns [in *McBroom's Zoo*] collect a quarter a head (children free) for admission to their zoo, which includes a wrong-legged Sidehill Gouger, a backward-swimming dryland catfish called a Desert Vamooser, and a Great Seventeen-Toed Hairy Prairie Hidebehind. Just pay no mind to Werth's less inventive tomato-colored notions of their appearance; McBroom is a genuine character and he never seems to run out of easy-reading, kid-pleasing whoppers.

Kirkus Reviews *(copyright © 1972 The Kirkus Service, Inc.), October 1, 1972, p. 1144.*

[Kurt Werth's] frolicsome drawings [echo] to perfection the blithe nonsense of [Sid Fleischman's] tall tale. As in earlier McBroom stories, the humor [in *McBroom's Zoo*] is both in the exaggeration of impossibilities and in the contrast between them and the straightforward manner in which they're described. . . . [The] fun is in the conception of such creatures as a Sidehill Gouger, a rabbit-like creature with legs shorter on one side—very convenient, those gouges, for the square eggs of the Galoopus Birds.

Zena Sutherland, in Bulletin of the Center for Children's Books *(© 1973 by the University of Chicago; all rights reserved), January, 1973, p. 75.*

Although Josh's unorthodox methods for outwitting a cyclone and retrieving his miraculous topsoil are not likely to be endorsed—officially—by the farm bureau, McBroom fans will be delighted with the addition of a Dr. Seuss-like menagerie to the familiar cast. And if these remarkable critters seem just a bit derivative, well, who can doubt a man who would "'rather sit on a porcupine than tell a fib'"? [Kurt Werth's] cartoon-like illustrations complement the droll text.

Mary M. Burns, in The Horn Book Magazine *(copyright © 1973 by The Horn Book, Inc., Boston), February, 1973, p. 43.*

OTHER CITATIONS

The Booklist, *January 15, 1973, p. 492.*

Alice D. Ehlert, in Library Journal, *February 15, 1973, p. 634.*

***MR. MYSTERIOUS & COMPANY* (1962)**

The Hacketts' warm relationship, Jane's yearning for a friend, young Paul's high jinks, all have the ring of reality [in "Mr. Mysterious & Company"]. But the author proves his genius by inventing Abracadabra Day. Once a year each child is entitled to be as wild as he likes, without fear of punishment. The day is a secret until Pa reaches for his switch. Only then does the child yell, "Abracadabra!" and all must be accepted, if not quite forgiven. A marvelous institution that may well sweep the country.

Dorothy M. Broderick, in The New York Times Book Review *(© 1962 by The New York Times Company; reprinted by permission), May 13, 1962 (Part 2), p. 30.*

Skillfully written with every event advancing the plot, imaginative but not fantastic, real but not realistic, and wholly delightful, [*Mr. Mysterious & Company*] can be added to the roster of children's books which are not only funny but truly humorous. It is hard to imagine a child who would not enjoy it.

Ruth Hill Viguers, in The Horn Book Magazine *(copyright, 1962, by The Horn Book, Inc., Boston), June, 1962, p. 279.*

OTHER CITATIONS

The Booklist and Subscription Books Bulletin, *June 15, 1962, p. 728.*

* * *

FOX, Paula

An American novelist and author of children's fiction, Paula Fox won the 1974 Newbery Medal for *The Slave Dancer*.

GENERAL COMMENTARY

It is time for people who care about children's books as literature to organize a society for the recognition of Paula Fox. In an era when youthful distrust of adults is rampant, Miss Fox remains true to the concept that children need adults if they are to grow though they must be fulfilled themselves and accept young people as individuals, not as pawns to be manipulated.

Dorothy M. Broderick, in The New York Times Book Review *(© 1969 by The New York Times Company; reprinted by permission), November 9, 1969 (Part 2), p. 34.*

The special gift of Paula Fox is that of seeing from the child's viewpoint and maintaining that viewpoint while feeling the sympathy of an adult and the detachment of an artist. Her children move our hearts because they are so true, yet there is neither sentimentality nor pity in her writing.

Zena Sutherland, in Bulletin of the Center for Children's Books *(© 1970 by the University of Chicago; all rights reserved), February, 1970, p. 96.*

Paula Fox is obviously much concerned with relationships between children and adults. She is conscious that in a complicated and changing society it is hard for the generations to live together satisfactorily. In her books the 'good' grown-ups are the flexible ones who appreciate the variousness of things and people. . . .

She is a very individual writer; and in view of this and an uncertainty about whom her books are trying to speak to, I would expect her to be a minority taste. I would not be nearly as confident of a child's liking Paula Fox as of his liking Meindert DeJong or Eleanor Estes. But the minority has its rights and is worth extending. Some of Miss Fox's books—most notably *How Many Miles to Babylon?* and *The Stone-Faced Boy*—are of striking quality and offer a kind of literary experience which is not too common in children's books. If they are read they will not be quickly forgotten.

John Rowe Townsend, in his A Sense of Story: Essays on Contemporary Writing for Children (copyright *© 1971 by John Rowe Townsend; reprinted by permission of J. B. Lippincott Company), Lippincott, 1971, p. 94.*

With the publication of *Maurice's Room* (1966) it became immediately clear that Paula Fox is one of the finest new writers in the field of children's literature. Her style is quiet, her vision penetrating, her understanding of children deep and sympathetic.

May Hill Arbuthnot and Zena Sutherland, in their Children and Books, *4th edition (copyright © 1947, 1957, 1964, 1972 by Scott, Foresman and Co.), Scott, Foresman, 1972, pp. 449-50.*

The durable world of DeJong may be contrasted with the fluid one of Paula Fox, a writer of a younger generation. With Miss Fox one has the impression that children would be all right if only grown-ups would let them develop in their own way.

John Rowe Townsend, in his Written for Children: An Outline of English Language Children's Literature, *revised edition (copyright © 1965, 1974 by John Rowe Townsend; reprinted by permission of J.B. Lippincott Company), Lippincott, 1974, pp. 276-77.*

BLOWFISH LIVE IN THE SEA (1970)

With her remarkable sensitivity and ability to express the problems of troubled youth, [Paula Fox] draws a portrait of long-haired Ben, eighteen, as he appears to his twelve-year-old sister Carrie. The reason for his compulsion to trace his private graffiti, "Blowfish live in the sea," on any free surface is the basis for a taut, penetrating, beautifully constructed piece of fiction. . . . The characterization is notable; each step in Ben's and Carrie's journeying relays something further in their tenuous gropings towards an understanding of themselves and of others.

Virginia Haviland, in The Horn Book Magazine *(copyright © 1970 by The Horn Book, Inc., Boston), December, 1970, p. 623.*

[In *Blowfish Live in the Sea*] Carrie is delightful and proves to be an apt storyteller with an eye for detail plus a sense of humor. Some scenes in Boston seem exaggerated, and there is an abundance of peculiar people, but then perhaps this is how an imaginative young girl would relate her experiences.

Ann P. Michalik, in School Library Journal *(reprinted from the January, 1971, issue of* School Library Journal, *published by R. R. Bowker Co., a Xerox company; copyright © 1971 by Xerox Corporation), January, 1971, p. 59.*

If this most perceptive book falls into the hands of adult readers, its message will be clear—that specific environments of body and spirit are needed for us to be ourselves. But Miss Fox presents the idea in such a subtle manner that younger readers may miss it, though still enjoying a wonderful story.

Mrs. John G. Gray, in Best Sellers *(copyright 1971, by the University of Scranton), February 15, 1971, p. 506.*

[*Blowfish Live in the Sea*] is a piercingly sweet and tender picture of a young girl's love for her brother. The book also is unusual in its sensitive characterization of Ben's father:

the failure, the drifter embarrassed at meeting his son, but so clearly lonely that he touches the heart.

Zena Sutherland, in Bulletin of the Center for Children's Books *(© 1971 by the University of Chicago; all rights reserved), March, 1971, p. 106.*

Though its title is a bit of a teaser, *Blowfish Live In the Sea* . . . is gentle with teen-age and adult idiosyncrasies. . . .

Paula Fox is too sophisticated a writer to make the boy a stereotype hippie—we see him always through the loyal, though not unquestioning eyes of his sister. . . . This is a compassionate book; Miss Fox knows how to touch sensitivities without bruising them.

Patience M. Canham, in The Christian Science Monitor *(reprinted by permission from* The Christian Science Monitor*; © 1971 The Christian Science Publishing Society; all rights reserved), May 6, 1971, p. B6.*

[In *The Stone-faced Boy* and *Portrait of Ivan*] Miss Fox was wobbling. Her sensitive feeling for dialogue and for the telling phrase was as alive as ever, but a degree of paralysis had gripped her command of plot. With *Blowfish* the wobbling has righted itself and the interplay of people, events, language is both subtle *and* compelling. . . . The set-up may sound commonplace, but such is Paula Fox's exactness in catching details and phrases that the 116 by no means closely printed pages of her story assume a remarkable density. The size, the remoteness, the squalor of mechanic civilisation is the more painful for the brevity and sharpness of her depiction of it; the hope for a measure of truth is the brighter for her masterly way with character. Everyone, from the aptly named Mr. Felix ('"Ben . . . there is such a thing in the world as not wanting *to do anything special*"'), to kindly barmy Mr. Krakowski (who walked 'rustling a little as though his clothes were lined with newspapers') may be finally a victim, but they are victims lovingly and honestly portrayed.

Brian W. Alderson, in Children's Book Review *(© 1973 Five Owls Press Ltd.), December, 1972, p. 184.*

OTHER CITATIONS

Kirkus Reviews, *November 1, 1970, pp. 1200-01.*

The Booklist, *February 15, 1971, p. 492.*

GOOD ETHAN (1973)

[*Good Ethan* tells how] Ethan, who is forbidden to cross the street, manages to retrieve his ball from the opposite gutter without disobeying his mother. . . . Lobel's soft, almost dreamlike pictures of the city scene show Ethan soaring through the air between two delicate, thin trees—which doesn't make his exploit seem more likely but does help to reinforce the muted slyness of Paula Fox's little joke on the world's oblivious grownups.

Kirkus Reviews *(copyright © 1973 The Kirkus Service, Inc.), April 1, 1973, p. 380.*

[Paula Fox's text] and [Arnold Lobel's] pictures are wonderfully balanced in a book which could have come straight out of the literal—yet endlessly imaginative—mind of a small child. . . . The tale [of *Good Ethan*] rises and falls like the arc described by the rubber ball: [after] reaching a triumphant peak, the story finishes as perfectly and as peacefully as it started. A little gem of a book.

Ethel L. Heins, in The Horn Book Magazine *(copyright © 1973 by The Horn Book, Inc., Boston), August, 1973, p. 374.*

[Good Ethan] conceives an ingenious method of [retrieving his ball]. In this part of the book the story moves into the improbable with blithe assurance, as Ethan climbs wires, swings from tree to tree, descends via wisteria vine to the other side of the street. [Paula Fox's] style of writing is bland and humorous, the story just the right length, complexity, and structure for the read-aloud audience; [Arnold Lobel's] brownstone-milieu pictures have a debonair simplicity.

Zena Sutherland, in Bulletin of the Center for Children's Books *(© 1973 by the University of Chicago; all rights reserved), September, 1973, p. 8.*

OTHER CITATIONS

Ethna Sheehan, in America, *December 1, 1973, p. 426.*

HOW MANY MILES TO BABYLON? (1967)

There is a dual sense of isolation [in "How Many Miles to Babylon?"]; both the isolation of a lonely childhood and the further isolation of an impoverished urban existence. And like the hero of a *nouveau roman*, James moves through this dream city, accepting what he sees. . . .

There is a plot. Perhaps too dense a plot. . . . But what is rare and valuable about this book is its unblunted vision of the way things are, and its capacity to evoke the sense of what it is to live as so many people do live in this city, in this time.

Margot Hentoff, in The New York Times Book Review *(© 1967 by The New York Times Company; reprinted by permission), September 24, 1967, p. 34.*

The writing [in *How Many Miles to Babylon?*] is subtle, making the understated story almost nightmarish in its excitement. Against the background, suggested rather than described, Jimmy is a small bewildered victim of an almost overwhelming situation. A story with great impact, it is far more important for young people who have no knowledge of Negro ghettos than it is for children to whom the setting may be all too familiar.

Ruth Hill Viguers, in The Horn Book Magazine *(copyright © 1967, by The Horn Book, Inc., Boston), October, 1967, p. 593.*

Miss Fox is an authentic novelist who can project herself into [the] mind of a ten-year-old black boy in Brooklyn with an unsentimental but deeply affecting understanding of what it is to be alone though loved, frightened though reasonably brave. Unlike most fiction for the young which is set in the ghetto, [*How Many Miles to Babylon?*] is not in the least homiletic. The boy James is himself, not a précis of sociological studies.

Nat Hentoff, "Fiction for Teenagers," in The Atlantic Monthly *(copyright © 1967, by The Atlantic Monthly Company, Boston, Mass.; reprinted with permission), December, 1967, (reprinted in* Only Connect: Readings on Children's Literature, *edited by Sheila Egoff, G. T. Stubbs, and L. F. Ashley, Oxford University Press, 1969, p. 402.*

The ending is inconclusively handled, the plot heavy, the characters not well differentiated; nevertheless, [*How Many Miles to Babylon?*] has several appealing aspects, the major one being the fine creation of mood and atmosphere. . . . [The] story makes James a sympathetic character even before he performs his one act of courage, but few readers of ten will appreciate the subtleties of the writing.

Zena Sutherland, in Bulletin of the Center for Children's Books *(copyright 1967 by the University of Chicago; all rights reserved), December, 1967, p. 59.*

How Many Miles to Babylon? is compellingly, if rather thickly, written. . . . As one follows James's desperate wanderings through the mean streets where junkies and the deranged are a commonplace and out by the sad autumn waves of Coney Island and its deserted fun fair the only warm thing that one remembers from this coldly terrifying story is the lick of the stolen dog's tongue on James's hand. It is a measure of the author's power that the sensation is so vivid, but it is difficult to understand how this can ever have been visualized as a book for children.

The Times Literary Supplement *(© Times Newspapers Ltd., 1968), June 6, 1968, p. 583.*

Mrs. Fox's talent for expressing a youngster's unique way of perceiving is evident . . . in *How Many Miles to Babylon*. . . . It is a moving testimony to a child's ability to escape from a terrifying experience and come away both wiser and more assured. The sophisticated line drawings by Paul Giovano Poulos lend an appropriate nightmarish quality to the book. . . .

This story emphasizes that if this reassurance [of familial love] is present, natural defenses will permit [a youngster] to handle frightening experiences and incorporate them into an increasing sense of self-confidence.

John Gillespie and Diana Lembo, in their Introducing Books: A Guide for the Middle Grades *(copyright © 1970 by Xerox Corp.), Bowker, 1970, pp. 11, 13.*

General appeal, along with black characterization, is achieved in Paula Fox's *How Many Miles to Babylon?* . . . Bored with school, the black boy who lives with three aunts leaves school and walks into the hands of thugs who kidnap him and use him as a decoy. Knowledge of the inner city is evident as the author interprets the spirit of boys as well as troubled adolescents.

Binnie Tate, "In House and Out House: Authenticity and the Black Experience in Children's Books," in The Black American in Books for Children: Readings in Racism, *edited by Donnarae MacCann and Gloria Woodard (copyright 1972 by Donnarae MacCann and Gloria Woodard), Scarecrow, 1972, p. 45.*

OTHER CITATIONS

Kirkus Service, *July 15, 1967, p. 807.*

THE KING'S FALCON (1969)

The story [of *The King's Falcon*] is beautifully written; like faceted crystal it is clear and sharp, with brilliant flashes and shifting opalescence that hint at deeper layers. It has the mournful bittersweetness of the closing incident: a troubador comes to the court, where nobody knows of Philip's rank, and sings of a king who disappeared; hiding his face, Philip smiles. "It is not often, he thought to himself, that a king can exchange his crown for a song."

Zena Sutherland, in Saturday Review *(copyright © 1969 by Saturday Review, Inc.; reprinted with permission), July 19, 1969, p. 43.*

[*The King's Falcon* is] a narrative of rare poetic beauty. . . . The simple reticent style is concrete in detail and at times humorous; its hushed effectiveness is derived from its overtones. The introspective king and the bullying queen are well contrasted, and the falconer plays the part of confidant to the king. . . . The seemingly abrupt ending invites one to reread the book. [Eros Keith's] illustrations of gray and gray-green washes over black line drawings echo the haunting mood of the story.

Paul Heins, in The Horn Book Magazine *(copyright © 1969 by The Horn Book, Inc., Boston), August, 1969, pp. 410-11.*

A LIKELY PLACE (1967)

[This is] a little more depressing than *Maurice's Room*, but written with the same natural, understated perception of how a young boy works, especially in relation to his parents. The characteristic quaintness of Edward Ardizzone's drawings doesn't seem quite consistent with the up-to-date tone of the story.

Virginia Kirkus' Service *(copyright © 1966 Virginia Kirkus' Service, Inc.), December 1, 1966, p. 1222.*

["A Likely Place"] is a very funny book, full of the lightning transitions from the matter-of-fact to fantasy which make an imaginative child's world continuously exciting. Paula Fox knows how children talk, think and act.

Aileen Pippett, in The New York Times Book Review *(© 1967 by The New York Times Company; reprinted by permission), March 12, 1967, p. 27.*

The writing [in *A Likely Place*] has distinctive style, the characterization is smooth, the humor is sophisticated: "Lewis shrugged. He knew his mother was smiling only because she wanted him to do something different from what he was going to do."

Zena Sutherland, in Bulletin of the Center for Children's Books *(copyright 1967 by the University of Chicago; all rights reserved), November, 1967, p. 41.*

MAURICE'S ROOM **(1966)**

Almost everybody has met, at some time, a small and imperturbable child who conquers adults by blandly refusing to be disturbed or persuaded by their ideas. . . . [Maurice] is enchantingly real, his family is real, and his friend Jacob (a satellite personality) is real. They are all charming, and their intended audience of middle-grade readers will be augmented by secret, older admirers.

Zena Sutherland, in Saturday Review *(copyright © 1966 by Saturday Review, Inc.; reprinted with permission), October 22, 1966, p. 62.*

[*Maurice's Room* is an] absolutely enchanting book, written in low key, with deadpan humor, and with marvelously real people. . . . [Paula Fox's] writing style is deft, [Ingrid Fetz's] illustrations engaging.

Zena Sutherland, in Bulletin of the Center for Children's Books *(copyright 1966 by the University of Chicago; all rights reserved), November, 1966, p. 42.*

Many boys will feel at home in Maurice's room which is so full of odd and sundry treasures, animate and inanimate, that there is scarely room to walk. . . . Black-and-white sketches [by Ingrid Fetz] emphasize the humor of the shrewdly discerning story about an engaging lad and his frustrated but understanding parents.

The Booklist and Subscription Books Bulletin *(© 1966 by the American Library Association), November 15, 1966, p. 376.*

OTHER CITATIONS

Virginia Kirkus' Service, *February 1, 1966, p. 109.*

Polly Burroughs, in The New York Times Book Review, *November 6, 1966 (Part 2), p. 46.*

Patience M. Daltry, in The Christian Science Monitor, *January 5, 1967, p. 7.*

PORTRAIT OF IVAN **(1969)**

On the surface, [*Portrait of Ivan*] is an acute portrait of an unhappy boy. But—and this is really what the book is about—things are never understood by their obvious properties, "'because *nothing* is exactly what it looks like.'" . . . As subtle as the book's essence is, children will comprehend the movingly told story and respond to this doubly meaningful equation of art and life.

Marilyn R. Singer, in School Library Journal, *(reprinted from the December, 1969, issue of* School Library Journal, *published by R. R. Bowker Co., a Xerox company; copyright © 1969 by Xerox Corporation), December, 1969, p. 50.*

Ivan is a lonely, motherless boy whose home life with a busy father who travels a lot and a friendly, sympathetic Haitian housekeeper is comfortable but circumscribed. . . . [This] quiet, introspective story is notable for its sensitive and discerning interpretation of a young boy's thoughts, feelings, and reactions to people, places, and situations.

The Booklist *(© by the American Library Association), February 1, 1970, p. 670.*

[*Portrait of Ivan* is a] penetrating story of an overprotected, yet lonely boy. . . . Despite the subtlety of the theme, the story is simple and clear. The author has an uncanny eye and ear for detail. . . . The writing is imagistic and sensitive. . . . Yet in honesty one must wonder whether the author is not interpreting childhood from a too objective adult point of view; whether the philosophical problems of identity and isolation, appearance and reality, can engage a child's interest.

Ethel L. Heins, in The Horn Book Magazine *(copyright © 1970 by The Horn Book, Inc., Boston), April, 1970, pp. 159-60.*

The plot is slight. . . . Yet the book stays in the mind, not only because the writer is able to convey so well Ivan's thoughts and feelings, but also because of the evocative atmosphere of the various scenes, the junkyards of the American countryside, the hot damp Florida riverbanks, the homely baking smells of the kitchen. Apart from the boy, the characters . . . are hardly drawn in the round, yet we see them as Ivan sees them in the way they impinge on his life, and it is a relief to find a book which has no villains, simply a failure in communication which has hitherto kept Ivan apart.

The Junior Bookshelf, *February, 1971, pp. 57-8.*

OTHER CITATIONS

Zena Sutherland, in Saturday Review, *December 20, 1969, p. 30.*

THE SLAVE DANCER **(1973)**

It's almost as if Paula Fox, in a twist on Stevenson's *Treasure Island* bet, had accepted a challenge to write a traditional sea story straight and make it live. . . . It must be admitted though that she meets the challenge brilliantly [with *The Slave Dancer*]; each of the sailors is sharply individualized, the inhuman treatment of the captives is conveyed straight to the nose and stomach rather than the bleeding heart, and the scenes in which Jessie is forced to play his fife to "dance the slaves" for their morning exercise become a haunting, focusing image for the whole bizarre undertaking.

Kirkus Reviews *(copyright © 1973 The Kirkus Service, Inc.), October 1, 1973, p. 1095.*

[*The Slave Dancer* is an] historical adventure story dealing with the fate of a shipload of ninety-eight Ashantis, illegally captured by slavers in 1840. . . . Hunger and thirst, hazardous voyaging under sail, a degraded crew's callousness, calculated torture, and greed are not minimized but have the veracity of the retelling in a journal. Jessie is a fully realized figure, whose perceptions and agonies are presented in depth. Demonstrating her versatility as well as her talent, [Paula Fox] deals impressively—in an epic storytelling manner—with a genre quite different from that of her stories about contemporary personal problems.

Virginia Haviland, in The Horn Book Magazine *(copyright © 1973 by The Horn Book, Inc., Boston), December, 1973, pp. 596-97.*

[*The Slave Dancer* is a] story that movingly and realistically presents one of the most gruesome chapters of history, with all its violence, inhuman conditions, and bestial aspects of human nature—exposed but never exploited in Fox's graphic, documentary prose.

The Booklist *(© American Library Association 1974), January 1, 1974, p. 484.*

Jessie is our window on the slave trade and it is here that the novel fails. As a character, Jessie simply is not interesting and thus his observations are not interesting. He becomes a mere device for the transmission of information about life on a slave ship and the slave trade in Africa and the Americas. The information, however, never takes on a living reality, because we do not care about Jessie. Thus it is difficult to care about what he sees. . . .

Jessie's reactions to the slave trade are "correct," i.e. he is horrified and sympathizes with the captured Africans. Exactly why is unclear, because he has grown up in the slave South and the author does not draw the character sharply enough to explain why he is atypical of his culture. We are asked to accept him on faith. I couldn't.

None of the characters, however, are much more than devices. The slave ship captain is a second-rate Wolf Larsen and the crew only a little less villainous. The Africans are depicted as rather pathetic and dumb creatures, so much so in fact that it is difficult to have sympathy for them. Maybe slave ship crews were villainous and African slaves pathetic, but their portrayal as such here simply isn't convincing.

What saves [this] book from being a failure is the quality of [Paula Fox's] writing, which is consistently excellent. With such good writing, it is too bad that the book as a whole does not succeed. This novel describes the horrors of the Middle Passage, but it does not re-create them, and if history is to become a reality, the reader must live that history as if it were his own life. In "The Slave Dancer" we are only spectators and we should have been fellow sufferers—as slave traders and slaves.

Julius Lester, in The New York Times Book Review *(© 1974 by The New York Times Company; reprinted by permission), January 20, 1974, p. 8.*

[*The Slave Dancer*] revolves essentially around the familiar theme of a white adolescent boy's initiation into manhood. The location of young Jessie's ritual is the slave ship *The Moonlight*. The evil white officers and crew are the masters of the ritual. The baptism occurs when Jessie emerges from the shipwrecked vessel as "the man," mastering the crisis and automatically assuming the leadership role in his relation with the one surviving Black. . . .

What is new in this particular sea adventure is the introduction of the Black Experience. The trade in African slaves becomes the backdrop for a white child's ritual. . . .

The Black people are *only* pathetic sufferers. No "fight back" qualities whatever are found in these characterless, chained objects on the ship *The Moonlight*. For them the author presents no balance. . . .

Jessie's experience with oppression on the slaver simply inactivates him. He shows that he is aware of oppression but makes no meaningful protest; he takes no stand against it. He is no model for today's young readers. At the end of the ritual of baptism, Jessie cannot play his fife, thus easing the uncomfortable memories. . . .

White readers who empathize with the misery of the Black Experience can feel virtuous. To feel virtuous is to feel superior. To put it into the terms of an R. D. Laing "Knot" or paradox: "I feel bad that this is happening to them. I feel good that I feel bad." But by thus feeling compassion, whites are relieved of the need to change society. Like Jessie, they end up feeling no real obligation to take a positive role. They merely take the passive role of not playing the fife—of not reacting to injustice in any meaningful way.

Albert V. Schwartz, in Interracial Books for Children *(reprinted by permission of* The Bulletin-Interracial Books for Children, *1841 Broadway, New York, N.Y.), Vol. 5, No. 5, 1974, pp. 5-8.*

[No] matter what the author's intent, [*The Slave Dancer*] presents grave problems for those of us concerned with eliminating children's materials which help perpetuate racism. . . .

As the story develops the author attempts to portray the slave ship's captain and crew as villains, but through the characters' words, she excuses the captors and places the blame for the slaves' captivity on Africans themselves. The author slowly and systematically excuses almost all the whites in the story for their participation in the slave venture and by innuendo places the blame elsewhere. . . .

In scenes aboard ship, the crew are generally portrayed as vile, coarse and vicious but the author even manages to cancel these qualities in most of the crew. . . .

The slaves in the story are completely dehumanized. They are often spoken of as "creatures." Many of the statements and incidents regarding them are prejudicial and totally unnecessary to the development of the story. . . .

Aside from the constantly repeated racist implications and negative illusions, there is a question of *The Slave Dancer's* historical accuracy. There is, for instance, some question about the slaves being "Ashantis captured in tribal wars with the Yoruba." I can find no evidence of these being warring peoples.

Certainly there is not enough evidence that African chiefs were a *primary* force in the slave trade to allow for the consistent projection of this theme.

One may also argue the credibility of the relationship that is portrayed between Jessie and the slave boy Ras. There was no basis for the trust which exists between them in the final passages of the story.

The author has assumed the task of dealing in this story

with a serious and critical issue in U.S. history. Slavery touches at the very "gut" of the Black Experience in America, and young children deserve a *fair* and *accurate* picture of it, even in a work of fiction. Instead, as presented, this story has clearly racist leanings.

Binnie Tate, in Interracial Books for Children *(reprinted by permission of* The Bulletin-Interracial Books for Children, *1841 Broadway, New York, N.Y.), Vol. 5, No. 5, 1974, p. 4.*

History does not cross frontiers as often as other fiction—for evident reasons. Nevertheless, one of the peak historical books of the year is American: *The Slave Dancer*, by Paula Fox. . . . Other books from this gifted writer . . . are brilliant, concise presentings of current situations. This is a document of another sort: with no acrobatics, but a compiling of point on insistent point.

Naomi Lewis, in The Listener *(© British Broadcasting Corporation 1974), November 7, 1974, p. 614.*

In a concise and carved style, Paula Fox once again gets into a child and looks out on a harsh and dangerous world [in *The Slave Dancer*]. For the nightmare of the voyage is shown in the very moments of realisation, growing fear and panic and disgust gripping the reader too at deep levels of consciousness. The ship is an evil place, and cruelty and degradation and fever and greed are its crew. The boy's groping understanding and the power of suggesting by few words both generate involvement to an unusual degree, involvement which like life itself has to be worked at and worked through. Jessie's horror of the fetid hold, the hatreds among the crew, the hypocrisy of the Mate and the crazed bravado of the Captain, and the terribly just fate of the ship build on one another to a crescendo that *must* be resolved. Like Jessie's the final escape cannot expunge the memory. This story . . . extends the belief that [Paula Fox] is one of the most exciting writers practising for children and young people today.

C. S. Hannabuss, in Children's Book Review *(© 1975 Five Owls Press Ltd.), Winter, 1974-75, p. 155.*

OTHER CITATIONS

Publishers' Weekly, *December 10, 1973, p. 36.*

Sister Avila, in Library Journal, *December 15, 1973, p. 3711.*

Zena Sutherland, in Bulletin of the Center for Children's Books, *January, 1974, pp. 77-8.*

THE STONE-FACED BOY (1968)

[*The Stone-Faced Boy*], wise and sometimes quite wonderful, is a little story that exists almost entirely below the surface, like Gus who's armored himself so securely that he can't break out. . . . Although Gus and his family have a quick, sharp reality, symbolic imagery is the nexus and the nucleus and the resolution. Which limits the readership to a reflective few.

Kirkus Service *(copyright © 1968 The Kirkus Service, Inc.), October 1, 1968, p. 1114.*

Miss Fox's concern [in "The Stone-Faced Boy"] is with people living in the prison of the self, and how they break out—if they can. . . .

More important than what happens in a Paula Fox book are the insights she offers into a world where silence can ring like a bell or roar; where blue rooms can terrify a child. . . . Although Gus is still stone-faced in the end, someday, when he is ready, he will break his shell as surely as he will break the geode stone given him by Great-aunt Hattie.

D. M. Broderick, in The New York Times Book Review *(© 1968 by The New York Times Company; reprinted by permission), November 3, 1968 (Part 2), p. 34.*

More wistful than sad, this percipient book contains both a keen, almost acid analysis of a family constellation and a shining symbolism. The characters have a sharp fidelity: eccentric Aunt Hattie, animal-loving Sabina, who prevails on a frightened Gus to hunt a lost dog in the night, and boisterous Zachary, "a thumper and a drummer."

Zena Sutherland, in Saturday Review *(copyright © 1968 by Saturday Review, Inc.; reprinted with permission), November 9, 1968, p. 66.*

[In *The Stone-Faced Boy*, Paula Fox] gives a vivid and poignant picture of a small and rather frightened boy surrounded by family members who are boisterous, secure, or complacent. The plot is believable but of minor interest, serving principally to round out the characterizations and relationships.

Zena Sutherland, in Bulletin of the Center for Children's Books *(copyright 1969 by The University of Chicago; all rights reserved), February, 1969, p. 92.*

Paula Fox has always been able to side with lonely children; she can even, as in [*The Stone-Faced Boy*], see the threat of loneliness in the "normal" environment of a happy middle-class home. . . . Paula Fox, like some modern psychological Andersen telling Snow Queen stories —stories of frozen children warmed by hot tears of love and friendship—has again provided an outstanding book; she offers the drama of a fairy tale, grounded in today's realities.

Jean C. Thomson, in School Library Journal *(reprinted from the April, 1969, issue of* School Library Journal, *published by R. R. Bowker Co., a Xerox company; copyright © 1969 by Xerox Corporation), April, 1969, p. 113.*

OTHER CITATIONS

Paul Heins, in The Horn Book Magazine, *February, 1969, pp. 53-4.*

Polly Goodwin, in Book World, *June 22, 1969, p. 12.*

G

GEISEL, Theodor Seuss 1904-
(Dr. Seuss, Theo LeSieg)

An American author-illustrator, Geisel is best known as Dr. Seuss and has published more than thirty picture books of nonsense verse for children. He has created such well-loved characters as Horton, Yertle the Turtle, Thidwick, the Grinch, and the Cat in the Hat. (See also *Contemporary Authors*, Vols. 15-16 and *Something About the Author*, Vol. 1.)

GENERAL COMMENTARY

However much adults may yawn over Dr. Seuss and sigh over their children's delight, he does seem to know exactly what children just beginning to read find unbearably funny, how to turn zany almost-logic topsy-turvy, how to make his rhymes sing and how to do it all in simple words.

Pamela Marsh, in The Christian Science Monitor *(reprinted by permission from* The Christian Science Monitor*; © 1960, The Christian Science Publishing Society; all rights reserved), May 12, 1960, p. 4B.*

[Dr Seuss] knows exactly what he is doing. He aims to create nothing more than what meets the eye or ear. He is not *using* his books for any purpose beyond entertaining himself and his readers. . . . They are ingenious solutions, exploited with unique humour and slyness and absurdity, of the standing problem of the juvenile-fantasy writer: how to find, not another Alice, but another rabbit hole. . . .

Dr Seuss is a craftsman, not an allegorist, or a satirist in disguise. . . . In his own way he is as mad about language as Flaubert was. . . .

Whatever may be the good Doctor's secret, there is no doubt that he is the most successful writer in his field today, and a true professional. Whether his work will last, as *The Wind in the Willows* has lasted, is another matter. Possibly the absence of that very ambiguous element you find in Kenneth Grahame, that teasing sense of other meanings and under-meanings, destine it to a shorter life than children's classics saturated with the confessional element. At the moment Dr Seuss is single-handedly changing the reading habits of hundreds of thousands of American children. That's enough for any one man. Somebody ought to give him that Ph.D. he's always hankered after.

Clifton Fadiman, "Professionals and Confessionals: Dr Seuss and Kenneth Grahame" (1962), in Only Connect: Readings on Children's Literature, *edited by Sheila Egoff, G. T. Stubbs, and L. F. Ashley (© Oxford University Press [Canadian Branch], 1969), Oxford University Press, 1969, pp. 320, 322.*

In all the morass of children's books Dr. Seuss stands out like a particularly welcome friend. He could not have worked from my basic word list *(snacks? bellies? fannies?)* but then Dr. Seuss makes his own rules, and has managed somehow to cover every step of reading growth from beginning to almost-sophisticated with a rich deposit of nonsense. . . .

If there are faults to be found with Dr. Seuss . . . they are certainly very small ones. There is a certain appearance of haste which creeps into the later books. . . . The animals are beginning to look alike, for one thing, with less crazy invention. . . .

Shirley Jackson, in Book Week *(©* The Washington Post*), November 10, 1963 (Part 2), p. 3.*

[Dr. Seuss'] depicted tales add to the confusion in a young child's life at a time when he is so earnestly trying to understand the complexities of the real. . . . There is a place for Dr. Seuss books, but be sure you are entertaining the child and not just the adult whose lot it is to read a bedtime story. In other words, "first things first" until the child can distinguish between "the real and the unreal."

Ruth S. Freeman, in her Children's Picture Books: Yesterday and Today *(copyright 1967 by Ruth S. Freeman; reprinted by permission of Century House, Watkins Glen, N.Y.), Century House, 1967, p. 100.*

Over the years Dr. Seuss's style has settled into a formula, as has Disney's, but Seuss's world is essentially a more fantastic and irrational visual world than Disney's; in Seuss's there is a greater proportion of distortions and outright inventions. . . .

In itself, the doggerel Seuss relies on eventually becomes

monotonous, and to some extent it leans on fairly common jokes and slang. Without the drawings, Seuss's humor is much quieter and much more ordinary than it is with the drawings. The very special fantasy of Dr. Seuss lies primarily in his visual creation.

James Steel Smith, in his A Critical Approach to Children's Literature *(copyright © 1967 by McGraw-Hill, Inc.), McGraw-Hill, 1967, pp. 313-14.*

Usually the Seuss stories sum up a moral, always easy to take. . . . In *The Sneetches*, for instance, Seuss rings the bell for equality and against snobbery. . . . [In *Horton Hears a Who*] the tiny Whos symbolize the Japanese people, defeated in war and seeking their own form of democracy. Probably the message of Dr. Seuss to the world of both children and grownups may be summed up in one line from that book. The line goes: "A person is a person no matter how small."

Donald Freeman, "'Who Thunk You Up, Dr. Seuss?'" (1969), in Authors and Illustrators of Children's Books: Writings on Their Lives and Works, *edited by Miriam Hoffman and Eva Samuels (copyright © 1972 by Xerox Corp.), Bowker, 1972, pp. 166-67.*

[In Dr. Seuss'] pictures the fractured legs and gangling arms have made his mad characters so beloved by children that Dr. Seuss is synonymous with laughter. This is cartoon art, but when it accompanies rhymed stories of great originality, whose words run and leap with the rhythmic lines of the pictures, the combination is irresistible. There is also a strange, wild grace about some of the pictures, with their great heights and depths, bright clear blues and reds, decorative touches to costumes or scenes. These make the grotesque arresting and even attractive.

May Hill Arbuthnot and Zena Sutherland, in their Children and Books, *4th edition (copyright © 1947, 1957, 1964, 1972 by Scott, Foresman and Co.), Scott, Foresman, 1972, p. 64.*

Seuss has managed, almost single-handedly, to provide a safety valve for the overscheduled, overburdened and overstimulated child of modern civilization. In recognizing that children's craving for excitement, in their books as in their lives, is often merely the means for releasing pent-up anxiety, Seuss cannily manages to magnify and multiply the sense of suspense in his stories. . . .

Every detail in a Seuss illustration is calculated to add its bit to increasing the child's vicarious anxiety. Nervous projections and curlicues wriggle everywhere. No drawing detail seems to be at rest. . . . The greatest pleasure in Seuss is derived from the sense of having a season pass to utter chaos with no personal responsibility for any of it . . . Seuss has a perfect understanding of grownups' love of order and the rule of their laws—and of the enormous anxiety burden this places on small children everywhere. . . .

For all his exaggerated zaniness (and subversive alliance with the child's free spirit against all forms of authoritarianism), the ultimate [anti-authoritarian] moral Seuss presents is always sane and mature, one to which adults as well as children can subscribe. . . .

Though there is a sameness of rhyme, occasionally even of ideas, in Seuss . . ., his audience has not dwindled because the good Doctor's inventiveness of language and zany hyperbole never flags. There are few places where a child can get a better sense of the richness of language, the infinite possibilities it offers a lively imagination.

Selma G. Lanes, in her Down the Rabbit Hole: Adventures and Misadventures in the Realm of Children's Literature *(copyright © 1971 by Selma G. Lanes), Atheneum, 1972, pp. 79, 83, 86, 88.*

AND TO THINK THAT I SAW IT ON MULBERRY STREET (1937)

The great secret of Dr. Seuss is that he keeps [children] turning the pages. *And to Think That I Saw It on Mulberry Street* was actually his first book, published in the United States in 1937. Those marvellously corny rhymes which can prod the slowest reader into response are already there. But what makes this book such fun is the ability of Marco, the small boy in it, to tell tall stories. . . . It is precisely for his gift of exaggerating the unexpected that Seuss will be remembered with gratitude.

The Times Literary Supplement *(© Times Newspapers Ltd., 1971), October 22, 1971, p. 1329.*

THE CAT IN THE HAT (1957)

Using a limited vocabulary but without sacrificing any of the rhythm, rhyme, or imaginative nonsense characteristic of his work, Dr. Seuss has produced a diverting picture book story which can be read independently and thoroughly enjoyed by first and second graders. . . . [The Cat in the Hat] is a welcome departure from the "Look! See!" fare which is the customary lot of children in the early stages of learning to read.

The Booklist and Subscription Books Bulletin *(© 1967 by the American Library Association), May 1, 1957, p. 459.*

In this reader Theodor Geisel has accomplished a *tour de force*. With only 223 different words he has created a story in rhyme which presents an impelling incentive to read. Parents and teachers will bless Mr. Geisel for this amusing reader with its ridiculous and lively drawings, for their children are going to have the exciting experience of learning that they *can* read after all.

Helen Adams Masten, in Saturday Review *(copyright © 1957 by Saturday Review, Inc.; reprinted with permission), May 11, 1957, p. 54.*

[*The Cat in the Hat* is a] hilarious account of what happened the day it rained and the Cat in the Hat came visiting while Mother was away. . . . The text is so simply written that beginning readers could handle it with ease, and it has all the spontaneous humor of Seuss nonsense at its best. Not only will the book bring welcome relief to beginning readers who are wearying of the stilted prose of their regular texts, but it will also be of use with older students, even into high school, who are severely retarded readers.

Bulletin of the Center for Children's Books *(published by the University of Chicago), September, 1957, p. 19.*

OTHER CITATIONS

Helen E. Walker, in Library Journal, *May 15, 1957, p. 1356.*

Heloise P. Mailloux, in The Horn Book Magazine, *June, 1957, p. 215.*

***DID I EVER TELL YOU HOW LUCKY YOU ARE?* (1973)**

[*Did I Ever Tell You How Lucky You Are?* is disappointingly] flat Dr. Seuss. In the usual manner of nonsense verse combined with familiar Seuss figures, an old, wise man enumerates for a youngster many situations that are much worse than the boy's present condition. . . . [Some] are mildly amusing, but most are not. . . . Lacking the light-hearted fun expected from Dr. Seuss, the tale leans too heavily on imaginary words which fail to prove the boy is indeed fortunate. The text is beyond early readers and not solid enough for story hour. *Did I Ever . . .* will circulate to Seuss devotees; however, budget-minded libraries can pass by this one.

Carol Chatfield, in School Library Journal *(reprinted from the Decmeber, 1973, issue of* School Library Journal, *published by R. R. Bowker Co., a Xerox company; copyright © 1973 by Xerox Corporation), December, 1973, pp. 41-2.*

[This is more] sheer Seuss nonsense, with wildly fantastic pictures of imaginary places and occupations, and with a rhyming text that uses invented words and names that match the drawings in extravagance. . . . Nothing like the charm of the earliest Seuss books here, but for those who are addicted, the razzle-dazzle will probably be appealing.

Zena Sutherland, in Bulletin of the Center for Children's Books *(© 1974 by the University of Chicago; all rights reserved), May, 1974, pp. 149-50.*

OTHER CITATIONS

Kirkus Reviews, *October 1, 1973, p. 1092.*

Publishers' Weekly, *November 26, 1973, p. 39.*

***DR. SEUSS'S ABC* (1963)**

Whether Dr. Seuss has any purpose or not, or whether a child will learn ABC's by mouthing phrases like "googoo goggles, quacking quacker-oo, and Fiffer-feffer-feff" is perhaps beside the point. Children seem to enjoy Seussy sauciness and although his googoo goggles gobbledygook may not fulfill all the needs of education it certainly puts any fear of letters completely at the mercy of a chubby Zizzer-zazzer-zuzz.

Guernsey Le Pelley, in The Christian Science Monitor *(reprinted by permission from* The Christian Science Monitor; *© 1963, The Christian Science Publishing Society; all rights reserved), November 14, 1963, p. 2B.*

Although intended for the pre-school child, [*Dr. Seuss's ABC*] will probably be read surreptitiously by aging Seuss devotees who are usually above such things as alphabet books. All of the zany creatures and the nonsense humor are used to good advantage in creating pages that encourage memorization. . . .

Zena Sutherland, in Bulletin of the Center for Children's Books *(copyright 1964 by the University of Chicago; all rights reserved), March, 1964, p. 116.*

[*Dr. Seuss's ABC* is an] alphabet book done in the author-illustrator's familiar zany drawings and nonsensical verse—"Big N, little n, what begins with those? Nine new neckties and a nightshirt and a nose." This title in the "Beginner books" series provides an entertaining way for small children to learn the letters and their sounds.

The Booklist and Subscription Books Bulletin *(© 1964 by the American Library Association), March 15, 1964, p. 703.*

OTHER CITATIONS

Margaret Sherwood Libby, in Book Week, *November 10, 1963 (Part 2), p. 43.*

Suzanne M. Glazer, in Library Journal, *December 15, 1963, p. 4847.*

***DR. SEUSS'S SLEEP BOOK* (1962)**

The zany pictures and catchy verses [in *Dr. Seuss's Sleep Book*], the best that the author-illustrator has produced in some time, provide entertaining if not sleep-inducing bedtime fare for both child readers and parents reading aloud.

The Booklist and Subscription Books Bulletin *(© 1962 by the American Library Association), November 1, 1962, p. 224.*

[*Dr. Seuss's Sleep Book* is a] read-aloud picture book with the familiar extravagant Seuss creatures in the illustrations, and a text that has a single theme embellished to ridiculous lengths. Various improbable creatures are described and pictured in a mad variety of sleep patterns.

Zena Sutherland, in Bulletin of the Center for Children's Books *(copyright 1963 by the University of Chicago; all rights reserved), January, 1963, p. 87.*

OTHER CITATIONS

Margaret Warren Brown, in The Horn Book Magazine, *February, 1963, p. 52.*

***FOX IN SOCKS* (1965)**

"When tweetle beetles battle with paddles in a puddle, they call it a tweetle beetle puddle paddle battle." Try blurting that one out in a hurry—or any of the other tongue trippers [in "Fox in Socks"]. . . . Let the beginner read and recite with sly Fox (in socks) the simple words which always accumulate into audible pandemonium. It will be a rigorous and riotous workout.

George A. Woods, in The New York Times Book Review *(© 1965 by The New York Times Company; reprinted by permission), April 18, 1965, p. 16.*

[*Fox in Socks* is the] usual Seuss daffiness in nonsense words and zany illustrations. The text does not tell a story, but plays with similar sounds and dissimilar spellings; identified on the jacket as a tongue twister for super children, the book will indeed appeal to those children who enjoy word-play. The text increases in difficulty, moving from "Knox in box. Fox in socks. Knox on fox in sox in box." to "Through three cheese trees three free fleas flew" and ". . . they call this a muddle puddle tweetle poodle beetle noodle bottle paddle battle." Fun, but not a beginner book.

Zena Sutherland, in Bulletin of the Center for Children's Books *(copyright 1965 by the University of Chicago; all rights reserved), May, 1965, p. 136.*

GREEN EGGS AND HAM **(1960)**

[*Green Eggs and Ham* is another] beginning reader with Dr. Seuss' usual ingenuity in rhyme, telling [the story] in a limited vocabulary but unlimited exuberance of illustration. . . . Of course, the children will love it, either as a read-aloud or as a beginning reader.

Mary Malone, in Junior Libraries *(reprinted from the September, 1960, issue of* Junior Libraries, *published by R. R. Bowker Co., a Xerox company; copyright © 1960 by Xerox Corporation), September, 1960, p. 59.*

The slight story line in this new Dr. Seuss concoction consists of the efforts of one fantastic creature to tempt another into eating some green eggs and ham. Real Seuss fans may regard the book as the silliest of nonsense but it does serve a purpose. It provides the beginning reader with tempting, easy material which employs a vocabulary of only 50 words and much repetition.

The Booklist and Subscription Books Bulletin *(© 1960 by the American Library Association), November 15, 1960, p. 188.*

HOP ON POP **(1963)**

For beginning independent readers, [*Hop on Pop* is] the Seuss substitute for a first book. [It is as] fragmented as Dick, Jane, Spot, up, down, but much more fun. The book has the usual mad Seuss drawings and many nonsensical combinations of words that will be easily remembered either because of association with illustrations or because they are such nonsense.

Zena Sutherland, in Bulletin of the Center for Children's Books *(copyright 1963 by the University of Chicago; all rights reserved), April, 1963, p. 133.*

Special arrangements of the words [in *Hop on Pop*] make new sounds and letters easily recognizable. There is no story, but each new group of words is used to establish a continuity of thought. The usual distinctive Seuss characters parade through the pages. Highly recommended.

Hope H. McGrady, in School Library Journal *(reprinted from the May, 1963, issue of* School Library Journal, *published by R. R. Bowker Co., a Xerox company; copyright © 1963 by Xerox Corporation), May, 1963, p. 96.*

HORTON HEARS A WHO! **(1954)**

There's a small sensible social message along with the big nonsense [in *Horton Hears a Who!*] as Horton the elephant helps the "whos"—minute beings living in a rather perfect little society atop a dust particle. . . . Silly rhymes and limpid pictures—those products of a wonderful imagination—make the story tops in excitement, too. Wonders will never Seuss!

Virginia Kirkus' Bookshop Service, *September 1, 1954, p. 581.*

The lengths to which Horton goes to protect the dust speck from destruction by his jungle friends who cannot hear the Whos as Horton can, and the way in which the Whos finally prove their existence, make a hilarious and fantastic tale. Although verses and pictures fall short of those in [*Horton Hatches the Egg*], the humor and imagination are as delightful as ever.

The Booklist, *October 1, 1954, p. 68.*

Straws in the wind hereabouts and elsewhere seem quite definitely to indicate that if, when, or wherever boys of eight or eleven are given a chance to select titles that are to be accorded space on their own jollity shelf "Who" is likely to be chosen for inclusion and with a generous margin of votes.

Della McGregor, in Saturday Review *(copyright © 1954 by Saturday Review, Inc.; reprinted with permission), November 13, 1954, p. 67.*

OTHER CITATIONS

Anne Izard, in Library Journal, *December 15, 1954, p. 2493.*

Bulletin of the Center for Children's Books, *December, 1955, p. 54.*

HOW THE GRINCH STOLE CHRISTMAS **(1957)**

Another Seuss-chimera joins the ranks of the unforgettable *Horton* and *Thidwick* with the advent of the Grinch—a sort of Yule Ghoul who lives in a cave just north of Whoville. . . . Youngsters will be in transports over the goofy gaiety of Dr. Seuss's first book about a villain—easily the best Christmas-cad since Scrooge. Inimitable Seuss illustrations of the Grinch's dog Max disguised as a reindeer are in black and white with touches of red. Irrepressible and irresistible.

Virginia Kirkus' Service, *September 15, 1957, pp. 687-88.*

Dr. Seuss's [*How the Grinch Stole Christmas*] is not his best in either pictures or rhymes but it is fun and different from the too frequently sentimental Christmas story; while the book does not reveal the religious meaning of Christmas it does show that Christmas is more than presents, trimmings, and feasting.

The Booklist and Subscription Books Bulletin (*© 1957 by the American Library Association), November 15, 1957, p. 176.*

The inimitable Dr. Seuss has brought off a fresh triumph in [*How the Grinch Stole Christmas*]. . . . The verse is as lively and the pages are as bright and colorful as anyone could wish. Reading the book aloud will be a fascinating exercise for parents or for older brothers and sisters, who will pretend they are entertaining the children while secretly enjoying the humor and the moral for themselves.

Aileen O'Brien Murphy, in Saturday Review *(copyright © 1957 by Saturday Review, Inc.; reprinted with permission), November 16, 1957, p. 72.*

I WISH THAT I HAD DUCK FEET (1966)

[*I Wish That I Had Duck Feet* is a] book for beginning independent readers . . . illustrated with lively cartoon-style drawings; both text and drawings give the details of a child's dreams of impossible glory. . . . The situations are not unfunny intrinsically, but they are fairly laboriously developed. Not bad, but a somewhat forced episodic story.

Zena Sutherland, in Bulletin of the Center for Children's Books *(copyright 1966 by the University of Chicago; all rights reserved), February, 1966, pp. 101-02.*

IF I RAN THE CIRCUS (1956)

There is the same fresh imaginative quality of the author's first books in [*If I Ran the Circus*]. . . . Fantastic animals and people drawn in the familiar Seuss manner—this time in yellow, blues, and pinks—with tongue-twisting names and rhymes, make this a book adults and children of all ages will enjoy.

Norma Rathbun, in Saturday Review *(copyright © 1956 by Saturday Review, Inc.; reprinted with permission), November 17, 1956, p. 49.*

In one of his best efforts since *Mulberry Street*, Dr. Seuss presents the famous Circus McGurkis [in *If I Ran the Circus*]. . . . There are the expected number of strange creatures with nonsensical names, but the real humor lies in the situations, and especially those involving Mr. Sneelock.

Bulletin of the Center for Children's Books *(published by the University of Chicago), December, 1956, p. 55.*

OTHER CITATIONS

Virginia Kirkus' Service, *October 1, 1956, p. 750.*

The Booklist and Subscription Books Bulletin, *November 1, 1956, p. 125.*

IF I RAN THE ZOO (1950)

If I Ran the Zoo by Dr. Seuss . . . has a range and freedom of extravaganza that I found utterly delightful in the verses and pictures. . . . Here, as it seems to me, is Dr. Seuss at the peak of his art and his imaginative power. . . .

Anne Carroll Moore, in The Horn Book Magazine *(copyrighted, 1950, by The Horn Book, Inc., Boston), September, 1950, p. 354.*

The illustrations [for *If I Ran the Zoo*]—some full page—are in three colors. It is true that some children do not take to unrelieved nonsense, and this book has little coordinated story—so feel out your readers and buyers. However, this will not disappoint the devoted.

Virginia Kirkus' Bookshop Service, *September 15, 1950, p. 558.*

Dr. Seuss has never imagined or created a better or funnier picture book than [*If I Ran the Zoo*]. . . . In a series of really extraordinary drawings we are shown exactly what Gerald McGrew brought together from the four corners of the earth. Page after page of impossible, fantastic, and exceedingly amusing creatures. . . . This is the creative faculty and creative humor at its best.

Rochelle Girson, in Saturday Review *(copyright © 1950 by Saturday Review, Inc.; reprinted with permission), November 11, 1950, p. 37.*

OTHER CITATIONS

Jennie D. Lindquist and Siri M. Andrews, in The Horn Book Magazine, *November, 1950, p. 466.*

THE LORAX (1971)

[This is the] redoubtable Dr. Seuss at his best. The Lorax is a little brown creature who has acted, in vain, as the voice of sanity in a sad story of ecological blight and pollution. . . . The message is too blithe, in Seuss style, to be burdensome; the rhyming text is cohesive, and the nonsense words are appealing.

Zena Sutherland, in Bulletin of the Center for Children's Books *(© 1972 by the University of Chicago; all rights reserved), September, 1972, p. 16.*

It was fortunate that the Once-ler, a manufacturer of Thneeds ('It's a shirt. It's a sock. It's a glove. It's a hat.') should have picked a name for his product which rhymes with 'greed' and 'need'. It enables Dr. Seuss, with just so much less effort, to bring out an additional emphasis in his little tract [*The Lorax*], laboriously billed on the cover as 'finding the answer to presenting the problems of conservation and ecology to young children'.

In summarising thus the doctor's intention, the publisher shows himself a good deal less subtle than his author, who, when it comes to moralizing, has the advantage of unabashed doggerel and *Beano* art-work. Truly it may be one and the same thing to say that the demands of global industry are degrading natural life, and to show this occurring with a Super-Axe-Hacker ('which whacked off four Truffula Trees at one smacker'), but the latter is vastly more impressive, not just because it is facetious but also because it is free from the deadening clichés that even the most honourable Causes attract.

Furthermore, Dr. Seuss succeeds in delivering much of his message with more subtlety than his reputation suggests. Only on the last pages, when he spells out the meaning of the Lorax's cryptic 'UNLESS' does he lapse into a sermon and even then it is within the frame of the story, a last general statement from the Once-ler after he has retracted his Whisper-ma-phone. . . . [*The Lorax* is] comparatively modest propaganda.

Brian W. Alderson, in Children's Book Review *(© 1973 by Five Owls Press Ltd.), December, 1972, p. 179.*

MARVIN K. MOONEY WILL YOU PLEASE GO NOW (1972)

Though it's never clear why, there's a long-fingered hairy arm, with a watch on the wrist, that is desperately eager to get rid of Marvin K. Mooney. . . . The pages of persistence and Marvin's final capitulation are reminiscent of *Green Eggs and Ham* (1960) though this doesn't strike us as quite that Bright, and with phrases like "bureau drawer" it won't be read all that Early either.

Kirkus Reviews *(copyright © 1972 The Kirkus Service, Inc.), August 15, 1972, p. 938.*

ON BEYOND ZEBRA (1955)

Dr. Seuss's own alphabet, made to order for anyone who thinks stopping at Z is a waste of time, cuts out nineteen new letters from *yuzz* to *hi!* and some fascinating new identifications for them which may or may not strike familiar chords. . . . Squirly-que, pluperfect, misty and bewildered pictures accompany each of the new categories.

Virginia Kirkus' Service, *October 15, 1955, p. 784.*

Although there is an increasing sameness about [Dr. Seuss'] weird animals and zany verse, children will undoubtedly find them hilariously funny and will be intrigued and delighted with the nonsensical alphabet—both the letters and what they stand for—that begins after Z.

The Booklist, *November 15, 1955, p. 131.*

ONE FISH TWO FISH RED FISH BLUE FISH (1960)

This is not a story but a collection of daffy verses about the daffiest of subjects and situations, done in the inimitable Seuss manner, complete with hypnotic rhymes, jokes, a picture-menagerie of Seuss-type animals that never were on land or sea. The words are mainly the one-syllable ones familiar to early readers but there are also, as a come-on, some brand new ones, which like the animals they stand for, are the author's own invention. . . .

[The] great thing about the Seuss books is that they never *seem* educational, just high-voltage fun to read, to look at and to listen to. This one is simple enough in vocabulary to encourage the pre-schooler who may already be trying to pick out words for himself. That is, of course, if he can just stop laughing long enough to take advantage of the opportunity.

Ellen Lewis Buell, in The New York Times Book Review *(© 1960 by The New York Times Company; reprinted by permission), March 20, 1960, p. 42.*

[*One Fish Two Fish Red Fish Blue Fish* is an] easy-to-read but hard-to-fathom pastiche. Seven- and eight-year-olds may be pleased with the frantic humor of this book. But whether or not younger children will be enticed into reading by the picture of a huge hairy monster sparring with a tiny box and the rhyme "In yellow socks/ I box my gox/ I box in yellow/ Gox box sox" is any five-year-old's parents' guess.

Saturday Review *(copyright © 1960 by Saturday Review, Inc.; reprinted with permission), May 7, 1960, p. 38.*

YERTLE THE TURTLE AND OTHER STORIES (1958)

Three fables by the inimitable Dr. Seuss, which originally appeared in *Redbook* magazine, are now available, by popular demand, in this book-form collection. . . . A must for both remedial reading and reading aloud, the sweeping illustrations and the spontaneous verse of these three stories make them a welcome addition to that nonsensical, but wise, wise world of the always popular Dr. Seuss.

Virginia Kirkus' Service, *May 1, 1958, p. 335.*

The strong sense of justice in children of elementary school age will be happily satisfied in these three fables about a dictator turtle, an envious young lady bird, and two animal braggarts, who are all jolted from their folly. . . . Dr. Seuss' talent in using ordinary, simple words with vividness, humor, and unflagging rhythm, coupled with his ability to draw eloquently funny illustrations, make his stories easily readable for young children and equally enjoyable for many a well-read adult.

Elizabeth Doak, in The Horn Book Magazine *(copyright, 1958, by the Horn Book, Inc., Boston), August, 1958, p. 262.*

[The] three fables [in *Yertle the Turtle and Other Stories*] portray in doggerel verse and Seuss pictures the calamitous consequences that are sure to befall all those who outbrag their betters be they mortal, mammal, or amphibian . . .

This three-in-one chuckle bargain in hard covers is sure to delight Seuss fans, even though they will not regard it as the supercolossal accomplishment characteristic of many of Seuss's more recent extravaganzas.

Della McGregor, in Saturday Review *(copyright © 1958 by Saturday Review, Inc.; reprinted with permission), September 20, 1958, p. 41.*

OTHER CITATIONS

The Booklist and Subscription Books Bulletin, *June 15, 1958, p. 591.*

Laura E. Cathon, in Library Journal, *June 15, 1958, p. 1940.*

GEORGE, Jean Craighead 1919-

Jean Craighead George is an American author-illustrator well-known for her books about nature. Her *Julie of the Wolves* won the 1973 Newbery Medal. (See also *Contemporary Authors*, Vols. 5-8, rev. ed., and *Something About the Author*, Vol. 2.)

ALL UPON A STONE (1971)

A poetic text [in *All Upon a Stone*] tells the story of a mole cricket who crawls from the earth deep under the stone, spends a summer day exploring, and after a brief, festive encounter with a host of other mole crickets, returns to "the silence, the darkness, the black hugging soil." Illustrations [by Don Bolognese] and text [by Jean Craighead George] are wholly integrated in a book uniquely designed and composed.

Ethel L. Heins, in The Horn Book Magazine *(copyright © 1971 The Kirkus Service, Inc.), April, 1971, p. 163.*

Together with [Jean Craighead George's] poetic story which describes the journey of a mole cricket from deep under the stone to the top in search of others of its kind, [Don Bolognese's] pictures uniquely and beautifully reveal the microcosm of the stone. Though lacking immediate appeal and not to every child's taste perhaps, the lovely, atmospheric book, if introduced, will delight the curious and the perceptive.

The Booklist *(© by the American Library Association), May 1, 1971, pp. 747-48.*

All Upon a Stone is a subtle and different science picture book. . . . Text and artwork are a poignant blend of beauty and sensitivity, with a valuable message as well: We just don't know why certain creatures behave as they do. Nature keeps some of its mysteries.

Julian May, in Book World *(© The Washington Post), May 9, 1971 (Part 2), p. 3.*

[*All Upon A Stone*] demonstrates rather well the idea of a miniature community. Although the population is well enumerated, little is said about relationships. A bright child, who reads the book, will most likely ask a number of questions. The information given is adequate for second- to fourth-grade students. [Don Bolognese's] illustrations are very good. The book will be useful in a classroom library. It will however, have limited usage because it is not sturdily bound. As a story to tell to children and illustrate by drawings (overhead projector), it could have a teaching impact.

Science Books *(copyright 1971 by the American Association for the Advancement of Science), Vol. VII, No. 2 (September, 1971), p. 143.*

OTHER CITATIONS

Judith K. Miller, in Library Journal, *May 15, 1971, p. 1795.*

Zena Sutherland, in Bulletin of the Center for Children's Books, *July, 1971, p. 169.*

COYOTE IN MANHATTAN (1968)

Although Tenny Harkness, the young teenage Harlem Negro girl responsible for releasing a wild coyote in New York City, plays an essential role in this unusual animal story, focus is on the coyote. The way in which the animal uses its innate instincts to survive in the city, establishing a private preserve in Central Park, foraging for food, mating, and evading capture by the health authorities, is told in detail in a story of mounting suspense.

The Booklist and Subscription Books Bulletin *(© 1968 by the American Library Association), April 15, 1968, p. 994.*

As in her other books, [Jean Craighead George] does a fine job of describing the life of an animal with remarkable and detailed authenticity, evoking real personality without endowing the animal with any semi-human traits. . . . [*Coyote in Manhattan*] is weakened by the fact that the substructure of the story seems out of proportion; there are several subplots and they are not fully developed, so that they neither stand alone nor add to the story of the coyote.

Zena Sutherland, in Bulletin of the Center for Children's Books *(copyright 1968 by The University of Chicago; all rights reserved), May, 1968, p. 141.*

Less successful than Mrs. George's earlier *My Side of the Mountain*, [*Coyote in Manhattan*] falls down on human characterization but redeems itself in its absorbing picture of a wild animal's efforts to carve out a life in the city.

Robin Gottlieb, in Book World *(©* The Washington Post*), May 5, 1968 (Part 2), p. 35.*

There are too many neatly-tied threads and points of view in this otherwise powerful book about a disease-carrying coyote on the loose in Harlem. A Negro girl's insecurity, a health official's hunt, and a Fifth Avenue boy's prejudice detract from the central drama—the struggle of the animal (and the inhabitants) to adapt to the ghetto. . . .

Nature-oriented readers will get some remarkable insights into the instincts and behavior of a wild animal, and a vivid view of the city with its extremes of blatant ugliness and hidden natural riches. And there's an important underlying point—that the city can be wider and warmer for those who open their eyes to its possibilities.

Alice Low, in The New York Times Book Review *(© 1968 by The New York Times Company; reprinted by permission), May 5, 1968 (Part 2), p. 36.*

OTHER CITATIONS

Kirkus Service, *March 1, 1968, p. 271.*

GULL NUMBER 737 (1964)

The information contained in ["Gull Number 737"] is so fascinating that the story and style are secondary. Briefly, it is the account of Dr. Rivers and his 16-year-old son—the eternal clash between the generations, as well as the tension between pure and applied science. . . . The story might well lag if it were not for the gulls. . . . The human characters pale beside the birds and the details of their habits. . . .

Still, the resolution of the story is neatly handled. Luke comes to terms with his father . . . [and] begins to sense both the patience and the imaginative insight that go into the making of a good scientist.

Chad Walsh, in The New York Times Book Review *(© 1964 by The New York Times Company; reprinted by permission), November 1, 1964 (Part 2) p. 16.*

This singularly compelling story tells of Luke Rivers and his ornithologist father, who study the habits of herring gulls at the Block Island Sea Bird Laboratory. The information about the gulls is fascinating, presented clearly and naturally. Equally interesting is the study of the boy's impatience with his father's passion for pure research in a field that seems of little importance, until he discovers how quickly the results of pure research can solve practical problems. . . .

Most important of all is the scientific attitude that pervades this book, an insistence on infinite patience and flexibility of approach.

Margaret Sherwood Libby, in Book Week (© The Washington Post), *January 24, 1965, p. 15.*

[*Gull Number 737* is a] fine novel, unusual in background and beautifully written; the scientific details and the island background are vivid; the characterization is perceptive. . . . There are in the book some fascinating scenes in which the herring gulls are described, and family relationships are sympathetically drawn—that between Luke and his father being almost a case-history struggle between father and son.

Zena Sutherland, in Bulletin of the Center for Children's Books *(copyright 1965 by the University of Chicago; all rights reserved), April, 1965, p. 117.*

OTHER CITATIONS

The Booklist and Subscription Books Bulletin, *November 15, 1964, p. 312.*

HOLD ZERO! (1966)

[In *Hold Zero!* four] high school boys secretly and happily pursue their interest in science and mechanics until it becomes known that they have built and plan to launch a three-stage rocket. . . . The problems and frustrations of the scientifically talented boys are sympathetically depicted in a story which offers some shrewd commentary on adult and youth relationships in the modern world.

The Booklist and Subscription Books Bulletin *(© 1966 by the American Library Association), November 1, 1966, pp. 323-24.*

[*Hold Zero!* is a] good story about four adolescent boys who have built a rocket of some proportions. . . . The scientific material is excellent, the many ingenious contrivances of the boys both impressive and believable, and the characterization good. The story is slowed considerably by the recurrent details about the natural setting, but the tempo of the tale picks up at the close for an exciting blast-off episode.

Zena Sutherland, in Bulletin of the Center for Children's Books *(copyright 1966 by the University of Chicago; all rights reserved), December, 1966, p. 58.*

JULIE OF THE WOLVES (1972)

Running away from an arranged marriage with simple-minded [Daniel], thirteen year-old Julie (she prefers Miyax, her Eskimo name) survives on the barren tundra by making friends with a family of wolves. Her patient, intelligent courting of the animals—observing their signs of leadership, submission, etc. and aping the appropriate ones—and her resourcefulness in keeping herself alive . . . are meticulously observed. . . . Though remarkable, Miyax and her experience are totally believable, her spirit living evidence of the magnitude of the loss.

Kirkus Reviews *(copyright © 1972 The Kirkus Service, Inc.), November 15, 1972, pp. 1312-13.*

[*Julie of the Wolves* is a] compelling story about 13-year-old Julie Edward Miyax Kapugen, an Eskimo girl caught between the old ways and those of the whites, between childhood and womanhood. . . . George has captured the subtle nuances of Eskimo life, animal habits, the pain of growing up, and combines these elements into a thrilling adventure which is, at the same time, a poignant love story.

Alice Miller Bregman, in School Library Journal *(reprinted from the January, 1973, issue of* School Library Journal, *published by R. R. Bowker Co., a Xerox company; copyright © 1973 by Xerox Corporation), January, 1973, p. 75.*

[This] novel is packed with expert wolf lore, its narrative beautifully conveying the sweeping vastness of tundra as well as many other aspects of the Arctic, ancient and modern, animal and human. At her best [Jean Craighead George] makes readers aware of new sights, sounds, tastes and odors. . . .

Mrs. George assumes readers will instantly accept the idea of Julie exchanging thoughts, bites, kisses, even breast feeding with an Arctic wolf. This is the kind of behavioral study a trained naturalist might explore for a doctorate in biology or a TV special. However, the Eskimos I know don't think that way. They would want plenty of white man's firewater before trying to kiss wolves. Still as Mrs. George portrays the wolf pack in almost-human terms the reader slowly comes to think of these wolves as dear friends.

James Houston, in The New York Times Book Review *(© 1973 by The New York Times Company; reprinted by permission), January 21, 1973, p. 8.*

A book of timeless, perhaps even of classic dimensions, the story of the phenomenal adventures and survival of Julie (Miyax in Eskimo) suggests both the author's *My Side of the Mountain* . . . and Scott O'Dell's *Island of the Blue Dolphins* . . . . [Jean Craighead George's] superb narration includes authentic descriptions and details of the Eskimo way-of-life and of Eskimo rituals. . . . Through the eyes of

Julie . . . the author lovingly describes the wildlife. . . . She evokes in full measure the terrors of losing directions and facing storms in abysmal temperatures. [*Julie of the Wolves*] has a rare, intense reality which [John Schoenherr] enhances beautifully with animated drawings.

Virginia Haviland, in The Horn Book Magazine *(copyright © 1973 by The Horn Book, Inc., Boston), February, 1973, pp. 54-5.*

The message [in *Julie of the Wolves*] tolls the death of an entire culture. Beautiful literary collages silhouette the intricate mesh of animal-man-earth, an interdependence that draws the best from each contributing member. Nothing makes the telling strictly topical. . . .

The story touches all bases gracefully and richly—cultural, ecological, natural, emotional. But personal experience tells me that it will only be read by the omnivorous bookworm. . . . [Unless] all librarians and teachers plan to execute a most comprehensive "Introduction to Julie" program, it will die on the shelf as has many a magnificent medal winner before.

Mrs. John G. Gray, in Best Sellers *(copyright 1973, by the University of Scranton), April 15, 1973, p. 45.*

Julie of the Wolves by Jean George . . . is a powerful novel about a 13-year-old girl lost on the Alaskan tundra. . . . The day-to-day specifics of Julie's struggle . . . are projected with engrossing precision. *Julie of the Wolves* is one of those triumphs of the imagination that meet and transcend coexisting trends: the magnificent [wolf] Amaroq dwarfs any of the current conservationist pack of semifictionalized wolves, and Julie/Miyax is all the more impressive a model of female strength and resourcefulness for being primarily an embodiment of the human spirit.

Sada Fretz, in Book World *(©* The Washington Post*), May 13, 1973 (Part 2), p. 6.*

[This] is undoubtedly a remarkable book, but it is its subject-matter, rather than its art or style, which is its great strength. . . . *Julie of the Wolves* gives the impression that Mrs. George has spent years in the country; the result is richly imagined and extremely thought-provoking. There are plenty of questions and no easy answers. . . .

No one reading the book can ever again think of wolves as frightening, shadowy predators; Mrs. George shows them capable of brotherly love and her story, moving and strange as it is, is firmly rooted in fact.

Times Literary Supplement *(© Times Newspapers Ltd., 1973), November 23, 1973, p. 1429.*

Julie of the Wolves is a fascinating oddity. . . . [Julie's] strange relationship with Amaroq, the leader of the [wolf] pack, and Kapu, the young wolf who plays with her, is described with the sharp accuracy of one who has really studied wolves and the tundra. The wolf lore is plainly correct, and there is a compelling reality to this story that forces one to believe in it, however inconceivable it may seem. There is no *Jungle Book* whimsy here, no anthropomorphic fantasy, simply a plain account of an extraordinary relationship that one somehow comes to accept as probable, possible and true.

Charity Blackstock, in Books and Bookmen *(© Hansom Books 1974), January, 1974, p. 84.*

Alongside Mrs. George's story of one girl's survival in ferocious natural conditions, there is a second story which is, in essence, a celebration of those conditions and of the discipline which they impose on all who dare to face them on their own terms. For when Miyax is alone on the tundra it is not so much the wolves who save her as her own native wit, her inborn sense of how to use, not fight, the elements. As her father, Kapugen, had said: 'We live as no other people can, for we truly understand the earth'—but the coming of 'civilisation' to the North forced upon that understanding a profoundly unhealthy compromise and one which Mrs. George is honest enough to leave unresolved. At the end of her story we find Kapugen himself a victim and Miyax—despite the lesson she has learnt—reverting to Julie.

[*Julie of the Wolves*] will appeal to our sociological critics because it shows a girl—and a girl from a 'racial minority' at that—acting resourcefully in adverse circumstances, and because it sustains a powerful case not only for conservation but also for the preservation of man's natural skills. It will appeal to the less rigid among us because of its integrity and its wholly convincing portrayal of its setting. . . .

Given so much that is so well-observed and thought-provoking, it may sound churlish to enter reservations; nevertheless, in two respects Mrs. George's book seemed less than perfect. In the first place the reader has, from time to time, a sense of the presence of the author outside the circle of her imagination—not a storyteller, preoccupied with the events as they impinge upon her eskimoes, but an American lady writing for American children. In the second place one might question the form which Mrs. George has chosen for her story: seventy pages bringing Miyax and the wolves together, twenty-nine pages of flashback, and sixty-one pages devoted to Miyax's journey. The story is a strong enough one to stand up without a literary device of this kind (which in such a short book proves rather clumsy) and, indeed one could say that the story is a strong enough one to warrant an altogether longer telling. It is not just that the people and events that we meet with here are strange to us, but more that they are imbued with a life and force that demands a more expansive treatment. Our short-winded readers of today may defend the book for dramatic conciseness—but I am not sure that an orderly exposition of events, with the graphic detail that Mrs. George has at her command, would not have made the book a richer one and, in the end, a more dramatic one too.

Brian W. Alderson, in Children's Book Review *(© 1974 Five Owls Press Ltd.), Spring, 1974, p. 18.*

OTHER CITATIONS

Publishers' Weekly, *February 12, 1973, pp. 66, 68.*

Zena Sutherland, in Bulletin of the Center for Children's Books, *March, 1973, p. 105.*

***MY SIDE OF THE MOUNTAIN* (1959)**

An amazing and unusual book, [*My Side of the Mountain*] is a first-person report by an adolescent boy who has decided to try his luck living off the land. . . . Vivid descriptions of animal life, and mouth-watering recipes dictated by necessity make Sam's record more real. The thoughts and attitudes he quotes from his diary indicate his maturation and deepening self-perception in a wholly convincing manner. Absorbing reading.

Zena Sutherland, in Bulletin of the Center for Children's Books *(published by the University of Chicago), June, 1960, p. 161.*

Jean George's knowledge of natural history lends conviction to [this] unlikely story. Indeed it is the aids to survival which Sam derives from what our grandmothers used to call "simples" which make the yarn just barely possibly true. At any rate the book is so well written that one's mental reservations do not matter much.

The Junior Bookshelf, July, 1962, p. 131.

My Side of the Mountain (1959) by Jean George made possible an extraordinary vicarious experience. . . . From the diary record of his mountain-forest year Sam's personality emerges clearly—his intelligence, his pleasure in animals and birds, his perseverance, and even his growing enjoyment of people, though he had chosen to separate himself completely from them to carry out his experiment. The book brings a great deal to its readers—an unforgettable year in the heart of nature.

Ruth Hill Viguers, in A Critical History of Children's Literature, *revised edition, by Cornelia Meigs, Anne Thaxter Eaton, Elizabeth Nesbitt, and Ruth Hill Viguers, edited by Cornelia Meigs (copyright © 1969 by The Macmillan Co.), Macmillan, 1969, p. 490.*

The boy's unsentimental love of nature and freedom is the dominant theme of [*My Side of the Mountain*]. His growing maturity and self-perception are well depicted. The novel also deals with the rewards of perseverance and strong will. The accurate and fascinating details on wildlife add an informational dimension to the book's usefulness.

John Gillespie and Diana Lembo, in their Introducing Books: A Guide for the Middle Grades *(copyright © 1970 by Xerox Corp.), Bowker, 1970, p. 146.*

OTHER CITATIONS

Virginia Kirkus' Service, *May 1, 1959, p. 323.*

Robert Hood, in The New York Times Book Review, *September 13, 1959, p. 58.*

The Booklist and Subscription Books Bulletin, *September 15, 1959, p. 56.*

SNOW TRACKS (1958)

[In *Snow Tracks*, Jean Craighead George] has taken a few typical tracks and let them tell their own tales of what happened to the white-footed mouse, the weasel, the skunk, the fox, and the boy, all of whom ventured out on a day following a fresh fall of snow. The style, having the tracks seem to speak, may prove slightly confusing to young readers at first, but the exceedingly clear drawings and the unfolding of the forest drama will capture and hold the reader's interest.

Zena Sutherland, in Bulletin of the Center for Children's Books, *(published by the University of Chicago), May, 1958, p. 94.*

[*Snow Tracks* is a] study of animal tracks—nose holes, wing and stomach prints, as well as tail and foot prints—presented with great imagination as a detective story told by a series of snow writers. . . . Mrs. George's illustrations are superb—lively and authentic, with clear impression of the fresh loveliness of winter scene. Children will be captivated by them and by the easy-to-read text.

Virginia Haviland, in The Horn Book Magazine *(copyright, 1958, by the Horn Book, Inc., Boston), June, 1958, p. 202.*

OTHER CITATIONS

Lucile W. Raley, in Saturday Review, *May 10, 1958, p. 48.*

SPRING COMES TO THE OCEAN (1966)

[*Spring Comes to the Ocean*] stands out in both literary and scientific terms and makes an excellent companion to the junior edition of Rachel Carson's *The Sea Around Us*. The author has captured and conveyed a sense of the simultaneity of ocean life and the awesome variety of its creatures.

Virginia Kirkus' Service *(copyright © 1965 Virginia Kirkus' Service, Inc.), November 15, 1965, p. 1161.*

Key episodes in the lives of these [marine] creatures provides drama [in "Spring Comes to the Ocean"]. While the book aims at scientific accuracy as well as good prose, scientists will shudder at such sentences as "The hermit crab wanted to be among these odd animals, for although his new house was splendid and colorful it was dangerous." From everything we know today of the senses and sensibilities of hermit crabs they do not "want" anything or know that colorful shells are dangerous. . . . Many such passages mar an otherwise gracefully written book.

Millicent E. Selsam, in The New York Times Book Review *(© 1966 by The New York Times Company; reprinted by permission), February 13, 1966, p. 30.*

[*Spring Comes to the Ocean*] is a tremendously impressive book written with quiet authority, imbued with a sense of wonder and pleasure in the marvelous intricacies of marine creatures. [Jean Craighead George] writes with great simplicity and dignity, her prose only just verging on the lyric; this is fine writing and a fine contribution to literature in the biological sciences.

Zena Sutherland, in Bulletin of the Center for Children's Books *(copyright 1966 by the University of Chicago; all rights reserved), October, 1966, p. 24.*

OTHER CITATIONS

The Booklist and Subscription Books Bulletin, *February 15, 1966, p. 584.*

***THE SUMMER OF THE FALCON* (1962)**

There is much beauty in the writing, as well as validity in emotional development, and warmth in family relationships. But ["The Summer of the Falcon"] has some basic flaws. Both the ease of June's final parting with her beloved falcon and the sub-theme of acceptance of death are premature for adolescents. . . . There may also be a handicap for readers in the fact that girls tussling with June's physical and emotional problems dislike an overt statement of them, and most younger girls will not understand the conflicts.

Miriam James, in The New York Times Book Review *(© 1962 by The New York Times Company; reprinted by permission), November 18, 1962, p. 52.*

OTHER CITATIONS

Charlotte Jackson, in The Atlantic Monthly, *December, 1962, p. 178.*

Books for Children 1960-1965: As Selected and Reviewed by *The Booklist and Subscription Books Bulletin* September 1960 through August 1965, *American Library Association, 1966, p. 297.*

THE THIRTEEN MOONS: *The Moon of the Owls; The Moon of the Bears; The Moon of the Salamanders; The Moon of the Chickarees; The Moon of the Fox Pups; The Moon of the Monarch Butterflies; The Moon of the Mountain Lions; The Moon of the Wild Pigs; The Moon of the Alligators; The Moon of the Deer; The Moon of the Gray Wolves; The Moon of the Moles; The Moon of the Winter Bird*

The thirteen moons of the year and who mates on each one is the basis of this new series, and as each animal moves about there is a reference to what he sees. . . . The staccato prose is simply tedious and there is a lot of moonshine with very little light.

Kirkus Service *(copyright © 1967 Virginia Kirkus' Service, Inc.), October 15, 1967, p. 1277.*

[*The Moon of the Bears, The Moon of the Salamanders*, and *The Moon of the Owls*] trace the hibernation and mating times of three completely different animals. How the female bear digs her den, awaits her cubs, and then begins another summer is told with Mrs. George's usual sensitivity and understanding. In the salamander book, Mrs. George shows us a living fossil seldom seen by man. She shows how hundreds of these primitive amphibians choose one night in spring to visit a pond and mate. Then back to land for the rest of the year. The great horned owl is put into his natural setting with vivid descriptions of the animals which live in the woods with him.

Marian Sorenson, in The Christian Science Monitor *(reprinted by permission from* The Christian Science Monitor; *© 1967 The Christian Science Publishing Society; all rights reserved), November 2, 1967, p. B11.*

[Jean George's] keen observations of nature and her gifts for telling a moving story are greatly in evidence [in *The Moon of the Salamanders*], and [John Kaufmann's] illustrations are equally as lively. The first three books of the series [*The Moon of the Owls, The Moon of the Bears*, and *The Moon of the Salamanders*] have set a good standard which we hope the others to come will sustain.

Science Books *(copyright 1967 by the American Association for the Advancement of Science), Vol. 3, No. 3 (December, 1967), p. 238.*

There is an incorrect assumption [in *The Moon of the Owls*] that an owl would vaguely remember the "two white eggs that had lain here [in the nest] last February." Birds respond to changes in their hormonal balance and as a result mate and nest. They do not "remember" anything. Neither does an owl get "bored." Other animals in the forest enter the story a bit too strongly and divert attention from the doings of the owl. Young readers will nevertheless get a sense of the beauty of a January night in the mountains, and the illustrations by Jean Zallinger beautifully complement the text. . . .

The Moon of the Salamanders tells of a male blue-spotted salamander who moves towards a spring pond in a Michigan forest to engage in a mating dance that precedes the ritual of fertilization. Some attempt should have been made to explain why these salamanders move towards ponds on one night of the year, during the first spring rain of the March moon. Saying that "instinct" guides them explains nothing.

Millicent E. Selsam, in Book World *(©* The Washington Post*), January 7, 1968, p. 10.*

Jean George's nature books have always been popular with children. These three ["The Moon of the Owls," "The Moon of the Bears," and "The Moon of the Salamanders"], launching a new series—The Thirteen Moons—which looks at wildlife in the light of the yearly moon cycle, will be no exception. . . .

Mrs. George's writing often achieves a lyric quality, and she is careful of her facts. One might wonder how she learned that the mating dance of the salamanders has been unchanged for 300-million years—but this may be a minor point. And it could just be correct.

Henry B. Kane, in The New York Times Book Review *(© 1968 by The New York Times Company; reprinted by permission), March 3, 1968, p. 30.*

[*The Moon of the Chickarees* and *The Moon of the Fox Pups* are staged] nature studies recording animal habits, each building up to one of the *Thirteen Moons* of the year. Sometimes the sympathetic elaboration of simple behavior detracts from the essential beauty, sometimes it overdignifies specific movements; usually animals encountered along the way receive momentary, precise representation.

Kirkus Service *(copyright © 1968 The Kirkus Service, Inc.), April 15, 1968, p. 463.*

Written with the keen insight of a trained and patient natural history observer, [*The Moon of the Chickarees* and *The Moon of the Fox Pups*] can be read to very young children—for they all learn early to recognize and enjoy squirrels. Although not so commonplace, they learn about foxes through other stories and are delighted to learn more about them. Older children can read these stories by themselves and learn a little forest ecology.

Science Books *(copyright 1968 by the American Association for the Advancement of Science), Vol. 4, No. 1 (May, 1968), p. 47.*

Mrs. George writes of the animal world with knowledge and enthusiasm, her descriptions of wild life untainted by melodrama or anthropomorphism. In [the books of The Thirteen Moons,] each illustrated by a different artist, the text is continuous and the tone verges on lyrical. The weakness of [*The Moon of the Fox Pups*] is its diffuseness, the story of the litter of fox pups being lost occasionally while the author focuses on some other creature. . . . Slow-paced, and the combination of diffused writing and the lack of index or table of contents means that this book, like others in the series, has browsing interest chiefly for the nature lover.

Zena Sutherland, in Bulletin of the Center for Children's Books *(copyright 1968 by The University of Chicago; all rights reserved), July-August, 1968, p. 174.*

The months of April, May, and June are the subjects of [*The Moon of the Chickarees, The Moon of the Fox Pups*, and *The Moon of the Monarch Butterflies*], similar in mood, writing style, and format to the earlier volumes [in the Moon series]. . . . The many animals and plants indigenous to the surroundings described are brought into all three stories, making readers aware of the entire natural environment in books that are both informative and satisfying to read. The black-and-white illustrations complement the text beautifully and, sometimes, dramatically.

Linda Lawson Clark, in School Library Journal *(reprinted from the September, 1968, issue of* School Library Journal, *published by R. R. Bowker Co., a Xerox company; copyright © 1968 by Xerox Corporation), September, 1968, p. 190.*

WHO REALLY KILLED COCK ROBIN? (1971)

[*Who Really Killed Cock Robin?*] is a fascinating new kind of mystery, delving into the obscure causes of a robin's sudden death, and the disasters that later befell its mate and her eggs. . . . [Tony and Mary] come to many puzzling and complex evidences of a dangerous imbalance in the area before they trace the troubles to their source and find the villains. The search, which eventually involves everyone, makes an absorbing, highly informative story that points up dramatically how difficult—and how important—it is for all of us [to] try to "live in balance with all beasts and plants, and air and water."

Polly Goodwin, in Book World *(©* The Washington Post*), November 7, 1971 (Part 2), p. 14.*

This engrossing ecological mystery will be read by many children, among them those who might not tackle standard non-fiction accounts on the subject. . . . Characterization is only fair, but the integration of factual material into a suspenseful story is outstanding.

Mary I. Purucker, in School Library Journal *(reprinted from the December, 1971, issue of* School Library Journal, *published by R. R. Bowker Co., a Xerox company; copyright © 1971 by Xerox Corporation), December, 1971, p. 58.*

[This is a] modern ecological mystery about the blight that killed thousands of migrating sparrows and thrushes. Light in tone, deft in style, but with a serious underlying theme, the story relates a small town's growing awareness of ecological relationships. . . . A great deal of sound ecological information is presented, and the story is timely and entertaining. Above all, the message is clear: "The Earth is one ecosystem."

Beryl Robinson, in The Horn Book Magazine *(copyright © 1971 by The Horn Book, Inc., Boston), December, 1971, p. 611.*

Who Really Killed Cock Robin? . . . is a book by Jean Craighead George for young readers who prefer asking questions to being told answers. . . .

[The] observations about wildlife and man's ecological bloopers are dropped as "clues," making the story a superb example of investigative learning which few classroom teachers could hope to match.

The Christian Science Monitor *(reprinted by permission from* The Christian Science Monitor; *copyright © 1971 The Christian Science Publishing Society; all rights reserved), December 30, 1971, p. 6.*

Although the current interest in curtailing pollution creates a sure audience for the story [*Who Really Killed Cock Robin?*], the obsession of adults and children in Saddleboro with such problems is not quite convincing. As an ecological problem superbly supported by meticulous facts this is intriguing; as a story it lacks balance.

Zena Sutherland, in Bulletin of the Center for Children's Books *(© 1972 by the University of Chicago; all rights reserved), January, 1972, p. 74.*

OTHER CITATIONS

The Booklist, *December 15, 1971, p. 366.*

Science Books, *May, 1972, p. 49.*

* * *

GLUBOK, Shirley 1933-

A lecturer at the Metropolitan Museum of Art in New York, American Shirley Glubok is noted for her books on art history and archaeology. She received a 1963 Lewis Carroll Shelf Award for *The Art of Ancient Egypt*. (See also *Contemporary Authors*, Vols. 5-8, rev. ed., and *Something About the Author*, Vol. 6.)

GENERAL COMMENTARY

[Shirley Glubok's] books are impressive because of the combination of authoritative knowledge, simple presentation, dignified format, and a recurrent emphasis on the relationships between an art form and the culture in which it was created. . . .

In all of Shirley Glubok's books the page layout and the quality of the reproductions are good; the correlation between the text and the pictures has been careful, and locations in museums are given for all of the objects pictured. . . . [Her art] series is unique in its field. It does not give a comprehensive art history of a culture, but it is unexcelled as an introduction for the beginner.

May Hill Arbuthnot and Zena Sutherland, in their Children and Books, *4th edition (copyright © 1947, 1957, 1964, 1972 by Scott, Foresman and Co.), Scott, Foresman, 1972, pp. 598-99.*

ART AND ARCHAEOLOGY (1966)

[*Art and Archaeology*] is undoubtedly the best visual introduction to man's search for his past and some of the beauty that the search has recovered. As one expects in Miss Glubok's books, the photographs are superb. . . . Children using the book will be left with the sense of all that is left to be discovered, problems posed by the past yet to be solved. Handsomely designed and of refresher interest to adults.

Virginia Kirkus' Service *(copyright © 1966 Virginia Kirkus' Service, Inc.), May 1, 1966, p. 476.*

As with [Shirley Glubok's] books on the arts of Africa, Ancient Greece, Ancient Rome, the design [of "Art and Archaeology"] is attractive and the photographs often excellent. Unhappily, the text tends to be stilted and staccato, and the innate drama of archaeology, its works and its findings, too often lost.

Henry Gilfond, in The New York Times Book Review *(© 1966 by The New York Times Company; reprinted by permission), May 8, 1966 (Part 2), p. 34.*

What is archaeology? Who were some great archaeologists? Miss Glubok with her usual clear style attempts to answer these questions in 48 pages. Some 27 sites from Lascaux (France) to Ohio are sketchily introduced with pictures and names of discoverers. Much, perhaps too much, is telescoped into a short space. The pages are sometimes crowded. Several photographs are murky and imposed on color, obscuring clear definition.

Marjorie Stephenson, in School Library Journal *(reprinted from the September, 1966, issue of* School Library Journal, *published by R. R. Bowker Co., a Xerox company; copyright © 1966 by Xerox Corporation), September, 1966, p. 246.*

The emphasis in this attractive book is the art, rather than the archeology. However, the well-chosen illustrations and the summarized text do provide highlights of famous archeological finds in various parts of the world. . . . The reader is afforded an appreciation, not only of the splendor, richness, and relevance of the finds, but also gains some insights into the painstaking care with which an archeologist does his work.

Science Books *(copyright 1966 by the American Association for the Advancement of Science), Vol. 2, No. 3 (December, 1966), p. 198.*

OTHER CITATIONS

Alice Dalgliesh, in Saturday Review, *May 14, 1966, p. 42.*

The Booklist and Subscription Books Bulletin, *July 15, 1966, p. 1086.*

Zena Sutherland, in Bulletin of the Center for Children's Books, *September, 1966, p. 10.*

THE ART OF AMERICA FROM JACKSON TO LINCOLN (1973)

[In *The Art of America from Jackson to Lincoln*], Glubok concentrates on formal rather than folk or popular art, and as always she chooses the most elegant, graceful examples of each style (there is only a hint here of some of the absurdities of the Greek and Gothic revivals). Perceptive students—who may wonder, for example, how Hiram Powers' Greek Slave relates to the earlier neo-classical movement, or want a more critical appraisal of paintings Glubok uses primarily for their social commentary—will have to look elsewhere. Still, a tasteful, judiciously selective sampler—further evidence of Glubok's remarkable consistency.

Kirkus Reviews *(copyright © 1973 The Kirkus Service, Inc.), November 1, 1973, p. 1206.*

The examples of art selected from the time when the American artist began to come into his own—even if he had to go abroad to do it—are excellent. Unfortunately, the quality of reproduction (exclusively black-and-white photographs) is fair to poor, and the narrative is lacklustre.

Sidney D. Long, in The Horn Book Magazine *(copyright © 1974 by The Horn Book, Inc., Boston), April, 1974, p. 166.*

The text [of *The Art of America from Jackson to Lincoln*] is written in a direct, unassuming style. . . . While this is not comprehensive, it is an excellent overview of the art of almost a half-century of life in America, and it should be of interest both to the art student and the history student.

Zena Sutherland, in Bulletin of the Center for Children's Books *(© 1974 by the University of Chicago; all rights reserved), April, 1974, p. 129.*

OTHER CITATIONS

Beverly B. Miller, in Library Journal, *January 15, 1974, p. 209.*

THE ART OF AMERICA IN THE GILDED AGE (1974)

[In *The Art of America in the Gilded Age*] the line between art and background becomes blurred and the nature of an object's importance (aesthetic, historical, or as commentary on some other item) uncertain. Glubok shows us so many different kinds and levels of achievements that none [stands] out, and so many unrelated names are paraded by with little or no commentary that it is difficult to remember any. . . . [One] wishes that the author had either limited her definition of art or her view of her series or better integrated the examples with her theme (if such it can be called) of the age's opulence and energy.

Kirkus Reviews *(copyright © 1974 The Kirkus Service, Inc.). April 1, 1974, pp. 365-66.*

[American art from 1865 to 1900] is the era Shirley Glubok documents in the latest of her "Art of . . ." series, employing her usual mixture of strong black-and-white and sepia illustrations, accompanied by brief explanatory notes. It is a formula that has served her well in many of her previous books, particularly when—as in "The Art of Ancient Egypt," "The Art of Africa," for instance—the art involved was largely sculptural. But in this volume, where so many of the works discussed are paintings, the lack of color plates is a real drawback. And this time the notes seem all too brief—two or three sentences about an artist and then on to the next subject, with no transitions, no connecting material. Certainly, Miss Glubok has covered a wide variety of artistic achievements in 48 pages, but even as an introduction to the period it seems unsatisfying, superficial. Perhaps the problem is that this time the subject matter demands a fuller treatment than the series format allows.

Margaret Berkvist, in The New York Times Book Review *(© 1974 by The New York Times Company; reprinted by permission), June 2, 1974, p. 8.*

Continuing [Shirley Glubok's] series of books on American art, [*The Art of America in the Gilded Age*] reflects the growing wealth and diversity of life in the years between the Civil War and the twentieth century. . . . The text describes the objects pictured and relates them to the life of the "Gilded Age." Not comprehensive, but an excellent overview, this latest volume is—like the others—a fine piece of bookmaking.

Zena Sutherland, in Bulletin of the Center for Children's Books *(© 1974 by the University of Chicago; all rights reserved), September, 1974, p. 8.*

OTHER CITATIONS

Publishers' Weekly, *May 6, 1974, p. 69.*

THE ART OF ANCIENT MEXICO (1968)

[*The Art of Ancient Mexico* is] a highly attractive display of representative—or awesome or curious—Mexican artifacts, excluding only the Mayan. . . . This approach gives primacy to experiencing art over studying art, which is not inappropriate for the age level, but it also has a built-in limitation: the author tells only what *she* thinks the child wants to know or should know. . . . On the other hand, the objects are handsome to look at and interesting for their associations, and the inclusion of an ancient ball game is a natural for boys. In sum, no synthesis, but strong, direct exemplification.

Kirkus Service *(copyright © 1968 The Kirkus Service, Inc.), May 1, 1968, p. 514.*

[In *The Art of Ancient Mexico*, Shirley Glubok] briefly describes a selection of artifacts well chosen to introduce children to the art and culture of the Aztec, Toltec, Olmec, and other civilizations of ancient Mexico. Photographs of the objects—ornaments, temples, jewelry, statues, and funerary urns—are clearly reproduced and invitingly displayed.

The Booklist and Subscription Books Bulletin *(© 1968 by the American Library Association), May 15, 1968, p. 1094.*

In the familiar format of this well-known, widely recommended series, religious and secular art in stone, clay, and metal introduce the Aztec and pre-Aztec world. . . . The book's pictorial value suggests use as enrichment or introduction despite the blandness and thinness of the text; it might be used to complement Beck's *First Book of the Aztecs*, which surveys their social and political scene.

Priscilla Moxom, in School Library Journal *(reprinted from the September, 1968, issue of* School Library Journal, *published by R. R. Bowker Co., a Xerox company; copyright © 1968 by Xerox Corporation), September, 1968, p. 190.*

OTHER CITATIONS

Zena Sutherland, in Saturday Review, *August 24, 1968, p. 43.*

THE ART OF ANCIENT PERU (1966)

The art objects . . . presented [in *The Art of Ancient Peru*] have been chosen with discernment and the descriptions of them are brief and simply expressed; together [Alfred H. Tamarin's] excellent photographs of Peruvian works of art and [Shirley Glubok's] informative text not only provide a stimulus to art appreciation but also give some insight into ancient civilizations.

The Booklist and Subscription Books Bulletin *(© 1966 by the American Library Association), December 1, 1966, p. 416.*

[*The Art of Ancient Peru*] is chiefly pictorial in interest. . . . There is a lack of imagination in the presentation of material, however. This book is simply another in what has become a somewhat stereotyped series. The younger readers, to whom the text in large print seems directed, are not made sufficiently aware of the differences in the various cultures that have been presented in the different books to be stimulated to read still another similar book. Yet, older readers need more written factual material and would bypass this large, profusely illustrated format.

Vera L. Coutard, in School Library Journal *(reprinted from the December, 1966, issue of* School Library Journal, *published by R. R. Bowker Co., a Xerox company; copyright © 1966 by Xerox Corporation), December, 1966, p. 53.*

[This] is a handsome, informative volume. [Shirley Glubok's] writing is simple and lucid, with professional authoritativeness but without technical terminology. The illustrations of art objects are stunning. . . . The text concentrates on the objects pictured, but in describing their uses or the ways in which they were made, also gives facts about their cultural matrix.

Zena Sutherland, in Bulletin of the Center for Children's Books *(copyright 1967 by the University of Chicago; all rights reserved), January, 1967, p. 73.*

***THE ART OF CHINA* (1973)**

Glubok manages to condense the 4000-year story of Chinese art into her familiar series format, with just enough judiciously integrated background information to make the examples meaningful and impressive. . . . [These examples are] surveyed in one coherent sweep, with emphasis on the subject matter of the work and the cultural context, passing but unobtrusive mention of dates and dynasties, minimal consideration of form and technique.

Kirkus Reviews *(copyright © 1973 The Kirkus Service, Inc.), April 15, 1973, pp. 459-60.*

Although no more unified than those of [Shirley Glubok's] previous books, the text—by meandering in and out of Chinese history, customs, culture, and religion—helps the reader develop an awareness of the variety and excellence of Chinese art. Touching briefly on the various forms of art . . . the book also explains some of the ancient Chinese inventions—porcelain, silk, and lacquer—which made various new art forms possible. The soft, colored backgrounds highlight the numerous scroll paintings, and interesting and aesthetic objects have been chosen as examples. [*The Art of China*] gives a glimpse of why Chinese art forms have flourished for over 4,000 years.

Anita Silvey, in The Horn Book Magazine *(copyright © 1973 by The Horn Book, Inc., Boston), August, 1973, p. 390.*

[*The Art of China*] does not attempt to be inclusive but serves nicely as an introduction to art forms. The material is more or less in chronological arrangement but stresses form and relates objects to their contemporary cultures. Designed with discrimination, the book is—like its predecessors—both handsome and informative, and it should lead readers to further examination of Chinese art.

Zena Sutherland, in Bulletin of the Center for Children's Books *(© 1973 by the University of Chicago; all rights reserved), September, 1973, p. 8.*

OTHER CITATIONS

The Booklist, *July 1, 1973, p. 1021.*

Anne Weaver Kemper, in Childhood Education, *January, 1974, p. 168.*

***THE ART OF INDIA* (1969)**

Shirley Glubok does not mention some of the minor Indian crafts, so [*The Art of India*] has less variety than various others in the series; the designer [Gerard Nook] has compensated for that by his use of color in the pages, and by the dignity of the format. The text is simply written, of necessity emphasizing religion rather than history in explaining the motifs of Indian art.

Zena Sutherland, in Saturday Review *(copyright © 1969 by Saturday Review, Inc.; reprinted with permission), November 8, 1969, p. 68.*

[*The Art of India*] is handsome in design, clearly written, and extremely useful, since there is comparatively little material available on Indian art for the elementary level. The illustrations are preponderantly sculpture and the lack of color is no limitation, but the miniatures lose effectiveness in black and white. There is no discussion of the Mogul period, although some miniatures are pictured, or of the ceramics or textiles in which it excelled.

Zena Sutherland, in Bulletin of the Center for Children's Books *(© 1969 by the University of Chicago; all rights reserved), December, 1969, p. 59.*

Stressing the contributions of Buddhism, Hinduism, and Jainism to the art of India, [this] book offers at least one illustration to a page, and confines brief but complete discussions of architecture, sculpture, or painting within the scope of two facing pages. The style and the explanations are effectively simple; but place-names and the names of divinities and of human personalities are never scanted. The photographs of architecture and sculpture—stône and bronze—have been especially chosen for their sharp interplay of light and shade; along with the reproduced paintings, they give the reader and viewer a sense of the linear power and rich detail of Indian art.

Paul Heins, in The Horn Book Magazine *(copyright © 1970 by The Horn Book, Inc., Boston), February, 1970, p. 52.*

OTHER CITATIONS

Margaret A. Dorsey, in Library Journal, *December 15, 1969, pp. 4604, 4606.*

***THE ART OF JAPAN* (1970)**

Of all Miss Glubok's books in the series [*The Art of Japan*] leaves the most to be desired—literally in that the distinctive qualities of Japanese art are not identified (or, in some cases, even represented); there is no apparent ordering principle (other than a vague chronology), little continuity or progression. The effect is of an assortment of works—painting, sculpture, architecture—attended to primarily for their subject-matter. . . . Some of the photographs, especially of architectural subjects, are muzzy: crisper, better composed views appear elsewhere. A sampler until superseded.

Kirkus Reviews *(copyright © 1970 The Kirkus Service, Inc.), April 1, 1970, pp. 386-87.*

Miss Glubok here performs with Japanese art her usual feat of explaining complex facts and ideas in concise, simple language. . . . Unfortunately, readers will find many of the illustrations in this book less helpful than those in some of the author's previous works. . . . Nevertheless, the text generally lives up to the standards set by Miss Glubok's other books and is a useful addition to the series.

Margaret A. Dorsey, in School Library

Journal *(reprinted from the September, 1970, issue of* School Library Journal, *published by R. R. Bowker Co., a Xerox company; copyright © 1970 by Xerox Corporation), September, 1970, p. 160.*

[Shirley Glubok's] writing [in *The Art of Japan*] is very simple, almost abrupt in places, giving both some historical background for, and some description of, the art object pictured. Much of the subject matter is religious or expresses appreciation of nature. . . . Perhaps the most impressive aspect of the book is in the reflection of the consistency of stylized elegance and economy in painting as opposed to the ornamentation in architecture and sculpture.

Zena Sutherland, in Bulletin of the Center for Children's Books *(© 1970 by the University of Chicago; all rights reserved), December, 1970, p. 58.*

OTHER CITATIONS

The Booklist, *September 1, 1970, p. 57.*

***THE ART OF LANDS IN THE BIBLE* (1963)**

Those who are bewildered by too much glory collected together in one museum will rejoice in the carefully chosen, cunningly displayed objects in [*The Art of Lands in the Bible*]. . . . Friezes and sculpture, vases and pottery are displayed on backgrounds of soft color so skillfully that the hand can imagine the feeling of smooth contours and satisfying balance. And the book has an added advantage. Not only does it help banish the dusty glass-case image of a museum but it gives young readers another glimpse of how life was at the time of Moses, David, Daniel—men who should feel like their friends.

Pamela Marsh, in The Christian Science Monitor *(reprinted by permission from* The Christian Science Monitor; *© 1963, The Christian Science Publishing Society; all rights reserved), April 4, 1963, p. C17.*

[This] is an introduction to the sculptures, great and small, of the ancient Near and Middle East, chiefly of Assyria, Babylonia and Persia. Miss Glubok and the designer, Gerard Nook, have not solved all the problems of scale—a tiny bronze stag loses something of its essential quality in enlargement and a drinking cup on one page dwarfs a heroic bas relief on the opposite page. Nevertheless, we have here a direct and pictorially impressive approach, and the author has cleverly related familiar Biblical stories to some of the art objects, thus bringing a sense of those remote civilizations closer to the reader.

Ellen Lewis Buell, in The New York Times Book Review *(© 1963 by The New York Times Company; reprinted by permission), April 14, 1963, p. 56.*

[*The Art of Lands in the Bible* presents a] collection of photographs of objects made in Biblical lands by peoples other than the Hebrews. The text is simple but informative; the format of the book is handsome and dignified. The book does not have the unity of *The Art of Ancient Egypt*, since it describes art objects from diverse cultures; in illustration it has less variety. The text occasionally—and a bit obtrusively—ties the illustrations to Biblical scenes or events in a rather desultory fashion.

Zena Sutherland, in Bulletin of the Center for Children's Books *(copyright 1963 by the University of Chicago; all rights reserved), June, 1963, p. 160.*

OTHER CITATIONS

Virginia Haviland, in The Horn Book Magazine, *April, 1963, p. 188.*

Alice Dalgliesh, in Saturday Review, *May 11, 1963, p. 50.*

***THE ART OF THE ETRUSCANS* (1967)**

[*The Art of the Etruscans* is] the closest this series has come to a random assortment of artifacts. . . . Descriptions of painting frescoes, casting solid bronze figures, and firing pottery supply a little solid information, but most of the text is informal commentary on the plates—a little iconography here, a little interpretation there. This approach works all right when kids are clustered around the object; here, without any preparation and with an art as offbeat as the Etruscan, it may seem like a lot of loose talk about a lot of queer characters.

Kirkus Service *(copyright © 1967 Virginia Kirkus' Service, Inc.), August 15, 1967, p. 962.*

[Shirley Glubok] respects her readers by not writing down to them as she identifies fact, myth, and legend [in *The Art of the Etruscans*]. Adult readers will be intrigued by new parcels of information about the enigmatic Etruscans. Of superior quality are the graphic designs by Gerard Nook including aesthetic placement of color and text with the clearly defined photographs by Alfred Tamarin.

Verle Mickish, in School Library Journal *(reprinted from the October, 1967, issue of* School Library Journal, *published by R. R. Bowker Co., a Xerox company; copyright © 1967 by Xerox Corporation), October, 1967, p. 187.*

Through her revealing presentation of carefully selected art objects [Shirley Glubok] introduces young readers not only to the art of the Etruscans but also to their civilization as well. As in her earlier books the descriptive text is brief and lucid and the clearly reproduced photographs of the art objects are strikingly displayed.

The Booklist and Subscription Books Bulletin *(© 1967 by the American Library Association), November 1, 1967, p. 330.*

Miss Glubok's text efficiently covers the known aspects of the Etruscans and their art. . . . The techniques and materials are explained simply. Stories derived from the illustrated work are apt and cogently told. And a genuine pleasure in the art is not swamped by a gush of epithets. The design of the book is imaginative, each page quite a different experience from the last. Plates are black and white on different colored backgrounds—far better than the usual fuzzy color reproductions.

Christopher Andreae, in The Christian Science Monitor *(reprinted by permission from* The Christian Science Monitor; *© 1967 The Christian Science Publishing Society; all rights reserved), November 2, 1967, p. B12.*

Unfortunately ["The Art of the Etruscans" is] not a wholly successful volume: the text is simple and direct, but contains a number of ambiguities and there's a disturbing sense of clutter in the format.

The New York Times Book Review *(© 1968 by The New York Times Company; reprinted by permission), January 21, 1968, p. 26.*

OTHER CITATIONS

Zena Sutherland, in Bulletin of the Center for Children's Books, *January, 1967, p. 27.*

Polly Goodwin, in Book World, *April 7, 1968, p. 14.*

***THE ART OF THE NEW AMERICAN NATION* (1972)**

Picking up where the *Art of Colonial America* left off, the *Art of the New American Nation* comes into its own with a sense of just acquired national dignity. . . . As always Glubok chooses her examples well . . . but her format is best suited to displaying the folk art which is somewhat less prominent here. . . . Glubok makes the most of her subject by minimizing her own role as critic. The commentary is all in the selection and presentation, and, seen here, even Stuart's George Washington becomes once again a visual experience instead of a schoolroom cliché.

Kirkus Reviews *(copyright © 1972 The Kirkus Service, Inc.), May 1, 1972, p. 538.*

The concise, informative text [of *The Art of the New American Nation*] smoothly interweaves history, information about the artists, comments on techniques and media, and discussions of the objects illustrated in the many fine black-and-white reproductions included in the book.

The Booklist *(© American Library Association 1972), July 1, 1972, p. 942.*

The photographs [in this book] are excellent, although a few color plates might have added a new dimension; the brief text is competent if unexciting, perhaps because so slim a volume can only suggest rather than explore so large a topic. A functional compilation.

Mary M. Burns, in The Horn Book Magazine *(copyright © 1972 by The Horn Book, Inc., Boston), August, 1972, pp. 386-87.*

[*The Art of the New American Nation* is an] excellent introduction to the early artists and craftsmen of this country. . . . The text is written simply, but it gives enough information about the artists and the art forms to read smoothly, and the chronological arrangement gives the book historical perspective.

Zena Sutherland, in Bulletin of the Center for Children's Books *(© 1972 by the University of Chicago; all rights reserved), November, 1972, p. 42.*

***THE ART OF THE NORTH AMERICAN INDIAN* (1964)**

It's a good idea to introduce children to the conceptual, non-realistic art of a "primitive" culture. Which is what is done [in "The Art of the North American Indian"], a fairly well-designed book with some good illustrations and adequate, if somewhat unimaginative commentary. The young child only needs the barest information to set the objects in some frame of reference related to life. Miss Glubok does this deftly and efficiently, although sometimes (especially for the help of parents who have to cope with questions) one wishes for a little more. . . . This book is a good idea. It will be interesting to see if it works.

Brian O'Doherty, in The New York Times Book Review *(© 1964 by The New York Times Company; reprinted by permission), March 29, 1964, p. 20.*

[*The Art of the North American Indian* is a] most handsome book, with photographs of varied and beautiful objects in a format of dignified simplicity. The text is clear and direct, referring to the illustrations briefly and extending to general remarks about the art form, tribal significance of the object or the form, or use of the object.

Zena Sutherland, in Bulletin of the Center for Children's Books *(copyright 1964 by the University of Chicago; all rights reserved), April, 1964, p. 124.*

[*The Art of the North American Indian*] samples Indian art from Florida to the Northwest and demonstrates that the North American Indians "all used the materials they found in nature for their art . . . [and] made beautiful works . . . from wood, sand, seashells, porcupine quills, and birch bark." The range of art reproduced comes from many museums, with a large share from the Museum of the American Indian. Many of the photographs are well produced against shades of yellow or orange brown. An attractive over-all introduction to pre-Columbian art.

Virginia Haviland, in The Horn Book Magazine *(copyright © 1964, by The Horn Book, Inc., Boston), June, 1964, p. 299.*

***THE ART OF THE NORTHWEST COAST INDIANS* (1974)**

The indigenous art of a region lends itself better to Glubok's overviewing than does the more eclectic material surveyed in her recent *Art of America* series, though here [in *The Art of the Northwest Coast Indians*] we notice that even on the purely factual level to which she limits herself, she is less enlightening on totem poles and potlatches than Glenn Holder . . . is in his far more prosaically got up introduction. And the more tours we take with Glubok, the more we pick up on the tired voice of the museum guide, informing children that the 19th century "is considered the most important period in Northwest Coast Indian Art" . . . but never thinking to satisfy their curiosity as to why so many of the figure paintings and carvings have smaller faces emerging, as if in the process of birth, from ovals down near the bottom of the trunk. Nevertheless Glubok has amassed a representative sampling of totem poles and screens, some powerful carvings and helmets, articulated masks that appeal to children's sense of the ingenious, and useful objects that would make any meal a feast—so that even though Glubok leaves much to be desired as a teacher of art appreciation, she is again to be thanked for bringing such work to the attention of young readers.

Kirkus Reviews *(copyright © 1975 The Kirkus Service, Inc.), April 15, 1975, p. 461.*

***THE ART OF THE SPANISH IN THE UNITED STATES AND PUERTO RICO* (1972)**

[In *The Art of the Spanish in the United States and Puerto Rico*] Ms. Glubok has chosen to dwell on the small decorated wooden statues called *bultos*—discussing techniques and costume styles while telling the religious stories they commemorate. Tinware *nichos* . . . , painted *retablos*, and many examples of religious and domestic architecture (shown for the most part through attractive 19th century sketches but treated almost purely descriptively in the text) round out the picture. Though the abstract patterns of several woolen blankets suggest a relationship to Indian designs there's no mention of possible cross-cultural influences, nor are there many specifics on how building styles differed from their Spanish prototypes.

Kirkus Reviews *(copyright © 1972 The Kirkus Service, Inc.), October 1, 1972, p. 1147.*

[Shirley Glubok's concise] descriptive text and [Alfred Tamarin's] clear photographs of representative artifacts, paintings, sketches, and restored or still extant buildings from Florida, New Mexico, Texas, Colorado, Arizona, California, and Puerto Rico unite to portray the rich Spanish contribution to the arts of America. . . . Similar in format, treatment, and the judicious selection of material displayed to Glubok's other books on the art of different cultures, this is an attractive introduction for readers, grades 4-7. Unfortunately there is no pronunciation guide to the many Spanish words used.

The Booklist *(© American Library Association 1973), January 1, 1973, p. 448.*

Profusely illustrated with photographs of architecture, room interiors, some craftwork objects, and—primarily—religious art objects, [*The Art of the Spanish in the United States and Puerto Rico* is] a good addition to Glubok's series of books in which art is related to the culture from which it emanates. . . . [Alfred Tamarin's] photography and [Gerard Nook's] design of the book are of excellent quality.

Zena Sutherland, in Bulletin of the Center for Children's Books *(© 1973 by the University of Chicago; all rights reserved), March, 1973, p. 106.*

OTHER CITATIONS

Publishers' Weekly, *January 15, 1973, p. 65.*

Virginia Haviland, in The Horn Book Magazine, *February, 1973, p. 64.*

***DISCOVERING THE ROYAL TOMBS AT UR* (1969)**

Despite the abridgment [from *Ur Excavations: The Royal Cemetery* by C. Leonard Woolley, *Discovering the Royal Tombs at Ur* is] a detailed factual account of what the famous archaeologist found in the Royal Cemetery of Ur of the Chaldees. . . . Slightly touching upon the practical details of dealing with local diggers, the text reveals the methods of rescuing and restoring the objects found, and offers conclusions and speculations regarding their significance. . . . The black-and-white photographs supply a visual documentation [and] attest to the richness of the discovery.

Paul Heins, in The Horn Book Magazine *(copyright © 1970 by The Horn Book, Inc., Boston), February, 1970, pp. 51-2.*

[*Discovering the Royal Tombs at Ur*] has captured the excitement and essence of the original book. It is revised in that the dating is more precise and minor errors of fact have been corrected. But by and large, this is still Woolley's report and reveals the story of the finding and excavation of the Royal Tombs of Ur. The book is well illustrated and contains plans of some of the graves. Detailed descriptions are given for many of the tombs. Its utility for reference is hindered by the lack of a bibliography, index, and suggested readings.

Science Books *(copyright 1970, by the American Association for the Advancement of Science), Vol. 6, No. 1 (May, 1970), p. 74.*

Although there have been new discoveries (some disproving facts previously held to be true) since the 1934 publication of Woolley's detailed and lengthy account of his findings at Ur, the basic material—here adapted and simplified [by Shirley Glubok]—is still of archeological interest. This is, however, still ponderously detailed enough to be dull fare for the reader with no special interest.

Zena Sutherland, in Bulletin of the Center for Children's Books *(copyright © 1970 by the University of Chicago; all rights reserved), July-August, 1970, p. 177.*

OTHER CITATIONS

Edward B. Garside, in The New York Times Book Review, *November 9, 1969 (Part 2), p. 28.*

***KNIGHTS IN ARMOR* (1969)**

[Shirley Glubok's] discussion of knighthood and the craftsmanship of medieval armorers has the directness and clarity of expression and the meaningful selection of content of one who knows children well. Equally as impressive as the selection for text is the choice of illustrations. In the handsome volume designed by Gerard Nook, there is a liberal selection of pictures concerned with castles, the Crusades, hand weapons, jousting and tournaments, and the King Arthur legends. . . . Illuminated manuscripts, paintings, and museum pieces of armor make graphic in book form the training and ideals of knights, details of armor construction, chivalric exploits, and the period pagentry.

Virginia Haviland, in The Horn Book Magazine *(copyright © 1969 by The Horn Book, Inc., Boston), June, 1969, pp. 316-17.*

[*Knights in Armor* is an] oversize book with a simply written text, some reproductions of paintings, and many photographs of armor. The labeled diagrams, the clear descriptions, and the many examples of armor for jousting or for fighting give the book minor reference use in addition to its historical and artistic relevance.

Zena Sutherland, in Bulletin of the Center for Children's Books *(© 1969 by the University of Chicago; all rights reserved), June, 1969, p. 158.*

Knight life becomes as clear as day in this sumptuous photographic essay which focuses on types of armor worn in the Middle Ages. . . . Unfortunately, each new topic discussed is not set off by a title or running head, and there is no table of contents. Further, the black-and-white reproductions are good but lack the excitement of color pictures. However, these reservations are minor, and the book remains an outstanding visual/verbal achievement, which will be used and appreciated by all students who study the age of chivalry, as well as a non-embarrassing source for older slow readers.

Anitra Gordon, in School Library Journal *(reprinted from the November, 1969, issue of* School Library Journal, *published by R. R. Bowker Co., a Xerox company; copyright © 1969 by Xerox Corporation), November, 1969, p. 120.*

OTHER CITATIONS

George A. Woods, in The New York Times Book Review, *April 6, 1969, p. 18.*

Polly Goodwin, in Book World, *May 4, 1969 (Part 2), p. 22.*

H

HAMILTON, Virginia 1936-

Virginia Hamilton, a Black American author, won the 1969 Edgar Allan Poe Award for *The House of Dies Drear*, and was awarded the 1975 Newbery Medal and National Book Award for *M. C. Higgins, The Great*. (See also *Contemporary Authors*, Vols. 25-28 and *Something About the Author*, Vol. 4.)

GENERAL COMMENTARY

Virginia Hamilton has written several superb pieces of literature about blacks with no attempt to present pseudointegrated circumstances. Her books are straightforward and literary, and present positive black imagery important for . . . appreciation by the white child. *Zeely* (. . . 1967) is an excellent example of positive symbolism. *Time-Ago Tales of Jahdu* (. . . 1969) . . . depicts blackness without reference or apology to whiteness; it is right in every emotional and literary sense. In turn, *House of Dies Drear* (. . . 1968) introduces the richness of 19th century black American history.

Binnie Tate, "In House and Out House: Authenticity and the Black Experience in Children's Books," in The Black American in Books for Children: Readings in Racism, *edited by Donnarae MacCann and Gloria Woodard (copyright 1972 by Donnarae MacCann and Gloria Woodard), Scarecrow, 1972, p. 44.*

THE HOUSE OF DIES DREAR (1968)

Unlike *Zeely*, Miss Hamilton's haunting first, [*The House of Dies Drear*] creates mystery only to reveal sleight-of-hand, creates a character who's larger than life only to reveal his double. . . . There are some sharp observations of, and on, the Negro church historically and presently, and an aborted ideological debate regarding use of the Negro heritage. Ideas abound, but when the focus shifts from Thomas' determination to take the measure of the house (literally and figuratively), the story becomes a charade.

Kirkus Service *(copyright © 1968 The Kirkus Service, Inc.), August 1, 1968, p. 818.*

Successful in presenting the seemingly occult, [Virginia Hamilton] does well, too, with the plain and everyday—the realistic details of household management and the service in the little African Methodist church. Satisfying every demand of the mystery story, [*The House of Dies Drear*] far more importantly deals with a boy's searching spirit and the history of a great cause. Thomas's responsiveness to the people in his life, including his twin baby brothers, reveals him to be an unusually sensitive child.

Virginia Haviland, in The Horn Book Magazine *(copyright © 1968 by The Horn Book, Inc., Boston), October, 1968, p. 563.*

"The House of Dies Drear" is written with poetic precision. Miss Hamilton polishes her sentences with care, develops her characters with imagination and love. Thomas is a sensitive boy, self-sufficient, sometimes lonely, his relationship with his father like nothing dreamed of in the Moynihan report. . . . "The House of Dies Drear" is not an angry book—although there is a need for anger too. Instead, Miss Hamilton has found her own way of saying "Black is beautiful."

Dorothy Sterling, in The New York Times Book Review *(© 1968 by The New York Times Company; reprinted by permission), October 13, 1968, p. 26.*

Let's admit right off that the plot [of *The House of Dies Drear*] is elaborate and the treasure found at tunnel's end rather too munificent. Never mind; it all makes titillating reading, and what really counts here are the poignant sense of a heroic past set against an eerie backdrop and the group-portrait of Thomas and his family, people who are very nice to meet.

Ellen Lewis Buell, in Book World *(©* The Washington Post*), November 3, 1968 (Part 2), p. 12.*

[*The House of Dies Drear*] is gifted writing; the characterization is unforgettable, the plot imbued with mounting tension. It is in a way irrelevant that the principles are black, for the haunting story and the author's craftsmanship are paramount, but, in a deeper sense, that this kind of book has been written about Negroes is of tremendous importance. Not a problem novel, *The House of Dies Drear* is memorable literature that gives dignity to black heritage.

Zena Sutherland, in Saturday Review *(copyright © 1968 by Saturday Review, Inc.; reprinted with permission), November 9, 1968, p. 69.*

The House of Dies Drear . . . is a complicated mystery-story and treasure-hunt set in the big old house of an abolitionist who had made it into an Underground Railroad station and had been murdered there. The story itself has a curious, almost-architectural resemblance to the house it describes: large, dark, rambling, rather frightening, and leading off in strange directions.

John Rowe Townsend, in his Written for Children: An Outline of English Language Children's Literature, *revised edition (copyright © 1965, 1974 by John Rowe Townsend; reprinted by permission of J.B. Lippincott Company), Lippincott, 1974, p. 274.*

OTHER CITATIONS

The Booklist and Subscription Books Bulletin, *November 1, 1968, p. 311.*

Zena Sutherland, in Bulletin of the Center for Children's Books, *December, 1968, p. 59.*

M. C. HIGGINS, THE GREAT (1974)

All of the characters [in *M. C. Higgins, the Great*] have vitality and credibility as well as a unique quality that makes them unforgettable. . . . Visual images are strong and vivid; and many passages are poetic in their beauty. M. C., however, is aware of a continuing note of sadness in the hills; for pervading the entire story is his dread that the huge pile of subsoil and trees bulldozed together and left behind by strip miners would begin to slide and suddenly crash down upon his home. All of the themes are handled contrapuntally to create a memorable picture of a young boy's growing awareness of himself and of his surroundings.

Beryl Robinson, in The Horn Book Magazine *(copyright © 1974 by the Horn Book, Inc., Boston), October, 1974, pp. 143-44.*

M. C. is not so very different from the characters in Virginia Hamilton's other books. A succession of solemn children—each one grasped by a mystic sense of significance and purpose—moves through space and time, passing among tall columnar presences of immense dignity (Zeely, Mr. Pluto, Mr. Pool, Banina, Jones), intent on strange random errands or journeys in which peculiar events are part of the circumscribing dailiness.

How does she do it? What ouija board does she write on? I find it baffling to describe the strength and rightness of her style. There is no weakening of the spell anywhere. Like a magician or prestidigitator, she leaves you levitated, sawed in half, and put back together—partially transformed. Like a sorcerer, she inhabits you with spirits. And they remain. The demon spell works for good. After reading *M. C. Higgins, The Great* . . ., you do not altogether get yourself back. It is Virginia Hamilton's most splendid book so far.

Jane Langton, "Virginia Hamilton, the Great," in The Horn Book Magazine *(copyright © 1974 by the Horn Book, Inc., Boston), December, 1974, pp. 671-73.*

The characterization, the creation of setting, the establishment of mood, and the writing style are all superb [in *M. C. Higgins, the Great*]; Virginia Hamilton has never written more beautifully. Her style is both intricate and graceful, with nuances of meaning that more mature readers may appreciate, but which are not essential for the average reader's comprehension.

Zena Sutherland, in Bulletin of the Center for Children's Books *(© 1974 by the University of Chicago; all rights reserved), December, 1974, p. 63.*

Virginia Hamilton writes in heavy but compelling prose. Characters lumber rather than leap from the page, but once in focus they make their mark. . . .

Certainly, this is a sincere and highly original work. . . . [The] story has enough force to keep most adult readers going. But not, surely, most young readers: the opening of the book is almost impenetrable, little use for any child accustomed to giving up after the first difficult page, let alone a whole chapter. For those that stay, there are rewards but some punishment. Emotion sometimes slides into over-intensity. There is an absence of the casual; everything from cooking meals to swimming takes on large significance. Silences between characters usually contain as many arguments as anything they happen to say. Like adolescence itself, so well described in this book, continual excess of feeling, although authentic, is sometimes hard to live with. While I admire Virginia Hamilton's achievement, honesty compels me to add that I was relieved as well as sorry to finish this strongly imagined story.

Nicholas Tucker, in The Times Literary Supplement *(© Times Newspapers Ltd., 1975), July 11, 1975, p. 766.*

OTHER CITATIONS

Donald J. Bissett and Ruth E. Moline, in Elementary English, *April, 1975, p. 485.*

PAUL ROBESON: THE LIFE AND TIMES OF A FREE BLACK MAN (1974)

In her preface—as significant as the book itself—[Virginia Hamilton] explains how her father was responsible for her initial appreciation of the great black artist, who is still alive but almost unknown to young people. Drawing information from an impressive list of sources, she painstakingly tells the story of Robeson's life. . . . Virginia Hamilton deals objectively and skillfully with the tangled complexities of Robeson's beliefs and with the American political climate of the Cold War period. . . . [This is an] important book for readers of all ages.

Ethel L. Heins, in The Horn Book Magazine *(copyright © 1975 by the Horn Book, Inc., Boston), April, 1975, pp. 159-60.*

THE PLANET OF JUNIOR BROWN (1971)

A stunningly good, absolutely compelling, weird and unique book, Virginia Hamilton's new novel is the story of three outsiders in New York City. . . . Through the story of the three, *The Planet of Junior Brown* presents an unforgettable evocation of madness—madness in the individual (overwhelming, generalized fear resulting from unrelieved spiritual/emotional/physical solitude) enforced by the madness of society which is indifference. . . . Hamilton's juxtapositions—of fantastical and realistic elements, of street dialogue and philosophical statement—work. . . . The book is like a perfectly executed piece of music; the author doesn't strike a single false note.

Michael Cart, in School Library Journal *(reprinted from the September, 1971, issue of* School Library Journal, *published by R. R. Bowker Co., a Xerox company; copyright © 1971 by Xerox Corporation), September, 1971, pp. 126-27.*

Buddy's altruism may be a bit overdone, and older street boys may not educate younger ones in quite the way Miss Hamilton describes, but it doesn't matter. Junior is entirely convincing, as is the character of his unbalanced mother. Virginia Hamilton tells this sad but loving story with authority, compassion, and skill. As a result, "The Planet of Junior Brown" can take its place among the best examples of recent children's literature.

Nancy Garden, in The Christian Science Monitor *(reprinted by permission from* The Christian Science Monitor; *© 1971 The Christian Science Publishing Society; all rights reserved), November 11, 1971, p. B5.*

Although [*The Planet of Junior Brown*] will have a more limited audience than the author's *Zeely* . . . and *The House of Dies Drear* . . . , it is a powerfully written story which can be read on many levels. Mature, sensitive readers will find it difficult to forget.

The Booklist *(© by the American Library Association), December 1, 1971, p. 333.*

[In *The Planet of Junior Brown*, Virginia Hamilton] has molded, rather than simply presented, experiences of black, inner-city children to create a narrative of unusual dimensions and unexpected facets. [She has combined] realism of detail and verisimilitude of speech with occasional touches of melodrama. . . .

Virginia Hamilton is not a strictly realistic writer, although the base of her operations may be said to be realism. . . . Actually, [she] overcomes the bonds of sordid reality. Her imagination, spilling over into metaphors and symbols, is a liberating force. For she feels "Perhaps the human race is yet to come. . . . We must make life ready." Ultimately, she writes of her aspirations—with a Dostoevskian intensity.

Paul Heins, in The Horn Book Magazine *(copyright © 1972 by The Horn Book, Inc., Boston), February, 1972, p. 81.*

The Planet of Junior Brown . . . is, if I interpret it correctly, a story of the creation in love and pain of small human refuges from loneliness and non-communication. It is not fantasy but is not wholly realistic either; for such conceptions as the 'planets' of homeless boys dotted around the big city, each with its 'Tomorrow Billy' as leader, are acceptable symbolically rather than literally.

John Rowe Townsend, in his Written for Children: An Outline of English Language Children's Literature, *revised edition (copyright © 1965, 1974 by John Rowe Townsend; reprinted by permission of J.B. Lippincott Company), Lippincott, 1974, p. 274.*

OTHER CITATIONS

Publishers' Weekly, *August 23, 1971, p. 81.*

Zena Sutherland, in Bulletin of the Center for Children's Books, *December, 1971, p. 57.*

TIME-AGO LOST: MORE TALES OF JAHDU (1973)

[In *Time-Ago Lost: More Tales of Jahdu*, Virginia Hamilton] ventures into the confusing symbolism of Yin and Yang, light and dark, warmth and cold, shadow and sun. The four stories deal with the finding of light, fire, and time —difficult concepts for average children to grasp, especially when the Yin-Yang symbol is intercepted. Moreover, the use of the symbol obscures the interesting, meaningful tie-up between the fantasy about the omniscient Jahdu and Lee Edward's acceptance of his role in life. Nevertheless, the style is vigorous and the description terse and vivid. Illustrations in black and white complement the text very well and add dimension to the stories.

Dorothy de Wit, in School Library Journal *(reprinted from the April, 1973, issue of* School Library Journal, *published by R. R. Bowker Co., a Xerox company; copyright © 1973 by Xerox Corporation), April, 1973, p. 67.*

The Jahdu stories [in *Time-Ago Lost*] are told with consummate skill, and the framing narrative has a warmth and substance that are a firm base for the tales. . . . Skilled writing, taut structure, and deep affection between the child and the adults of his world, "a fine, good place called Harlem" make this a distinguished book.

Zena Sutherland, in Bulletin of the Center for Children's Books *(© 1973 by the University of Chicago; all rights reserved), April, 1973, p. 124.*

In spite of the fact that these tales deal with the classic subjects of myth and folklore—creation, rebirth, magic, the power of fire, the forces of darkness—the treatment is superficial and unsatisfying. The existential weariness pervading the book makes the reader feel that perhaps these stories were not really meant for children. [Ray Prather's] illustrations match the mood of the stories; they are stark and sometimes distorted.

Sidney D. Long, in The Horn Book Magazine *(copyright © 1973 by The Horn Book, Inc., Boston), June, 1973, p. 278.*

Although [the] stories [in *Time-Ago Lost*] are somewhat confusing and heavy with symbolism in a way that *The Time-Ago Tales of Jahdu*—also set in Harlem with the same characters—were not, Hamilton's writing is still strong and Lee Edward's relationship with his baby sitter, Mama Luka, and with his own parents is reassuringly warm.

The Booklist *(© American Library Association 1973), June 15, 1973, p. 988.*

OTHER CITATIONS

Kirkus Reviews, *January 1, 1973, p. 5.*

The New York Times Book Review, *August 5, 1973, p. 8.*

Jennifer Farley Smith, in The Christian Science Monitor, *October 3, 1973, p. 10.*

***THE TIME-AGO TALES OF JAHDU* (1969)**

[The] Jahdu stories themselves are not well paced enough to be engrossing and the Harlem and characters depicted by Miss Hamilton are much too flaccid when compared to the reality of black places and people. The sensitivity with which the story is spun might recommend this book to the few children who enjoy a poetic style of fantasy. But to the vast majority of action-oriented young library users, it will have small appeal.

Lynne Stewart, in School Library Journal *(reprinted from the December, 1969, issue of* School Library Journal, *published by R. R. Bowker Co., a Xerox company; copyright © 1969 by Xerox Corporation), December, 1969, p. 53.*

The message that Virginia Hamilton is trying to convey [in *The Time-Ago Tales of Jahdu*] has dignity and strength and substance. But despite the brilliantly conceived and executed framework of her story, the book is weak because the Jahdu tales themselves, excepting the last, are contrived and tasteless. They lack drama and excitement, and their symbolism is vague. . . . The book is recommended for the power of [Nonny Hogrogian's] pictures; the poetry of [Virginia Hamilton's] prose; the strength of the characterizations of Mama Luka and Lee Edward; and the significance of the theme—with regret that the author's development of the theme in the device of Jahdu falls so short of success.

Diane Farrell, in The Horn Book Magazine *(copyright © 1970 by The Horn Book, Inc., Boston), February, 1970, p. 36.*

OTHER CITATIONS

Dorothy M. Broderick, in The New York Times Book Review, *October 12, 1969, p. 34.*

Zena Sutherland, in Bulletin of the Center for Children's Books, *November, 1969, p. 45.*

***W.E.B. DU BOIS: A BIOGRAPHY* (1972)**

For the most part, [*W.E.B. Du Bois* is] a cool and careful study which avoids the dramatic improvisations of Emma Gelders Sterne's *His Was the Voice* (1971) and concentrates heavily, and perhaps too didactically, on placing Du Bois' leadership into a historical context. . . . Unfortunately, there is . . . less about Du Bois' ideas than one might wish for. . . . Indeed, if Hamilton had given us more straight Du Bois and resisted the temptation to deliver elaborately hedged pronouncements of her own . . . this would have been a better book. As it is, it is a useful compilation of background facts, but is unlikely to inspire in others the reverence which Ms. Hamilton so obviously feels.

Kirkus Reviews *(copyright © 1972 The Kirkus Service, Inc.), May 15, 1972, p. 591.*

Carefully researched and documented, sympathetic toward the subject yet candid about his failings, this is a sober record of the long career of William Du Bois. . . . This lacks the warmth that characterizes Virginia Hamilton's fiction, but it makes a particular contribution in placing the events of Du Bois' life not just in the stream of black history but against the background of what was happening in the United States and how it inevitably affected what was happening to William Du Bois.

Zena Sutherland, in Bulletin of the Center for Children's Books *(© 1972 by the University of Chicago; all rights reserved), September, 1972, p. 8.*

With grace and dignity [Virginia Hamilton] has recounted the story of W.E.B. Du Bois. . . . The book is an affirmation of Du Bois' life, and a fascinating historical document of the Black Movement in America. Comprehensive Notes, Bibliography, and Index complete a fine, scholarly work. Unfortunately, there are often more facts than characterization, and a young reader may find it, at times, a little dry and difficult. Still, this is unequivocally the best of all the biographies of Du Bois for young people—and clearly conveys the sense of his intellectual struggle, frustration, and search.

Sheryl B. Andrews, in The Horn Book Magazine *(copyright © 1972 by The Horn Book, Inc., Boston), October, 1972, p. 476.*

OTHER CITATIONS

The Booklist, *October 1, 1972, p. 148.*

***ZEELY* (1967)**

[*Zeely* is a] quiet, slow-moving story of an important summer in a young girl's life. . . . The characterization of a young girl absorbed in herself isn't fully realized; the big confrontation to which the author has carefully built, though quietly and realistically handled, is anti-climactic. Nevertheless, the author uses language well to create a mood piece that may appeal especially to girls feeling growing pains. . . . The plot bypasses civil rights concerns to arrive at an unselfconscious story employing Negro characters in a situation with which any young girl can empathize.

Amy Kellman, in School Library Journal *(reprinted from the May, 1967, issue of* School Library Journal, *published by R. R. Bowker Co., a Xerox company; copyright © 1967 by Xerox Corporation), May 1967, pp. 59-60.*

Miss Hamilton tells with perfect, nostalgic descriptions of

the uncle's old farmhouse, of country days and doings, good country things to eat, and of summer nights slept in the dewy outdoors, of moonlight tricks and exchanged whispers in the dark. . . .

Zeely is a fresh, sensitive story, with a lingering, serene, misty quality about it which the reader can save and savor. There are some fine illustrations by Symeon Shimin.

Elinore Standard, in Book Week *(© The* Washington Post*), June 25, 1967, p. 12.*

This glimpse into a pre-adolescent's fanciful and half-formed musings about her heroine makes an unusual story. . . . The tentative solution rings true, and strengthens both the realistic and imaginative quality of the story. The illustrations, by Symeon Shimin, capture the ordinary characteristics of the people and locale, as well as the natural exaggeration in a child's fantasy.

John Gillespie and Diana Lembo, in their Introducing Books: A Guide for the Middle Grades *(copyright © 1970 by Xerox Corp.), Bowker, 1970, p. 63.*

This is a book without bitterness or paranoia, but it is deeply concerned with black dignity: the splendour of Zeely in contrast with her humble occupation, the associations of night travelling with escape from slavery. It is easy to read a message into the book—walk tall—but this does not detract from its merit.

John Rowe Townsend, in his Written for Children: An Outline of English Language Children's Literature, *revised edition (copyright © 1965, 1974 by John Rowe Townsend; reprinted by permission of J.B. Lippincott Company), Lippincott, 1974, pp. 273-74.*

OTHER CITATIONS

Virginia Haviland, in The Horn Book Magazine, *April, 1967, p. 205.*

The Booklist and Subscription Books Bulletin, *June 1, 1967, pp. 1045-46.*

Zena Sutherland, in Bulletin of the Center for Children's Books, *July-August, 1967, p. 170.*

* * *

HENTOFF, Nat 1925-

An American author, editor, journalist, and jazz critic, Nat Hentoff has written several young adult novels, including his well-known *Jazz Country*. (See also *Contemporary Authors*, Vols. 1-4, rev. ed.)

I'M REALLY DRAGGED BUT NOTHING GETS ME DOWN (1968)

[*I'm Really Dragged But Nothing Gets Me Down* is an] episodic story in which believable, sincere, intelligent and philosophically opposed characters discuss their differences, don't resolve them, and are left with nagging frustration and a sense of solitude. . . . Echoing the occasionally blasphemous and raunchy sound of ordinary conversation . . . the extensive dialogues constitute confrontations between young and old, black and white, dove and hawk, head and straight opinion in America today. This relevance gives the book its value and at the same time flaws it—for readers may easily find themselves being persuaded from side to side in a series of editorials and losing track of the minimal plot and story.

Diane G. Stavn, in School Library Journal *(reprinted from the November, 1968, issue of* School Library Journal, *published by R. R. Bowker Co., a Xerox company; copyright © 1968 by Xerox Corporation), November, 1968, p. 96.*

Although timely and important in theme, ["I'm Really Dragged But Nothing Gets Me Down"] falls short as a novel for basic reasons. It lacks driving power; it becomes, instead of a story that moves the reader, a philippic that instructs. The welding of a moral and philosophic discussion to a dramatic form is never easy to do but done well that is precisely what makes great books great. Because the surface of this one remains so flat, the characters so blurred, the arguments so objective, the impact of Mr. Hentoff's theme is largely ineffective.

John Weston, in The New York Times Book Review *(© 1968 by The New York Times Company; reprinted by permission), November 3, 1968 (Part 2), p. 66.*

Jeremy is . . . a stencil of today's "alienated youth," and his parents are stencils of today's puzzled progenitors. Jeremy and his father and mother are stupid and boring. It is bad enough to be a bore in real life, but to be a bore in a book is unpardonable. The Wolfs and their tiresome, spoiled, and priggish son. . . . have surrendered to every cliché popular with the makers of the mass media, and the conflict with which Jeremy attempts to mask his mediocrity is no conflict at all. Jeremy is not assailed by self-doubt or torn by opposed loyalties. He . . . stands forth as complete a stereotype as an end man in a minstrel show. His decision to become a draft counselor in the end seems altogether too easy to be true.

All of this would do very well if the author had taken time and space to discuss what really "bugs" these people, as Jeremy would say. He doesn't. He merely "tells it like it is," and "like it is" doesn't even scratch the surface of what ails Jeremy. . . . [He] and his woebegone parents deserve more exacting and more humane treatment than they receive in this too slight and humorless novelette.

Martha Bacon, in The Atlantic Monthly *(copyright © 1968 by The Atlantic Monthly Company, Boston, Mass.; reprinted with permission), December, 1968, p. 152.*

[Very] rarely does *I'm Really Dragged* give us the look either of human beings or of places; we are not, strangely enough, made aware of any particular place. And in losing the particularity of place, we lose somehow the sense of reality, and I mean an intense sense of reality. We are all but blind—like the chambered mole. Nor do we feel the surfaces of solid objects; they seem scarcely to exist. We never smell anything. As readers, we seem stripped of all senses except hearing. . . .

Eleanor Cameron, in The Horn Book Magazine *(copyright © 1972 by The Horn Book, Inc., Boston), December, 1972, p. 578.*

In *I'm Really Dragged But Nothing Gets Me Down* (1968) not a great deal happens, but a great deal is there: it is the scope of understanding and the depth of perception that give vitality and impact to a story of the unsure adolescent and the generation gap. Jeremy and his father don't understand each other, but then Jeremy hardly understands himself. . . . *I'm Really Dragged* makes both viewpoints understandable.

May Hill Arbuthnot and Zena Sutherland, in their Children and Books, *4th edition (copyright © 1947, 1957, 1964, 1972 by Scott, Foresman and Co.), Scott, Foresman, 1972, p. 467.*

OTHER CITATIONS

Zena Sutherland, in Bulletin of the Center for Children's Books, *January, 1969, p. 78.*

IN THE COUNTRY OF OURSELVES (1971)

Unfortunately, some of the episodes [in *In the Country of Ourselves*] are a bit strained, and the responses of the characters are occasionally overdrawn in an attempt to make the philosophies they espouse clear. Nevertheless, most of the kids behave believably—and, thankfully, not always predictably—and the book is very wittily written. All in all, it's one of the fairest and most entertaining titles available about politically aware young teens today.

Jack Forman, in School Library Journal *(reprinted from the December, 1971, issue of* School Library Journal, *published by R. R. Bowker Co., a Xerox company; copyright © 1971 by Xerox Corporation), December, 1971, p. 64.*

[*In the Country of Ourselves* is a] novel of unrest and rebellion in a high school, the trouble fomented by a group of students and encouraged by a radical teacher. . . . [The] implication is that the young people of conviction, black and white, will continue to press after the agitators have been sloughed off. The characters are developed well, yet each seems a type, without being a sterotype, that represents a point of view—so that the fate of each seems less important than the solution and resolution of their cause.

Zena Sutherland, in Bulletin of the Center for Children's Books *(© 1972 by the University of Chicago; all rights reserved), January, 1972, p. 74.*

OTHER CITATIONS

Publishers' Weekly, *November 1, 1971, p. 55.*

JAZZ COUNTRY (1965)

[In *Jazz Country*, Nat Hentoff] manages to sustain the tone of a young boy's viewpoint in the vivid idiom of Negro jive talk, coherently used. . . . Some of the other characters too often sound like mouthpieces for a crusade rather than people; the intensity and bitterness of the race situation have been caught without the harsh laughter that usually accompanies it as a safety valve. Tom himself is never phony and Godfrey, though idealized, is a complex and memorable man. Here is a book with something important to say about the sacrifices demanded of the artist in a way that makes a strong appeal to boys—and that's a rare combination.

Virginia Kirkus' Service, *March 1, 1965, p. 252.*

Jazz Country is a novel directed at young people struggling to realize themselves; it is also a gem of a book that talks rare sense about the ambiguities of race, the difficulties of a child's growth, and the ironies of artistic life. . . .

Mr. Hentoff has chosen not so much to compare or contrast lives as to let them be, separately and together. Such restraint, enabling a touching and real story, deserves our surprised, grateful recognition.

Robert Coles, in Book Week *(©* The Washington Post*), May 9, 1965 (Part 2), p. 5.*

Not only does ["Jazz Country"] render the experience of jazz with passion, with what strikes an uninformed reader as veracity; it presents its Negro characters with honesty and dignity. . . . Yet it is precisely in so far as it is tailored for teen-agers that the book fails. Its teen-age hero is cardboard, its plot an outrageous tissue of coincidences which do not, as coincidences should, mirror inner compulsions of the characters. The setting is New York, but the hero keeps tripping over people he knows as though he were strolling around a town of 500 people.

Carolyn Heilbrun, in The New York Times Book Review *(copyright © 1965 by The New York Times Company; reprinted by permission), May 9, 1965, p. 3.*

In several ways, [*Jazz Country* is] a most unusual book: honest, perceptive, and sophisticated. . . . [It is a] good story about New York, a wonderfully candid story about racial attitudes, and a fine book about jazz.

Zena Sutherland, in Bulletin of the Center for Children's Books *(copyright 1965 by the University of Chicago; all rights reserved), June, 1965, p. 150.*

Despite [the] preceptive analyses of youthful malaise [in *Jazz Country*, it is] markedly flawed by the treatment accorded [Tom's girlfriend]. . . . The quality of honesty that Tom considers unique to Jessica isn't really, of course, and it's a disservice to imply to boys that it is. In fact, there is nothing in Jessica's actions or responses that makes her a special, individual person in any way; she's merely a mouthpiece to relate information about other characters in the book and a sounding board for their ideas and problems.

Diane G. Stavn, in School Library Journal *(reprinted from the January, 1971, issue of* School Library Journal, *published by R. R. Bowker Co., a Xerox company; copyright © 1971 by Xerox Corporation), January, 1971, p. 67.*

OTHER CITATIONS

The Booklist and Subscription Books Bulletin, *July 1, 1965, p. 1025.*

Margaret C. Scoggin, in The Horn Book Magazine, *October, 1965, p. 517.*

The Times Literary Supplement, *May 19, 1966, p. 442.*

* * *

HUNT, Irene 1907-

Irene Hunt, an American author who won the 1967 Newbery Medal for *Up a Road Slowly*, wrote the highly acclaimed *Across Five Aprils*. (See also *Contemporary Authors*, Vols. 19-20 and *Something About the Author*, Vol. 2.)

ACROSS FIVE APRILS (1964)

[This] book abounds in southern Illinois folkway and folksay. Indeed, it is a conversation-piece of a novel, where most of the action is something talked about, as in a Greek play. Yet, it is withal an intriguing and beautifully written book—a prize to those who take the time to read it, whatever their ages.

John K. Bettersworth, in The New York Times Book Review *(© 1964 by The New York Times Company; reprinted by permission), May 10, 1964 (Part 2), pp. 8, 10.*

[*Across Five Aprils*] gives the reader an intense experience because of the reality of the characters. Because she knows them so well . . ., [Irene Hunt] can create a whole person with a very few lines. She was wise to confine her story within a small frame . . .; and she is so skillful that the reader is not aware of the limitations. Even while different points of view are a necessary part of the story, she consistently keeps Jethro at the center, relating events and impressions through him. Very rarely does she emphasize a message, but in her understatement the message is clear, and readers—boys, girls, and adults—will not be quite the same again.

Ruth Hill Viguers, in The Horn Book Magazine *(copyright © 1964, by The Horn Book, Inc., Boston), June, 1964, p. 291.*

[*Across Five Aprils* is a] memorable story of the tragic years of the Civil War as experienced by a boy, his family, and neighbors in a backwoods community in southern Illinois. . . . Drawing from family records and from stories told by her grandfather [Irene Hunt] has, in an uncommonly fine narrative, created living characters and vividly reconstructed a crucial period of history.

The Booklist and Subscription Books Bulletin *(© 1964 by the American Library Association), July 1, 1964, p. 1002.*

[This is an] impressive book both as a historically authenticated Civil War novel and as a beautifully written family story. . . . [The] realistic treatment of the intricate emotional conflicts within a border-state family is superb. The details of battles and campaigns are deftly integrated into letters and conversations, and the characters are completely convincing.

Zena Sutherland, in Bulletin of the Center for Children's Books *(copyright 1964 by the University of Chicago; all rights reserved), July-August, 1964, p. 171.*

[In *Across Five Aprils*] Irene Hunt skillfully conveys the impact of the [Civil War] through the medium of letters from the front. Through conversation and experience, the issues in the war gradually become clearer to Jehro, and the main theme of the book is the effect of outside events upon a child growing up. For all that, the novel is fast moving and exciting. The characterization of the family is beautifully executed and the rifts that divide them are described without any disjuncture in the prose style or bowdlerization of history.

The Times Literary Supplement *(© The Times Publishing Company Ltd. 1965), December 9, 1965, p. 1147.*

Mrs. Hunt's description of a young boy whose adolescence coincides with the period of American Civil War is both perceptive and moving. . . . [*Across Five Aprils* is a] superior historical novel. . . .

This story nobly emphasizes the futility of aggression. The American Civil War with its drama is expertly presented through the lives of an ordinary family. It will provide young adults with a clearer understanding of and compassion for this country's conflict. In addition, the worthy values of a devoted family relationship and the traditional American emphasis on education are stressed.

John Gillespie and Diana Lembo, in their Juniorplots: A Book Talk Manual for Teachers and Librarians *(© 1967 by the R. R. Bowker Co.), Bowker, 1967, pp. 181, 183.*

OTHER CITATIONS

Patricia H. Allen, in Library Journal, *April 15, 1964, pp. 1871-72.*

Patience M. Daltry, in The Christian Science Monitor, *June 11, 1964, p. 9.*

NO PROMISES IN THE WIND (1970)

The incidents [in *No Promises in the Wind*] provide a thin soup of Depression background—the barest pinch of Republican/Democratic politics, radio, movies, garnished with a bootlegger and two economic reform radicals (drawn as tetched), with floating lumps of first love for Josh before the boys get home, more understanding of their now chastened father. Dirty gray storm clouds on the jacket and the hopelessness implicit in the title won't attract voluntary readers.

Lillian N. Gerhardt, in School Library Journal *(reprinted from the March, 1970, issue of* School Library Journal, *published by R. R. Bowker Co., a Xerox company; copyright © 1970 by Xerox Corporation), March, 1970, p. 144.*

The personal relationships are sensitively drawn, and the changes in Josh are natural, but the book—despite the background of the Depression—is so colored by the exotic carnival atmosphere that it does not give a true picture of the era.

Zena Sutherland, in Saturday Review *(copyright © 1970 by Saturday Review, Inc.; reprinted with permission), May 9, 1970, p. 69.*

The bleakness of [*No Promises in the Wind*] is relieved by kindness, for even in such times [as the Depression] there were people whose mercy was not quenched. . . . It will be hard for many [young people today] to believe that so many tragedies could occur, that such conditions could exist, that so many decent, hard-working people could become so degraded, but the reality of this absorbing book should help them to understand. With all the problems that exist today such an honest picture of one of our country's most tragic periods may give readers a wider perspective. It is a deeply moving story.

Ruth Hill Viguers, in The Horn Book Magazine *(copyright © 1970 by The Horn Book, Inc., Boston), June, 1970, p. 301.*

Although the economic hardships of the Depression years form the basis of events [in this book], the story's major emphasis is on a fifteen-year-old boy's growth in understanding himself and the ways of the world. . . . Although marred by an overly earnest tone and a tendency toward sentimentality, the story of Josh's reactions to occurrences, including the death of Howie, points up some of the truths of the human condition and offers interesting sidelights on the period.

The Booklist *(© by the American Library Association), June 15, 1970, p. 1279.*

[*No Promises in the Wind*] is strong in style, in its relationships, and in the perception with which [Irene Hunt] invests Josh, who learns from his own relationship with Joey how it is possible for one depressed and worried to lash out at a loved person. It is weak in plot and construction: the carnival episode is long and seems out of balance; the character of the friend-in-distress is not quite convincing; the several episodes on the road seem isolated by the absence of other such wandering boys, a marked phenomenon of the period.

Zena Sutherland, in Bulletin of the Center for Children's Books *(© 1970 by the University of Chicago; all rights reserved), September, 1970, p. 11.*

OTHER CITATIONS

Kirkus Reviews, *March 15, 1970, p. 329.*

Pamela Marsh, in The Christian Science Monitor, *May 7, 1970, p. B6.*

***TRAIL OF APPLE BLOSSOMS* (1968)**

Johnny Appleseed, part myth, part reality, has captured the imagination of many writers, but [in "Trail of Apple Blossoms"] Irene Hunt has written one of the best accounts of the gentle man who would harm neither man nor beast. . . .

The brevity of the story, written for a younger audience than her previous books, . . . has led Miss Hunt to sharpen her prose; the poetic quality of the writing glimmers on every page. Don Bolognese, one of the best illustrators, has created perfect pictures. . . . Between Miss Hunt and Mr. Bolognese, Johnny and the apple trees he loved have both come alive.

Dorothy M. Broderick, in The New York Times Book Review *(© 1968 by The New York Times Company; reprinted by permission), April 14, 1968, p. 20.*

John Chapman, the legendary Johnny Appleseed, lives again in this brief fictional narrative which emphasizes his gifts of healing, feeling of kinship with wild creatures, courage, and love of peace. Beginning when Chapman is a well-known adult in Pennsylvania, the story centers on the Bryant family whose lives he touches. [Irene Hunt] has endowed her subject with a spiritual quality which shines through the story.

Helen Armstrong, in School Library Journal *(reprinted from the May, 1968, issue of* School Library Journal, *published by R. R. Bowker Co., a Xerox company; copyright © 1968 by Xerox Corporation), May, 1968, p. 79.*

[*Trail of Apple Blossoms* is a] story about John Chapman that emphasizes his philosophy and his personality rather than the role that won him the nickname of Johnny Appleseed. . . . [Irene Hunt's] writing has an almost lyric quality in parts of the book, a note echoed in [Don Bolognese's] illustrations; the story moves slowly and has curiously little impact despite the drama of some events and the appealing figure of Chapman himself, a humanitarian in the rough world of the frontier.

Zena Sutherland, in Bulletin of the Center for Children's Books *(copyright 1968 by the University of Chicago; all rights reserved), May, 1968, p. 143.*

OTHER CITATIONS

The Booklist and Subscription Books Bulletin, *June 15, 1968, p. 1186.*

***UP A ROAD SLOWLY* (1966)**

With "Up a Road," Miss Hunt demonstrates that she is a writer of the first rank—and a daring one as well, as she brings off a difficult tour de force and turns personal reminiscence into art. . . .

"Up a Road" may not appeal to every girl but it will to those who love Millay's poetry and weep over beauty as well as ugliness. Those who follow Julie's growth—from a tantrum-throwing 7-year-old to a gracious young woman of 17—will find this book has added a new dimension to their lives.

Dorothy M. Broderick, in The New York Times Book Review *(© 1966 by The New York Times Company; reprinted by permission), November 6, 1966 (Part 2), pp. 8, 12.*

The Julie from 7 to 17 [in *Up a Road Slowly*] is an unusually intelligent girl who feels things deeply and is extremely sensitive to her environment. The adult Julie supposedly writing it all down can be perceptively articulate about young Julie's experiences without the smallest jarring note. . . . Irene Hunt demonstrates that she can tell a compelling story about people who come to grips with truly important matters. She has a way of getting straight to the heart of things—and to the heart of the reader, as well.

Robin Gottlieb, in Book Week *(©* The Washington Post*), November 6, 1966, p. 22.*

Julie's maturing wisdom and the subtlety of her perceptions mark [*Up a Road Slowly*] as a teen-age book; her extreme youth at the beginning should be considered only *as* a beginning. Unfortunately, the title and the cover are forbidding, and the heavy binding suggests a juvenile—handicaps that the wise librarian will know how to overcome. The author is adept at distinguishing the genuine from the spurious: Julie *is* a genuine character, and girls who go up the road with her will share in her growing up.

Virginia Kirkus' Service *(copyright © 1966 Virginia Kirkus' Service, Inc.), November 15, 1966, p. 1188.*

The problems of jealousy, first love, parental relations, and snobbishness are handled with ease and honesty [in *Up a Road Slowly*]; the more serious problems of alcoholism and of emotional disturbance in adult characters are handled with dignity. A moving and beautifully written book.

Zena Sutherland, in Bulletin of the Center for Children's Books *(copyright 1967 by the University of Chicago; all rights reserved), January, 1967, p. 75.*

Perhaps the people who make up Julie Trelling's world [in *Up a Road Slowly*] are no more unusual and varied than are most people's families and friends, but [Irene Hunt] sees them so much more clearly than most of us see people and gives them such vivid life that the reader is quickly and intensely interested in them. . . . Brett, [Julie's] first love, is the only unconvincing character. He fits too slickly into a contemporary mold. Julie herself is just selfish and exasperating enough to reassure girls reading about her and identifying with her. . . . [This is an] absorbing, beautifully written book.

Ruth Hill Viguers, in The Horn Book Magazine *(copyright © 1967, by The Horn Book, Inc., Boston), February, 1967, p. 73.*

A book that escapes the sterotyped superficiality of many teen-age novels is . . . *Up a Road Slowly*, by Irene Hunt. Miss Hunt relates with warmth and sympathetic insight the story of a young girl's growth to maturity. . . .

There are no really dramatic adventures in Julie Trelling's life, but the story of her problems with her family and friends, her loves, her quarrels, her small triumphs and disasters form a book that is, on the whole, a delight. The story is real, it has dimension, its characters are alive, it moves with a fine pace, and it is beautifully written.

Constantine Georgiou, in his Children and Their Literature *(copyright © 1969 by Prentice-Hall, Inc.), Prentice-Hall, 1969, p. 379.*

OTHER CITATIONS

Marilyn Gardner, in The Christian Science Monitor, *November 3, 1966, p. B12.*

The Booklist and Subscription Books Bulletin, *January 1, 1967, p. 490.*

The Times Literary Supplement, *November 30, 1967, p. 1141.*

K

KEATS, Ezra Jack 1916-

Ezra Jack Keats is a popular American author-illustrator. His picture book *The Snowy Day*, which won the 1963 Caldecott Medal, introduced Peter, who has appeared in subsequent works.

GENERAL COMMENTARY

Ezra Jack Keats is certainly no new voice, but the consistency with which he transmutes the everyday life of poor American children living in seedy city apartment buildings into something rich and teeming with possibilities has established him as one of the most exciting contemporary makers of picture books.

The Times Literary Supplement *(© Times Newspapers Ltd., 1972), November 3, 1972, p. 1326.*

Ezra Jack Keats has not yet shown any remarkable gift as a writer, but he has succeeded where many artists have failed in creating effective picture books without the collaboration of an author. In his most successful books his concepts have been such as can be expressed and developed pictorially, without requiring too much help from the written word. As an artist he demonstrates incidentally that although economy of means is a sound principle there is nothing *wrong* with using vivid colour and all the technical panoply of the day.

John Rowe Townsend, in his Written for Children: An Outline of English Language Children's Literature, *revised edition (copyright © 1965, 1974 by John Rowe Townsend; reprinted by permission of J.B. Lippincott Company), Lippincott, 1974, p. 315.*

APT. 3 (1971)

On slickest slick paper, with luscious brush strokes of rich colors, Keats impressionistically recreates a somber world of crumbling plaster wall, bare light bulbs and exposed wiring [in "Apt. 3"]. Always fond of reproducing textures in his books, Keats here reaches for the very fabric of tenement life. But his plot . . . is so frail that its intended audience is likely to grow restive with an introductory lesson in urban sociology unrelieved by any red-blooded action.

Selma G. Lanes, in The New York Times Book Review *(© 1971 by The New York Times Company; reprinted by permission), September 19, 1971, p. 8.*

Though Keats doesn't glamorize the dreary setting [in *Apt. 3*], he does convey—largely through his lavish, double-page spread paintings on shiny, slick paper contrasting dim, dark and a few bright colors—the richness of possibilities when many varied people live closely together.

Melinda Schroeder, in School Library Journal *(reprinted from the October, 1971, issue of* School Library Journal, *published by R. R. Bowker Co., a Xerox company; copyright © 1971 by Xerox Corporation), October, 1971, p. 104.*

One wonders about the necessity of the somber naturalism of words and pictures which tell a story of urban squalor . . . and of two lonely boys who stumble into a bittersweet friendship with a harmonica-playing blind man. [Keats'] subtle, shadowy paintings—done with deep, rich colors on large, elegantly glossy pages—say much more than is implied in [his] brief text. But some of the words are as needlessly sumptuous as the paper and paint. . . .

Ethel L. Heins, in The Horn Book Magazine *(copyright © 1971 by The Horn Book, Inc., Boston), December, 1971, p. 601.*

[*Apt. 3*] is not the Ezra Jack Keats of *The Snowy Day, Whistle for Willie* and *Goggles*. Gone are the bright contrasting gay colours, gone are the appealing 'identifiable' stories to be replaced by a sombreness of blurred illustration and outline which I found rather depressing. . . . No doubt the author is trying to convey the image of something beautiful and memorable amid the drabness of tenement life. . . .

Apt. 3 has prompted me to once again pose the basic question 'For whom do we create children's picture story books and why?' The first part is easier to answer than the second for today there are a great many motives other than for sheer enjoyment, and surely enjoyment should be high on anyone's list of criteria. There is little to enjoy in *Apt. 3*.

Edward Hudson, in Children's Book Review *(© 1973 Five Owls Press Ltd.), December, 1972, p. 179.*

OTHER CITATIONS

Zena Sutherland, in Bulletin of the Center for Children's Books, *December, 1971, pp. 58-9.*

The Junior Bookshelf, *April, 1972, p. 368.*

DREAMS (1974)

[Ezra Jack Keats'] skillful use of a combination of acrylic painting and collage has never been more effectively employed than in this quiet tale of a hot summer night in the city. The rich hues of sunset, the muted sky of night, and the brilliant blue of early morning form an impressive but not overwhelming background; and the evanescent nature of dreams is delightfully conveyed.

Beryl Robinson, in The Horn Book Magazine *(copyright © 1974 by the Horn Book, Inc., Boston), December, 1974, p. 684.*

How often it can be said of the many picture books published today that they lack a sense of atmosphere. This charge could never be levelled at Ezra Jack Keats however, for one of his many talents is that of being able to paint moods and temperatures. In *Dreams* he catches the hot, sultry atmosphere as night falls over the city tenements. Through the windows, we see the colours of the dreams of the children who live there. . . .

Ezra Jack Keats's involvement with life as it is for 'kids' in the streets of New York bears a remarkable parallel to Charles Keeping's sensitive picture books based on his impressions of situations in the East End of London. The use of short, sharp incident to illustrate a mood or sensation, an 'atmosphere' if you like, is also a common feature. In the hands of less skilled artists, the result would probably be a failure, but ability, combined with a true insight into the reaction of children from rough backgrounds in particular circumstances has resulted in a group of books which have added new dimensions to the world of picture books. *Dreams* is, perhaps, not the best example from Ezra Jack Keats, for the incident is too fleeting in its effect on the main character and the subject of the title is not really developed to any degree, but the artist's use of acryllic paint and collage to create mood is as marvellous as ever.

Edward Hudson, in Children's Book Review *(© 1975 Five Owls Press Ltd.), Spring, 1975, p. 12.*

OTHER CITATIONS

Zena Sutherland, in Bulletin of the Center for Children's Books, *January, 1975, p. 80.*

GOGGLES! (1969)

Peter, the charming small child of *Snowy Day*, is now old enough to encounter the power structure that exists in every urban neighborhood. . . . [Keats'] illustrations are lovely: big, clear, colorful pictures with a city background, excellent for using with a group. The story [*Goggles!*] is slight but realistic; a situation encountered by most small boys should evoke the pleasure of recognition and the added pleasure of vicarious triumph.

Zena Sutherland, in Bulletin of the Center for Children's Books *(© 1969 by the University of Chicago; all rights reserved), December, 1969, p. 61.*

Goggles! . . . is professional in the extreme as well as being rich in humanity and shrewd observation. Mr. Keats' technique depends less than usual on collage and is none the worse for that. His clever little story catches the excitement and urgency of the city slums, the terror of gangs and the warmth of friendship, all with the minimum of words.

The Junior Bookshelf, *February, 1971, p. 19.*

Those already familiar with the work of Ezra Jack Keats will know what to expect [in *Goggles!*] and perhaps not be disappointed. . . . Were it not for the skill of the author-artist and his sympathy for all things childish, [his] stories would have neither relevance nor interest. At times the background illustration tends to be rather theatrical, but generally, these minor-key . . . adventures are more directly satisfying than many of the social-conscience-torn extravaganzas of some artists.

Jeff Jackson, in Children's Book Review *(© 1971 by Five Owls Press Ltd.), February, 1971, p. 15.*

OTHER CITATIONS

Zena Sutherland, in Saturday Review, *October 18, 1969, p. 56.*

Lillian N. Gerhardt, in School Library Journal, *December 15, 1969, p. 66.*

HI, CAT! (1970)

The sixth book about Peter is really a story about Peter's friend Archie and the inquisitive, nondescript half-grown alley cat that tags after him and manages to make a shambles out of the boys' street carnival. . . . The text [of *Hi, Cat!*] is a preschooler's tall tale, but it provides an adequate framework for the author-artist's bold bright paintings of a lively city neighborhood and Peter's widening circle of friends.

Diane Farrell, in The Horn Book Magazine *(copyright © 1970 by The Horn Book, Inc., Boston), December, 1970, p. 606.*

Peter's back again [in *Hi, Cat!*] but Archie holds the stage, his Afro moderate, his glasses gleaming over a pert nose, and his sense of fun in firm control. . . . The pages are gay with color and movement, the children of the city neighborhood are engaging, and the story has a natural ease and humor that compensate for the slight story line.

Zena Sutherland, in Bulletin of the Center for Children's Books *(© 1971 by the University of Chicago; all rights reserved), January, 1971, p. 75.*

Ezra Jack Keats is a master of the contemporary scene, as much at ease in the back streets of New York as Charles

Keeping is in Joseph's Yard. What is more, he sees fun as well as beauty among the dustbins. . . . The little black and white cat is explosive. The tiny scrap of story is handled with great dexterity, in vivid and hilarious pictures and with a thread of unobtrusively perfect narrative.

The Junior Bookshelf, *June, 1971, p. 161.*

Ezra Jack Keats's illustrations are as skilful and dramatic as ever, but the story in this book leaves much to be desired. . . .

The superb pictures are richly coloured, and striking in form and movement; boldly patterned and textured across the landscape double-spreads. Some are theatrical, giving the feeling of stage sets for some juvenile *West Side Story*; but without the bones of a real plot it cannot add up to an entirely successful picture-story book for children.

John A. Cunliffe, in Children's Book Review *(© 1971 by Five Owls Press Ltd.), June, 1971, p. 83.*

OTHER CITATIONS

The Booklist, *October 15, 1970, p. 193.*

Nicholas Tucker, in The Times Literary Supplement, *July 2, 1971, p. 769.*

JENNIE'S HAT (1966)

[*Jennie's Hat* consists of a] slight story, but a riotously vernal and charming set of illustrations; the gay and colorful cumulations in collage-and-painting are exactly right for spring. . . . The move from fancy to fantasy is smooth enough, but the ending of the story, right on the heels of [the] climax, seems abrupt: Jennie walks home, the birds fly off with the nest of baby birds that had topped the hat, and Jennie and her mother wrap and box the beautiful hat.

Zena Sutherland, in Bulletin of the Center for Children's Books *(copyright 1966 by the University of Chicago; all rights reserved), June, 1966, p. 165.*

Although the gaily colored pictures tend to produce a slick magazine effect, the transformation of Jennie's plain hat into a marvelous pink-valentine, colored-egg, flower-bedecked creation topped with a nest of fledglings will no doubt entrance many little girls.

The Booklist and Subscription Books Bulletin *(© 1966 by the American Library Association), June 1, 1966, p. 960.*

OTHER CITATIONS

Alice Dalgliesh, in Saturday Review, *April 16, 1966, p. 49.*

JOHN HENRY: AN AMERICAN LEGEND (1965)

Like most retellings, Mr. Keats' narration [of *John Henry*] for 5-8's reads a little as if it were a translation in Basic English, padded out by footnotes. But the illustrations—big, bright, and powerful—make this a valuable book. Only read the original lyrics as you look at them.

The Christian Science Monitor *(reprinted by permission from* The Christian Science Monitor; *© 1965 The Christian Science Publishing Society; all rights reserved), May 6, 1965, p. 7B.*

In a huge book, John Henry seems to dwarf everyone, and the marbled backgrounds suggest the gloom of tunnels lit by flares or the flashes from hammers and drills. The finest work [Ezra Jack Keats] has done, both words and pictures catch the very essence of John Henry's fierce pride—a man to shame mere machines.

Margaret Sherwood Libby, in Book Week *(©* The Washington Post*), May 9, 1965 (Part 2), p. 30.*

[In *John Henry: An American Legend*] the prose is adequate; the illustrations are superb. The pages are bold and vibrant, all of the paintings being double-spread; the use of color here is even more impressive than it was in [Keats'] previous books. Because of the color and layout, the book lends itself particularly well to being used with a group of children.

Zena Sutherland, in Bulletin of the Center for Children's Books *(copyright 1965 by the University of Chicago; all rights reserved), July-August, 1965, p. 163.*

This picture-book presentation has vigor and excitement even though the exaggeration of the tall tale and the larger-than-life qualities of the folk hero are to a great extent missing, with the result that John Henry emerges more as a man of uncommon strength and courage than as a mighty folk hero.

The Booklist and Subscription Books Bulletin *(© 1965 by the American Library Association), November 1, 1965, p. 273.*

OTHER CITATIONS

George A. Woods, in The New York Times Book Review, *April 25, 1965, p. 26.*

Margaret Poarch, in Library Journal, *June 15, 1965, p. 2881.*

Helen Bogle, in The Horn Book Magazine, *August, 1965, p. 383.*

A LETTER TO AMY (1968)

[The] storm—lowering clouds, explosive lightning, wind and water and glistening sidewalks—is as vital [in *A Letter to Amy*], transforming the look and feel of the city, as the snow in *The Snowy Day*. . . . In a refreshing switch, the kids are dis-integrated: all but one are black, or rather varying shades of brown. Other apt touches: the lightning that crosses from the flaps to the endpapers, the mailbox as imposing as a Buckingham Palace guard. *In toto*, a top artist in top form.

Kirkus Service *(copyright © 1968 The Kirkus Service, Inc.), October 1, 1968, pp. 1106-07.*

In the everyday world children are often surrounded by crisis, sometimes the product of their own creation. Such a story is *Letter to Amy* by Ezra Jack Keats . . ., the fourth book about Peter . . . . The tale of a small boy inviting a girl to his birthday party is primarily played out in the city streets in the midst of a storm. Once again this artist-author proves his power to understand children and to see and re-create the beauty around him.

Anne Izard, in Book World *(© The Washington Post), November 3, 1968 (Part 2), p. 5.*

[In *A Letter to Amy*] Keats uses collage most effectively: thunderclouds roil the lowering skies and the yellow slicker below couldn't be brighter or more wet; lightning crackles across the pages. The birthday guests (in assorted colors) are realistically raucous, the story satisfying and low-key.

Zena Sutherland, in Saturday Review *(copyright © 1969 by Saturday Review, Inc.; reprinted with permission), January 18, 1969, p. 41.*

OTHER CITATIONS

Ethel L. Heins, in The Horn Book Magazine, *February, 1969, p. 41.*

George A. Woods, in The New York Times Book Review, *February 2, 1969, p. 26.*

***THE LITTLE DRUMMER BOY* (1968)**

Ezra Jack Keats has vividly illustrated, primarily in brilliant yellow, red, and orange, the lyric of a popular recent carol, *The Little Drummer Boy*. . . . These paintings, using occasional elements of paper collage, are an attractive and energetic visualization of the verses.

Margaret A. Dorsey, in School Library Journal *(reprinted from the October, 1968, issue of* School Library Journal, *published by R. R. Bowker Co., a Xerox company; copyright © 1968 by Xerox Corporation), October, 1968, p. 144.*

Separated from [the rhythm, melody and performance of the song] the words [of *The Little Drummer Boy*] are blunt and flat in their isolation. Mr. Keats has the burden of making music, as it were, in his illustrations. He plays a pretty tune in this account of the Wise Men honoring the Child and the poor boy offering his reverberating drum beat. But there are jarring notes: too much lavish color and patterns, multicolored skies, an El Greco pose, clichés of animals. What should be a subtle depiction inspiring awe and reverence is instead very close to a traditional spectacular.

George A. Woods, in The New York Times Book Review *(© 1968 by The New York Times Company; reprinted by permission), December 1, 1968, p. 74.*

OTHER CITATIONS

Kirkus Service, *September 15, 1968, p. 1042.*

Pamela Marsh in, The Christian Science Monitor, *November 7, 1968, p. B2.*

***PET SHOW!* (1972)**

Archie of *Hi Cat* (1970) is back [in *Pet Show!*] and so is the Keats of brightly patterned collage, exuberant thick-smudged paint, and general good will. . . . Even Keats' ubiquitous row of background doors appear in popsicle colors for the jubilant occasion.

Kirkus Reviews *(copyright © 1972 The Kirkus Service, Inc.), April 15, 1972, p. 473.*

Archie and Peter of *Goggles!* and *Hi Cat!* are back, participating in the excitement of a neighborhood pet show. The pictures in rich acrylic hues, less heavy than those in some of the author's recent books, extend a story which has an original twist. . . . The special touch in this happy, childlike picture book is that every pet gets an award.

Virginia Haviland, in The Horn Book Magazine *(copyright © 1972 by The Horn Book, Inc., Boston), August, 1972, p. 363.*

Everything embraced by the Keats formula for success is here [in *Pet Show!*]. There is brilliant colour on every page, his use of browns and reds being particularly masterly. There is the usual mixture of coloured and white children and the double-page spread of all the children with their pets queueing up for the judges, catches all the feeling and excitement of the event better than any camera's eye. All this combined with Ezra Jack Keats's understanding of the way the child's mind works, presents a picture book of rare quality and sensitivity.

Edward Hudson, in Children's Book Review *(© 1973 Five Owls Press Ltd.), December, 1972, p. 180.*

OTHER CITATIONS

The Booklist, *July 15, 1972, p. 1004.*

Zena Sutherland, in Bulletin of the Center for Children's Books, *September, 1972, p. 10.*

***PETER'S CHAIR* (1967)**

With artful artlessness, this very simple story of sibling dethronement suggests the behavior patterns of the resentful child but does so with an amused affection that robs the book of either minatory or purposive message. . . .

Zena Sutherland, in Saturday Review *(copyright © 1967 by Saturday Review, Inc.; reprinted with permission), June 17, 1967, p. 35.*

[In "Peter's Chair"] Peter runs away—but fortunately, not far. And fortunately, too, Ezra Jack Keats doesn't overdo the theme of jealousy—Peter's is only a mild case, which quite easily gives way to playfulness—besides, the boy is too big for that little chair anyway. If Keats overdoes anything in this otherwise attractive visual display, it's the use of flowered and textured wallpaper backgrounds.

George A. Woods, in The New York Times Book Review *(© 1967 by The New York Times Company; reprinted by permission), June 18, 1967, p. 30.*

The text [of *Peter's Chair*] is very slight but pertinent to the situation, and the drawings and artistic collage work in rich, warm colors are appealing and tellingly portray Peter's temporary qualms.

The Booklist and Subscription Books Bulletin *(© 1967 by the American Library Association), July 15, 1967, p. 1194.*

The familiar lesson [in *Peter's Chair*] is suggested rather than told, and little children enjoying the delightful pictures will have the satisfaction of working out the meaning for themselves and will feel themselves growing along with Peter. In the handsome collage drawings Peter is the same little boy who was the hero of *The Snowy Day* and *Whistle for Willie*. . . . A simple, tasteful, charming book.

Ruth Hill Viguers, in The Horn Book Magazine *(copyright © 1967, by The Horn Book, Inc., Boston), October, 1967, p. 582.*

Among later Keats books, *Peter's Chair* . . ., with its simple visual story, is notably successful. Yet a degree of sameness has set in; Keats the artist seems in need of more varied stimuli than Keats the originator of ideas can provide.

John Rowe Townsend, in his Written for Children: An Outline of English Language Children's Literature, *revised edition (copyright © 1965, 1974 by John Rowe Townsend; reprinted by permission of J.B. Lippincott Company), Lippincott, 1974, p. 316.*

OTHER CITATIONS

Kirkus Service, *March 1, 1967, p. 265.*

Publishers' Weekly, *May 22, 1967, p. 64.*

Patience M. Daltry, in The Christian Science Monitor, *August 31, 1967, p. 5.*

PSSST! DOGGIE— (1973)

A scraggly cat invites a shaggy dog to dance [in *Pssst! Doggie—*]. . . . Only the costume changes and attitudes struck by the colorfully cartooned animals give the clue to what they are up to; it's an almost wordless book except for the cat's invitation to the dance. There's no story here for pre-readers to tell from the pictures, and little likelihood that today's three- and four-year-olds could identify the patterned dances of yesterday.

Lillian N. Gerhardt, in School Library Journal *(reprinted from the September, 1973, issue of* School Library Journal, *published by R. R. Bowker Co., a Xerox company; copyright © 1973 by Xerox Corporation), September, 1973, p. 114.*

OTHER CITATIONS

Zena Sutherland, in Bulletin of the Center for Children's Books, *November, 1973, p. 46.*

SKATES! (1973)

The humor [in *Skates!*] derives from [the two dogs'] evident unsteadiness in an upright position, as they slip and tumble through the mobile, popsicle-colored pages with a long fringed purple scarf billowing in their wake. It ends on a note of typical Keatsian harmony, with the pair treating a quartet of dressed-up kittens to a doggy-back roller skate ride, and as long as you don't expect the sustaining warmth and personality of the Peter books (and can overlook the kittens' wide-eyed cuteness) it's a fetching enough free-wheeling diversion.

Kirkus Reviews *(copyright © 1973 The Kirkus Service, Inc.), October 15, 1973, p. 1153.*

The action and the situation [in *Skates!*] will probably appeal to pre-readers; the pictures are lively and colorful, the text weakened by the fact that after one double spill the dogs, bandaged, say, "I've had it!" and "Yeah! Who wants to skate anyway?" yet are somehow still on skates for the final episode.

Zena Sutherland, in Bulletin of the Center for Children's Books *(© 1974 by the University of Chicago; all rights reserved), April, 1974, p. 131.*

OTHER CITATIONS

Judith Kronick, in Library Journal, *February 15, 1974, p. 564.*

THE SNOWY DAY (1962)

[*The Snowy Day* contains] Mr. Keats's technically brilliant, artistically delightful illustrations. . . . Blocks of color, tinted drifts, smoky swirls, blue footprints, snow-flaked end papers, a checked dress, a tiled floor—every page has its little shock of pleasure for an adult—and, one hopes and expects, for the 3-6's who will recognize every thrill of Peter in the snow.

Roderick Nordell, in The Christian Science Monitor *(reprinted by permission from* The Christian Science Monitor; *© 1962, The Christian Science Publishing Society; all rights reserved), November 15, 1962, p. 2B.*

Most attractively illustrated, [*The Snowy Day* is] a read aloud picture book with only a few lines of text on each page. The writing is quiet and simple, describing a small boy's day as he plays alone in the snow, his return to home and a bath, and his anticipation when he wakes the next morning to see that there is a fresh fall of snow.

Zena Sutherland, in Bulletin of the Center for Children's Books *(copyright 1962 by the University of Chicago; all rights reserved), December, 1962, p. 60.*

[This] story is merely a simple narration of the little boy's joyous doings but it is enough to support the charming, unpretentious illustrations which are fresh and appealing in composition and color.

The Booklist and Subscription Books Bulletin *(© 1963 by the American Library Association), February 1, 1963, p. 450.*

The colours [in *The Snowy Day*] are bright and bold (bits of material, scraps of wool, and so on, were used to make the original pictures), but there is no attempt at a story, and the boy has no individual character whatever.

The Times Literary Supplement *(© Times Newspapers Ltd., 1967), November 30, 1967, p. 1152.*

[*The Snowy Day*] combines skilful collage technique and a universal experience. Peter happens to be coloured, not to be modish but possibly because it is more artistically satisfying in these snowy settings. This was one of Ezra Jack Keats' first experiments with collage and uses less texture than later books; his draughtsmanship is uncertain but his placement fine and he transmits both the feel of snow and of being a child in the snow. Making tracks, making snow-angels, sliding—it is all here.

The Junior Bookshelf, *December, 1967, p. 373.*

In one sense there is not much story [in *The Snowy Day*]; what is offered is an atmosphere, a discovery of the strange in the familiar; but in another sense this discovery *is* the story. *The Snowy Day* comes closer than most books to reconciling the two viewpoints on 'pure' picture-book art and story-telling art: to look at it is to perceive and grant at once that pictures are indeed arrangements of colours, lines, shapes, and textures, and that a picture-book page can provide an aesthetic experience for the reader.

John Rowe Townsend, in his Written for Children: An Outline of English Language Children's Literature, *revised edition (copyright © 1965, 1974 by John Rowe Townsend; reprinted by permission of J.B. Lippincott Company), Lippincott, 1974, pp. 315-16.*

OTHER CITATIONS

George A. Woods, in The New York Times Book Review, *November 11, 1962, p. 57.*

Alice Dalgliesh, in Saturday Review, *December 15, 1962, p. 27.*

Mabel B. Bell, in Library Journal, *January 15, 1963, p. 336.*

Virginia Haviland, in The Horn Book Magazine, *February, 1963, p. 51.*

WHISTLE FOR WILLIE (1964)

Using the same technique as he did in *The Snowy Day* . . ., with no less originality and somewhat more universality, Mr. Keats [in *Whistle for Willie*] gives eloquent expression to a child's solitary play. Peter is small, but he is all-important in his wall-and-sidewalk world. Vividly colored, exquisitely simple, his spacious environment is a place of texture, shape, and belonging. . . . The essence of joy in spontaneous activity and accidental discovery are for a child's sharing now—for his remembering later.

Priscilla L. Moulton, in The Horn Book Magazine *(copyright © 1964, by The Horn Book, Inc., Boston), October, 1964, pp. 490-91.*

[*Whistle for Willie* is a] delightful picture book. The story has a universal quality and a simplicity that are most appealing. . . . The illustrations are beguiling, especially the first picture of Peter: a small child leaning against a stop-light, his little brown face bored and wistful. The use of color and the sense of design are perhaps more impressive than in *The Snowy Day*.

Zena Sutherland, in Bulletin of the Center for Children's Books *(copyright 1964 by the University of Chicago; all rights reserved), November, 1964, p. 37.*

One has the enchanting impression that the words of [*Whistle for Willie*] are the lyrics to the music of the illustrations. . . . It is warm and simple and real, and what small child hasn't felt the wonder of that first whistle when it appears? Any child will feel it in this delightful book and love the feeling, as bright as the glowing modern pictures which tell the story—especially 3-7's.

Barbara S. McCauley, in The Christian Science Monitor *(reprinted by permission from* The Christian Science Monitor; *© 1964, The Christian Science Publishing Society; all rights reserved), November 5, 1964, p. 2B.*

OTHER CITATIONS

George A. Woods, in The New York Times Book Review, *September 13, 1964, p. 34.*

The Booklist and Subscription Books Bulletin, *October 15, 1964, p. 219.*

* * *

KONIGSBURG, E(laine) L(obl) 1930-

An American author-illustrator, E. L. Konigsburg won the Newbery Medal in 1968 for *From the Mixed-Up Files of Mrs. Basil E. Frankweiler* and was runner-up the same year for *Jennifer, Hecate, Macbeth, William McKinley, and Me, Elizabeth*. (See also *Contemporary Authors*, Vols. 21-22 and *Something About the Author*, Vol. 4.)

GENERAL COMMENTARY

Mrs. Konigsburg is far more than a skillful technician. . . . The situations in both [*From the Mixed-Up Files of Mrs. Basil E. Frankweiler* and *Jennifer, Hecate, Macbeth, William McKinley, and Me, Elizabeth*] are in tune with the personalities and imaginations of the children involved. The style in *Jennifer* . . . maintains the flavor of an articulate fifth-grader; in *From the Mixed-Up Files* . . . it has the dignity and wry humor of a well educated, literate woman, enlivened by her enjoyment of the discoveries she has made about the children's characters and personalities. The books are very much alive.

Ruth Hill Viguers, in A Critical History of Children's Literature, *revised edition, by Cornelia Meigs, Anne Thaxter Eaton, Elizabeth Nesbitt, and Ruth Hill Viguers, edited by Cornelia Meigs (copyright © 1969 by The Macmillan Co.), Macmillan, 1969, p. 575.*

***ABOUT THE B'NAI BAGELS* (1969)**

Mark narrates [*About the B'nai Bagels*] in the same wrily perceptive tone that made *Jennifer, Hecate* . . . (Atheneum, 1967) and *From the Mixed-Up Files of Mrs. Basil E. Frankweiler* (Atheneum, 1967) so appealing. Unfortunately, the author makes him strain too hard to dramatize the sterotyped comic character of his oh-so-Jewish mother and the other adults, and his story continuity is dissipated by the quantity of problems and intrigues. Fans of Mrs. Konigsburg will enjoy playing along with the B'nai Bagels, but this year her team isn't strong enough for any pennants in the Newbery/Caldecott League.

Elinor Cullen, in School Library Journal *(reprinted from the March, 1969, issue of* School Library Journal, *published by R. R. Bowker Co., a Xerox company; copyright © 1969 by Xerox Corporation), March, 1969, p. 183.*

The ups and downs of the Little League season are happily scrambled with observations on the crafty manipulations of one of the most endearing Jewish mothers in print, the difficulties of preparing for a Bar Mitzvah, the delightful embarrassment of having a girl friend—sort of—and the problem of an irksome relationship with one anti-Semitic team member. The last is deftly handled, as is Mark's encounter with the centerfold in a girlie magazine. Warm, humorous, and devastatingly real.

Zena Sutherland, in Saturday Review *(copyright © 1969 by Saturday Review, Inc.; reprinted with permission), March 22, 1969, p. 63.*

While ostensibly about Little League baseball, ["About the B'nai Bagels"] is really a book about growing up: about sorting out the difference between "right and wrong" and "fair and unfair." . . .

While unlike either of Konigsburg's previous books, this is as good, if not better. There may be children who won't know a bagel from a baseball: it won't matter. The universality of Mother Setzer assures an audience. So enough, already. Read and enjoy.

Dorothy M. Broderick, in The New York Times Book Review *(© 1969 by The New York Times Company; reprinted by permission), March 30, 1969, p. 30.*

Continuing to explore aspects of suburban life, [E. L. Konigsburg] has written a Little League baseball story, featuring, as chief character, a delightful example of that increasingly familiar literary heroine, the Jewish Mother. . . . Penetrating characterizations emerge by implication; and the author's unfailing humor and her deep understanding of human nature are as noticeable as ever. Yet the story, in scope and originality, does not equal her two previous books.

Ethel L. Heins, in The Horn Book Magazine *(copyright © 1969 by The Horn Book, Inc., Boston), June, 1969, p. 307.*

Whatever the merits of *About the B'nai Bagels* as a growing-up or a baseball story, from the Jewish point of view the Setzers represent a dying Jewishness. The understanding that gives meaning to folkways has long since leaked out of their lives. It is very significant that in [Isaac Bashevis] Singer's *A Day of Pleasure*, the older brother argues the relevance of Judaism in a modern society with his mother, while in Ms. Konigsburg's book, Spencer, who has nothing to do with anything Jewish, argues with his mother about the proper way to cook stuffed cabbage.

Eric A. Kimmel, in The Horn Book Magazine *(copyright © 1973 by The Horn Book, Inc., Boston), April, 1973, p. 179.*

OTHER CITATIONS

Laura Polla Scanlon, in Commonweal, *May 23, 1969, p. 297.*

***ALTOGETHER, ONE AT A TIME* (1971)**

The children in E. L. Konigsburg's "Altogether, One at a Time" may be short in stature, but they are long on mental acuity. As spies in the adult camp, they understand its inhabitants almost too well. . . .

Not all of the stories in this book are equally successful. . . . But even the weaker items in the collection have the virtue of respecting their audience enough to demand some mental work in the midst of the fun. Assistance is given by the illustrations of the four artists, whose various styles underline the individuality of the stories.

Georgess McHargue, in The New York Times Book Review *(© 1971 by The New York Times Company; reprinted by permission), May 30, 1971, p. 8.*

Told with economy, subtlety, and considerable humor, each story [in *Altogether, One at a Time*] conveys a child's perception of personal relationships; . . . best of all, Momma describes for her child her experiences of being bussed to school in Ohio and becoming recognized for her talent in art ("Momma was poor at that time, too, and she was as black then as she is now . . ."). The situations are deftly established, leading the bright child to clear insights.

Virginia Haviland, in The Horn Book Magazine *(copyright © 1971 by The Horn Book, Inc., Boston), August, 1971, p. 384.*

[These four] short stories . . . are varied in plot, alike in excellence, and united by the theme of compromise. . . . The compromise is not in action, but in the acceptance of the fact that life consists of good things and bad. In "Inviting Jason," a boy gets a new perspective on a handicapped child who comes to his birthday party and in "The Night of the Leonids" another child comes to a new understanding of his grandmother. "Camp Fat" is the only story with a fanciful twist; "Mamma at the Pearly Gates" has a wry humor in the story of an interracial friendship that develops from enmity, due to the acumen of the black child. [Konigsburg's] writing is deft and polished, the development of relationships subtly percipient.

Zena Sutherland, in Bulletin of the Center for Children's Books *(© 1971 by the University of Chicago; all rights reserved), September, 1971, p. 10.*

OTHER CITATIONS

Publishers' Weekly, *February 15, 1971, p. 79.*

Ruth Robinson, in Library Journal, *May 15, 1971, p. 1805.*

The Booklist, *July 1, 1971, p. 908.*

Amy Kellman, in Grade Teacher, *September, 1971, p. 153.*

***FROM THE MIXED-UP FILES OF MRS. BASIL E. FRANKWEILER* (1967)**

[This] is the kind of book our increasingly sophisticated pre-teens ask for, and it has almost all they hope for in a book: humor, suspense, intrigue, and their problems acknowledged seriously but not somberly. . . . Anybody rejecting this book on the grounds that resolute Claudia and canny Jamie should not be shown cleverly flouting museum rules or so apparently unconcerned over their parents' anguish would be denying their patrons the reading pleasure of an unusual book, extremely well written.

> *Elva Harmon, in* School Library Journal *(reprinted from the October, 1967, issue of* School Library Journal, *published by R. R. Bowker Co., a Xerox company; copyright © 1967 by Xerox Corporation), October, 1967, p. 175.*

[*From the Mixed-up Files of Mrs. Basil E. Frankweiler*] is told in the first person by a wealthy elderly lady—an art collector—as a letter to her lawyer. Such a description might put off the potential reader, but if it does the reader has missed not only one of the most original stories of many years but one of the most humorous and one with characters wholly alive.

> *Ruth Hill Viguers, in* The Horn Book Magazine *(copyright © 1967, by The Horn Book, Inc., Boston), October, 1967, p. 595.*

Claudia Kincaid deserves an award for launching the most imaginative protest movement of the year. Not only is she agitating for a sorely neglected cause—the fair treatment of big sisters—but she also chooses a unique form of demonstration: a secret live-in at New York's Metropolitan Museum of Art. . . . E. L. Konigsburg is a lively, amusing and painlessly educational storyteller.

> *Alice Fleming, in* The New York Times Book Review *(© 1967 by The New York Times Company; reprinted by permission), November 5, 1967 (Part 2), p. 44.*

All the plaudits that greeted the author's earlier book, *Jennifer, Hecate, Macbeth, William McKinley, and Me, Elizabeth*, once more are in order. [*From the Mixed-up Files of Mrs. Basil E. Frankweiler*] too is an exceptional story, notable for superlative writing, fresh humor, an original theme, clear-eyed understanding of children, and two young protagonists whom readers will find funny, real and unforgettable.

> *Polly Goodwin, in* Book World *(©* The Washington Post*), November 5, 1967 (Part 2), p. 22.*

[*From the Mixed-Up Files of Mrs. Basil E. Frankweiler*] is an engaging romp of a story, trembling on the brink of unbelievability—but not quite getting there, since the setting is real and the children seem no less so—a sturdy, rational, thoughtful pair.

> *Zena Sutherland, in* Bulletin of the Center for Children's Books *(copyright 1968 by The University of Chicago; all rights reserved), March, 1968, p. 112.*

The theme of helping the heroine to understand the basic value of her escapade—the need to seek answers to satisfy her own intellectual nature—is well developed [in *From the Mixed-up Files of Mrs. Basil E. Frankweiler*]. In addition, the nature of individuality and the need to develop one's strengths is presented dramatically in the sharply etched characterizations of the children.

> *John Gillespie and Diana Lembo, in their* Introducing Books: A Guide for the Middle Grades *(copyright © 1970 by Xerox Corp.), Bowker, 1970, p. 72.*

OTHER CITATIONS

Kirkus Service, *July 1, 1967, p. 740.*

The Booklist and Subscription Books Bulletin, *October 1, 1967, p. 199.*

John Allen, in The Christian Science Monitor, *November 2, 1967, p. B10.*

***(GEORGE)* (1970)**

Combining delightful conversations between Benjamin and George with a realistic portrayal of Benjamin's school experiences, home life with an impractical but understanding divorced mother and beloved obstreperous younger brother, and holiday visits with a remarried father, [*(George)*] reveals, with humor and discernment, the character and unique problems of a precocious but shy, insecure child.

> The Booklist *(© by the American Library Association), November 15, 1970, p. 269.*

George is Benjamin's alter ego, living inside him. . . . As [Ben's] schizophrenic symptoms become clear, he is sent to a psychiatrist—and the book ends on a cheerful note of recovery. Although the book deals with a serious problem, it is not somber. There is tenderness in Ben's relationships with his mother and brother, humor in the description of the sedate courtship, and contrast and action in a dramatic school problem in which Ben becomes involved. The characters are vividly portrayed, the writing style vigorous.

> *Zena Sutherland, in* Bulletin of the Center for Children's Books *(© 1971 by the University of Chicago; all rights reserved), February, 1971, p. 94.*

A collection of question-marks gather round any book by Mrs. Konigsburg and (*George*) is no exception. Is it writing of a high literary quality? Yes. Is there a strong story line? Yes. Are the characters credible and sensitively drawn? Yes. Are the books for children? Yes. Do children read and enjoy them? Er . . . Her originality, both in material and treatment, is indisputable—but may it not in fact prove her downfall? It appears to me to put her stories in a league of their own—one in which few children will even recognise the game which is being played. This is a pity, as Mrs. Konigsburg has some sharp comments to make on relationships, though the examples she uses to illustrate her case must, surely, remain incomprehensible even to those whose condition comes closest to it. . . .

I read this book in my own right as an adult and enjoyed its originality, sensitivity and wit, but for twelve-year-olds, fourteen-year-olds? The questions gather again.

Margot Petts, in Children's Book Review *(© 1971 by Five Owls Press Ltd.), June, 1971, pp. 89-90.*

In *The Mixed-up Files* Mrs. Konigsburg wrote as Mrs. Frankweiler, in *Jennifer, Hecate* . . . she wrote as Elizabeth. In *(George)* she writes as herself, and somehow her own voice is not as consistent or as beguiling as the voices of the personae she invented. . . .

Mrs. Konigsburg could not write a dull book if she tried, but it should be made clear that [*(George)*] is a book of much narrower appeal than [*The Mixed-up Files* or *Jennifer, Hecate*]: it is strictly for older readers, who are prepared to accept a foreign idiom, who will be intrigued by the notion of symbiosis, and who like being made to think.

The Times Literary Supplement *(© Times Newspapers Ltd., 1971), July 2, 1971, p. 765.*

(George) . . . deals with a serious problem, the schizoid personality, yet the book has high humor, tenderness, and a lively plot. The distinctive achievement of *(George)* is that it enables the reader to see that the child with psychological problems is not beyond the pale: Ben is human, intelligent, loving.

May Hill Arbuthnot and Zena Sutherland, in their Children and Books, *4th edition (copyright © 1947, 1957, 1964, 1972 by Scott, Foresman and Co.), Scott, Foresman, 1972, p. 452.*

OTHER CITATIONS

Kirkus Reviews, *October 15, 1970, p. 1148.*

Paul Heins, in The Horn Book Magazine, *December, 1970, pp. 619-20.*

Amy Kellman, in Grade Teacher, *February, 1971, p. 137.*

JENNIFER, HECATE, MACBETH, WILLIAM McKINLEY, AND ME, ELIZABETH (1967)

In the tart juvenile vernacular of a New York suburb, Elizabeth recounts the rigors and rewards of her apprenticeship [to master witch Jennifer]. . . . The sudden resolution of their relationship is unconvincing, and the adults are either satirized sharply or borne stoically, but Elizabeth's narrative has considerable pertinence and vitality. With the important difference that the girls do not hurt anyone, this raises some of the questions attending the reception of *Harriet the Spy*. On balance, we find it a fresh, funny spoof of the adult Establishment and the clichés of conjuring.

Kirkus Service *(copyright © 1967 Virginia Kirkus' Service, Inc.), February 1, 1967, pp. 131-32.*

[*Jennifer, Hecate, Macbeth, William McKinley, and Me, Elizabeth* contains] an original plot and [two] natural characters who are both outsiders in their suburban New York community. This is a funny and distinctively unpatronizing presentation of the relationship between a white girl and a Negro. . . . Despite the girls' careful preparations, Elizabeth flunks the witch test, and her failure culminates in a very satisfying way, allowing both girls to relax into a comfortable friendship the strength of which is developed without moralizing by contemporary characters in an entertaining tale that has staying power.

Elinor Cullen, in School Library Journal *(reprinted from the May, 1967, issue of* School Library Journal, *published by R. R. Bowker Co., a Xerox company; copyright © 1967 by Xerox Corporation), May, 1967, p. 58.*

]This is an] unusual and engrossing story about sustained imaginative play. . . . Elizabeth's acceptance of the fantasy finally disappears, but it is convincingly described; her descriptions of the events at school are amusing, especially her acid comments on another classmate: "Every grown-up in the whole U.S. of A. thinks that Cynthia is perfect." Jennifer contributes zealously to the demolition of that myth. [E. L. Konigsburg] treats with commendable irrelevance the fact that Jennifer is Negro and Elizabeth white: they are simply two little girls.

Zena Sutherland, in Bulletin of the Center for Children's Books *(copyright 1967 by the University of Chicago; all rights reserved), June, 1967, p. 155.*

In a fresh, lively story, skillfully expressed as though by a ten-year-old, Elizabeth recounts the trials and satisfactions of her apprenticeship and her association with her mysterious tutor. [Konigsburg's] writing is crisp, the narrative, which ends with the stormy transformation of pretend witches into ordinary friends, abounds in humor, and the two witches, especially inscrutable Jennifer, who is a Negro, are characters to be long remembered.

The Booklist and Subscription Books Bulletin *(© 1967 by the American Library Association), June 1, 1967, p. 1048.*

[*Jennifer, Hecate, Macbeth, William McKinley, and Me, Elibabeth* is a] book to make you laugh out loud, yet beneath its gaiety it handles the passionate attachment between the girls with delicacy and truth. Like the best adult novels, it illuminates a situation we can all recognize. Strongly recommended.

The Times Literary Supplement *(© Times Newspapers Ltd., 1968), October 3, 1968, p. 1112.*

OTHER CITATIONS

Ruth Hill Viguers, in The Horn Book Magazine, *April, 1967, pp. 206-07.*

Publishers' Weekly, *April 10, 1967, p. 80.*

A PROUD TASTE FOR SCARLET AND MINIVER (1973)

Viewing Eleanor [of Aquitaine] as a "modern" heroine doesn't make for a very subtle appreciation of the woman of her times, but it does create a sparkling framework for the old story in which John is the villain and Eleanor and Henry's love affair survives perversely through her fifteen years of imprisonment. . . . [Much] of the credit for her salvation must go to Konigsburg's diffuse but energetic delight in words—a quality so rare in juvenile literature that even Henry's arrival [in Heaven] on the arms of Winston Churchill and Abraham Lincoln can be forgiven.

Kirkus Reviews *(copyright © 1973 The Kirkus Service, Inc.), July 1, 1973, p. 685.*

One of the most fresh, imaginative, and deft biographies to come along in a long, long time, this story of Eleanor of Aquitaine is unusual both in format and in the sophisticated vitality of the writing style. . . . The style of telling is beautifully adapted to each speaker, the biography of the amazing Eleanor is vivid, the historical complexities of French and English history are made lucid, and—bonus—[E. L. Konigsburg's] wit is both delightful in itself and eminently suitable for the volatile, shrewd heroine.

Zena Sutherland, in Bulletin of the Center for Children's Books *(© 1973 by the University of Chicago; all rights reserved), September, 1973, pp. 10-11.*

Konigsburg fans will be disappointed in [*A Proud Taste for Scarlet and Miniver*, an] out-of-sync approach to history as fiction. . . . Konigsburg's writing and treatment of history is witty and urbane but blithely undercuts the importance of the era. Middle graders, without a better foundation in 12th-Century history than most American curriculums offer, will be confused by the catalog of events, will lose track of who's telling which part of the story, and may not recognize any of the cast except Lincoln and Churchill—who escort Henry to Heaven on his day of judgment.

Alice Miller Bregman, in School Library Journal *(reprinted from the October, 1973, issue of* School Library Journal, *published by R. R. Bowker Co., a Xerox company; copyright © 1973 by Xerox Corporation), October, 1973, p. 117.*

With great ingenuity and wit [E. L. Konigsburg] has fashioned a novel based on the life of Eleanor of Acquitaine and has succeeded in making history amusing as well as interesting. . . . The characterization is superb—not only of Eleanor, who dominates the Tales, but of aesthetic Abbot Suger, who was responsible for the invention of Gothic architecture, and of William the Marshal, who always backed the winning Plantagenet. . . . The [author's] black-and-white drawings are skillfully as well as appropriately modeled upon medieval manuscript illuminations and add their share of joy to the book.

Paul Heins, in The Horn Book Magazine *(copyright © 1973 by The Horn Book, Inc., Boston), October, 1973, pp. 466-67.*

Perhaps it would be best to say that "A Proud Taste for Scarlet and Miniver" is the portrait of a remarkable woman, a portrait as selective, fast-paced, idiosyncratic and colorful as a slide show produced by Eleanor herself. . . . Though the anachronisms remind us of [T. H. White's] "The Sword in the Stone," the book's use of fantasy is not nearly so creative or its narrative power so great. As a highly personal view of a vivid woman, it is at its worst mildly irritating and at its best good and provocative fun.

Georgess McHargue, in The New York Times Book Review *(© 1973 by The New York Times Company; reprinted by permission), October 14, 1973, p. 8.*

[In *A Proud Taste for Scarlet and Miniver*] Eleanor is vibrant, dynamic, and headstrong—a delight to read about—except that the biographical flow is interrupted by flimsy celestial scenes. . . . Each tale, smooth in itself, is followed by a "back in heaven" scene in which the dynamics of Eleanor's personality are sacrificed to artificial conversations. Still, in spite of structural gimmickry, the corporeal Eleanor is eminently worth the readers' while.

The Booklist *(© American Library Association 1973), November 1, 1973, p. 292.*

[E. L. Konigsburg] unravels her tale of Eleanor of Aquitaine by means of a rather mod Chaucerian device. Eleanor, her mother-in-law, an abbot, and a Knight sit on a cloud in heaven, waiting for Henry's ascendance and whiling the time away by telling stories, like Canterbury pilgrims. . . .

Miss Konigsburg's crisp prose and wealth of anecdotes make this complex era—usually remembered as a list of names and dates—come so alive that the reader will feel he is laughing at the same jokes and sharing the same frustrations and sorrows of 700 years ago.

And Eleanor—ambitious, intelligent, energetic—will delight youngsters who crave an emancipated heroine. . . . "A Proud Taste" is a good example of how enthralling history can be in the hands of an imaginative writer.

Jennifer Farley Smith, in The Christian Science Monitor *(reprinted by permission from* The Christian Science Monitor*; © 1974 The Christian Science Publishing Society; all rights reserved), May 1, 1974, p. F1.*

There is no need to avoid the anachronisms which are the nightmare of the historical novelist, for Up in Heaven the actors are also audience of everything which has gone on Below. Apart from this rather negative advantage, it is difficult to see much benefit in Mrs. Konigsburg's device, and although Eleanor's story is one worth telling over and over again it might just as well have been told straight.

The Junior Bookshelf, *April, 1975, p. 119.*

[The] anachronisms [in *A Proud Taste for Scarlet and Miniver*] are at times most useful and pertinent, enabling Mrs Konigsburg to sum up historical events in a way which preserves the past, yet is wholly comprehensible now.

[The] gap between Eleanor and Mrs Konigsburg's previous heroines is perhaps not after all so great. Eleanor as seen here is nothing if not the prototype of Claudia, Jennifer, et al. The Queen who set her sons against her husband and dressed as a man to escape him, eight centuries ago, would understand and be understood by Claudia with her equally jaundiced view of family life. The real and fictional characters have, too, a certain ruthlessness in common. Eleanor's of course is on a much larger scale—her somewhat cavalier disregard for human life is not glossed over.

Penelope Farmer, in The Times Literary Supplement *(© Times Newspapers Ltd., 1975), April 4, 1975, p. 370.*

OTHER CITATIONS

Publishers' Weekly, *August 6, 1973, p. 65.*

Ethna Sheehan, in America, *December 1, 1973, p. 431.*

L

LEAR, Edward 1812-1888

An English artist who specialized in drawings of birds and animals, Edward Lear is best remembered for writing and illustrating his nonsense verse and limericks. He created such well-loved characters as the Jumblies, the Dong with the luminous nose, and the Owl and the Pussy-cat.

GENERAL COMMENTARY

Lear's was an odd, maybe a unique genius. His brand of Nonsense was different from that of 'Lewis Carroll', and we should perhaps not compare them. For Lear at his best seems to have been catching a real echo from early childhood, and his later Nonsense poems prove that he was a greater poet than 'Lewis Carroll'; but the discoverer of Wonderland was far cleverer, more skilful, and had an infinitely finer imagination. 'The mystical Edward Lear, the one who wore the runcible hat, is one of the great masters of English literature,' wrote G. K. Chesterton—and 'The Dong with the Luminous Nose' goes far to substantiate this claim . . . but it is not a good piece of Nonsense. Lear got much nearer to the essence of childhood in the best of his limericks, and fused that essence with his poetic inspiration best of all in the superb simplicity of 'The Owl and the Pussy Cat' and 'The Pobble who has no Toes'.

Roger Lancelyn Green, in his Tellers of Tales: British Authors of Children's Books from 1800 to 1964, *revised edition (copyright 1946, © 1965 by Edmund Ward, Publishers, Ltd.), Kaye & Ward Ltd., 1965, p. 44.*

Lear coined a vocabulary, and he did so with gusto. I think it is in his gusto that he differs most from [Lewis] Carroll. One never feels with Lear that his nonsense is an intellectual recreation; one never has the sense of contrivance. . . . And yet what art, deliberate or natural, lies behind those apparently casual verses! Lear is the master of the incompatible, the wildly impossible. . . . He is master, too, of the totally unexpected: of the line which catches the reader unawares. . . .

Lear understands every kind of humour: the humour of words and the humour of situation; he can be dry, rumbustious, zany, slapstick, and, sometimes, macabre. Occasionally he anticipated—and parodies in advance—the 'automatic writing', the irrational inspiration of the Surrealists. . . .

Lear is often compared with his contemporary in nonsense, Lewis Carroll; but a world divides them. Carroll approached his nonsense by way of logic and mathematics, Lear approached it through his paintings and through poetry, and—which is most important—through life itself. Lear was intensely human—and his humanity, warm and honest and spontaneous, cannot ever fail to be endearing.

Joanna Richardson, in her Edward Lear *(© Joanna Richardson 1965), Longmans, Green, 1965, pp. 34-6.*

[Because he thought himself to be physically grotesque] Edward Lear . . . peopled the world of his imagination with figures even more stricken than he: sappy, goofy Simple Simons—aspects of himself, as of everyone else. That is the secret of their universality. . . .

Death is a leading topic of Lear's limericks. . . . Here . . . are the baked people, the choked people, the smashed people. The comic violence is that of our frenetic film cartoons. Lear's limericks must have brought into Victorian parlours welcome release of licensed rudeness. And the ultimate rudeness is violent death. Also, in his limericks Lear, like all of us, is trying to get used to death, to dull its sting. . . .

[Of] all his poems, [the limericks] are by far the most spontaneous. They must have emerged from his subconscious virtually unedited. Not nearly all of them are alarming or dire. Some convey the deep charm he must have had. . . .

Edward Lear had genius. His creations have a strange dignity. It is perhaps only by the—for us—fortunate circumstance of the poet's despair and self-deprecation that his intense poetic phantasms should have emerged humbly as owls and pussycats, ducks and kangaroos. They form an indispensable part of English poetry; and because of them the days of Lear's pilgrimage are unlikely to vanish.

Alison White, "With Birds in his Beard" (1966), in Only Connect: Readings on Children's Literature, *edited by Sheila Egoff, G. T. Stubbs, and L. F. Ashley (© Oxford University Press [Canadian Branch], 1969), Oxford University Press, 1969, pp. 281, 283-85.*

[Far] better than any sentimentalist, [Edward Lear] could apparently meet children on their own ground. . . . As [his] limericks care not a rap for morality or manners, so [his] pictures give not a fig for Art. Lear's nonsense drawings have the directness of a young child's and also have the controlled line of the practiced draughtman. . . . [Lear's] verbal associations may have [risen] up from a Freudian unconscious; but the line that gave them form was directed by an artist who knew exactly what he was doing.

Ruth S. Freeman, in her Children's Picture Books: Yesterday and Today *(copyright 1967 by Ruth S. Freeman; reprinted by permission of Century House, Watkins Glen, N.Y.), Century House, 1967, p. 99.*

Lear's verses were as free from any attempt to sugar coat a moral as was Lewis Carroll's prose. . . . [His] nonsense created a world of its own, different from the real world but a logical and consistent world according to the laws of nonsense. . . . All of [Lear's books] were illustrated by [his] enormously original, imaginative, and hilarious drawings, with their apparent naiveté produced by the skillful hand of a master.

Anne Thaxter Eaton, in A Critical History of Children's Literature, *revised edition, by Cornelia Meigs, Anne Thaxter Eaton, Elizabeth Nesbitt, and Ruth Hill Viguers, edited by Cornelia Meigs (copyright © 1969 by The Macmillan Co.), Macmillan, 1969, pp. 198-99.*

Lear is an excellent craftsman. His meters are exact, his rhymes neat and musical, and his verse has a pleasant sound even at its wildest. Much of it is decidedly melodious. Undoubtedly part of the appeal of "The Owl and the Pussy Cat" for young children is its melody. They chant it happily and linger over the refrains.

Children also like the ridiculous and eccentric characters in these verses and are especially entertained by the mad troop that populates the limericks.

May Hill Arbuthnot and Zena Sutherland, in their Children and Books, *4th edition (copyright © 1947, 1957, 1964, 1972 by Scott, Foresman and Co.), Scott, Foresman, 1972, p. 333.*

With [Edward] Lear, freedom made its appearance in children's literature. . . . His whimsical and rather provocative rhymes . . . openly [oppose] didacticism and boring explanations; [they have] the candour and vivacity of the best nursery rhymes and an inexhaustible fund of inventiveness. . . . The mechanical, ritualistic nature of [his rhyme] casts a spell over the reader and conjures up a completely distorted world which is, nonetheless, perfectly organized and absolutely inevitable; a world where things are what they are because words make them so; . . . once the words have been pronounced one can no more escape from the spell than one can escape from a dream.

Isabelle Jan, in her On Children's Literature, *edited by Catherine Storr with a preface by Anne Pellowski (translation copyright © Allen Lane, 1973), Schocken, 1974, p. 58.*

Lear was a poet, in a sense in which the word cannot quite be applied to Lewis Carroll. As Lear's biographer, Vivien Noakes, truly says, his development as a nonsense writer 'is increasingly away from pure nonsense into sad and moving poetry.' There is an imaginative richness, but in the later work also a growing melancholy, in Lear's stories of wandering and travel in distant, exotic, and surely unhappy lands. One would not wish to spend one's summer holidays roving with the forsaken Dong across the great Gromboolian plain, or among the hills of the Chankly Bore.

John Rowe Townsend, in his Written for Children: An Outline of English Language Children's Literature, *revised edition (copyright © 1965, 1974 by John Rowe Townsend; reprinted by permission of J.B. Lippincott Company), Lippincott, 1974, p. 138.*

***ABC* (written c. 1871)**

Printed on cream paper, with black ink, and with borders and the letters of the alphabet in red or blue on alternating pages, [*ABC*] is a dignified volume. Its appeal will be primarily for the countless adults who number among Lear's loyal fans and to large libraries. Children will find the script difficult to decipher, though some may enjoy trying. The verses, repeated at the end in clear readable type, are delightful and timeless.

Harriet B. Quimby, in School Library Journal *(reprinted from the May, 1965, issue of* School Library Journal, *published by R. R. Bowker Co., a Xerox company; copyright © 1965 by Xerox Corporation), May, 1965, pp. 93-4.*

[This is a] recently discovered Lear manuscript, here published for the first time [by McGraw-Hill], with each page having a verse in script and an illustration; the alphabet verses are repeated in type at the back of the book. Not particularly good as an alphabet-learning device, but enjoyable nonsense indeed. An example of the light humor and the style: "X was King Xerxes Who most of all Turks is Renowned for his fashion of fury and passion—X!—Shocking old Xerxes!"

Zena Sutherland, in Bulletin of the Center for Children's Books *(copyright 1965 by the University of Chicago; all rights reserved), May, 1965, p. 131.*

[Edward Lear's] verses and pen-and-ink sketches [in *ABC*] are a joy, and the handwriting which gives the volume a distinctive flavor is legible enough for children who are able to read script. The verses are also printed in regular type at the back of the book. For adults, a fascinating period piece; for children, an entertaining book of rhymes.

The Booklist and Subscription Books Bulletin *(© 1965 by the American Library Association), June 1, 1965, pp. 958-59.*

OTHER CITATIONS

Virginia Kirkus' Service, *March 15, 1965, p. 307.*

Priscilla L. Moulton, in The Horn Book Magazine, *August, 1965, p. 394.*

***THE DONG WITH A LUMINOUS NOSE* (written c. 1877)**

Edward Lear's lonely *Dong With a Luminous Nose* [Scott, 1969] . . . is newly captured in evocative drawings by Edward Gorey—though Lear's own drawings cannot be improved on. But Mr. Gorey is clearly the only modern illustrator to do justice to the Victorian master.

William Jay Smith, in Book World *(© The* Washington Post*), May 4, 1969 (Part 2), p. 24.*

[*The Dong with a Luminous Nose* (Scott, 1969), a] companion volume to *The Jumblies* (Scott, 1968) written in Lear's style of distinguished nonsense, tells of a creature called the Dong who falls in love with a Jumbly girl. . . . Edward Gorey's pen-and-ink drawings are beautifully eerie and enforce the mood of the story.

Laurie Rand, in School Library Journal *(reprinted from the September, 1969, issue of* School Library Journal, *published by R. R. Bowker Co., a Xerox company; copyright © 1969 by Xerox Corporation), September, 1969, p. 157.*

***THE FIRST ABC* (written c. 1871)**

For each letter the verso page gives a Lear verse in addition to upper and lower case letters (although the title page ignores Edward Lear) and on the recto page, two or three drawings of objects or creatures whose names begin with that letter. In a few instances, two letters are given on a page. No poem for X, Y, or Z, and the four-line verse is dropped on the I-and-J page for Lear's "I was once a bottle of ink . . .". The illustrations are pleasant, the whole as useful as any other alphabet book but far from outstanding.

Zena Sutherland, in Bulletin of the Center for Children's Books *(© 1972 by the University of Chicago; all rights reserved), February, 1972, pp. 93-4.*

***LIMERICKS BY LEAR* (written c. 1846-1861)**

Though [Lois Ehlert's] illustrations may be confusing to some children, they bear enough resemblance to reality for most to find them as amusing as [Edward Lear's] limericks. Since the illustrations are more readily identifiable when seen from a distance, the book will be very useful for storytelling.

School Library Journal *(reprinted from the September, 1965, issue of* School Library Journal, *published by R. R. Bowker Co., a Xerox company; copyright © 1965 by Xerox Corporation), September, 1965, p. 142.*

The casual nonsense of Lear's limericks has been well served by [Lois Ehlert's] deceptively casual looking blobs of color to represent the nonsense people and animals, with overlays of stamping and some features drawn in. The limericks [in this 1965 World edition] have been reduced to their original four line form and one to a page with these measurements leaves an unconscionable amount of white space around the text.

Virginia Kirkus' Service *(copyright © 1965 Virginia Kirkus' Service, Inc.), September 1, 1965, p. 899.*

***NONSENSE BOOK* (written c. 1846-1861)**

In spite of the big colorful pictures by Tony Palazzo, drawn especially for his selection of eighteen Lear rhymes [for *Nonsense Book* (Garden City, 1956)], it is still the rhymes themselves that hold most of the enchantment. Perhaps any new edition of a classic is always something of a disappointment to hard and fast fans. While Mr. Palazzo's pictures are lush and gay and sometimes witty, one misses the dry, wizened quality of some of the older drawings, a certain something that carried out the nonsense rather than prettying it up for contemporary tastes.

Virginia Kirkus' Service, *August 1, 1956, p. 516.*

[*Nonsense Book* contains seventeen] of Lear's poems, limericks, and an alphabet selected and interpreted in pictures by [Tony Palazzo]. While many will prefer the original Lear drawings which so aptly mirror the nonsense of the verses, contemporary young children will undoubtedly enjoy the entertaining four-color pictures in this oversized book.

The Booklist and Subscription Books Bulletin *(© 1956 by the American Library Association), September 15, 1956, p. 52.*

***THE OWL AND THE PUSSY-CAT* (written c. 1868)**

The gay pink jacket and the small size will immediately attract the youngest child to this fresh new edition [Doubleday, 1962] of an old favorite [*The Owl and The Pussy-Cat*]. Mr. du Bois uses bright hues of all the colors of the rainbow for his lively interpretation. The two pictures of the cat rowing—an immaculate gray cat with blue eyes and neckribbon to match, against a background of blue-sky—are particularly appealing.

Margaret Warren Brown, in The Horn Book Magazine *(copyright, 1962, by The Horn Book, Inc., Boston), April, 1962, p. 166.*

One look into the coldly calculating blue eyes of Mr. du Bois's Pussy Cat makes one marvel that the henpecked Owl does not remember he has wings. Children will probably not get the fine points of all this, and find it good fun. Color is skilfully used to suggest more colors than four, but the book seems too small for its pictures.

William Lipkind, in Saturday Review *(copyright © 1962 by Saturday Review, Inc.; reprinted with permission), May 12, 1962, p. 36.*

OTHER CITATIONS

Roderick Nordell, in The Christian Science Monitor, *May 10, 1962, p. 2B.*

Thomas Lask, in The New York Times Book Review, *May 13, 1962 (Part 2), p. 37.*

***THE QUANGLE WANGLE'S HAT* (written c. 1877)**

Helen Oxenbury has an attractive version of "The Quangle Wangle's Hat" (Watts, [1969]).

All her beasts have amiable, slightly balmy and dubious faces and her Dong with the luminous nose is done in something approximating a cross between paisley and psychedelic dayglo.

> *Nora L. Magid, in* The New York Times Book Review *(© 1969 by The New York Times Company; reprinted by permission), November 9, 1969 (Part 2), p. 65.*

In this delectable picture book the humor of Lear's nonsense verse about the Quangle Wangle who let all manner of strange creatures build their homes in his 102-foot wide beaver hat is happily matched by Oxenbury's highly imaginative page-filling colored illustrations.

> The Booklist *(© by the American Library Association), January 1, 1970, p. 566.*

TWO LAUGHABLE LYRICS (written c. 1877)

The Quangle Wangle's Hat and *The Pobble Who Had No Toes* are nicely complemented by Paul Galdone's gaily colored drawings which add just the right humorous touch. . . . Children will find the pictures as truly funny as the made-up words and ridiculous situations in the two verses. This should create an audience for Lear that might not have discovered the original.

> School Library Journal *(reprinted from the April, 1966, issue of* School Library Journal, *published by R. R. Bowker Co., a Xerox company; copyright © 1966 by Xerox Corporation), April, 1966, p. 84.*

Galdone's diverting colored drawings amusingly portray the action and capture the flavor of Lear's nonsense verses. The fact that the two "laughable lyrics," one printed on green pages and the other on lavender, are bound together back to back in reverse order adds to the fun of the book.

> The Booklist and Subscription Books Bulletin *(© 1966 by the American Library Association), July 15, 1966, p. 1088.*

THE TWO OLD BACHELORS (written c. 1862)

[Though] not so well-known as others of Edward Lear's narrative nonsense, [*The Two Old Bachelors* (McGraw, 1962)] should certainly now reach a wide audience. The book is both beautiful and very funny. The drawing of the Old Bachelors climbing the "nearly purpledicular crags" to reach the old Sage needed for their Stuffin' is characteristic of [Paul Galdone's] way of having his own fun even while perfectly interpreting Lear's nonsense.

> *Ruth Hill Viguers, in* The Horn Book Magazine *(copyright © 1962, by The Horn Book, Inc., Boston), October, 1962, p. 483.*

[*The Two Old Bachelors*] isn't truly a horror story—though it builds up towards being one—because the two old bachelors tumbling from a high cliff remain perfectly intact, and the mouse they intend to eat escapes. Paul Galdone's pictures add to the humor of the rhyme and give it a suitably strange atmosphere. This is really above the picture-book age, and is wisely not printed in large, picture-book size.

> *Alice Dalgliesh, in* Saturday Review *(copyright © 1962 by Saturday Review, Inc.; reprinted with permission), November 10, 1962, p. 37.*

OTHER CITATIONS

The Times Literary Supplement, *November 28, 1963, p. 972.*

WHIZZ! (written c. 1846-1861)

Janina Domanska's sharp, patchwork pictures unite six of Lear's limericks in a cumulative farce as a narrow bridge fills up with the old man in a tree with his bee, a second old man with a cow, others with a bird in a bush, a bear, and eight birds in a beard, and finally a young lady in blue upon whose "Whizzz!" the bridge breaks and the whole company heads for a ducking. Lear's words are upstaged by all the gratuitous visual frenzy, but some will find the elaboration diverting.

> Kirkus Reviews *(copyright © 1973 The Kirkus Service, Inc.), April 15, 1973, p. 453.*

The merry nonsense of six of Edward Lear's familiar limericks has been matched with drawings [by Janina Domanska] as delightfully wacky as the verse and embodied in a blithe procession that marches across the arch of a bridge. . . . The action takes place against a backdrop composed of stylized hills, rectangular fields, and neat row houses, whose windows gradually fill with cheering spectators. The inventive humor of the mini-drama adds a new dimension to the distinguished body of the artist's work. An exuberant and joyous expression.

> *Beryl Robinson, in* The Horn Book Magazine *(copyright © 1973 by The Horn Book, Inc., Boston), August, 1973, pp. 370-71.*

Six limericks by Edward Lear are used as a continuous text, the humor echoed by the details of the small figures marching, as they are introduced, across a long, narrow bridge. The background is somewhat stylized, although this has less of the geometric quality than Domanska has shown in earlier books. As the sixth character joins the line, the bridge collapses. . . . The illustrations bring a measure of cohesion to the separate verses, and the collapse of the bridge gives a dramatic focus to a bit of gay nonsense.

> *Zena Sutherland, in* Bulletin of the Center for Children's Books *(© 1973 by the University of Chicago; all rights reserved), September, 1973, pp. 11-12.*

OTHER CITATIONS

Publishers' Weekly, *April 30, 1973, p. 55.*

The Booklist, *June 1, 1973, p. 948.*

Ruth M. McConnell, in Library Journal, *September 15, 1973, p. 2641.*

Lois Belfield Watt, in Childhood Education, *October, 1973, p. 30.*

* * *

L'ENGLE, Madeleine 1918-

Madeleine L'Engle, an American, won the Newbery Medal in 1963 for her space fantasy *A Wrinkle in Time*. She is also widely known for her family stories about the Austins. (See also *Contemporary Authors*, Vols. 1-4, rev. ed., and *Something About the Author*, Vol. 1.)

GENERAL COMMENTARY

Madeleine L'Engle is a curiously-gifted, curiously-learned, curiously-imperfect writer. Her novels for young people seem to me to be full of contradictions. They are so often exciting and stylishly written, yet so often complicated beyond endurance or unintentionally comic or embarrassing. . . .

And yet I find her an extraordinarily interesting writer. She aims high, and will risk a few misses for the sake of the hits. She is not afraid of strong feeling. . . . [Her books are] faulty but intriguing, irritating but likeable, unsatisfactory in various ways but stimulating to the mind and the emotions. They belong, I believe, in the small, frustrating but fascinating category of good bad books.

John Rowe Townsend, in his A Sense of Story: Essays on Contemporary Writing for Children *(copyright © 1971 by John Rowe Townsend; reprinted by permission of J. B. Lippincott Company), Lippincott, 1971, pp. 120, 125-26.*

THE ARM OF THE STARFISH (1965)

Taking sides (right vs. wrong) and teaming up provides both the suspense and the philosophical tug-of-war in this imaginative story of a 16 year old high school graduate who unwittingly becomes involved in international intrigue. . . . As the conflict becomes more pronounced, the story gets weaker. The personal probe is valid although many may disagree with the answers, and it accompanies some solidly detailed, excitingly sustained adventure.

Virginia Kirkus' Service, *January 1, 1965, p. 12.*

The plot [of *The Arm of the Starfish*] moves with such speed and variety, and emotions are so tautly stretched, that if there are weaknesses, the reader is much too occupied to be aware of them. At the end he might wish that the restraint and subtlety had held to the last page. . . .

The story lasts beyond the reading and can be turned to again and again because it is based on the conviction of the power in humanity's essential yearning to build for the future. Being so based, it can give courage as well as enjoyment.

Ruth Hill Viguers, in The Horn Book Magazine *(copyright © 1965, by The Horn Book, Inc., Boston), April, 1965, p. 161.*

Tense, tricky, well-plotted, "The Arm of the Starfish" has all the stuff of which adult spy novels are made. From the moment you meet the 16-year-old hero, until the conclusion of his exotic adventures, the story moves like a missile to target. The author quickly envelops you in an ominous atmosphere; opening with a foggy scene at Kennedy International Airport, she drops the magic name, Lisbon—that capital of intrigue.

Robert Hood, in The New York Times Book Review *(© 1965 by The New York Times Company; reprinted by permission), April 18, 1965, p. 16.*

The Arm of the Starfish entertains with the intriguing story of a serious-minded boy who discovers the almost overwhelming responsibility of the scientist but remains sensitive to the warm and personal love of those close to him. . . . The motives of most characters seem real. Admirable characters are individualized, but undesirable characters are often stereotypes of the fanatic or psychopathic international agent. But, realistically, not all the "good guys" win nor do all the "bad guys" come to justice. . . . The serious theme is borne lightly by a fascinating array of people, exotic settings, lively plot action, and a familiar, recurring motif.

Stuart Huff, in English Journal *(copyright, 1965, by the National Council of Teachers of English), May, 1965, p. 457.*

OTHER CITATIONS

Julia Losinski, in Library Journal, *February 15, 1965, p. 974.*

Zena Sutherland, in Bulletin of the Center for Children's Books, *March, 1965, p. 105.*

CAMILLA (1965)

As in her other books, [Madeleine L'Engle] has incorporated in her characters a deep concern for matters of the conscience—life and death, God, war, responsibility, love, family relationships. Camilla undergoes a painful process of self reckoning as she approaches maturity from a sheltered youth. . . . Camilla's separate reactions to her parents are honestly described, and poignantly realized, but then made puzzling as she tries to fit them into the scheme of life in her extended discussions with Frank. The introspective passages are lengthy; while they are obviously sincere they seem more author-imposed than true to character, and the relating of personal problems to abstractions does both less than justice. An earnest, not entirely successful effort, but one that merits selection attention.

Virginia Kirkus' Service, *July 15, 1965, pp. 688-89.*

[There] are few novels that present with so much wisdom and compassion some of the tragic realities affecting people of widely different ages and backgrounds. *Camilla* sidesteps nothing that belongs in the story of the growing-up in present-day New York City of a highly intelligent child of attractive, wealthy, and sadly mismated parents. . . . The characters have the extraordinary individuality and reality that keep the story deeply absorbing.

Ruth Hill Viguers, in The Horn Book Magazine *(copyright ©, by The Horn Book, Inc., Boston), October, 1965, pp. 505-06.*

[*Camilla*] is . . . the sensitive first-person portrayal of a 15-year-old girl who faces the reality of her parents' failures and her own maturity. . . . There is no happy ending, but the result is a penetrating, realistic study of bare human emotion with few holds barred. The long discussions about the existence of God do not give the book an undue religious emphasis but provide food for thought. Well written and sensitive, this is for the mature reader only.

Julia Losinski, in School Library Journal *(reprinted from the November, 1965, issue of* School Library Journal, *published by R. R. Bowker Co., a Xerox company; copyright © 1965 by Xerox Corporation), November, 1965, p. 83.*

First published in another version in 1951 under the title *Camilla Dickinson*, [this is] a candid and perceptive story of an adolescent girl in New York. Camilla, fifteen and an only child of wealthy parents, is faced with adult problems and, in responding to the problems, moves to a deeper and more adult understanding of herself and of her parents. . . . Although the story reflects the conflict and tension of marital incompatibility, it is neither bitter nor lurid: Camilla has an integrity and a sense of intelligent wonder about her world and about her future that are impressive.

Zena Sutherland, in Bulletin of the Center for Children's Books *(copyright 1965 by the University of Chicago; all rights reserved), November, 1965, p. 46.*

OTHER CITATIONS

Mary Louise Hector, in The New York Times Book Review, *November 7, 1965 (Part 2), p. 12.*

Stephen A. Dunning, in English Journal, *January, 1966, p. 105.*

***DANCE IN THE DESERT* (1969)**

Whether or not one reads into the story one more legendary comment on the Holy Family's flight into Egypt, [*Dance in the Desert*] is a tender, beautiful allegory. In the luminous pictures [by Symeon Shimin] the contrasts of desert darkness and glowing firelight are stunning. Story and illustrations are harmonious and completely right together; but, probably in an effort to create unity, type has unfortunately been superimposed on the illustrations.

Ruth Hill Viguers, in The Horn Book Magazine *(copyright © 1969 by The Horn Book, Inc., Boston), August, 1969, p. 401.*

The interest level [of "Dance in the Desert"] is baffling; the parable is too sweetly unbelievable and oft-told for adults, and children would surely find the blocks of narrative (almost lacking in conversation) unappealing. There is a cryptic Latin epigraph to the effect that one does not understand what words mean until one has a grasp of what they do not mean. This leaves me wondering if I've failed to grasp the essence of the book, only reading what *seems* to be there. The problem is that children would do the same.

Mary Stolz, in The New York Times Book Review *(© 1969 by The New York Times Company; reprinted by permission), August 10, 1969, p. 20.*

The text [of *Dance in the Desert*] has a gentle charm, although I could wish that it had been written in the form of a ballad. Verse convinces where prose has a tendency merely to assert. [Symeon Shimin's] pictures, however, brilliantly adorn and support the statement. They are magical.

Martha Bacon, in The Atlantic Monthly *(copyright © 1969, by The Atlantic Monthly Company, Boston, Mass.; reprinted with permission), December, 1969, pp. 148, 150.*

OTHER CITATIONS

Polly Goodwin, in Book World, *May 4, 1969, p. 14.*

Elinor S. Cullen, in Library Journal, *July, 1969, p. 2672.*

***THE JOURNEY WITH JONAH* (1967)**

The reluctant prophet comes full circle with the aid of various percipient animals in Mrs. L'Engle's verse-drama [*The Journey With Jonah*], offering an unusual entree into biblical themes. . . . The philosophical interplay between Jonah and the animals advances with an easy, ironical wit that only occasionally turns into farce, and the characterization of each is distinctive and vivid. This can be staged (and has been) but it makes intriguing reading also for receptive young persons.

Kirkus Service *(copyright © 1967 Virginia Kirkus' Service, Inc.), August 15, 1967, p. 975.*

[This] miniature drama is flawless in construction, and its freshness and sparkle are irresistible. . . . The beasts are winningly and consistently in character, being variously pert, foolish or solemn, while Jonah is properly irascible and preoccupied as he ponders the frustrating paradox of God's wrath and God's compassion. Children's plays are too often little more than graceless, idiotic travesties; Miss L'Engle in contrast has produced a wise and witty little masterpiece.

Houston L. Maples, in Book World (© The Washington Post), *November 5, 1967 (Part 2), p. 34.*

The play's cast seems appropriate for a rather young audience (for example, three little rats named Huz, Buz, and Hazo) while some of the dialogue is quite sophisticated. Indeed, some of it is beautifully phrased, some delightfully witty. The discrepancy of levels suggests that the best use of the script would be, perhaps, to have the performance given by older children for younger ones. As a play to read, however, [*The Journey with Jonah*] seems not to be quite right for either group.

Zena Sutherland, in Bulletin of the Center for Children's Books *(copyright 1967 by the University of Chicago; all rights reserved), December, 1967, p. 62.*

The prophet Jonah and his God-given mission to warn the people of Nineveh of their excesses [provide] the basis of this short, effective morality play elaborating the Biblical story. . . . [Madeleine L'Engle's] drama is simple, direct, poetic yet not without humor and depth of meaning. Helpful production notes are included based on performances given by students in New York City. Fisher's black-and-white illustrations add beauty and dignity.

Julia Losinski, in School Library Journal *(reprinted from the January, 1968, issue of* School Library Journal, *published by R. R. Bowker Co., a Xerox company; copyright © 1968 by Xerox Corporation), January, 1968, p. 87.*

["The Journey with Jonah"] offers opportunities for dressing up and for metaphysical speculation about [the play's] meaning. However, all the action occurs offstage, leaving the audience with tedious dialogue, and an offensive conglomeration of Biblical language and modern idiom.

The New York Times Book Review *(© 1968 by The New York Times Company; reprinted by permission), January 21, 1968, p. 28.*

[Madeleine L'Engle's] dramatization of the story found in the Old Testament Book of Jonah amplifies the humor of the original and retains its basic meaning. Jonah, the somewhat pompous prophet, may be at odds with God and man, but he is not left alone. On every step of his way he is confronted by animal creation. . . . Through the prose and the verse, the rhymes and the puns, is witnessed the animal world's revelation of the incomprehensibility of God's mercy, which Jonah finally acknowledges.

Paul Heins, in The Horn Book Magazine *(copyright © 1968 by The Horn Book, Inc., Boston), April, 1968, p. 184.*

OTHER CITATIONS

Best Sellers, *October 1, 1967, p. 263.*

Melvin Maddocks, in The Christian Science Monitor, *November 2, 1967, p. B7.*

Geraldine E. LaRocque, in English Journal, *May, 1968, pp. 752-53.*

LINES SCRIBBLED ON AN ENVELOPE AND OTHER POEMS (1969)

Madeleine L'Engle is at her most successful in these 40-odd poems when she turns her whimsical imagination loose and explores at will. . . .

Her insights always ring true, yet her language is often inadequate to the truth she is expressing. She tends to slip into trite phrases or plain, flat-bottomed prose. . . .

Chad Walsh, in The New York Times Book Review *(© 1969 by The New York Times Company; reprinted by permission), November 30, 1969, p. 42.*

[The poems in *Lines Scribbled on an Envelope and Other Poems*] have variety in mood, subject, and form; they have wry humor, wide understanding, and imagination. Most of all, they have the emotion of a poet's very personal expression of joy and pain, of facing the inevitable, and discovering that rebellion is not enough. Although the poems have more for those who have lived awhile, they should be known by many of the young people who have already made their own discoveries in the author's other books.

Ruth Hill Viguers, in The Horn Book Magazine *(copyright © 1969 by The Horn Book, Inc., Boston), December, 1969, pp. 680-81.*

OTHER CITATIONS

Neil Millar, in The Christian Science Monitor, *November 6, 1969, p. B10.*

MEET THE AUSTINS (1960)

[*Meet the Austins* is an] unusually good family story, told in convincing style by Vicky, who is twelve. . . . The story line is realistic, the characters are nicely differentiated and consistent. It is, however, the family itself that is wonderful: warmth, intelligence, humor, and kindness pervade the Austin atmosphere with no suggestion of sentimentality or precocity.

Zena Sutherland, in Bulletin of the Center for Children's Books *(copyright 1961 by the University of Chicago; all rights reserved), March, 1961, p. 112.*

[This] is an unusual book, far better than most in style and in sensitivity, yet suffering from an overly weak story line. There are intimate details of home life which everyone will recognize with pleasure; there is great warmth in the family relationship, and it is movingly communicated to the reader. There are also, unfortunately, moments when the Austins become just a little too good to be true, and the going gets a wee bit sticky.

Alberta Eiseman, in The New York Times Book Review *(© 1961 by The New York Times Company; reprinted by permission), March 12, 1961, p. 30.*

[*Meet the Austins*] is a beautiful book and very difficult to describe without making it seem commonplace. . . . [The story] is one of the most convincing bits of living I have experienced in a book in a long time. It is full of warmth and love and idealism but is intensely real, and so is absorbing reading. I felt that this author's *And Both Were Young* . . . showed remarkable perception of young people. This book is an even greater exercise of that perception. We not only "meet the Austins" here, we know and love them.

Ruth Hill Viguers, in The Horn Book Magazine *(copyright, 1961, by the Horn Book, Inc., Boston), April, 1961, pp. 162-63.*

The Austins, in *Meet the Austins*, are one of the idyllic families that seem to be part of the American dream; a dream because they are much too good to be real. . . . The adults, in fact, especially the saintly grandfather, are pure fairy-tale, but the children in their relations with each other are a true and natural mixture of good and bad. Especially vivid is the spoilt child Maggy, who tries to bully everyone into being sorry for her, and her gradual improvement and acceptance by the others are the best part of the book.

The Times Literary Supplement *(© The Times Publishing Company Ltd. 1966), May 19, 1966, p. 433.*

In [*Meet the Austins*] there are incidents and discussions that explore the nature of God and the meanings of infinity and death. As in many of her books, [Madeleine L'Engle] reveals a faith in the power of love as a positive force to change men's lives. The inner serenity and strength of the Austin family, as contrasted with an outward appearance of disunity and confusion, is well presented.

John Gillespie and Diana Lembo, in their Introducing Books: A Guide for the Middle Grades *(copyright © 1970 by Xerox Corp.), Bowker, 1970, p. 16.*

OTHER CITATIONS

The Booklist and Subscription Books Bulletin, *February 15, 1961, p. 362.*

THE MOON BY NIGHT (1963)

[*The Moon by Night* is] a sequel to *Meet the Austins*. . . . The viewpoint [of Vicky] is kept consistent in the writing; characterization and family relationships are particularly good. One of the most valuable assets of the book is in the calibre of the Austin family: they are intelligent and thoughtful people with broad interests.

Zena Sutherland, in Bulletin of the Center for Children's Books *(copyright 1963 by the University of Chicago; all rights reserved), April, 1963, p. 129.*

Madeleine L'Engle presents in "The Moon By Night" . . . a skillful combination of travel adventure, family relationships and adolescent growing pains. . . . I wish there had been a little more comedy to leaven this plummy mixture, but this is probably quibbling since Miss L'Engle offers so much reassurance to girls who, like Vicky, are full of fears and confusion.

Ellen Lewis Buell, in The New York Times Book Review *(© 1963 by The New York Times Company; reprinted by permission), April 14, 1963, p. 56.*

Perceptively written with natural dialog and good characterization and family relationships, this story of an intelligent, lifelike family is far superior to the average fare for the early teens.

The Booklist and Subscription Books Bulletin *(© 1963 by the American Library Association), July 1, 1963, p. 900.*

THE TWENTY-FOUR DAYS BEFORE CHRISTMAS (1964)

[*The Twenty-four Days Before Christmas* is a] brief Christmas story in which the author goes back in the family life of the Austins (*Meet the Austins, The Moon by Night*) to the December of Vicky's seventh year. . . . The story moves through the days of Advent and the preparations for Christmas, giving vividly the feeling of pendant anticipation. [It is a] bit more sentimental than the previous Austin stories, but appropriately so, both as a Christmas story and as a family story for younger readers. Simply written in present tense, and—since Vicky is only seven—a very good story for reading aloud to younger children.

Zena Sutherland, in Bulletin of the Center for Children's Books *(copyright 1964 by the University of Chicago; all rights reserved), November, 1964, p. 38.*

A WIND IN THE DOOR (1973)

The audacity of Ms. L'Engle's mytho-scientific imagination and her undoubted storytelling abilities keep the reader involved in Meg's quest [in *A Wind in the Door*], but one wonders whether its chief appeal doesn't lie in the all too natural desire to believe that our difficulties, like the Murrys', are personal attacks by the forces of cosmic evil. . . . Unfortunately, Meg learns to love the universe with unconvincing ease, and L'Engle seems to be straining unusually hard to relate what's wrong with America to the double-talk phenomenon of mitochondria and farandolae.

Kirkus Reviews *(copyright © 1973 The Kirkus Service, Inc.), April 15, 1973, p. 463.*

The chief characters of L'Engle's Newbery Award winner, *A Wrinkle in Time* (. . . 1962), return in [this] complex sci-fi/fantasy adventure that is both similar and superior. . . . Once again it is love that enables Meg to overcome evil, and L'Engle reaches mystical ecstasy in describing Meg's apprehension of the beauty and unity of the universe. Complex concepts of space and time are handled well for young readers, and the author creates a suspenseful, life-and-death drama that is of believable cosmic significance. Complex and rich in mystical religious insights, this is breathtaking entertainment.

Margaret A. Dorsey, in School Library Journal *(reprinted from the May, 1973, issue of* School Library Journal, *published by R. R. Bowker Co., a Xerox company; copyright © 1973 by Xerox Corporation), May, 1973, p. 81.*

At the risk of supreme danger of being X-ed out of existence by a Farandela from a Mitochondria from a prokaryocyte despite the help of a cherubim named Proginoskes and the dangers of the Echthroi—are you sensing the strain of even the best readers to wade through extremes of science-fiction while trying to dig out those "levels of truth" advertised in the publicity blurb?

The message [in *A Wind in the Door*] is perceivable—when we have an identity, when we are loved, when we matter, then there is a purpose to everything and a depth to living. Seems that such a valuable philosophy could be made a shade more available. . . .

Mrs. John G. Gray, in Best Sellers *(copyright 1973, by the University of Scranton), May 15, 1973, p. 98.*

[As] she does in "A Wrinkle in Time," Madeleine L'Engle mixes classical theology, contemporary family life, and futuristic science fiction to make a completely convincing tale that should put under its spell both readers familiar with the Murrys and those meeting them for the first time. It isn't any advance on Miss L'Engle's earlier work—readers of "A Wrinkle in Time" will be able to predict the sequence of events of "A Wind in the Door"—but the formula works as well a second time as it did the first, which is, after all, no small accomplishment.

Michele Murray, in The New York Times Book Review *(© 1973 by The New York Times Company; reprinted by permission), July 8, 1973, p. 8.*

In *A Wrinkle in Time* the author encased her philosophy of life in the form of compelling fantasy, but in [*A Wind in the Door*] she has forsaken the fantasy to write about her philosophy, and the story—burdened by page after page of her commentary on evil, the violence of American society, the individual worth of human life—lacks the consistency and the believable motivation needed to keep fiction from becoming dogma.

Anita Silvey, in The Horn Book Magazine *(copyright © 1973 by The Horn Book, Inc., Boston), August, 1973, p. 380.*

The protagonists of *A Wrinkle in Time* are embroiled in a new fantasy in a story that has the same level of polished writing but a rather more intricate plot, not as compelling as its predecessor. . . . Throughout this heavily complicated plot, there are precepts of behavior, morals, psychological interpretations, and a trace of didacticism. It is Madeleine L'Engle's triumph that she is able, despite the layered intricacy, to make her characters interesting and her story moderately suspenseful.

Zena Sutherland, in Bulletin of the Center for Children's Books *(© 1973 by the University of Chicago; all rights reserved), September, 1973, p. 12.*

[In A *Wind in the Door*,] Madeleine L'Engle returns to the strange world of her classic novel, *A Wrinkle in Time*, a world where time and space are immaterial, where all things are possible, yet ordinary life manages to continue unabashed. Few writers are more able to combine the cosmic with the comic, and no one can match Miss L'-Engle's treatment of the powers of darkness. . . .

The domestic and the galactic come together in the three trials that Meg must undergo in order to save Charles Wallace's life and, ultimately, that of the universe. It is a tribute to the author's imagination that this is not quite as absurd as it sounds; Meg's helper in the trials . . . is a typical product of that imagination.

The huffy, arrogant farandola and the mad dance of disharmony it almost joins are brilliantly described but . . . in the final crashing bars, during which the cherubim annihilates himself and Meg embraces the Ecthrol, the reader retires, deafened by a barrage of concepts, exhausted and jaded by a plethora of heavy messages of love and empathy.

Miss L'Engle's virtues have in the end become faults: her wild imagination has overreached itself; her sensuous prose has become purple: and the family life she describes so well suddenly seems rather silly.

Sarah Hayes, in The Times Literary Supplement *(© Times Newspapers Ltd., 1975), April 4, 1975, p. 360.*

OTHER CITATIONS

Publishers' Weekly, *April 16, 1973, p. 54.*

The Booklist, *June 1, 1973, pp. 948-49.*

A WRINKLE IN TIME (1962)

[*A Wrinkle in Time* is a] science fantasy that incorporates the concepts of time travel, extrasensory perception, and inhabited planets in outer space. . . . The plot is involved and extended, weakening a story that, were it more unified, would be quite absorbing. Characterization is good, details of some of the episodes are freshly imaginative, and the writing style is excellent.

Zena Sutherland, in Bulletin of the Center for Children's Books *(copyright 1962 by the University of Chicago; all rights reserved), March, 1962, p. 113.*

Stories like ["A Wrinkle in Time"], with its overtones reminiscent of Orwell's "1984," of Hans Christian Andersen and C. S. Lewis, are not for the casual or strictly realistic reader. Imaginative readers with a taste for speculation, a feeling for intricate symbolism, should find it wholly absorbing—for in her highly accelerated spin through space Miss L'Engle never loses sight of human needs and emotions.

Ellen Lewis Buell, in The New York Times Book Review *(© 1962 by The New York Times Company; reprinted by permission), March 18, 1962, p. 26.*

Here is a confusion of science, philosophy, satire, religion, literary allusions, and quotations that will no doubt have many critics. I found it fascinating. To children who read and reread C. S. Lewis' fairy tales I think [*A Wrinkle in Time*] will be absorbing. It makes unusual demands on the imagination and consequently gives great rewards.

Ruth Hill Viguers, in The Horn Book Magazine *(copyright, 1962, by The Horn Book, Inc., Boston), April, 1962, p. 177.*

[This] has the general appearance of being science fiction, but it is not, except that by means of "a tesseract"—a wrinkle in time—the children are transported from one planet to another without time seeming to elapse. There is mystery, mysticism, a feeling of indefinable, brooding horror. . . . One feels that this book quests desperately for something it never quite touches. It is original, different, exciting—and in some parts frustrating.

William Lipkind, in Saturday Review *(copyright © 1962 by Saturday Review, Inc; reprinted with permission), May 12, 1962, p. 40.*

[*A Wrinkle in Time*] is an impressive rather than an entertaining book, but for the receptive child, who can give himself to the splendour and the terror of Miss L'Engle's imagination, it may well be a lasting experience. . . . The book is deeply sincere and intensely serious. It offers no easy solution to the problems it propounds. Its weakness is partly stylistic, but more in portrayal of character; the ideas remain ideas instead of being fused into the narrative.

The Times Literary Supplement *(© The Times Publishing Company Ltd. 1963), June 14, 1963, p. 427.*

[This is] an unusual, thought-provoking book. . . . Although this can be read superficially as an exciting science fiction adventure, [Madeleine L'Engle] has tried to explore such serious themes as: the need for individuality and respect for others' differences, the power of love and the nature of good and evil.

John Gillespie and Diana Lembo, in their Juniorplots: A Book Talk Manual for Teachers and Librarians *(© 1967 by the R. R. Bowker Co.), Bowker, 1967, pp. 188, 190.*

[*A Wrinkle in Time* is an] exciting, mysterious fantasy in which three children—Meg and Charles Wallace Murry and Calvin O'Keefe—travel in search of Mr. Murry. . . . There are overtones of science fiction. Characterizations are marvelously drawn, especially that of Meg, the twelve-year-old daughter, who demonstrates typical adolescent insecurities and concerns.

Constantine Georgiou, in his Children and Their Literature *(copyright © 1969 by Prentice-Hall, Inc.), Prentice-Hall, 1969, p. 299.*

Madeleine L'Engle took some of the ideas and some of the techniques of science fiction to the making of an extraordinary fantastic novel. In the event the mixture proved almost too explosive to be controlled, and the resulting story, for all its wit and occasional gaiety, failed to achieve total communication. *A Wrinkle in Time* remains an experiment, an uneasy blending of physics and metaphysics, but an experiment entirely in the spirit of the age in which it was conceived.

Marcus Crouch, in his The Nesbit Tradition: The Children's Novel in England 1945-1970 *(© Marcus Crouch 1972), Ernest Benn, 1972, p. 56.*

OTHER CITATIONS

Patricia D. Beard, in Library Journal, *March 15, 1962, p. 1332.*

The Booklist and Subscription Books Bulletin, *April 1, 1962, p. 535.*

Dorothy Light, in English Journal, *May, 1965, pp. 457-58.*

William Jay Jacobs, in Teachers College Record, *October, 1966, p. 90.*

May Hill Arbuthnot and Zena Sutherland, in their Children and Books, *Scott, Foresman, 4th edition, 1972, p. 260.*

***THE YOUNG UNICORNS* (1968)**

What more unlikely setting for a novel of suspense than New York City's Cathedral Church of St. John the Divine? What less likely suspects for massive villainy than the highly placed clergy? Yet Madeleine L'Engle spins her complicated new tale of street gangs and unscrupulous scientists in, around and even under the great Manhattan church and involves its leaders in the fast-paced plot. . . . Like the polyglot neighborhood in which the story takes place, [*The Young Unicorns*] seems somewhat over-populated with protagonists, problems and plots. . . . But it's a first-rate suspense story, complete with missing formulae.

John Beck, in Book World *(©* The Washington Post*), May 5, 1968 (Part 2), p. 5.*

The Austins, well-met once, have become increasingly cloying in succeeding books, and Miss L'Engle's philosophic concerns, which gave urgency to *A Wrinkle in Time*, have begun to seem pretentious, their expression sententious. *The Young Unicorns* is a kind of *aggiornamento* of the Austin series and *The Arm of the Starfish*—via cross-references and a congeries of characters—and *Wrinkle*—the latter because seven-year-old Rob Austin speaks with the same precocious wisdom as Charles Wallace and, in the clinch, withstands evil with the same indomitable innocence: the roles are interchangeable.

Kirkus Service *(copyright © 1968 The Kirkus Service, Inc.), May 15, 1968, p. 555.*

What makes "The Young Unicorns" exciting is Dr. Austin's invention, a Micro-Ray, capable of changing a personality, of taking away identity. It could transform a killer into a docile human being. A miraculous cure in the offing or a curse?. . .

I believe that young readers will let Miss L'Engle know that they are grateful for her having written this novel. What "critics" will say could hardly matter in her case. She is a juvenile author in the very best sense of those words. Children read her with joy. And the rest of us authors can only wish for the same luck.

Maia Wojciechowska, in The New York Times Book Review *(© 1968 by The New York Times Company; reprinted by permission), May 26, 1968, p. 30.*

[*The Young Unicorns*] is packed with almost everything that makes good reading: human problems, scientific challenges, suspense, mystery (with a surprise ending), and a great variety of characters with many different backgrounds. . . . A superb storyteller, Miss L'Engle is deeply concerned with fundamental values that are integral to the story, and what might have been a very complicated plot is smoothly woven together. The book is contemporary in feeling—the time actually is in the future—and its color, excitement, and variety offer a tremendous relief from many dull current books with urban settings.

Ruth Hill Viguers, in The Horn Book Magazine *(copyright © 1968 by The Horn Book, Inc., Boston), June, 1968, pp. 329-30.*

OTHER CITATIONS

Zena Sutherland, in Bulletin of the Center for Children's Books, *June, 1968, pp. 161-62.*

Martha Bacon, in The Atlantic Monthly, *December, 1969, p. 150.*

* * *

LINDGREN, Astrid (Ericsson) 1907-

A Swedish winner of the 1958 Hans Christian Andersen

Medal, Astrid Lindgren is well-known for her series of books about Pippi Longstocking. (See also *Contemporary Authors*, Vols. 13-14.)

GENERAL COMMENTARY

Astrid Lindgren's books are the outstanding masterpieces of much-larger-than-life portraiture. In Pippi she embodies all the dreams of small children who weave fantasies about total freedom from adult supervision, enormous physical strength, escape from the conventions of a civilization invented by grown-ups. . . .

This is great fun, and that might be enough. It would not sustain Pippi through a whole series of books. Pippi, however, is not a simple exaggeration. There is considerable subtlety in this portrait, so that the reader is constantly being surprised.

Marcus Crouch, in his The Nesbit Tradition: The Children's Novel in England 1945-1970 *(© Marcus Crouch 1972), Ernest Benn, 1972, p. 103.*

***BILL BERGSON AND THE WHITE ROSE RESCUE* (1965)**

[*Bill Bergson and the White Rose Rescue*] is the usual thriller, in which the young adventurers escape from one hair-raising situation to another—a plot similar to the author's earlier *Bill Bergson, Master Detective*, but the style has unfortunately deteriorated: the suspense is forced; the characters, both children and adults, are never more than one-dimensional; the dialogue is stiff and marked by the heavy use of the sort of insulting exchange that often passes for humor at the middle point of this age level. Good triumphs and evil loses in the end, but that was telegraphed from the beginning.

Virginia Kirkus' Service, *February 15, 1965, p. 176.*

In a third story about Bill Bergson, Astrid Lindgren piles on the excitement for the 11 to 13-year-olds as Bill, Anders and Eva-Lotte attempt to foil the evil men who kidnap Professor Anders and his little son Eric. With a fine disregard for probability Miss Lindgren never hesitates to give the children extra thrills, just as she employs exaggeration to produce constant laughter in her tales about Pippi Longstocking.

Margaret Sherwood Libby, in Book Week *(©* The Washington Post*), July 18, 1965, p. 10.*

OTHER CITATIONS

The Booklist and Subscription Books Bulletin, *September 15, 1965, p. 97.*

***BILL BERGSON LIVES DANGEROUSLY* (1954)**

Good characterization, the vivid picture of the little Swedish village which is the scene of the Bill Bergson adventures, and, above all, real humor, along with a well-worked-out plot, make [*Bill Bergson Lives Dangerously*] a good addition to the mystery shelf for young readers. Bill and his friends, Anders and Eva-Lotta—always ready for any excitement—are the kind of children American boys and girls as well as Swedish ones take to their hearts.

Jennie D. Lindquist, in The Horn Book Magazine *(copyrighted, 1954, by The Horn Book, Inc., Boston), October, 1954, p. 334.*

OTHER CITATIONS

Kirkus Reviews, *August 1, 1954, p. 489.*

Helen M. Brogan, in Library Journal, *December 15, 1954, p. 2497.*

***BILL BERGSON, MASTER DETECTIVE* (1952)**

How Bill and his friends, Anders and Eva-Lotta, catch three thieves is an unusually well-worked-out mystery story full of ingenuity and hilarious situations. There is nothing run-of-the-mill about it.

Jennie D. Lindquist, in The Horn Book Magazine *(copyrighted, 1952, by The Horn Book, Inc., Boston), October, 1952, p. 325.*

[*Bill Bergson, Master Detective*] is a hilarious story of a boy detective in a little town in Sweden. . . . Perhaps the funniest part of the story lies in Bill's imaginary conversation with his admiring public. The grown-ups in the story are as amusing and satisfying as the three children.

Mary Gould Davis, in Saturday Review *(copyright © 1952 by Saturday Review, Inc.; reprinted with permission), November 15, 1952, p. 54.*

OTHER CITATIONS

Elizabeth Johnson, in Library Journal, *November 1, 1952, p. 1908.*

The Booklist, *December 1, 1952, pp. 129-30.*

***THE CHILDREN OF NOISY VILLAGE* (1962)**

Nothing very important happens in any of [the] stories [in *The Children of Noisy Village*]—just the exciting ordinariness of everyday. But there is a special delight about them—partly because they are told by nine-year-old Lisa who is a dear, partly because they happen in Sweden, mostly because the reader, too, is drawn deep into the tale so that even grownups remember how it felt to take an endless age walking home from school. Ilon Wikland's line drawings show the children just as we had imagined them.

Pamela March, in The Christian Science Monitor *(reprinted by permission from* The Christian Science Monitor*; © 1962, The Christian Science Publishing Society; all rights reserved), November 15, 1962, p. 4B.*

[The episodes in "The Children of Noisy Village"] are leisurely incidents, some gently amusing, others interesting for the light they throw on old Swedish customs. And there is great warmth in some of the relationships, especially that of the children to the old gentleman they all call Grandfather. Yet the pace is too much the same throughout and the children are not drawn as individuals.

Alberta Eiseman, in The New York Times Book Review *(© 1962 by The New York Times Company; reprinted by permission), November 18, 1962, p. 52.*

[*The Children of Noisy Village* is a] timeless story—the author's recollections, perhaps?—of an idyllic country childhood in Sweden. . . . Each chapter has its account of highly inventive fun and the distinctively gay Swedish festivities around the year. All are enjoyed in a happy relationship between children and adults (as in Jennie Lindquist's American-Swedish stories, which this sometimes brings to mind), in general high spirits, and in jokes and friendly rivalries between girls and boys.

Virginia Haviland, in The Horn Book Magazine *(copyright © 1962, by The Horn Book, Inc., Boston), December, 1962, p. 599.*

The writing style [in *The Children of Noisy Village*] is subdued and appropriately ingenuous, describing daily events, neighbors, observance of holidays, etc. The book's chief appeal is the Swedish background. The anecdotes are realistic detailings of small events; there is, however, a bland quality to the writing—slightly sweet, slightly self-consciously childlike—that may limit reader interest. . . .

Zena Sutherland, in Bulletin of the Center for Children's Books *(copyright 1963 by the University of Chicago; all rights reserved), February, 1963, pp. 96-7.*

OTHER CITATIONS

The Booklist and Subscription Books Bulletin, *November 15, 1962, p. 256.*

***CHRISTMAS IN NOISY VILLAGE* (1964)**

As in the other books about Noisy Village, the story [*Christmas in Noisy Village*] is told by Lisa, and the first person is used with fair success—being just slightly self-conscious. The format is that of a picture book, the text more brief and simple than are the other stories [about Noisy Village]. . . . The Swedish background is delightful; the story has holiday appeal; the writing is uncluttered and ingenuous, verging occasionally on quaintness. The book should appeal to a younger read-aloud audience, too.

Zena Sutherland, in Bulletin of the Center for Children's Books *(copyright 1964 by the University of Chicago; all rights reserved), December, 1964, p. 58.*

OTHER CITATIONS

The Booklist and Subscription Books Bulletin, *December 1, 1964, p. 348.*

***CHRISTMAS IN THE STABLE* (1962)**

The story [*Christmas in the Stable*] is a very simplified version of the Christmas story—told by a mother to a small child who sees the manger scenes in terms of the farm life with which she is familiar. The writing has a simple dignity and no trace of sentimentality; the whole book has a quiet strength. The religious interpretation is left to the adult; beyond the title and the reference on one page to Christmas, the text is not specific.

Zena Sutherland, in Bulletin of the Center for Children's Books *(copyright 1963 by the University of Chicago; all rights reserved), November, 1963, p. 46.*

OTHER CITATIONS

The Booklist and Subscription Books Bulletin, *November 1, 1962, p. 224.*

Ruth Hill Viguers, in The Horn Book Magazine, *December, 1962, p. 590.*

***EMIL AND PIGGY BEAST* (1973)**

[In *Emil and Piggy Beast*, Emil continues] to bedevil the straightlaced population of old-time rural Sweden, where the accidental drunkenness of a small farm boy and his pet pig is enough to arouse the town and preoccupy the local temperance society. . . . Lindgren's light touch and her sympathetic projection of Emil's world allow readers to accept the "noble deed" and enjoy the mischief.

Kirkus Reviews *(copyright © 1973 The Kirkus Service, Inc.), March 15, 1973, p. 317.*

Emil's mischievous ventures [in *Emil and Piggy Beast*] are imaginative and funny, while each person on his Swedish farm is characterized warmly and clearly in relation to him. Berg's illustrations are as zany as Emil's pranks.

The Booklist *(© American Library Association 1973), June 1, 1973, p. 949.*

As fresh and spontaneous as its predecessors, *Emil in the Soup Tureen* and *Emil's Pranks*, this new collection of loosely connected anecdotes about the irrepressible little Swedish farm boy tells of a succession of hiliarious events triggered as much by Emil's quick mind as by his love of mischief. . . . The lively incidents, the sprightly style, and the humor of [Björn Berg's] cartoon-like drawings all contribute to a light-hearted and very funny book.

Beryl Robinson, in The Horn Book Magazine *(copyright © 1973 by The Horn Book, Inc., Boston), August, 1973, p. 380.*

An episodic and humorous story about a Swedish child of long ago is told with vigor [by Astrid Lindgren] and translated [by Michael Heron] so that the idiomatic flow of writing is preserved. Emil is a precocious and indefatigably energetic child of five whose ploys and pranks frequently drive his father to despair and occasionally make his parents very proud.

Zena Sutherland, in Bulletin of the Center for Children's Books *(© 1973 by the University of Chicago; all rights reserved), September, 1973, p. 12.*

***EMIL'S PRANKS* (1971)**

Several of [Emil's pranks], fortunately for the reader, are recorded here in an intimate, affectionate, and very funny fashion. Whether Emil, in trying to catch a rat, catches his father's toe, and causes general chaos . . . or whether in doing a kindly deed for poor hungry old folk he deprives an upcoming family gathering of a holiday dinner, the well-meaning if disrupting Emil will win all hearts.

Polly Goodwin, in Book World *(©* The Washington Post*), November 7, 1971 (Part 2), p. 10.*

Descriptions of [Emil's] exploits introduce farm animals, celebrations, and a humorous relationship between the hired helpers, Alfred and Lina (the pursued and the pursuing). It all bespeaks the turn of the century and a way of life remote from that of today, giving [*Emil's Pranks*] the immediacy and the tone of a grandmother's reminiscences.

Virginia Haviland, in The Horn Book Magazine *(copyright © 1972 by The Horn Book, Inc., Boston), April, 1972, p. 146.*

***HAPPY TIMES IN NOISY VILLAGE* (1963)**

While some of [the children's] adventures [in *Happy Times in Noisy Village*] seem too mild to be interesting and none are really exciting, a few are quite funny and some will have a strong appeal for little girls. Unessential but pleasant; likable drawings [by Ilon Wikland].

The Booklist and Subscription Books Bulletin *(© 1963 by the American Library Association), November 1, 1963, p. 262.*

While Astrid Lindgren is inclined to exploit the unconscious naivete of children for laughs—a humorous technique more appreciated by adults—children 8 to 10 will respond, nevertheless, to the unflagging gaiety and zest of [*Happy Times in Noisy Village*].

Houston Maples, in Book Week *(©* The Washington Post*), November 10, 1963 (Part 2), p. 26.*

In her own highly individual but typically nine-year-old manner, Lisa tells the story of the happy times. In any country, children brought up in rural areas learn to draw on their own imagination and resources for their fun. Anyone who ever had such a childhood can relive it with Lisa and her friends, and rural and town children alike will enjoy every minute of the "happy times" right along with the boys and girls from "Noisy Village."

Marian Sorenson, in The Christian Science Monitor *(reprinted by permission from* The Christian Science Monitor*; © 1963, The Christian Science Publishing Society; all rights reserved), November 14, 1963, p. 11B.*

[*Happy Times in Noisy Village* is a] sequel to *The Children of Noisy Village*. . . . The writing style is light and informal, with a note (as in the first book) of cuteness that palls; for example, "Mommy says she can't understand why it takes more than twice as long to walk home as it does to walk to school. I don't understand it either. But it just can't be helped."

Zena Sutherland, in Bulletin of the Center for Children's Books *(copyright 1964 by the University of Chicago; all rights reserved), July-August, 1964, p. 173.*

OTHER CITATIONS

Mary Louise Hector, in The New York Times Book Review, *November 10, 1963 (Part 2), p. 14.*

***LOTTA ON TROUBLEMAKER STREET* (1963)**

Bad or not, both the story and pictures [in *Lotta on Troublemaker Street*] make chubby little Lotta who left home to start her own "house-hole" one of this season's heart-stealers. Older girls who love to mother younger ones will enjoy this as much as the 5-7's for whom it is intended. And the 5-7's who start off the day being sad and bad may remember Lotta and think again.

Pamela Marsh, in The Christian Science Monitor *(reprinted by permission from* The Christian Science Monitor*; © 1963, The Christian Science Publishing Society; all rights reserved), May 9, 1963, p. 3B.*

[*Lotta on Troublemaker Street* is a] lightly humorous and realistic read-aloud story about one ploy of a child of five. . . . Lotta's mischief is apologized for and pardoned; her parents are gentle, but her older brother is realistically scornful. Written with realism and simplicity [by Astrid Lindgren], and engagingly illustrated [by Ilon Wikland].

Zena Sutherland, in Bulletin of the Center for Children's Books *(copyright 1963 by the University of Chicago; all rights reserved), July-August, 1963, p. 178.*

***OF COURSE POLLY CAN RIDE A BIKE* (1972)**

[This story] has a hint of the didactic, but is saved from the worst aspect of didacticism by the fact that Polly is so firmly self-centered a child, and perhaps will appeal to the audience for this read-aloud book precisely because she goes right on bellowing and getting her way rather than either getting punished or becoming wiser and meeker.

Zena Sutherland, in Bulletin of the Center for Children's Books *(© 1973 by the University of Chicago; all rights reserved), April, 1973, p. 128.*

Wikland's idyllic full-color illustrations buoy up a rather loose plot and artificial ending [in *Of Course Polly Can Ride a Bike*]. Polly's personality is strongly drawn and her stubborn independence will endear her to children.

The Booklist *(© American Library Association 1973), April 1, 1973, p. 765.*

[In *Of Course Polly Can Ride A Bike*] Astrid Lindgren reproduces with devastating accuracy the grumbling monologue of the frustrated five-year-old, and Ilon Wikland's pictures are engaging, cheerful and easy to understand.

The Times Literary Supplement *(© Times Newspapers Ltd., 1973), April 6, 1973, p. 389.*

[This is a] delightful story based on a theme with which young readers will identify: the transition from tricycle to bicycle. . . . Not overly moralistic in its treatment of theft, the story ends happily when Polly's father brings her a smaller two-wheeler which she can handle. Colorful, cartoon-like illustrations [by Ilon Wikland] reflect Polly's changing moods and complement the text.

Patricia M. Cuts, in School Library Journal *(reprinted from the May, 1973, issue of* School Library Journal*, published by R. R.*

Bowker Co., a Xerox company; copyright © 1973 by Xerox Corporation), May, 1973, p. 64.

***PIPPI GOES ON BOARD* (1957)**

Sweden's small fry Paul Bunyan, feminine gender, continues her miraculous adventures as enfant terrible and again leads her friends, Tommy and Annika. . ., down the primrose path. Part of the magic of her tales lies in the enchantment of reading about other children doing the things one would not dare to do. . . . Somehow [*Pippi Goes on Board*] doesn't quite come off. One has the same sense of anti-climax that one did in the disappointing sequel to the imperishable *Heidi*.

Virginia Kirkus' Service, *July 15, 1957, p. 483.*

Lovers of Pippi Longstocking will welcome [*Pippi Goes on Board*, which presents] rollicking tales of a topsy-turvy world in which Pippi and her next door neighbors put into practice some ideas about good times. Their hilarious, absurd adventures, sometimes motivated by generous impulses, fascinate Pippi's friends.

Inger Boye, in Junior Libraries *(reprinted from the December, 1957, issue of* Junior Libraries, *published by R. R. Bowker Co., a Xerox company; copyright © 1957 by Xerox Corporation), December, 1957, p. 28.*

***PIPPI IN THE SOUTH SEAS* (1959)**

Throughout the expedition [in the South Seas] Pippi manifests her tremendous capacity for humor, imagination, and extraordinary physical strength in a manner which will delight those readers already familiar with her and win for her many ardent new friends.

Virginia Kirkus' Service, *August 1, 1959, p. 550.*

[*Pippi in the South Seas*] will be greeted with wild joy by the huge number of children who found the first two Pippi books so different from any others, so funny and so free. . . . Pippi's tongue is as caustic as ever, her remarks to adults as shocking (and as close to what many children would often like to say). . . . The particular mixture of realism and magic in these stories is unique. Besides being so hilarious to most children, they seem to be saying something important but elusive.

Margaret Warren Brown, in The Horn Book Magazine *(copyright, 1959, by the Horn Book, Inc., Boston), October, 1959, p. 387.*

Pippi, in [*Pippi in the South Seas*], once more copes triumphantly with the adult world. . . . [This is gay], rather slapstick fantasy, with a heroine who has the ability and courage to put grownups in their place. Not as original and amusing as "Pippi Longstocking," but still appealing for grades 4-6, and for reading and storytelling to grades 3-5.

Dorothy Garey, in Junior Libraries *(reprinted from the December, 1959, issue of* Junior Libraries, *published by R. R. Bowker Co., a Xerox company; copyright © 1959 by Xerox Corporation), December, 1959, p. 51.*

OTHER CITATIONS

Lavinia R. Davis, in The New York Times Book Review, *January 3, 1960, p. 16.*

***PIPPI LONGSTOCKING* (1950)**

[This is a] fresh delicious fantasy that children will love. In the character of 9-year-old Pippi Longstocking, who was lucky to have no parents to tell her what to do, is a juvenile Robin Hood with the authority of a Mammy Yokum and a Mighty Mouse. . . . Champion of fun, freedom and fantasy and long happy thoughts, Pippi is an inspired creation knit from daydreams.

Virginia Kirkus' Bookshop Service, *September 1, 1950, p. 515.*

It would be unfair to judge the quality of Astrid Lindgren's writing by the fantastic and often nonsensical actions performed by Pippi, who is the central figure in three of the writer's most popular books. The success of this trilogy demonstrates how much children appreciate nonsense and, by the reactions of adults towards Pippi's every day antics and bravado, how little many grown up people appreciate the unreality and immaturity of the child's world. . . . There can be few adults, however, who would deny the uncommonly fresh humour, the wealth of bright ideas and genuine hearty character of Pippi Longstocking.

Stein Hagliden, "Astrid Lindgren, The Swedish Writer of Children's Books," in The Junior Bookshelf, *July, 1959, p. 114.*

[Astrid Lindgren] has endowed her outrageous superchild [Pippi Longstocking] with a carefree existence that will be the envy of every young reader. Louis Glanzman's drawings contribute to the humor and strength of the tale. . . .

These episodes were designed purely for reading pleasure. They appeal because most children, at some time, wonder how pleasant life might be if only they were free of parental restrictions and could do the many things their fancy dictates.

John Gillespie and Diana Lembo, in their Introducing Books: A Guide for the Middle Grades *(copyright © 1970 by Xerox Corp.), Bowker, 1970, pp. 269, 271.*

Pippi Longstocking is a prime example of the anti-authoritarian book. . . . Pippi stands for every child's dream of doing exactly what he or she wants to (regardless of any prohibitions). . . . The main difference between Pippi and the libertarian characters of, say, James Barrie, Antoine de Saint-Exupéry, Maurice Druon, and Penelope Farmer—to mention only a few authors—is that Pippi is strong, cheerful, and generally happy, while the other children are delicate and mournful and bear all the trouble of the world on their small shoulders.

Mary Orvig, in The Horn Book Magazine *(copyright © 1973 by The Horn Book, Inc., Boston), February, 1973, pp. 17-18.*

Pippi Longstocking personifies the most cherished and secret dream of any child—that of being omnipotent and able to function without any interference from the adult world. Independent and disobedient children are not uncommon in children's literature, but they are seldom girls. And Pippi is super girl, tomboy, feminist or plain horror, all wrapped into one delicious creature. . . . For although Pippi herself is a bit too "unreal" to truly identify with, she inhabits a world which is very real indeed, a world which most *white* children of any nationality can recognize very easily. It is a world filled with overt racism and hidden sexism, very much in the Western tradition of children's literature. . . .

It is soon apparent that Pippi isn't a girl at all, even a tomboy, but a boy in disguise, Astrid Lindgren has simply equipped Pippi with all the traits we have come to think of as male. . . .

Pippi embodies a complete set of glorified but questionable white, male values; strength, wealth, success, definance and staunch unemotionalism.

Kik Reeder, "Pippi Longstocking–Feminist or Anti-Feminist," in Interracial Books for Children *(reprinted by permission of* The Bulletin-Interracial Books for Children, *1841 Broadway, New York, N.Y.), Vol. 5, No. 4, 1974, pp. 1-2, 12.*

OTHER CITATIONS

Siri M. Andrews and Jennie D. Lindquist, in The Horn Book Magazine, *September, 1950, p. 376.*

RASMUS AND THE VAGABOND (1960)

[*Rasmus and the Vagabond*] is no "everyday" story, although nine-year-old Rasmus . . . is, until one gets to know him, a stock character. But once known, he will not be forgotten or confused with any other book hero. . . . Everything is here that children could want: appealing characters, adventures on the open road, much humor, suspense and excitement, and even robbers whom Oscar and Rasmus bring to justice.

Ruth Hill Viguers, in The Horn Book Magazine *(copyright, 1960, by the Horn Book, Inc., Boston), April, 1960, p. 133.*

[Rasmus and Paradise Oscar] have some incredible adventures which children will find absorbing and amusing. The chief value [of the book], however, lies in the relationship between the boy and the vagabond. Written with a sure, deft touch, in an unpretentious style but a masterful choice of words, there emerges a clear picture of the Swedish countryside and a poignant unforgettable figure of a boy whose search for love and security ends in a most satisfying manner.

Marian Herr, in Junior Libraries *(reprinted from the May, 1960, issue of* Junior Libraries, *published by R. R. Bowker Co., a Xerox company; copyright 1960 by Xerox Corporation), May, 1960, pp. 60-1.*

Astrid Lindgren's descriptions of pre-motor-age Sweden are delightful and her main characters both original and appealing. Over-literal minds may find Rasmus' escape from the orphanage and his ultimate discovery of a perfect home somewhat fortuitous. However, Mrs. Lindgren's writing is so convincingly gay and so radiant with genuine happiness and affection that most readers will credit this book with that greater-than-reality truth which is usually only found in myth and poetry.

Lavinia R. Davis, in The New York Times Book Review *(© 1960 by The New York Times Company; reprinted by permission), May 8, 1960 (Part 2), p. 18.*

OTHER CITATIONS

Kirkus Reviews, *February 1, 1960, p. 90.*

Pamela Marsh, in The Christian Science Monitor, *May 12, 1960, p. 3B.*

SEACROW ISLAND (1969)

[*Seacrow Island*] is pleasant and lively, and should provide the average child with plenty to laugh at, enough excitement to keep him interested, and the occasional hint of near-tragedy and disappointment by way of contrast. A closer look at the story might arouse some doubts—isn't it all too idyllic, too warm-hearted, too rose-coloured? . . . Such questions are of course unfair and irrelevant when the story is so obviously intended for amusement only. Amusing it certainly is, and charming and wholesome, but with nothing to disturb the mind or prick the imagination.

The Times Literary Supplement *(© Times Newspapers Ltd., 1968), June 6, 1968, p. 588.*

Probably limited in appeal, [*Seacrow Island* is] a pleasant, leisurely story. . . . Pace varies and points of view shift as the loosely plotted story records the feelings, friendships, and activities of bumbling, affectionate Mr. Melkerson, seven-year-old animal-loving Pelle, the adventurous young teen-agers John and Niklas, and romantic nineteen-year-old Malin who is both sister and mother to the three boys.

The Booklist *(© by the American Library Association), March 1, 1970, pp. 847-48.*

[*Seacrow Island*] is a book for many ages, certainly the nine- to twelve-year-olds. Even eight-year-olds who love to read and are too often limited to slim volumes will appreciate a book that has some substance, is full of humor, amusing personal relationships, and people they will enjoy and have time to know well. The work of [Astrid Lindgren] gives children what they need most in books: wonder, joy, love, hope, refreshment, and excellent storytelling.

Ruth Hill Viguers, in The Horn Book Magazine *(copyright © 1970 by The Horn Book, Inc.; Boston), April, 1970, p. 164.*

The day-to-day adventures of the Swedish family [in *Seacrow Island*] are enlivened by their encounters with some delightful local residents—particularly two sturdy, lively little girls. Some of the episodes are about animals, some about Malin's suitors, and the sustaining theme is the family's love of the island and their acquisition of the cottage they have come to love. The style is vigorous, the characterization and dialogue good; the book may be rather difficult for the reader most likely to enjoy the material—but it can be read aloud to third and fourth graders.

Zena Sutherland, in Bulletin of the Center for Children's Books *(© 1970 by the University of Chicago; all rights reserved), September, 1970, p. 14.*

SIA LIVES ON KILIMANJARO (1959)

A series of [Anna Riwkin-Brick's] fine black-and-white photographs linked together by a minimum of [Astrid Lindgren's] text shows us a day in the life of a little African girl who lives on the slopes of beautiful Mt. Kilimanjaro. . . . The setting is exotic, the costumes strange, but the childhood curiosity, mischief and fun are universal.

Marian Sorenson, in The Christian Science Monitor *(reprinted by permission from* The Christian Science Monitor; *© 1959, The Christian Science Publishing Society; all rights reserved), May 14, 1959, p. 12.*

The story is slight and is, unfortunately, built on an incident of disobedience; nevertheless, [*Sia Lives on Kilimanjaro*] is recommended for [Anna Riwkin-Brick's] fine photographs which give an excellent view of the East African background and a feeling of kinship with children of another land.

The Booklist and Subscription Books Bulletin *(© 1959 by the American Library Association), June 15, 1959, p. 577.*

OTHER CITATIONS

Elvajean Hall, in Library Journal, September 15, 1959, p. 2724.

M

MILNE, A(lan) A(lexander) 1882-1956

An English editor, novelist, playwright, and poet, A. A. Milne was the creator of the well-loved *Winnie-the-Pooh* series. Milne's own son, Christopher Robin, and Christopher Robin's toys served as models for the popular characters in his books.

GENERAL COMMENTARY

Christopher Robin is not one of those innocently feral children Milne intellectually believed in; the little boy is loving and forgiving, godlike in a Christian sense. Some of the animals, like Tigger, *are* innocently feral. In other words, Christopher Robin can be a nice little boy because there are no adults in the stories.

Donald Barr, in Book Week *(© The Washington Post), October 31, 1965 (Part 2), p. 42.*

After the slight archness of the 'frame' dialogue in the first chapter, *Winnie-the-Pooh* (1926) and *The House at Pooh Corner* (1928) spring to life on their own, dictate themselves to Milne and blow away every trace of the faults latent in his other works. The humour, with its touch of nonsense held in place by irresistible logic, and the sure and inevitable creation of character after character make *Pooh* the greatest work of its kind since *Alice*. Indeed, it is almost the only completely successful and original work of that kind. . . .

The *Pooh* stories, wrote Kathleen Lines, 'are known and loved and quoted the world over', and in quotability at least they are only surpassed by *Alice*, though . . . the *Just So Stories* run them a close second. Beatrix Potter had much of this quality, but her whole practical feminine outlook kept her from stepping over the boundary between fancy and fantasy. This was a boundary that Kenneth Grahame could cross, notably in 'The Reluctant Dragon', but it is only a momentary glimpse that he gives us before summoning us back to the deeper magic of *The Wind in the Willows*. . . . Pooh and his companions are the only immortal toys of fiction, and appear likely to remain so.

Roger Lancelyn Green, in his Tellers of Tales: British Authors of Children's Books from 1800 to 1964, *revised edition (copyright 1946, © 1965 by Edmund Ward, Publishers, Ltd.), Kaye & Ward Ltd., 1965, pp. 256-57.*

Because of their craftsmanship, wit, and rhythmical qualities [the works of A. A. Milne] defy criticism and remain gems of verse and prose. Matched with apt drawings by E. H. Shepard, [they] seem to call up something elemental in children that gives these books their deserved immortality. The prose fantasies especially seem to stem from a genuine creative impulse. . . . Pooh, a teddy bear, undeniably expresses best the author's ability to bestow life and personality on a plaything as well as warmth of genuine affection that a child gives it.

Constantine Georgiou, in his Children and Their Literature *(copyright © 1969 by Prentice-Hall, Inc.), Prentice-Hall, 1969, pp. 263-64.*

Perception of the child's world, of his imaginative play caught and enchantingly expressed in A. A. Milne's poetry of childhood, is the substance of his whimsical tales, *Winnie-the-Pooh* (1926) and *The House at Pooh Corner* (1928). . . .

The fun and surprise in [*When We Were Very Young* and *Now We Are Six*] and the gaiety evoked by their exact meter, amusing rhymes, and pictorial quality have made them almost universally known among English-speaking children. . . .

[The] child who emerges from these verses is a composite picture of childhood. In [Milne's] poems children can see themselves, while adults catch nostalgic glimpses of the children they once were. . . .

Mr. Milne quickly became the acknowledged master at capturing both the supreme egotism and the artless beauty of little children.

Ruth Hill Viguers, in A Critical History of Children's Literature, *revised edition, by Cornelia Meigs, Anne Thaxter Eaton, Elizabeth Nesbitt, and Ruth Hill Viguers, edited by Cornelia Meigs (copyright © 1969 by The Macmillan Co.), Macmillan, 1969, pp. 465, 658-59.*

The stories [about Winnie-the-Pooh] are unusual in that

Christopher goes in and out of them on a familiar forest-dwelling level with the animals, but in the end he brings everything back to reality when he sets off up the stairs of his own house, headed for a bath, dragging Pooh by one leg. The stories are finished, Christopher is himself, and Pooh is Pooh. This is not only a tale about toys come to life, but also a clever fantasy for the youngest. . . .

May Hill Arbuthnot and Zena Sutherland, in their Children and Books, *4th edition (copyright © 1947, 1957, 1964, 1972 by Scott, Foresman and Co.), Scott, Foresman, 1972, p. 236.*

Pooh has only one bearlike characteristic, which is that he likes honey. Piglet has one piggy characteristic, which is that he likes Haycorns. Otherwise the characterization is quite arbitrary: Tigger (the tiger) is bouncy, Eeyore the donkey is gloomy, Rabbit is an organizer, and so on; and none of these qualities has anything to do with animal nature. . . .

Apart from any nostalgic pleasure, the adult returning to the Pooh books is bound to appreciate the sheer grace of craftsmanship. Milne was a most accomplished professional writer. He knew and accepted that he was a happy lightweight, and used to say merely that he had the good fortune to *be* like that. In children's as in adult literature, the lightweight of true quality is a rare and welcome phenomenon. The Pooh stories are as totally without hidden significance as anything ever written. . . . For all his rotundity Pooh—bless him—is one-dimensional.

John Rowe Townsend, in his Written for Children: An Outline of English Language Children's Literature, *revised edition (copyright © 1965, 1974 by John Rowe Townsend; reprinted by permission of J.B. Lippincott Company), Lippincott, 1974, pp. 171-72.*

It is, precisely, the limitations imposed on them that give the Christopher Robin books their timelessness. By mythicizing his own social world in terms of a small boy and a group of nursery animals, Milne at last broke through the restrictions of his own class, age, and country, to achieve the immortality which his "adult" writing always missed.

Peter Green, in The Times Literary Supplement *(© Times Newspapers Ltd., 1975), April 4, 1975, p. 375.*

ONCE ON A TIME (1922)

Ostensibly [*Once on a Time*] tells the story of two kings who go to war, and of the women who rule in their absence. Symbolically, it is a good natured spoof of all fairy tales, and in the long run, of the uncontrollable but forgivable foibles of human nature. Children who cannot yet go below the surface will be rewarded nevertheless by the activities [of the rulers] and by the hilarious conduct of men at war. Adults will delight in the typical Milne humor and the allegorical meanings. Susan Perl's comic, current illustrations are perfectly attuned to the text.

Virginia Kirkus' Service, *December 15, 1961, p. 1086.*

The sly tongue-in-cheek humor [of *Once On a Time*] has an adult quality, and the length of the story will limit its appeal to older boys and girls. The story of King Merriweg, the fair Princess Hyacinth, the brave Coronel, the pretentious Prince Udo, and the wicked Countess Belvane reaches a surprisingly happy climax.

Allie Beth Martin, in School Library Journal, *(reprinted from the February, 1962, issue of* School Library Journal, *published by R. R. Bowker Co., a Xerox company; copyright © 1962 by Xerox Corporation), February, 1962, pp. 42-3.*

It's a welcome return trip through an ever-ever land of wars and witches, king and fairies, and magic rings with A. A. Milne's timeless "Once on a Time" (New York Graphic Society [1962]), back in print after an absence of forty years. . . . A pretty young princess, a conniving, beautiful countess, and a rabbit-headed, lion-tailed prince of Araby skip, glide, and sometimes stumble through all the grand deceits and petty follies of modern mortals, but with a proper dash of wizardry. It's all in a royal day's work. Moral: people, especially as depicted in print by Milne and picture by Susan Perl, can be enchanting.

Saturday Review *(copyright © 1962 by Saturday Review, Inc.; reprinted with permission), February 24, 1962, p. 29.*

OTHER CITATIONS

Aileen Pippett, in The New York Times Book Review, *March 4, 1962, p. 34.*

Barbara A. Bannon, in Publishers' Weekly, *June 13, 1966, p. 131.*

THE POOH STORY BOOK (1965)

[*The Pooh Story Book*] is presumably a blast of the authentic Pooh against the Disney heresy. One sympathises. Yet it rarely pays to meddle with perfection and most lilies are best ungilded. The small scale of the original Shepard pictures matched that of the text. Blown up, they lose their intimacy. Coloured, they lose their touch of mystery. Pooh in line is more than Bear. In colour he seems just a teddy-bear. Christopher Robin, not the most successful of Shepard's interpretations, is now sentimentalised still further. The new pictures do not amount to much although there are small and pleasing touches in the sketching on of landscape. Some of the redrawn pictures are definitely less good than the originals, notably the favourite one of Pooh and Christopher Robin playing Pooh-sticks; the altogether pleasing frontispiece of *The House at Pooh Corner* is now provided with a technicolour sunset and with the fine balance of the original lost.

The Junior Bookshelf. *December, 1967, pp. 379-80.*

Two stories from *The House at Pooh Corner* and one from *Winnie-the-Pooh* are illustrated with new pictures by Mr. Shepard very much like those drawings he did for the original Milne editions. An attractive book with some pictures in color, but this seems expensive and unnecessary. . . . Why frustrate a child by giving him only these three stories? Too much packaging and not enough substance for the price.

School Library Journal *(reprinted from the October, 1965, issue of* School Library Journal, *published by R. R. Bowker Co., a Xerox company; copyright © 1965 by Xerox Corporation), October, 1965, p. 220.*

OTHER CITATIONS

Thomas Lask, in The New York Times Book Review, *November 7, 1965 (Part 2), p. 60.*

***PRINCE RABBIT AND THE PRINCESS WHO COULD NOT LAUGH* (1966)**

One of those books that are fun for the reader as well as the read-to is *Prince Rabbit and The Princess Who Could Not Laugh*. . . . These A. A. Milne stories, not previously published in book form, may not have been handed down through the centuries. But they have the fairy-tale atmosphere of tests to be taken and brides to be won. The difference is a slight teasing of the conventions . . . rabbit becomes the hero, for example, and the Chancellor becomes the victim of the King's repartee. Fairy tales are not naturally funny, but these are.

Roderick Nordell, in The Christian Science Monitor *(reprinted by permission from* The Christian Science Monitor; *© 1966 The Christian Science Publishing Society; all rights reserved), November 3, 1966, p. B2.*

These two stories [*Prince Rabbit and the Princess Who Could Not Laugh*] are in a manner of which the best known and the most successful exponent was Andrew Lang. That is, they are mock-fairy tales playing lightly with the conventions of the authentic folk-tale. *Prince Rabbit* is the more successful. It was a happy idea to make a rabbit the best contender for the title of King's Heir. Inevitably the rabbit turns into a prince in the end but most readers will prefer him in his earlier shape. The second story is much less funny. Mary Shepard's illustrations are thin and flat. They lack altogether the depth of character of her father's work, and indeed of her own for Mary Poppins. The book gives a little pleasure, but Milne's great reputation rests still on his Pooh and Christopher Robin books.

The Junior Bookshelf, *December, 1966, p. 372.*

OTHER CITATIONS

Lavinia Russ, in Publishers' Weekly, *October 10, 1966, p. 74.*

***TOAD OF TOAD HALL* (1929)**

[This 1965 Scribner edition of *Toad of Toad Hall* contains] no changes . . . in text from the first 1929 edition and only slight changes in format: e.g., character's names appear above rather than on a line with narration, and a different typeface with lighter characters and closer spacing give a slightly more crowded appearance. Biographies of [Kenneth] Grahame and Milne are included. Unavailable for many years, this is a welcome addition to all libraries.

Marguerite Bagshaw, in School Library Journal *(reprinted from the March, 1965, issue of* School Library Journal, *published by R. R. Bowker Co., a Xerox company; copyright © 1965 by Xerox Corporation), March, 1965, p. 186.*

A. A. Milne created [*Toad of Toad Hall*] from [Kenneth Grahame's] *The Wind in the Willows*. . . . The unifying theme of [the play] is the story of Toad and his friends; and the flavor of the [original] book is captured, despite some typically Milne touches of whimsey and sentimentality.

Ethel L. Heins, in The Horn Book Magazine *(copyright © 1965, by The Horn Book, Inc., Boston), August, 1965, p. 407.*

OTHER CITATIONS

Books for Children 1960-1965: As Selected and Reviewed by *The Booklist and Subscription Books Bulletin* September 1960 through August 1965, *American Library Association, 1966, p. 162.*

***THE WORLD OF CHRISTOPHER ROBIN* (1958)**

A companion to *The World of Pooh*, this collection offers the complete poetic adventures of Pooh Bear's companion, Christopher, as he wanders through the enchanted pages of *When We Were Very Young* and *Now We Are Six*. Six or sixty, one will inevitably be delighted by the Milne verses and the E. H. Shepard illustrations which appear in their complete form along with eight new color illustrations done by the artist for this edition.

Virginia Kirkus' Service, *September 1, 1958, p. 658.*

***THE WORLD OF POOH* (1957)**

The immortal nursery animals that brought the world of Pooh alive to small listeners some 26 years ago are perennial favorites with the next generation today. [In *The World of Pooh*] Mr. Milne has combined their adventures, including the complete *Winnie the Pooh* and *The House at Pooh Corner*, and the original illustrator, E. H. Shepard, has redrawn some of the old pictures and made some new colored ones for this onmibus volume for the delectation of the small fry in today's nurseries.

Virginia Kirkus' Service, *November 1, 1957, p. 811.*

O

O'DELL, Scott 1903-

An American historian, journalist, and author of books for both adults and children, Scott O'Dell received the 1961 Newbery Medal for *Island of the Blue Dolphins* and the 1972 Hans Christian Andersen Award.

GENERAL COMMENTARY

One suspects that a quick, light step is not natural to Scott O'Dell. His is a more measured tread. And probably he is a long-distance man. His most substantial books have been his most successful, and *The King's Fifth*—a sombre, almost stately novel—is his best of all. . . . His best stories grow, moreover, from roots which are planted in known experience, actual places, historical fact, books; and there is neither wit nor humour in them. His imagination is strong but it does not soar or sparkle. He is a natural heavyweight.

John Rowe Townsend, in his A Sense of Story: Essays on Contemporary Writing for Children *(copyright © 1971 by John Rowe Townsend; reprinted by permission of J. B. Lippincott Company), Lippincott, 1971, p. 159.*

THE BLACK PEARL (1967)

[This] legendlike story, as well as the setting and characters, has a strong feeling of authenticity. Overtones, symbolism, unique atmosphere, inevitability make a memorable tale, but first of all it is a gripping story that will hold practically any age enthralled, and so well written that it can be read aloud with pleasure.

Ruth Hill Viguers, in The Horn Book Magazine *(copyright © 1967, by The Horn Book, Inc., Boston), October, 1967, p. 603.*

[*The Black Pearl*] is a curiously compelling story. Not perhaps as moving as the author's exquisite *The Island of the Blue Dolphins*, it seems more in the spirit of *The King's Fifth*, as with strength, simplicity and subtle overtones it probes man's eternal struggle between good and evil.

Polly Goodwin, in Book World *(©* The Washington Post*), November 5, 1967 (Part 2), p. 32.*

Once more Scott O'Dell has demonstrated his mastery of simple, rhythmic first-person narrative. Whether the reader can accept Ramon's conclusion has no effect on the validity of the plot; the boy himself is completely believable, and his sincerity is communicated from the first words to the final page. The other characters . . . all have the air of authenticity evoked by the story-teller's suspenseful, cadenced prose. The added dimension of the age-old struggle between reason and superstition, between the sense and the senses, makes ["The Black Pearl"] a worthy successor to "The Island of the Blue Dolphins" and "The King's Fifth."

Della Thomas, in The New York Times Book Review *(© 1967 by The New York Times Company; reprinted by permission), November 5, 1967 (Part 2), p. 20.*

[*The Black Pearl*] is vividly and simply told by Ramon himself, in an archaic "I, Ramon" style that is not overdone but gives the story a distinctive flavour. The characters are few and strongly contrasted, and the story moves through tragedy and danger to a dramatic conclusion.

The Times Literary Supplement *(© Times Newspapers Ltd., 1968), June 6, 1968, p. 588.*

OTHER CITATIONS

Publishers' Weekly, *October 23, 1967, p. 52.*

Zena Sutherland, in Bulletin of the Center for Children's Books, *December, 1967, p. 64.*

The Booklist and Subscription Books Bulletin, *December 1, 1967, p. 450.*

THE CRUISE OF THE ARCTIC STAR (1973)

Only Scott O'Dell could turn an uneventful cruise up the Pacific coast into a suspenseful adventure based entirely on his growing suspicions about the reliability of the *Arctic Star*'s hired skipper and, at the same time, conduct a grand tour from the confines of the boat's cabin. . . . While the *Arctic Star* is real, this is definitely a novelist's interpretation, the voyage a framework for all those scenes from the California past which the author has obviously long had in his imagination. It's worth going along.

Kirkus Reviews *(copyright © 1973 The Kirkus Service, Inc.) February 1, 1973, p. 128.*

["The Cruise of the Arctic Star"] is open-ended, for on the last page Alaska is still far away and, as life, leaves many questions unanswered. . . . What is the significance of the Arctic Star to Island Eagle, or man to man, sea to land, heaven to hell?

In prose that ranges from the clipped speech of men fixing a motor to the rich cadence of storytelling and the sensuous naming of ships, landmarks, creatures and places, the reader may drink in O'Dell's passions. "We are still at sea," he writes, "where anything can happen." What happens, in the plot, requires that we, like the author, re-examine a few of our own myths.

Myra Cohn Livingston, in The New York Times Book Review *(© 1973 by The New York Times Company; reprinted by permission), March 25, 1973, p. 8.*

[This] account of a sea trip . . . blends reminiscences from the author's past with passages from the books he loves, his views on wildlife preservation, and episodes from the history of California. . . . Only so adept a writer [as Scott O'Dell] could achieve success with the mixture, sometimes spellbinding, consisting of a wealth of incidental information about history, marine ecology, and seamanship. Seven pictorial coastal maps [by Samuel Bryant] are placed in proper sequence for elucidating the sailing course—some 2,000 miles from San Diego to the Columbia River.

Virginia Haviland, in The Horn Book Magazine *(copyright © 1973 by The Horn Book, Inc., Boston), August, 1973, p. 390.*

Interwoven in the adventures experienced by O'Dell on a small-craft voyage from San Diego, California to Portland, Oregon are vignettes of California history . . . as well as informal lessons on ecology. . . . Navigational problems, such as an account of the seven U.S. Navy ships that crashed into the cliffs of Honda Head rock in September of 1923, add tension, and the complex relationships between O'Dell, his wife and friend, and Rod Lambert, a handsome and daring but unreliable young hired man, provide an interesting personal dimension.

Kathryn A. Litsinger, in School Library Journal *(reprinted from the December, 1973, issue of* School Library Journal, *published by R. R. Bowker Co., a Xerox company; copyright © 1973 by Xerox Corporation), December, 1973, p. 57.*

OTHER CITATIONS

Kirkus Reviews, *February 1, 1973, p. 128.*

Publishers' Weekly, *March 12, 1973, p. 64.*

Zena Sutherland, in Bulletin of the Center for Children's Books, *July-August, 1973, p. 174.*

THE DARK CANOE (1968)

["The Dark Canoe"] is a piggyback novel, an ill-advised literary exercise in which Scott O'Dell . . . draws on a classic ["Moby Dick"] hoping to add depth to a simple story. Not that this is cheating; Mr. O'Dell honestly hoped to ride the immortal white whale to new glory—But his Ahab-like character and Queequeg's eternally floating canoe merely muddy the waters. Too bad, because the author has narrative flair when he follows his own course.

Robert Hood, in The New York Times Book Review *(© 1968 by The New York Times Company; reprinted by permission), November 3, 1968 (Part 2), p. 22.*

[No] summary can do justice to a brooding, twilit quality which makes [*The Dark Canoe*] an adventure more of the mind than of the sea. . . . Figures and events from *Moby Dick* are given eerie, shadowy counterparts in *The Dark Canoe*. So quietly, so persuasively, is this accomplished that when Ishmael's ocean-going coffin drifts out of Melville's seas into O'Dell's, it carries no shock for either Nathan or the reader. And when the *Alert* finally stands out to sea, we do not know whether she is commanded by Caleb Clegg bound homeward for Nantucket, or by Captain Ahab sailing once more in vengeful pursuit of the White Whale.

Digby B. Whitman, in Book World *(©* The Washington Post*), November 3, 1968 (Part 2), p. 12.*

Whether or not the story gains from its intertwining with Melville's masterpiece of "Moby Dick" is a point that can be argued. Also, the splendid description, and the moments of lofty symbolism, at times almost sink the fragile story. But nonetheless, reading "The Dark Canoe" is an enjoyable voyage. Like other modern stories in this category it is almost a plotless narrative, a sort of unfolding of events rather than an attempt to shape them.

Guernsey Le Pelley, in The Christian Science Monitor *(reprinted by permission from* The Christian Science Monitor; *© 1968 The Christian Science Publishing Society; all rights reserved), November 7, 1968, p. B12.*

OTHER CITATIONS

Bruce L. MacDuffie, in Library Journal, *December 15, 1968, pp. 4733-34.*

Zena Sutherland, in Saturday Review, *December 21, 1968, p. 40.*

ISLAND OF THE BLUE DOLPHINS (1960)

[*Island of the Blue Dolphins* is a] most unusual story, based on historical incident, of an Indian girl whose tribe was evacuated from her home island. . . . Told in the first person, Karana's record is convincing—a tour de force for a male author—and the writing style is distinctive and appropriate in flavor to the background. Since the far greater part of the book is concerned with Karana's long years of solitude, there is perhaps too much time devoted to minute details of hunting, fishing, weaving, etc., but for the reader who spurns teen-age romances, this will be a refreshingly different book.

Zena Sutherland, in Bulletin of the Center for Children's Books *(published by the University of Chicago), April, 1960, p. 134.*

The rare quality of [*Island of the Blue Dolphins*] lies in Mr. O'Dell's ability to depict the majesty of the heroine's lonely struggle. . . . The story is well written and the main character is vividly presented. . . .

The heroine's control of her emotions and her realistic appraisal of the situation are stressed by [Mr. O'Dell]. The motivations of the Indian girl are examined in greater depth than is usually accorded the fictional Indian. Young adults will admire and respect Karana's fortitude. Her transformation from her early instincts of fear and revenge to her acceptance of love for all living things is well presented. The author's knowledge of the marine life gives added interest.

John Gillespie and Diana Lembo, in their Juniorplots: A Book Talk Manual for Teachers and Librarians *(© 1967 by the R. R. Bowker Co.), Bowker, 1967, pp. 47, 49.*

O'Dell has used choice bits of history about the Ghalas-at Indians to tell a story of a girl who finds herself marooned on an island. Told in the first person, her strange and beautiful story reveals the strongest of human attributes: courage, endurance, and greatness of spirit. Nor are loyalty, beauty, serenity, and peace overlooked. Perfectly blended together, these qualities portray a character who arouses in the reader the fullest sense of character identification so that the whole story becomes a living and lasting experience.

Constantine Georgiou, in his Children and Their Literature *(copyright © 1969 by Prentice-Hall, Inc.), Prentice-Hall, 1969, pp. 316-17.*

Most unusual of all the survival stories, both for subject and for beauty of literary style, is *Island of the Blue Dolphins* (1960). . . . [Scott O'Dell] has Karana tell her own story of being left behind when her people evacuated the island. . . . Her strange, beautiful account reveals courage, serenity, and greatness of spirit, and is a lasting experience for children who have the chance to know her.

Ruth Hill Viguers, in A Critical History of Children's Literature, *revised edition, by Cornelia Meigs, Anne Thaxter Eaton, Elizabeth Nesbitt, and Ruth Hill Viguers, edited by Cornelia Meigs (copyright © 1969 by The Macmillan Co.), Macmillan, 1969, p. 491.*

[*Island of the Blue Dolphins*] is the beautifully told story of [Karana's] survival on the island for eighteen years. . . . Shining through her struggles and hardships are her quiet resignation, her endurance, her genuine love for her island home, and the great fortitude and serenity she developed.

May Hill Arbuthnot and Zena Sutherland, in their Children and Books, *4th edition (copyright © 1947, 1957, 1964, 1972 by Scott, Foresman and Co.), Scott, Foresman, 1972, p. 519.*

The isolation of Karana, the Indian girl in *Island of the Blue Dolphins*, is total and involuntary; it lasts through all the years of youth. Yet she manages to be sane; to grow in wisdom and in dignity; her strength of character transforms an intrinsically sad story into an inspiring one.

John Rowe Townsend, in his Written for Children: An Outline of English Language Children's Literature, *revised edition (copyright © 1965, 1974 by John Rowe Townsend; reprinted by permission of J.B. Lippincott Company), Lippincott, 1974, p. 213.*

OTHER CITATIONS

Ellen Lewis Buell, in The New York Times Book Review, *March 27, 1960, pp. 40-1.*

The Booklist and Subscription Books Bulletin, *April 1, 1960, p. 489.*

Miriam S. Mathes, in Library Journal, *April 15, 1960, p. 1702.*

JOURNEY TO JERICHO **(1969)**

If the author of "Journey to Jericho" were anyone but Scott O'Dell, this book would be dismissed as a slight tale that shows promise. Indeed, the story . . . is hardly more than an extended magazine story. But the author is Scott O'Dell, Newbery winner; the writing is clean, sparkling and direct. . . . Perhaps it is critical carping but I wish this were just the opening of a longer, deeper book, with full-bodied characters instead of the work we have here—especially from such a proven, mature writer.

Jane Yolen, in The New York Times Book Review *(© 1969 by The New York Times Company; reprinted by permission), November 16, 1969, p. 56.*

Not as outstanding as *The Black Pearl* (1967) or *Island of the Blue Dolphins* (1960 . . .), [*Journey to Jericho*] is a long short story that captures mood and character while it presents just enough action to carry readers along. The economic use of words produces a deceptively simple story; its overtones will echo in readers' minds long after the action is forgotten.

School Library Journal *(reprinted from the December, 1969, issue of* School Library Journal, *published by R. R. Bowker Co., a Xerox company; copyright © 1969 by Xerox Corporation), December, 1969, p. 58.*

[*Journey to Jericho* is a] sedate story, competently written but slow-paced and not wholly cohesive; [Leonard Weisgard's] illustrations are attractive in sophisticated black, brown and white. . . . The first half of the book describes the life in Big Loop and the decision to go west, a few pages are devoted to the summer in which David misses his father, and the rest of the story is about the trip; the long, slow beginning robs the journey of importance.

Zena Sutherland, in Bulletin of the Center for Children's Books *(© 1970 by the University of Chicago; all rights reserved), February, 1970, p. 104.*

OTHER CITATIONS

Zena Sutherland, in Saturday Review, *December 20, 1969, p. 29.*

Ethel L. Heins, in The Horn Book Magazine, *April, 1970, p. 164.*

***THE KING'S FIFTH* (1966)**

The theme of Conquistador betraying Indian, betraying his fellows and inevitably betraying himself, has been given no more powerful expression than in Newbery winner Scott O'Dell's second novel for young people. . . . The author uses the first person, near-diary form to heighten the immediate moment—the trial—and confer a documentary value on the retrospective narrative. And the ending eschews, in large measure, the contrived solution of many juveniles. . . . Unloose the adjectives for [*The King's Fifth*]: a stunning novel of compelling interest and mounting impact.

Virginia Kirkus' Service *(copyright © 1966 Virginia Kirkus' Service, Inc.), September 1, 1966, p. 913.*

Mr. O'Dell must have been deeply immersed in the history and literature of the conquistadores, for Indians, villages, landscapes, lake of gold, all are vivid. As would be expected from the author of *Island of the Blue Dolphins*, the writing is subtly beautiful, often moving, and says more than may be caught in one reading.

Ruth Hill Viguers, in The Horn Book Magazine *(copyright © 1966, by The Horn Book, Inc., Boston), December, 1966, p. 722.*

[Scott O'Dell's] low-keyed, powerful writing and the first-person narration, which skillfully interweaves Estéban's chronicle of the past with his report of the ongoing trial, give a strong sense of reality and immediacy to this compelling, deeply felt story of a boy who, almost too late, comes to realize the awful cost of the lust for gold in honor and human life.

The Booklist and Subscription Books Bulletin *(© 1966 by the American Library Association), December 15, 1966, p. 452.*

The characters [in "The King's Fifth"] are brave and cruel, and they fit without being memorable. . . . But the story is first-rate with a fast, suspenseful pace set and sustained from the beginning. The treasure hunt is treated in retrospect during Estéban's trial for withholding the "King's fifth," the author doing a masterful job intertwining the two story lines.

James Forman, in The New York Times Book Review *(© 1967 by The New York Times Company; reprinted by permission), January 15, 1967, p. 28.*

OTHER CITATIONS

Lavinia Russ, in Publishers' Weekly, *October 10, 1966, p. 74.*

Zena Sutherland, in Saturday Review, *November 12, 1966, p. 53.*

Zena Sutherland, in Bulletin of the Center for Children's Books, *January, 1967, p. 78.*

***SING DOWN THE MOON* (1970)**

[This] story is told quietly as if in keeping with the natural stoical dignity of the American Indian, permitting the facts of "man's cruelty to man" to speak for themselves. [*Sing Down the Moon* is not] as powerful or as complex as the author's previous novels, but just as significant for its depiction of the triumph of the human spirit.

Paul Heins, in The Horn Book Magazine *(copyright © 1970 by The Horn Book, Inc., Boston), December, 1970, p. 623.*

Bright Morning is the young Navaho girl who tells the story of her people [in *Sing Down the Moon*]; like the heroine of *Island of the Blue Dolphins*, she has a quiet courage that prevails over circumstance. . . . The very simplicity of [O'Dell's] writing, at times almost terse, makes more vivid the tragedy of the eviction and the danger and triumph of the return.

Zena Sutherland, in Bulletin of the Center for Children's Books *(© 1971 by the University of Chicago; all rights reserved), January, 1971, p. 78.*

In a style that combines simplicity and intensity, Scott O'Dell shows a centuries-old way of life broken by forces it cannot understand, a proud and independent people reduced to accepting grudging hand-outs, a race of hunters and pastoralists treated like cattle. The story is told by Bright Morning, a young Navaho girl, whose simple belief in the fitness of her people's ways sustains her through a private ordeal when she is sold into slavery, and the degradation of her tribe when they are harried from their homes. [*Sing Down the Moon* is a] worthy addition to the work of a fine children's novelist.

C.E.J. Smith, in Children's Book Review *(© 1973 Five Owls Press Ltd.), February, 1973, p. 16.*

OTHER CITATIONS

Kirkus Reviews, *October 15, 1970, p. 1149.*

The Booklist, *November 1, 1970, p. 230.*

***THE TREASURE OF TOPO-EL-BAMPO* (1972)**

Scott O'Dell, who is at his best in high adventure ("The King's Fifth") or in a stark background ("Island of the Blue Dolphins," . . .), seems impatient and ill at ease in a Mexican village with only two displaced donkeys to worry about. It's too bad for we would like to get inside . . . "The Treasure of Topo-el-Bampo" . . . and feel at home with at least some of [the] characters. . . . But Mr. O'Dell is almost impersonal, shifting his focus so that we are never inside one character long enough to feel much of anything.

Jean Fritz, in The New York Times Book Review *(© 1972 by The New York Times Company; reprinted by permission), April 23, 1972, p. 8.*

[*The Treasure of Topo-el-Bampo* is a] story set in Mexico two hundred years ago. . . . [Scott O'Dell's] style is sprightly, [Lynd Ward's] illustrations attractive, and the story of historical interest; the picture of the poverty-stricken peasants and the conditions of mining are smoothly enough presented. The story is somewhat overburdened, however, by the convenience of the bandit-incident and the detailed account of the mayor's family, a beginning that has too much emphasis for a story that doesn't, for a large portion of the book, concern them.

Zena Sutherland, in Bulletin of the Center for Children's Books *(© 1972 by the University of Chicago; all rights reserved), May, 1972, pp. 143-44.*

The narrative [in *The Treasure of Topo-el-Bampo*] has a folkstory-like quality and moves swiftly along in uncomplicated sentences; it is direct in telling and interspersed with bits of humor. Although the donkeys occupy the center of attention, the characters—children, mayor, village priest, owners of the silver mine—are remarkably well delineated despite the brevity of their appearance. And terrain, story, and characters are all superbly served by Lynd Ward's paintings—gray on yellowish tan against a white background. . . . Both story and pictures are perfectly compatible in their combination of seriousness and joy.

Paul Heins, in The Horn Book Magazine *(copyright © 1972 by The Horn Book, Inc., Boston), June, 1972, p. 265.*

How the two donkeys help Topo-el-Bampo, the poorest village in Mexico, to become the richest village is told with restraint and grace in a story which, though not one of the author's best, is nonetheless warmly satisfying. Forceful two-color drawings [by Lynd Ward] accentuate the Mexican setting.

The Booklist *(© American Library Association 1972), July 1, 1972, p. 943.*

P

POTTER, Beatrix 1866-1943

An English author-illustrator, Beatrix Potter is most remembered for her classic, *The Tale of Peter Rabbit*, first published in 1902. Others of her still-loved books include *The Tale of Jemima Puddle-Duck, The Tale of Squirrel Nutkin*, and *The Tailor of Gloucester*.

GENERAL COMMENTARY

'It is said that the effect of eating too much lettuce is soporific.' It is with some such precise informative sentence that one might have expected the great Potter saga to open, for the obvious characteristic of Beatrix Potter's style is a selective realism, which takes emotion for granted and puts aside love and death with a gentle detachment reminiscent of Mr. E. M. Forster's. Her stories contain plenty of dramatic action, but it is described from the outside by an acute and unromantic observer who never sacrifices truth for an effective gesture. (p. 232)

Miss Potter is seldom at her best with human beings . . . though with one human character she succeeded triumphantly. I refer of course to Mr. MacGregor, who made an elusive appearance in 1904 in *The Tale of Benjamin Bunny*, ran his crabbed earth-mould way through *Peter Rabbit*, and met his final ignominious defeat in *The Flopsy Bunnies* in 1909. (p. 233)

From 1904 to 1908 were [her] vintage years in comedy; to these years belong *The Pie and the Patty Pan, The Tale of Tom Kitten, The Tale of Mrs Tiggy Winkle*, and only one failure, *Mr Jeremy Fisher*. Miss Potter had found her right vein and her right scene. The novels were now set in Cumberland; the farms, the village shops, the stone walls, the green slope of Catbells became the background of her pictures and her prose. She was peopling a countryside. Her dialogue had become memorable because aphoristic: *'I disapprove of tin articles in puddings and pies. It is most undesirable—(especially when people swallow in lumps).'* (pp. 235-36)

Graham Greene, "Beatrix Potter" (1933), in his Collected Essays *(copyright 1951, © 1969 by Graham Greene; all rights reserved; reprinted by permission of Viking Press, Inc.), Viking, 1969, pp. 232-40.*

It is not for me to evaluate [Beatrix Potter's] art in relation to that of others. What is of far more interest is why her books are so beloved. Certainly it is not only because of their small size, as someone suggested. There are others just as little. Nor because people like to see animals dressed in human clothes. So many dressed-up animals prance through children's books and are gone tomorrow. Is it because in spite of being put into books and clothes, Peter Rabbit, Hunca Munca, Mrs. Tiggy-Winkle, Tom Kitten and all the others stay pretty much themselves? . . .

Beatrix Potter never ridicules or caricatures animals or distorts their small features with human expressions. She must have loved them too much just as they were. And when she dresses them up she is like a little girl who, stuffing her kitten into doll's clothes, laughs with delight to see how absurd and how darling it looks! . . .

Every bit of an animal that sticks out of those clothes, as well as all the creatures wearing only their own skins, is as accurately, carefully and beautifully drawn as if each was a portrait of an individual animal, as indeed many of them were. Perhaps that is why her books have been taken to so many hearts in various countries.

Dorothy P. Lathrop, in The Horn Book Magazine *(copyrighted, 1955, by The Horn Book, Inc., Boston), October, 1955, pp. 335-36.*

I have always been glad that my own first impressions of Beatrix Potter as an artist were taken from *The Tailor of Gloucester* and from *Squirrel Nutkin*, published in the same year, rather than from *Peter Rabbit*. The individuality of character and setting of each little book remains clearer in mind in consequence and the value of her contribution to children's books, as her own direct communication of the natural world to children, more fully appreciated. To me they have always been Beatrix Potter's books rather than the Peter Rabbit books.

Anne Carroll Moore, "An Appreciation" (1955), in The Art of Beatrix Potter, *with notes by Enid and Leslie Linder (© 1972 Frederick Warne & Co. Ltd), Warne, revised edition, 1972, p. xiii.*

It is given to only a few writers to add something to the

total of experience. Beatrix Potter's creation of character is comparable in kind, though not in degree, to that of Dickens. Both had the power of drawing individuals who represented also a summary of experience. It is this timeless universal quality which has embedded Tom Kitten, Jemima Puddle-Duck and Pigling Bland deep in the hearts of those who have met them at the right timc and in the right company. Such characters are not less orginial and memorable for being conveyed in a few words and a few lines.(p. 216)

Everyone who loves Beatrix Potter loves and remembers the pictures; her prose is often taken for granted when it is not condemned. She was in fact as great a master of word as of line. The mannerisms are always calculated; they give an atmosphere of formality and elegance where the mood of the story needs it. In ordinary narrative she is clean and economical, never a word too many and every one in its place. She is particularly successful in dialogue, which is beautifully expressed and always coloured by the characters of the speakers. There are obvious advantages in being one's own illustrator; equally it helps for an illustrator to be her own author. Drawing is a slow process compared with writing, and while putting in the perfections of detail in her pictures Beatrix had ample time to ponder her story and to distil the fine essence of every word. (p. 217).

Marcus Crouch, "Beatrix Potter's World" (© Marcus Crouch 1960), in Henry Treece, C. S. Lewis and Beatrix Potter, *by Margery Fisher, Roger Lancelyn Green and Marcus Crouch, Bodley Head, 1969, pp. 215-18.*

[Beatrix Potter's] English country-side animals are depicted as real, even when wearing clothes; her stories have a detailed directness and also show real understanding of animal character. Her stories have some moral and always have some kind of a happy ending. . . . Her pictures are good art with faithfulness to animal character. In [*The Tale of Peter Rabbit*] and all her 30 other books there is nothing grotesque or deceiving or really gruesome. Beatrix Potter was really the Queen of them all when presenting personified animals in pictures and words for young children.

Ruth S. Freeman, in her Children's Picture Books: Yesterday and Today *(copyright 1967 by Ruth S. Freeman; reprinted by permission of the Century House, Watkins Glen, N.Y.), Century House, 1967, p. 97.*

Aside from the fact that [Beatrix Potter] was not afraid to use quite long words for the very young if they were just the right words, here is neither prettiness, preciousness, nor sentimentality in her pages. . . . One even finds in her books a kind of faint irony of expression, a wonderful pithiness, dryness, toughness, which are quite astonishing qualities when you consider the youth of her readers. . . . Her humor *is* expressed in spare, chastened prose, using exactly the right words to convey in unbelievably brief compass precisely the scene or feeling or action she had in mind.

Eleanor Cameron, in her The Green and Burning Tree: On the Writing and Enjoyment of Children's Books *(copyright ©1962, 1964, 1966, 1969 by Eleanor Cameron; reprinted by permission of Little, Brown and Co. in association with The Atlantic Monthly Press), Little, Brown, pp. 27-8.*

It is the delicate and discerning quality of imagination, the exquisite, disciplined economy of incident, detail, and words, the unusual perception of what pleases little children, which give [Beatrix Potter's stories] distinction and which mark her as an author of authentic genius. . . .

[Underlying] her stories are the eternal verities of life—love of home and countryside, the dignity of work, the decency of simple, average beings, the mingled humor and pathos of existence. It is the reflection of these imperishable truths which makes the tales of Beatrix Potter classics in miniature.

Elizabeth Nesbitt, in A Critical History of Children's Literature *revised edition, by Cornelia Meigs, Anne Thaxter Eaton, Elizabeth Nesbitt, and Ruth Hill Viguers, edited by Cornelia Meigs (copyright © 1969 by The Macmillan Co.), Macmillan, 1969, pp. 323, 327.*

[Beatrix Potter's] stories are invariably built on the neverfail formula of a beginning, a middle, and an end, with plenty of suspense to bring sighs of relief when the conclusion is finally reached. Children chuckle over the funny characters, the absurd predicaments, and the narrow escapes. They pore over the clear watercolor illustrations, which are full of action. Even at four they absorb delightedly the lovely details of landscape, old houses, fine old furniture and china, and at forty, learn why they liked them.

May Hill Arbuthnot and Zena Sutherland, in their Children and Books, *4th edition (copyright © 1947, 1957, 1964, 1972 by Scott, Foresman and Co.), Scott, Foresman, 1972, p. 224.*

Beatrix Potter's little books give small children the pleasure they do, not because they are childlike in their view, but because they are so thoroughly sensible and wholly forthright about the realities with which they deal. From story to story, the tales mesh in countless small ways that only a mature and thoroughly engaged mind . . . could conceive and control. . . . A palpable reality, as solid as the world's, was created by Miss Potter from the elements of her various animal adventures. And those larger truths that she encounters in her tales are never sidestepped. Of the pigs in one of her books, she wrote: "They led prosperous uneventful lives and their end was bacon". . . .

Selma G. Lanes, in her Down the Rabbit Hole: Adventures and Misadventures in the Realm of Children's Literature *(copyright © 1971 by Selma G. Lanes), Atheneum, 1972, pp. 206-07.*

Graham Greene's essay on Beatrix Potter was written no doubt with tongue in cheek; his references to her 'vintage years in comedy' and 'the period of the great near-tragedies' are not to be taken too seriously; but behind his gentle satire there obviously lies a genuine respect for her work. . . . The firm ring of the words, the precise composition and characterization of the drawings, the dry humour and the decisive and satisfying conclusions are common to all of her books. They differ in their individual nature but they are alike in excellence and they are all parts of a body of work that has a country-grown flavour and firmness.

John Rowe Townsend, in his Written for Children: An Outline of English Language Children's Literature, *revised edition (copyright © 1965, 1974 by John Rowe Townsend; reprinted by permission of J.B. Lippincott Company), Lippincott, 1974, p. 156.*

***THE SLY OLD CAT* (1972; written 1906)**

Beatrix Potter's *The Sly Old Cat* is now published for the first time, illustrated with her preliminary sketches, and we must be grateful that it has been finally brought to light. The book was written as a companion to *The Story of a Fierce Bad Rabbit* and *The Story of Miss Moppet*, and it shares with these two the same continuous-present narrative form and the same strong, simple story line. . . . The pictures, sketchy as they are, have life and character.

The Times Literary Supplement *(© Times Newspapers Ltd., 1971), October 22, 1971, p. 1324.*

The story [of *The Sly Old Cat*] is comparatively slight (and older than Aesop) and the pictures, from Miss Potter's preliminary sketches, have a bare look about them, but Potter followers will discern flashes of the well-known diminutive charm.

Kirkus Reviews *(copyright © 1972 The Kirkus Service, Inc.), March 15, 1972, p. 322.*

[In *The Sly Old Cat*] Potter deftly establishes character, brief as the tale is, by referring to "Mr. Rat" but—more brusquely—to "Cat": no title for a miscreant. Yet Cat comes to no real harm, and if there is a lesson, it is a gentle one, the softness and humor of the illustrations robbing the story of any didacticism.

Zena Sutherland, in Bulletin of the Center for Children's Books *(© 1972 by the University of Chicago; all rights reserved), July, 1972, p. 175.*

OTHER CITATIONS

The Booklist, *July 1, 1972, p. 943.*

Ethel L. Heins, in The Horn Book Magazine, *August, 1972, p. 365.*

Nora L. Magid, in The New York Times Book Review, *May 20, 1973, p. 8.*

***THE TAILOR OF GLOUCESTER* (1903)**

Frederick Warne & Co. have brought out *The Tailor of Gloucester* as Beatrix Potter originally wrote it. This [1968] version is much longer than the tiny book to which most of us are accustomed. . . . Beatrix Potter sacrificed a thousand words for the original Warne edition, and it is interesting to see how the work reads in its first form. Beatrix Potter's economy of style required no cutting. She was a mistress of brevity, and the complete *Tailor of Gloucester* remains admirably direct and uncluttered.

Martha Bacon, in The Atlantic Monthly *(copyright © 1968, by The Atlantic Monthly Company, Boston, Mass.; reprinted by permission), December, 1968, p. 153.*

This large-sized (9½" x 7⅜") edition [Warne, 1968] of Miss Potter's own favorite story contains the complete original text and illustrations, a glossary, and a foreword by Leslie Linder. . . . Most children will probably prefer the 1903 version for clarity but this attractive edition of the original text should be in children's literature collections.

Katherine Heylman, in School Library Journal *(reprinted from the February, 1969, issue of* School Library Journal, *published by R. R. Bowker Co., a Xerox company; copyright © 1969 by Xerox Corporation), February, 1969, p. 68.*

A small picture story book of great beauty is Beatrix Potter's *The Tailor of Gloucester*, a miniature classic for younger children. As an example of total integration of visual and verbal elements, this tiny fantasy is woven from an old tailor's fevered dream, a legend of Christmas Eve, and an ancient city silenced in snow and moonlight.

Constructed with great skill and precision, *The Tailor of Gloucester* is as subtle a fantasy as any that has rolled off the printing press. The whole book rustles with light, gentle sounds of mouse feet in the night and the fevered breath of a deliriously ill tailor. . . .

Based on very close observation of the habits of small animals as well as of details of architecture, landscape, china, and original embroideries, the story takes on an air of actuality that makes the fantasy come convincingly alive in cadenced prose style. . . .

The pictures, exquisitely detailed, are an integral part of this miniature classic. Suffused in soft pastels of pink, sepia, and rose matched with greens, grays, and browns, the full beauty of the embroideries, particularly, comes into clearest focus only under a magnifying glass. This artistry in the water colors produces an exact pictorial equivalent for the well-turned text that makes *The Tailor of Gloucester* a fine example of literature and art scaled to the world of children.

Constantine Georgiou, in his Children and Their Literature *(copyright © 1969 by Prentice-Hall, Inc.), Prentice-Hall, 1969, pp. 252-54.*

***THE TALE OF THE FAITHFUL DOVE* (1955; written 1907)**

It is easy to see why [Beatrix Potter] may have laid [*The Tale of the Faithful Dove*] aside: the story of the pigeons of Winchelsea and Rye is itself more finicky and circumferential, less vigorous and direct, than her best work. There is much badinage between Mr. and Mrs. Tidler before her entrapment down a chimney . . . enlists his devoted attention. There is also not a little of the quaint in the dialogue among the sexton, the plumber and his apprentice anent their plight. Less a tale than a little history, and less for children than for the Potter following.

Kirkus Reviews *(copyright © 1970 The Kirkus Service, Inc.), October 15, 1970, p. 1141.*

The new [Warne, 1970] edition [of *The Tale of the Faithful Dove*] has been elegantly reset and suggests in format the familiar Beatrix Potter picture books. The meticulously detailed and delicately colored paintings by [Marie Angel] suggest elements in Beatrix Potter's pictures but have a sharp, obvious individuality of their own. One must disagree with Margaret Lane, who in her biography of Beatrix Potter characterizes the story as a "slight tale." The story of the pigeon, Mr. Tidler . . . is supported by a bevy of bird characters, some convivial mice, and three delightfully but realistically portrayed human creatures: a sexton, a plumber, and his boy-apprentice.

Paul Heins, in The Horn Book Magazine *(copyright © 1970 by The Horn Book, Inc., Boston), December, 1970, pp. 604-05.*

Parts of [*The Tale of the Faithful Dove*] are prime Potter: Amabella's chimney conversations with some genteel, "Gloucester" . . . ("'I loikes pigeon poy!' said the objectionable plumber"). But there are technical difficulties . . ., the kind children will spot and question. Amabella was tending another egg before her misfortune; it is forgotten once she is caught in the chimney. Introduction of the plumber and his assistant is too abrupt, without suitable transition.

What compensates for these minor flaws and explains the book's appearance now . . . are the elegant illustrations by Marie Angel. Like Miss Potter's watercolors in other works (she did none for this book), they are appreciative of gesture and scale, time and texture.

Nancy Klein, in The New York Times Book Review *(© 1971 by The New York Times Company; reprinted by permission), February 14, 1971, p. 20.*

Although [this] tiny book looks appropriate for the read-aloud audience, the vocabulary, the style, and the dialect used in human dialogue are quite sophisticated; this perhaps is better read aloud to the middle grades than read independently by them. The story is gentle, especially in its humor, and old-fashioned enough to be, perhaps, of primary interest to confirmed fans and students of Beatrix Potter's work.

Zena Sutherland, in Bulletin of the Center for Children's Books *(© 1971 by the University of Chicago; all rights reserved), March, 1971, p. 113.*

[*The Tale of the Faithful Dove*] has many characteristic touches, and the writing is, as ever, immaculate; there is, however, a vein of sentimentality in it which would scarcely have survived the revising hand of the ruthless author, and the story—at least as a vehicle for illustrations—lacks variety.

The story has, on the whole, only a little more than curiosity value. Miss Angel's charming watercolours may bring it to a wider audience. They are softer than Beatrix Potter's, more competent in handling the human characters, and successful in catching the mild tenderness of the story and the pretty Rye settings.

The Times Literary Supplement *(© Times Newspapers Ltd., 1971), July 2, 1971, p. 768.*

OTHER CITATIONS

Phyllis Shumberger, in Library Journal, *April 15, 1971, p. 1498.*

***THE TALE OF TUPPENNY* (written 1903)**

Any version of a Potter story is of interest to her fans, but this [1973 Warne edition of *The Tale of Tuppenny*] is really rather slight and only moderately humorous. [Marie Angel's] illustrations are prettier than those [by Beatrix Potter], but lack the humor and spontaneity of [the original] drawings.

Zena Sutherland, in Bulletin of the Center for Children's Books *(© 1973 by the University of Chicago; all rights reserved), September, 1973, p. 16.*

Written in 1903 . . . *Tuppenny* was reworked by [Beatrix Potter] for use as the first chapter of the 1929 *Fairy Caravan*, her only lengthy work. Presented here in its original form, it is better written than it was as the opening of the longer book. . . . Unfortunately, the book has been issued in the small format of the *Peter Rabbit* series. While [Marie Angel's] style is appropiately reminiscent of Potter, her skillfully detailed, softly colored illustrations would be more effective in a larger book. Nevertheless, the tale retains the charm, directness, and lack of sentimentality for which Beatrix Potter is so highly regarded.

Avi Wortis, in School Library Journal *(reprinted from the March, 1974, issue of* School Library Journal, *published by R. R. Bowker Co., a Xerox company; copyright © 1974 by Xerox Corporation), March, 1974, p. 100.*

Beatrix Potter's animal characters continue to appeal to new generations. *The Tale of Tuppenny* . . . offers readers another chance to make Miss Potter's acquaintance—this time as an author only (illustrations are by a contemporary artist, Marie Angel).

The story is purely "Potteresque": a morality tale in which the inescapable moral is neatly evaded. . . . Beatrix Potter's tongue-in-cheek humor is still as fresh as it was in 1903, when this story was written. While Miss Angel's animals may not be as distinctly individual as their forebears, the stronger lines and bolder colorings will probably have more appeal for today's youngsters.

Jennifer Farley Smith, in The Christian Science Monitor *(reprinted by permission from* The Christian Science Monitor; *© 1974 The Christian Science Publishing Society; all rights reserved), March 6, 1974, p. F2.*

OTHER CITATIONS

Kirkus Reviews, *May 15, 1973, p. 557.*

R

RASKIN, Ellen 1928-

Ellen Raskin is an American who is noted for her humorous stories and illustrations. (See also *Contemporary Authors*, Vols. 23-24 and *Something About the Author*, Vol. 2.)

***A & THE; OR WILLIAM T.C. BAUMGARTEN COMES TO TOWN* (1970)**

Anyone can read A & THE—the words that is, printed in boldface throughout the text; but *the* child who looks for them assiduously is apt to lose *the* thread of *a* tricky story, while on *the* other hand if he doesn't see T & C and recognize them when he sees them, he may miss *the* point. . . . Miss Raskin's insight matches her outreach and usually she balances the two better.

Kirkus Reviews *(copyright © 1970 The Kirkus Service, Inc.), August 1, 1970, p. 796.*

The street scenes [in *A & THE*] look like those in *Nothing Ever Happens on My Block*, with a great deal of zany activity taking place in seemingly static pictures. Accompanying the story of the Norman Conquest are pictures of the schoolroom with authentically drawn scenes from the Bayeux Tapestry floating above like a musical descant. The "book is dedicated to everyone who can read a and the"; and for encouragement, the articles are printed throughout in boldface. A delightfully original picture book for all ages.

Ethel L. Heins, in The Horn Book Magazine *(copyright © 1970 by The Horn Book, Inc., Boston), October, 1970, pp. 471-72.*

[This is not] very substantial, not quite as witty as most of the author-illustrator's previous books, but [it is] an amusing book with a mild lesson about prejudgement, some English history (a bit too much for a picture book) and a use of heavy type for "a" and "the" whenever they appear as words or within words that is slightly obtrusive. . . . The most engaging thing in the book is the everchanging backdrop of the houses in the block. . . .

Zena Sutherland, in Bulletin of the Center for Children's Books *(© 1971 by the University of Chicago; all rights reserved), June, 1971, pp. 161-62.*

***AND IT RAINED* (1969)**

[*And It Rained* is a] slight but amusing story about some silly animals, [Raskin's] illustrations showing the three protagonists in white against busy, stylized green and gold scenes of a tropical rain forest; when the rain comes down on schedule each afternoon, the other animals turn pale green, while the potto, pig, and parrot turn blue. . . . The dialogue (in balloon) functions as a refrain to the dialogue of the text, always consisting of a comment from the pig on the tea, from the parrot on the biscuits, from the potto on the party ("Ruined!").

Zena Sutherland, in Bulletin of the Center for Children's Books *(© 1970 by the University of Chicago; all rights reserved), February, 1970, pp. 105-06.*

***FRANKLIN STEIN* (1972)**

Once again [Ellen Raskin] has concocted a hilariously improbable story [*Franklin Stein*] and allowed the outpourings of her visual imagination to take shape in neat and monstrous line drawings. . . . The pure-white pages of the book are a perfect background for the clear blues and greens coloring the drawings; in practically each picture Fred appears in blatant red. The illustrations are rich with impossible details that are only hinted at in the text; and if the youngest of readers or viewers [fails] to catch the implied irony (the inconsistency of human reactions and opinions), he can, at least, give himself unreservedly to the exuberance of the slapstick.

Paul Heins, in The Horn Book Magazine *(copyright © 1972 by The Horn Book, Inc., Boston), April, 1972, pp. 138-39.*

A moralistic tale with somewhat sterotyped characters, this is about friendless Franklin Stein who lives on the top floor of a deteriorating apartment house with his parents, nosey sister, and a variety of peculiar neighbors. . . . The text is enhanced by the ink drawings filled with areas of bright red, blue, and green in Raskin's familiar cheerful style. Although Raskin fans might appreciate Franklin and his monster, the vicissitudes of public opinion are rather obviously portrayed.

Phyllis Yuill, in School Library Journal *(re-*

printed from the May, 1972, issue of School Library Journal, *published by R. R. Bowker Co., a Xerox company; copyright © 1972 by Xerox Corporation, May, 1972, p. 71.*

[*Franklin Stein*] is written with sparkling wit and in a sophisticated style, and the illustrations—which echo the humor of the text—are effective both in the use of color . . . and in the way in which they complement and supplement the story.

Zena Sutherland, in Bulletin of the Center for Children's Books *(© 1972 by the University of Chicago; all rights reserved), June, 1972, p. 162.*

Although the story's off-beat humor will not appeal to every child, some readers will find the tale [of *Franklin Stein*] highly amusing and will enjoy the many comical details in the brightly colored illustrations.

The Booklist *(© American Library Association 1972), November 1, 1972, p. 246.*

OTHER CITATIONS

Kirkus Reviews, *February 1, 1972, p. 132.*

Saturday Review, *September 19, 1972, p. 75.*

The Booklist, *November 1, 1972, p. 246.*

GHOST IN A FOUR-ROOM APARTMENT (1969)

The text [of *Ghost in a Four-Room Apartment*] is interspersed with the author's distinctively stylized, delightfully detailed, bright illustrations in shades of blue, green, red, and yellow; they, and the repetitive rhyming of family names, depiction of the spirited poltergeist's activities, and final tantalizing "Here is Boris,/ Whose favorite is Horace./ Guess who he might be!" will wow the young at read-aloud time.

Patricia G. Hodapp, in School Library Journal *(reprinted from the May, 1969, issue of* School Library Journal, *published by R. R. Bowker Co., a Xerox company; copyright © 1969 by Xerox Corporation), May, 1969, p. 78.*

The text [of "Ghost in a Four-Room Apartment"] is in two parts: a monologue by the unseen, uninvited ghost, and a cumulative, rhyming roster of the visiting relatives. The illustrations are a series of stained-glass showcases for Miss Raskin's considerable talents. . . . Yet there is less here than meets the eye. One feels let down after being introduced to a unique leading character in a humorous situation and discovering that while a lot goes on nothing actually happens. It's a little like looking at an animated still life—interesting, unusual but strangely static.

Katherine Perry, in The New York Times Book Review *(© 1969 by The New York Times Company; reprinted by permission), June 15, 1969, p. 26.*

OTHER CITATIONS

Virginia Haviland, in The Horn Book Magazine, *June, 1969, p. 297.*

MOE Q. McGLUTCH, HE SMOKED TOO MUCH (1973)

Instead of dressing up an anti-smoking message in comic clothing, Ellen Raskin outdoes the Victorian spoof [in *Moe Q. McGlutch, He Smoked Too Much*], using Moe's dangerous habit as an occasion for pure farce—and for parading her stylishly flamboyant menagerie. . . . It's fun to read the pictures for details the words don't tell, but it's sometimes hard to see the smoke signals for all of Raskin's brilliant visual patterns.

Kirkus Reviews *(copyright © 1973 The Kirkus Service, Inc.), September 15, 1973, p. 1032.*

In this heavy-handed anti-smoking tract, . . . the plot is overshadowed by the propaganda. Moreover, the message is off-target: smoking is bad only because it annoys others and causes accidents. In contrast, the full-color drawings have a rich enamelled look and give the animals a vitality that is missing in the text. . . . Still, cigarette warnings are better left to the Surgeon General.

Jane Abramson, in School Library Journal *(reprinted from the October, 1973, issue of* School Library Journal, *published by R. R. Bowker Co., a Xerox company; copyright © 1973 by Xerox Corporation), October, 1973, p. 110.*

THE MYSTERIOUS DISAPPEARANCE OF LEON (I MEAN NOEL) (1971)

[In "The Mysterious Disappearance of Leon (I Mean Noel)," Ellen Raskin] has relied on words, and her visual humor translates admirably into word-plays: puns, puzzles, codes, name games. She has also set up the wackiest cast of characters this side of "Charlie and the Chocolate Factory." . . .

The story moves in amusing fits and starts (sometimes slowly, I admit) across the U.S., as Mrs. Carillon, along with her adopted children and assorted friends, seeks the missing Leon (I mean Noel). . . . [Even] after two readings [I] am still marveling at the funny twists and turns of Ellen Raskin's mind.

Jane Yolen, in The New York Times Book Review *(© 1972 by The New York Times Company; reprinted by permission), December 12, 1971, p. 8.*

To read [*The Mysterious Disappearance of Leon (I Mean Noel)*] place tongue firmly in cheek. . . . The [mystery] is solved, and the whereabouts of the missing Leon discovered, but only after a series of incidents that have the lighthearted frenzy of a French farce. The story bubbles with fun, sly humor, and straight-faced nonsense like solemn footnotes and provocative clues.

Zena Sutherland, in Bulletin of the Center for Children's Books *(© 1972 by the University of Chicago; all rights reserved), January, 1972, p. 79.*

[Ellen Raskin's] first full-length story begins on a note of lighthearted madness which continues, unabated, until the end of the book. . . . It is difficult to see how children could resist the story, crammed as it is with baffling word puzzles, a dozen zany characters, uproariously funny situations, and unmitigated slapstick. [The book is illustrated] very suitably with ingenious word pictures, literally made of pen-and-ink lines and letters.

Ethel L. Heins, in The Horn Book Magazine *(copyright © 1972 by The Horn Book, Inc., Boston), February, 1972, pp. 51-2.*

OTHER CITATIONS

Zena Sutherland, in Saturday Review, *December 11, 1971, p. 46.*

Diane Gersoni Stavn, in Library Journal, *December 15, 1971, p. 4186.*

The Booklist, *January 1, 1972, pp. 394-95.*

NOTHING EVER HAPPENS ON MY BLOCK (1966)

[In *Nothing Ever Happens on My Block*, Ellen Raskin's young anti-hero] sits the day away on a sidewalk curb, a raffish, Sendak-type young man with a Beatle haircut and the expression of someone who works in the garment trade, and he laments that nothing ever happens on his block while, of course, all hell is breaking loose behind him. A familiar theme. In my own memory it dates back to *Just Kids and Nancy*, but at no time have I seen it done with such freshness of humor. . . .

It is to Miss Raskin's credit that her humor is not programmed to teach but exists only to entertain, which she winningly does.

Jules Feiffer, in Book Week *(©* The Washington Post*), March 20, 1966, p. 2.*

In *"Nothing Ever Happens on My Block"* . . . Ellen Raskin presents Chester Filbert, a "dull" little boy who is too involved with his interior fantasies to see the extraordinary things that are really happening around him. . . . [In] all fairness to Chester, all those thefts and parachute jumps never happened on *my* block either. This in no way detracts from the inventive excellence of the book, which is a delight. The brilliant line drawings, spotted strategically with color, show us the *real* happenings, while the captions deal with the youngster's unfulfilled wishes, cleverly conveying the division between Chester's inner experience and actuality.

Barbara Novak O'Doherty, in The New York Times Book Review *(© 1966 by the New York Times Company; reprinted by permission), May 22, 1966, p. 26.*

OTHER CITATIONS

Virginia Kirkus' Service, *February 1, 1966, p. 104.*

Alice Dalgliesh, in Saturday Review, *April 16, 1966, p. 49.*

WHO, SAID SUE, SAID WHOO? (1973)

In a delightful variation on the old joke about fitting elephants into a Volkswagen, the tiny two-seater and its diminutive driver pick up a zoofull of riders. . . . As the passengers increase in this unlikely ark, so does the ingenuity of Miss Raskin's design, a blend of visual elegance and pure slapstick.

Ann Sperber, in The New York Times Book Review *(© 1973 by The New York Times Company; reprinted by permission), April 1, 1973, p. 10.*

The pictures [in this book] have a Rousseau-like charm, with animals peering out from exotic sunlit foliage (the artist can make even a cornfield look bizarre), but the style of both illustration and text is uniquely [Ellen Raskin's]. The book can hold its own with the best nonsense anywhere.

Sidney D. Long, in The Horn Book Magazine *(copyright © 1973 by The Horn Book, Inc., Boston), June, 1973, p. 261.*

[*Who, Said Sue, Said Whoo?* is made up of nonsense] questions which concern unusual animals [as well as repetitive] and humorous use of words and colorful, amusing pictures. [It is particularly] good for listening skills [and is recommended] to be read to children. [This book is included in Ms. Altemus' list, Books for Younger Disabled Readers.]

Evelyn Goss Altemus, in School Library Journal *(reprinted from the October, 1973, issue of* School Library Journal, *published by R. R. Bowker Co., a Xerox company; copyright © 1973 by Xerox Corporation), October, 1973, p. 132.*

OTHER CITATIONS

Kirkus Reviews, *February 15, 1973, p. 183.*

The Booklist, *July 15, 1973, p. 1073.*

Publishers' Weekly, *July 30, 1973, p. 67.*

Zena Sutherland, in Bulletin of the Center for Children's Books, *September, 1973, p. 17.*

THE WORLD'S GREATEST FREAK SHOW (1971)

In this brief moral tale [*The World's Greatest Freak Show*], nasty Alastair Pflug, an exceedingly handsome and vain impresario, gets his due. . . . Despite the turnabout, it is a touchy business to focus attention on physical disabilities, no matter how gross. . . . Additionally, the book suffers from the problem of a picture-book format coupled with a text too turgid for the youngest and lacking the easy rhythms which might make it acceptable for reading aloud.

Janet French, in School Library Journal *(reprinted from the May, 1971, issue of* School Library Journal, *published by R. R. Bowker Co., a Xerox company; copyright © 1971 by Xerox Corporation), May, 1971, p. 61.*

Alastair Pflug may be the most insufferable anti-hero of the current picture-book season. . . . It's enough to turn you off by the second page of this odd and garish tale. . . .

The bright, raucous pictures are sometimes gorgeous, though usually grotesque. But the book lacks the laugh-at-yourself fun of the same author's "Nothing Ever Happens on My Block." The idea of deriding freaks is more discomforting than comic, no matter how conspicuous the moral.

Nancy Griffin, in The New York Times Book Review *(© 1971 by The New York Times Company; reprinted by permission), May 2, 1971, p. 44.*

S

SELSAM, Millicent E(llis) 1912-

An American, Millicent Selsam is widely known for the more than fifty science books she has written for children, including such works as *Birth of an Island, How Animals Tell Time,* and *Questions and Answers About Ants*. (See also *Contemporary Authors*, Vols. 9-12, rev. ed., and *Something About the Author*, Vol. 1.)

GENERAL COMMENTARY

Mrs. Selsam's nature books are remarkable for their accuracy and always interesting. She never talks down to children but has a gift for channeling their natural curiosity about their fellow creatures into the beginnings of scholarly investigation. Her prose is consistently beautiful, with poetic rhythms and literary tempos.

Millicent Taylor, in The Christian Science Monitor *(reprinted by permission from* The Christian Science Monitor; *© 1964 The Christian Science Publishing Society; all rights reserved), November 5, 1964, p. 108.*

Mrs. Selsam never goes beyond the conclusions the child can draw from the observations he himself can make. This is important because children trust their sensory experiences more than the logic of grown-ups. . . .

Another strength of Mrs. Selsam's books is her use of language. She avoids two equally serious, although opposite, pitfalls: she never talks down to the child, and she never uses sophisticated scientific jargon. Her language is very simple, and yet everything she says is absolutely accurate and free from over-simplifications.

Luitgard Wundheiler, "A Psychological Basis for Judging Children's Literature Dealing with Nature and Science," in A Critical Approach to Children's Literature: The Thirty-first Annual Conference of the Graduate Library School August 1-3, 1966, *edited by Sara Innis Fenwick (© 1967 by The University of Chicago; all rights reserved), University of Chicago Press, 1967, pp. 28-9.*

Millicent Selsam, one of the most dependably competent authors of science books, writes for all age levels, but she is undoubtedly best known for her books for young readers. Her style is simple and clear, with no extraneous material and no trace of popularization.

May Hill Arbuthnot and Zena Sutherland, in their Children and Books, *4th edition (copyright © 1947, 1957, 1964, 1972 by Scott, Foresman and Co.), Scott, Foresman, 1972, p. 605.*

***ANIMALS AS PARENTS* (1965)**

As in Mrs. Selsam's previous books on animal lore, the writing [in *Animals as Parents*] is unusually clear and responsive to the needs and interests of younger readers. The index includes references to the very satisfying illustrations of John Kaufmann as well as to the text. There is a bibliography of easily available books, some adult, as a guide to further reading.

Virginia Kirkus' Service *(copyright © 1965 Virginia Kirkus Service, Inc.), September 15, 1965, p. 986.*

[In this book, Millicent Selsam] records observations made both in the laboratory and in the wild by behavioral scientists. In a clear, crisp style she tells of their findings on parental care—or lack of it—shown by some sea animals, fishes, toads and frogs, reptiles, mammals and birds. [This is a] good introduction to some aspects of animal behavior.

Thomas Foster, in The New York Times Book Review *(© 1965 by The New York Times Company; reprinted by permission), November 7, 1965 (Part 2), p. 52.*

[*Animals as Parents* is a] good science book. Mrs. Selsam writes in a straightforward style, moving easily from one topic to the next; the material is well-organized and nicely illustrated; most important, there are repeated references to scientific principles. Without punching it, the author stresses the value of observation, correlation, corroboration, and objectivity.

Zena Sutherland, in Bulletin of the Center for Children's Books *(copyright 1966 by the University of Chicago; all rights reserved), March, 1966, p. 120.*

OTHER CITATIONS

Marian Sorenson, in The Christian Science Monitor, *November 4, 1965, p. B9.*

The Booklist and Subscription Books Bulletin, *November 15, 1965, pp. 332-33.*

***THE APPLE AND OTHER FRUITS* (1973)**

[*The Apple and Other Fruits* is a] visual demonstration of pollination. Selsam, as usual, teaches by repetition so that the material on pears, peaches, cherries, etc. merely reinforces the lesson on apples. But her concise text and Wexler's close-ups of flower parts and stage-by-stage photos of a fuzz covered ovary gradually turning into a ripe fruit should put some life into a lesson that children often find abstract and confusing.

Kirkus Reviews *(copyright © 1973 The Kirkus Service, Inc.), August 15, 1973, p. 887.*

[This is a] well-written account of [the apple's] flower structure, fertilization, and fruit growth . . .; other fruits are considered briefly and serve as reinforcement. Unfortunately, [Jerome Wexler's] diagrams of the pistil and stamens are not sufficient to explain the technical words. However, all the photos are clear and good (especially the handsome color plates); the 14 point bold type is easy to read; and there's more emphasis here on the function of flower parts and on the growth process than is found in such books as Barbara Beck's *The First Book of Fruits*. . . .

George Gleason, in School Library Journal *(reprinted from the November, 1973, issue of* School Library Journal, *published by R. R. Bowker Co., a Xerox company; copyright © 1973 by Xerox Corporation), November, 1973, p. 55.*

OTHER CITATIONS

Zena Sutherland, in Bulletin of the Center for Children's Books, *February, 1974, p. 100.*

***BIRTH OF A FOREST* (1964)**

[*Birth of a Forest* presents the] story of change from lake to forest as plant life gradually replaces water. Steps in changing vegetation and animal life are vividly described in a brief text, which explains satisfactorily such technical matters as *climax community*. The illustrative material adds and clarifies information.

Virginia Haviland, in The Horn Book Magazine *(copyright © 1964, by The Horn Book, Inc., Boston), August, 1964, p. 391.*

[*Birth of a Forest* is excellent] science writing: lucid, simple, accurate, and well organized, with no extraneous material and no popularization. [Barbara Wolff's] illustrations are delicate in technique and meticulous in detail. . . . [Millicent Selsam's] text is specific enough to be used in a beginning botany course, yet informal enough to be an enticing introduction to the outdoors for the amateur.

Zena Sutherland, in Bulletin of the Center for Children's Books *(copyright 1964 by the University of Chicago; all rights reserved), September, 1964, p. 19.*

OTHER CITATIONS

Elizabeth F. Grave, in Library Journal, *May 15, 1964, p. 2222.*

The Booklist and Subscription Books Bulletin, *October 1, 1964, pp. 161-62.*

***BIRTH OF AN ISLAND* (1959)**

A straightforward explanation of how islands are formed, this text, elaborately illustrated by Winifred Lubell, achieves intensity from the core of its subject. . . . Woven into the framework of [the island's] progress is the consideration of natural selection which is deftly explained by the author, who unobtrusively uses her island as a microcosm in which to explore natural growth.

Virginia Kirkus' Service, *February 1, 1959, p. 92.*

[In *Birth of an Island,* the] evolution of a volcanic island is described in text that, despite its simplicity, communicates a sense of excitement at the wonder of natural processes. . . . In describing one island, the patterns of all islands are reflected in the action of the elements, the migration of life forms and the differentiation of isolated species. Illustrations are striking, using one or two vibrant colors with bold black and white.

Zena Sutherland, in Bulletin of the Center for Children's Books *(published by the University of Chicago), May, 1959, p. 157.*

[*Birth of an Island*] is marked for the 7-10's, but it is so charmingly written and so delightfully illustrated in color that with a little imaginative ad libbing it could be read aloud to even younger children. The concepts are simple while the unfolding story of how the various plants and island creatures come floating in over the sea or through the air, finally to make a unique community isolated from all others, should delight both the young listener and the older reader alike.

Robert C. Cowen, in The Christian Science Monitor *(reprinted by permission from* The Christian Science Monitor; *© 1959, The Christian Science Publishing Society; all rights reserved), May 14, 1959, p. 11.*

OTHER CITATIONS

The Booklist and Subscription Books Bulletin, *May 1, 1959, pp. 488-89.*

***THE BUG THAT LAID THE GOLDEN EGGS* (1967)**

Besides a little information (bugs as a subdivision of insects) and some tips on the technique of catching insects, [*The Bug That Laid the Golden Eggs* presents] a discourse on method developed in the course of informal trial-and-error. It's good for kids to know that answers don't come easily (even to experts), that there is a proper time and place for each investigation, that patience pays; they will have to be patient (and forbearing) to put up with false starts and dead ends, the snapshots and posed shots, of Millie and her friends.

Kirkus Service *(copyright © 1967 Virginia Kirkus' Service, Inc.), October 1, 1967, pp. 1203-04.*

Considering Millicent Selsam's undeniable skill as a writer, her book "The Bug That Laid the Golden Eggs" . . . is something of a mystery. A curiously self-conscious report of what apparently was a real experience (with a photographer handy to help record it), it tells of the futile attempts of a group of children, aided by Mrs. Selsam, to identify some insect eggs they find at the beach. Their efforts come to nothing—not even a museum entomologist can help them. If all this is meant to show the frustrations of scientific research, it would be helpful to state the point.

Paul Walker, in The New York Times Book Review *(© 1967 by The New York Times Company; reprinted by permission), November 5, 1967 (Part 2), p. 57.*

OTHER CITATIONS

Science Books, *December, 1967, p. 241.*

***BULBS, CORMS AND SUCH* (1974)**

In characteristic format, [Millicent Selsam] presents information about the different parts of plants and their growing cycle as well as directions for raising various types of bulbous and tuberous vegetation. [Jerome Wexler's] clear and explicit photographs and the concise, detailed text have been well-integrated, creating another informative book by the author-photographer team.

Anita Silvey, in The Horn Book Magazine *(copyright © 1975 by the Horn Book, Inc., Boston), February, 1975, p. 64.*

Selsam's writing is always informed and lucid, and her experience as a science teacher enables her to assess accurately the scope and vocabulary of a book for the intended audience. [Jerome] Wexler, whose photographs have illustrated so many of the author's books on plants, has outdone himself here, the full-color pictures of plants in bloom contrasting dramatically with black and white pictures—often with plant parts cut away—of stages in the growth of bulbs, corms, tubers, tuberous roots, and rhizomes. . . . This is an example of the best kind of science writing: clear and informative, with the text and illustrations nicely integrated.

Zena Sutherland, in Bulletin of the Center for Children's Books *(© 1975 by the University of Chicago; all rights reserved), February, 1975, p. 99.*

***THE COURTSHIP OF ANIMALS* (1964)**

Mrs. Selsam has written a fascinating text about what constitutes male and female, and what the function of courtship is . . . . [She] goes into all the technicalities of mating and conceiving with the lower animals, but turns a little evasive with the higher. She tells how Indian elephants gently touch each other with their sensitive trunks, how bears hug and paw each other. The child may wonder where little elephants and little bears come from.

Nora Magid, in Book Week *(© The Washington Post), November 1, 1964 (Part 2), p. 39.*

With simple clarity, most of [*The Courtship of Animals*] describes the myriad and fascinating courtship patterns of fishes, amphibians and reptiles, birds, mammals, insects and spiders. Scientific observation is stressed. A matter-of-fact approach lays a solid base for questions and for books on human reproduction that will later engage a child's attention. In going surely and directly to the essentials, a feeling for nature's intricacies and marvelous mysteries is in no way sacrificed.

Priscilla L. Moulton, in The Horn Book Magazine *(copyright © 1965, by The Horn Book, Inc., Boston), February, 1965, p. 68.*

[Millicent Selsam's] simple, frank yet dignified explanation of the function of all animal courtship is followed by individual chapters on the rituals performed by fish, reptiles, amphibians, birds, mammals, insects, and spiders. . . . Although this is an excellent introduction to a subject fascinating in itself, the true value of the book lies in its overall message that without this necessary and sometimes elaborate prolog to mating there would be no new life upon the earth. Recommended for libraries needing more material on this one phase of animal behavior than is available in other books.

The Booklist and Subscription Books Bulletin *(© 1965 by the American Library Association), February 1, 1965, p. 528.*

OTHER CITATIONS

Margery and Lorus Milne, in The New York Times Book Review, *November 1, 1964 (Part 2), p. 60.*

Zena Sutherland, in Bulletin of the Center for Children's Books, *December, 1965, p. 68.*

***EGG TO CHICK* (1946)**

Anticipating common questions, Mrs. Selsam notes that "most of the eggs you buy in the grocery store have not been joined by sperm" (no such term as 'fertilize' appears); explains the insignificance of blood spots, the embryonic nature of white spots (which may then discomfort some children). The illustrations [by Barbara Wolff] are workmanlike, well-labeled and not insensitive—you won't blanch at the rooster mounting the hen. Without any to-do, it all seems part of a grand design and an individual accomplishment.

Kirkus Reviews *(copyright © 1970 The Kirkus Service, Inc.), September 15, 1970, p. 1034.*

Departing from the storybook style of her other Science I Can Read books such as *Let's Get Turtles* and *Plenty of Fish*, [Millicent Selsam] factually and clearly presents the development of the chicken until its hatching. The narrative is conversational in tone, allowing the author to suggest in a natural sort of way that the fertilization process is universal in the animal kingdom. . . . The author wisely explains why "you cannot hatch a chick from your breakfast egg" in the early pages of this informative little book.

Sheryl B. Andrews, in The Horn Book Magazine *(copyright © 1971 by The Horn Book, Inc., Boston), April, 1971, p. 180.*

[*Egg to Chick* is a] revised edition of the book first published under the same title in 1946 by International Publishers. The new illustrations [by Barbara Wolff] are an improvement. . . . The writing is simplified in one way: some of the longer sentences have been broken down into separate sentences for easier reading. In the way the material is handled, the new edition is more sophisticated, without the trace of oversimplification that was in the earlier book.

Zena Sutherland, in Bulletin of the Center for Children's Books *(© 1971 by the University of Chicago; all rights reserved), April, 1971, pp. 128-29.*

A FIRST LOOK AT BIRDS (with Joyce Hunt, 1973)

[*A First Look at Birds* is a] primer of ornithology—not a catalog of species but a set of lessons on how to observe and identify birds of all kinds. . . . The value of the book lies in its single, uncomplicated purpose and in the simplicity of its approach to the study of birds. [This is a] good companion to more colorful, encyclopedic volumes.

The Booklist *(© American Library Association 1974), March 15, 1974, p. 824.*

[Harriet Springer's clearly] drawn pictures, some in color, are nicely integrated with [Millicent Selsam's and Joyce Hunt's] simply written text, much of it comprising directions addressed to the reader. Since the drawings are explicit, it seems redundant to ask the reader "How can you tell them apart? The hawk is usually a smaller bird," when the pictures show a large bird (an eagle) and smaller one. However, any reader will be encouraged; he can answer every question. . . . The book encourages comparison and observation.

Zena Sutherland, in Bulletin of the Center for Children's Books *(© 1974 by the University of Chicago; all rights reserved), July-August, 1974, p. 185.*

OTHER CITATIONS

Publishers' Weekly, *February 18, 1974, p. 74.*

A FIRST LOOK AT LEAVES (1972)

A very simple book with well-integrated text and pictures uses repetition and comparison to encourage observation of differences in leaves, and concludes with pictures of familiar tree-leaves and instructions for making leaf prints. The text is a bit more stilted than the texts of Mrs. Selsam's books usually are, and there are occasional statements that may not be as clear as her explanations usually are. . . .

Zena Sutherland, in Bulletin of the Center for Children's Books *(© 1973 by the University of Chicago; all rights reserved), June, 1973, p. 162.*

OTHER CITATIONS

Kirkus Reviews, *December 1, 1972, p. 1357.*

A FIRST LOOK AT MAMMALS (with Joyce Hunt, 1973)

The drawing of an opossum (looking, unfortunately, like a hollow toy stuffed with babies) shows why that animal is related to the kangaroo, but the word marsupial is never introduced, nor are the names of any of the other mammal groups except primates. And some of the visual puzzles here—matching a trunkless elephant to a trunk and a wingless bat to a pair of wings—are unlikely to challenge any age group. The concept approach seems a good way to teach what mammals are and how they are divided into orders, but exceptions prove troublesome to explain . . . and Springer's pictures don't invite more than a desultory first look.

Kirkus Reviews *(copyright © 1973 The Kirkus Service, Inc.), May 15, 1973, p. 566.*

The intended audience won't get a clear idea of what a mammal is from [Millicent Selsam's and Joyce Hunt's *A First Look at Mammals*]. Animals with hair or fur and some with very little hair are depicted and confirmed to be members of the mammal family. After several examples of these animals, there is a confusing shift to teeth, flippers, toes, wings, etc. as characteristics of a group of mammals. . . . When children are ready to learn about mammals, they can start with the much more informative *The First Book of Mammals* by Margaret Williamson. . . .

Annabelle R. Bernard, in School Library Journal *(reprinted from the October, 1973, issue of* School Library Journal, *published by R. R. Bowker Co., a Xerox company; copyright © 1973 by Xerox Corporation), October, 1973, p. 111.*

HOW ANIMALS LIVE TOGETHER (1963)

[*How Animals Live Together*] is a serious study in the social habits of certain animals, birds, and insects, skillfully adapted to the understanding and interest of the 10-to-14's. It is written in Mrs. Selsam's naturally rhythmic prose, and effectively illustrated by Kathleen Elgin's full-page and half-page pencil sketches. Migration organization in birds and monarch butterflies is one of the "togetherness" examples described. Breeding colonies of penguins and herring gulls is another. Particularly fascinating is the class consciousness of hierarchy represented by the "pecking order" among birds—including barnyard fowl—and the social order discovered among flocks made up of several different kinds of birds. This and a great deal of information of other sorts in the social life and organization of the creatures make this a fascinating book.

Millicent J. Taylor, in The Christian Science Monitor *(reprinted by permission from* The Christian Science Monitor; *© 1963, The*

Christian Science Publishing Society; all rights reserved), May 9, 1963, p. 7B.

HOW ANIMALS TELL TIME (1967)

[In *How Animals Tell Time*, interest] is captured by specific examples and held by perceptive analysis. In raising *Questions for the Future*, Mrs. Selsam reviews and previews research, and so reveals something of the rhythm of science itself. Literate text and inviting illustrations [by John Kaufmann] also—the duo that did *Animals As Parents* and *The Courtship of Animals* do it again.

> Kirkus Service *(copyright © 1967 Virginia Kirkus' Service, Inc.), February 15, 1967, p. 205.*

[*How Animals Tell Time*] is an extremely important up-to-date account of theories relating to the rhythmical activities and adaptations of a wide variety of animals. Experiments are described in which data are gathered on the day-night activity rhythms of fruit flies, cockroaches, bees, mice, and men. . . . Questions that are awaiting answers are also discussed, e.g., in a single cell is the "regulating force" inside or outside the nucleus? . . . Pictures and diagrams [by John Kaufmann] help clarify the text.

> *Alphoretta Fish, in* School Library Journal *(reprinted from the May, 1967, issue of* School Library Journal, *published by R. R. Bowker Co., a Xerox company; copyright © 1967 by Xerox Corporation), May, 1967, pp. 59-60.*

In a fascinating study of biological clocks, Mrs. Selsam discusses the relationship between the earth's daily, seasonal, and tidal rhythms and animal breeding, hibernation, migration, and other behavior. Her simple, lucid analyses of numerous scientific experiments explains current theories about time-related behavior and describes research being done on the unsolved problem of the internal location of biological clocks.

> The Booklist and Subscription Books Bulletin *(© 1967 by the American Library Association), May 1, 1967, p. 951.*

OTHER CITATIONS

Isaac Asimov, in The Horn Book Magazine, *June, 1967, p. 366.*

Zena Sutherland, in Bulletin of the Center for Children's Books, *July-August, 1967, p. 175.*

HOW PUPPIES GROW (1972)

[*How Puppies Grow*] doesn't give as much information as do most Selsam books, but it is written with her usual gift for very simple prose that avoids being stilted; easy enough for beginning independent readers, the text is smooth enough to read aloud well, and can be used with preschool children.

> *Zena Sutherland, in* Bulletin of the Center for Children's Books *(© 1973 by the University of Chicago; all rights reserved), January, 1973, p. 81.*

OTHER CITATIONS

Kirkus Reviews, *September 15, 1972, p. 1104.*

The Booklist, *February 15, 1973, p. 574.*

IS THIS A BABY DINOSAUR? (1971)

Adding bits of nature lore to the photographic guessing game introduced by Tana Hoban, Selsam invites children to *Look Again* again [in *Is This a Baby Dinosaur?*]. . . . Hoban's camera eye is more startlingly ingenious and the educational value of Selsam's text is minimal, but that dewy spider web and vertical porcupine quill are sure to fool you and it's all set forth most attractively.

> Kirkus Reviews *(copyright © 1972 The Kirkus Service, Inc.), August 15, 1972, p. 937.*

Handsome photographs, some magnified, and a lucid, informally written text make an enticing book for the very young naturalist. . . . [*Is This a Baby Dinosaur?* is a] book to sharpen perception, to enjoy for its beauty.

> *Zena Sutherland, in* Bulletin of the Center for Children's Books *(© 1972 by the University of Chicago; all rights reserved); December, 1972, p. 64.*

Another in Selsam's long line of excellent science materials, [*Is This a Baby Dinosaur?*] will be particularly valuable in developing a spirit of inquiry in young children. The clear vocabulary and photographs and the emphasis on similarities and differences make the book a valuable learning aid. The black-and-white photographs stress the importance of careful observation—things are often not what they seem to be. . . . The reviewer is reminded of Rachel Carson's *Sense of Wonder* and *The Seeing Eye*, other books which also teach an appreciation of the variety of nature.

> Science Books *(copyright © 1973, by the American Association for the Advancement of Science), Vol. IX, No. 4 (March, 1973), p. 300.*

OTHER CITATIONS

The Booklist, *March 15, 1973, p. 718.*

MICROBES AT WORK (1953)

[In *Microbes at Work*, a] short introduction, on location, activity and types [of microbes] leads logically into main chapters on the discouragement of bad microbes, the encouragement of good ones, and finally, their role as agents in the breakdown of dead plants to nitrates. Causes are carefully if not completely related and the assumptions should provoke the right kinds of questions. Interesting home experiments with food and its preservation help make a lively text. Attractively illustrated by Helen Ludwig.

> Virginia Kirkus' Bookshop Service, *July 1, 1953, p. 388.*

[*Microbes at Work* is a] fascinating book that clearly and accurately explains the many different effects and uses of the various microbes. . . . The many experiments that can be done in any kitchen, informative illustrations by Helen Ludwig, and the easy-to-read style make the book a necessity for all libraries.

Harriet Morrison, in Library Journal *(reprinted from the October 1, 1953, issue of* Library Journal, *published by R. R. Bowker Company, a Xerox Company; copyright © 1953 by Xerox Corporation), October 1, 1953, p. 1699.*

OTHER CITATIONS

Bulletin of the Center for Children's Books, *September, 1953, pp. 7-8.*

The Booklist, *September 1, 1953, p. 20*

***MILKWEED* (1967)**

[*Milkweed*] is a rather skimpy presentation using the weed to make some general botanical observation perhaps, although it is in no way obvious. The format is rather childish (large print, oversized illustrations and little text), and this alone would probably deter the age group most likely to gain something from it. The photographs [by Jerome Wexler] are quite beautiful. As a picture essay this might have appeal, but as a sample of science literature it leaves much to be desired.

Kirkus Service *(copyright © 1967 Virginia Kirkus' Service, Inc.), August 15, 1967, p. 963.*

Written clearly and simply, and illustrated with fascinating photographs in color and black and white, this is an excellent account of the growth and pollination of the milkweed plant. . . . Although parts of the milkweed's reproductive cycle are unique, the principles of growth common to all plant life are brought out here. Included in the text are several pages about the use to which this common weed has been put.

Ann D. Schweibish, in School Library Journal *(reprinted from the October, 1967, issue of* School Library Journal, *published by R. R. Bowker Co., a Xerox company; copyright © 1967 by Xerox Corporation), October, 1967, p. 166.*

[*Milkweed* is a] good first science book, illustrated with [Jerome Wexler's] clear and attractive photographs. [Selsam] does not attempt to discuss every aspect of plant physiology (there is no mention of photosynthesis or of respiration) but describes in simple language the growth of a milkweed plant from a seed, the reproductive parts, pollenation, and distribution.

Zena Sutherland in Bulletin of the Center for Children's Books *(copyright 1967 by the University of Chicago; all rights reserved), October, 1967, p. 33.*

OTHER CITATIONS

Helen B. Crawshaw, in The Horn Book Magazine, *October, 1967, p. 607.*

Science Books, *December, 1967, p. 234.*

The Booklist and Subscription Books Bulletin, *December 1, 1967, p. 451.*

***PLENTY OF FISH* (1960)**

One of the most delightful ways for a child to learn is through play. Miss Selsam is cognizant of this in her whimsical little book about the care, feeding, and habits of two goldfish. . . . Eric Blegvad's lively illustrations give added emphasis to the playful approach to information in a book which encourages both reading and nature study.

Virginia Kirkus Service, *August 1, 1960, p. 617.*

[*Plenty of Fish* is a] delightful book: it is enjoyable as a story, having sequence and humor; it gives accurate science information with clarity; it is excellent material for the beginning independent reader; it has enchanting illustrations [by Erik Blegvad].

Zena Sutherland, in Bulletin of the Center for Children's Books *(published by the University of Chicago), October, 1960, p. 34.*

OTHER CITATIONS

Margaret C. Farquhar, in Library Journal, *September 15, 1960, p. 3211.*

The Booklist and Subscription Books Bulletin, *December 15, 1960, p. 250.*

***THE QUEST OF CAPTAIN COOK* (1962)**

[*The Quest of Captain Cook* is an] interesting account of Cook's three great voyages (1768-1779) of exploration and discovery, and of their enormous contribution to science. . . . The book has no bibliography, a serious omission, for surely readers will want to know what sources were used by the author and, since the subject is so interesting and so briefly treated here, where to go for further reading. The maps of each voyage are useful; but [Lee J. Ames'] pictures, of which there are far too many, are intrusive rather than illustrative.

Margaret Warren Brown, in The Horn Book Magazine *(copyright © 1962, by The Horn Book, Inc., Boston), October, 1962, p. 495.*

[In this book] Mrs. Selsam communicates her admiration for Cook as a humanitarian, amateur anthropologist, explorer, and navigator. The illustrations [by Lee J. Ames] are adequate, the writing style straightforward, with a minimum of embellishment. An index is appended. The combination of subject interest, dignified style, and simplicity of narration will make the book useful to slow readers in high school.

Zena Sutherland, in Bulletin of the Center for Children's Books *(copyright 1963 by the University of Chicago; all rights reserved), February, 1963, p. 100.*

OTHER CITATIONS

Joanna R. Long, in Library Journal, *October 15, 1962, p. 3898.*

The Booklist and Subscription Books Bulletin, *November 1, 1962, p. 225.*

QUESTIONS AND ANSWERS ABOUT ANTS (1967)

Millicent E. Selsam's "Questions and Answers About Ants" . . . blends a lucid, easy-going text, written without clichés or condescension, and [Arabelle Wheatley's] precise, beautiful drawings. The question-answer format covers concisely many points about ant anatomy and ant behavior, yet never bogs down in dry details. The questions are calculated to arouse a child's interest (How do ants sleep? How do they wake up? How do they find their way?), and the answers are enlivened by the author's personal experiences and reports of some unusual laboratory experiments.

Paul Walker, in The New York Times Book Review *(© 1967 by The New York Times Company; reprinted by permission), November 5, 1967 (Part 2), p. 56.*

Ants are a fascinating subject, and, although the recent books by Shuttlesworth and Hutchins on this subject are excellent, this one will be useful for younger children. Mrs. Selsam has arranged her information, based on a year's study of an ant colony, in a question and answer format that can easily be used by a child and will be equally useful to the adult who must answer, simply, the questions asked by those too young to read.

Ann D. Schweibish, in School Library Journal *(reprinted from the January, 1968, issue of* School Library Journal, *published by R. R. Bowker Co., a Xerox company; copyright © 1968 by Xerox Corporation), January, 1968, p. 75.*

Based on a thorough one-year series of observations on an ant colony, Millicent Selsam has prepared a question-and-answer book that encourages children to make their own studies and observations and learn the facts of their life history. The question-and-answer format, happily, encourages personal investigation because there is some open-endedness. . . . Appropriate scientific words are used and explained. The book may be read to or with preschool children or other nonreaders while the adult shares observations of ants with them. Young readers can easily take off on their own with this learning guide.

Science Books *(copyright 1968 by the American Association for the Advancement of Science), Vol. 4, No. 4 (March, 1968), p. 321.*

OTHER CITATIONS

The Booklist and Subscription Books Bulletin, *March 1, 1968, pp. 787-88.*

QUESTIONS AND ANSWERS ABOUT HORSES (1974)

Selsam's question and answer format makes [*Questions and Answers About Horses*] attractive to new or reluctant readers, especially the reality-oriented among them who have no use for [fictionalized horse stories], and yet within this structure she manages to cover the horses's evolution from *eohippis* and the origin and qualities of eight special breeds. . . . [Robert J. Lee's] soft brown and green water colors take up at least half of each double page, which adds to the browsable appearance.

Kirkus Reviews *(copyright © 1974 The Kirkus Service, Inc.), February 1, 1974, p. 118.*

[*Questions and Answers About Horses*] provides clear and concise descriptions of ten popular horse breeds, their habits, care, and equine evolution. There are minor inaccuracies—e.g., the statement that "The American Saddle Horse is the most popular riding horse today" is unsupportable; the draft horse is designated as a breed rather than a type . . .—and omissions of references to the Arabian's intelligence and slight stature and threats to wild mustangs. . . . [The book] is greatly enhanced and enlarged by [Robert J. Lee's] brown-and-green water-color paintings. . . . Providing browsing material and fodder for simple school reports, this title will also stimulate the interest of older reluctant readers.

Patricia G. Harrington, in School Library Journal *(reprinted from the April, 1974, issue of* School Library Journal, *published by R. R. Bowker Co., a Xerox company; copyright © 1974 by Xerox Corporation), April, 1974, pp. 52-3.*

Selsam is always accurate and informative, but her gift for clear and simple writing is hampered by the format [of *Questions and Answers About Horses*], although the book gives many facts about equine evolution, breeds, taking care of a horse, and some information about gestation period, diet, ways of communicating, et cetera.

Zena Sutherland, in Bulletin of the Center for Children's Books *(© 1974 by the University of Chicago; all rights reserved), June, 1974, p. 164.*

OTHER CITATIONS

Publishers' Weekly, *January 28, 1974, p. 300.*

SEE THROUGH THE SEA (with Betty Morrow, 1955)

Three creative individuals combined their resources to produce this simple explanation of the life that is to be found in the sea: Miss Selsam, a biologist, assures the scientific accuracy of the text; Miss Morrow, a poet, illuminates the facts with a sense of wonder; Miss Lubell, an artist, draws on the sea itself for the colors of her imaginative illustrations—sea-green, sand-gold, and coral-red. . . .

An attractive introduction to sealore, this, which may, in this day of skin-diving, appeal to more than the younger readers for whom it is intended.

Eulalie Steinmetz Ross, in Saturday Review *(copyright © 1955 by Saturday Review, Inc.; reprinted with permission), December 17, 1955, p. 35.*

OTHER CITATIONS

Good Books for Children: A Selection of Outstanding Children's Books Published 1950-65, *compiled by Mary K.*

Eakin, University of Chicago Press, third edition, 1966, p. 292.

***TERRY AND THE CATERPILLARS* (1962)**

[This is easy] reading, easy science—made something more than merely functional by a certain dry wit in both [Selsam's] text and [Lobel's] pictures. These make the caterpillar-to-cocoon-to-moth process so interesting that the young reader will want to bring up the next caterpillar he finds, and so clear that he will know how to do it.

Margaret Warren Brown, in The Horn Book Magazine *(copyright © 1962, by The Horn Book, Inc., Boston), October, 1962, p. 479.*

[*Terry and the Caterpillars* is a] small masterpiece. Terry puts three caterpillars in jars, feeds them, and hovers over the cocoons until three moths emerge. The accuracy and simplicity of the writing, regarded as introductory science, is impressive; the book is doubly impressive because the text is at the same time simple enough for beginning readers and interesting enough to read aloud. [Arnold Lobel's] illustrations echo the humor of [Millicent Selsam's] writing. . . .

Zena Sutherland, in Bulletin of the Center for Children's Books *(copyright 1963 by the University of Chicago; all rights reserved), January, 1963, p. 87.*

OTHER CITATIONS

The Booklist and Subscription Books Bulletin, *December 1, 1962, p. 291.*

Dorothy Winch, in Library Journal, *December 15, 1962, p. 4615.*

***VEGETABLES FROM STEMS AND LEAVES* (1972)**

The vocabulary [used in *Vegetables from Stems and Leaves*] may raise some questions, as the use of terms like "set seed" and the references to fruits in the botanical sense ("A package of lettuce seed contains fruits without the parachutes") are not self-explanatory. The potato . . . and the onion . . . are the most surprising and illuminating inclusions, but more vegetables are introduced (with less detail about each) than in previous Selsam volumes. Still, [this is] an eye-opening visual experience, particularly for the city child, but perhaps [it will be] used to best advantage by an informed teacher.

Kirkus Reviews *(copyright © 1972 The Kirkus Service, Inc.), October 1, 1972, p. 1149.*

[*Vegetables from Stems and Leaves*] encourages curiosity and experimentation while presenting facts of interest to the young child. . . . The author delineates, for example, the life cycle of asparagus in a matter-of-fact but not prosaic manner, making each stage in the evolution of the mature plant exciting for the young reader. A lovely format and interesting style enhance the attractiveness of the book and make it more useful for the elementary school science teacher. . . . The book should serve to dispel some of the misconceptions children may have of how things grow, how they reproduce, how the fruit is obtained, etc. Altogether a worthy contribution!

Science Books *(copyright 1973 by the American Association for the Advancement of Science), Vol. IX, No. 4 (March, 1973), p. 330.*

The writing [in *Vegetables from Stems and Leaves*] is clear, concise, and informative, the information accurate and geared in its lack of complexity to the level of the intended audience. Since Mrs. Selsam writes even the simplest book with dignity, this can be used by slow older readers also. The title is third in a series of books that describe categories of vegetables, the others being roots and fruits; the series serves as a good introduction to botany.

Zena Sutherland, in Bulletin of the Center for Children's Books *(© 1973 by the University of Chicago; all rights reserved), May, 1973, p. 144.*

OTHER CITATIONS

The Booklist, *March 15, 1973, p. 718.*

* * *

SENDAK, Maurice 1928-

Maurice Sendak, an American author and illustrator who received the Caldecott Medal (1964) for *Where the Wild Things Are* and the Hans Christian Andersen illustrator's medal (1970), is widely known for his distinctive, compelling illustrations and for his controversial *Where the Wild Things Are* and *In the Night Kitchen*. (See also *Contemporary Authors*, Vols. 5-8, rev. ed., and *Something About the Author*, Vol. 1.)

GENERAL COMMENTARY

[Maurice Sendak's] pictures are in the best tradition: wry, gentle, witty, subtle. As an original creator, his work, disguised in fantasy, springs from his earliest self, from the vagrant child that lurks in the heart of all of us. His illustrations are a corrective to the many published sins of adulthood against childhood—the sops, the cozy insults, the condescensions. He knows that children live in wonder, a state that opens them nakedly to joy, desire and a world full of sudden and fearful possibilities.

Brian O'Doherty, in The New York Times Book Review *(© 1963 by The New York Times Company; reprinted by permission), May 12, 1963, p. 3.*

What makes Maurice Sendak the best children's illustrator in America is his attitude to his imagination. For he approaches it, and his work, with a prosaic professionalism that is part of a practical belief in the facts of fantasy. . . . His best work is in fact an addition to the 19th-century's tradition of illustration. . . . In connecting with it across the break caused by photography and "modern" art . . . Sendak is pioneering, just as he has pioneered in restoring the majestic sense of fright, and its magical control, that have been streamlined out of children's literature.

Brian O'Doherty, in Book Week *(© The Washington Post), November 28, 1965, p. 20.*

[Maurice Sendak] does not subscribe to the credo that childhood is a time of innocence. . . . The young in Sendak's books—particularly the books he writes himself—are sometimes troubled and lonely, they slip easily into and out of fantasies, and occasionally they are unruly and stubborn. Nor are they the bright, handsome boys and softly pretty little girls who are so numerous in so many picture books. The Sendak boys and girls tend to appear truncated, having oversized heads [and short arms and legs]. . . .

His drawings . . . are oddly compelling. Intensely, almost palpably alive, they seem to move on the page and, later, in memory.

Nat Hentoff, "Among the Wild Things" (1966), in The New Yorker *(© 1966 by The New Yorker Magazine, Inc.), January 22, 1966 (and reprinted in* Only Connect: Readings on Children's Literature, *edited by Sheila Egoff, G. T. Stubbs, and L. F. Ashley , Oxford University Press, 1969, pp. 325-26).*

[Maurice Sendak's versatility] has made him one of the most exciting illustrators at work today. The key to Sendak's attractiveness lies in the way he combines pen-drawing and colour-wash and the command which this gives him over detail and atmosphere. He is able to adapt his technique to the demands of a given text, whether of his own devising or not.

Bettina Hürlimann, in her Picture-Book World, *translated and edited by B. W. Alderson (© Oxford University Press 1968), Oxford University Press, 1968, pp. 84-5.*

Unlike [Arthur] Rackham, Sendak is never distracted by the details of what his characters may be wearing nor the particulars of their objective milieu. . . . His illustrations . . . spring from the emotional reality of the child's world. . . . Nostalgia and pain—all entirely absent from Rackham's inventions—are often evoked by Sendak. . . .

Sendak's work is freighted with the memories of a solemn and even somber child. . . . There is an element of compulsion, of underlying psychological necessity to [his] work that gives it its tension and deep truth. We cannot take it lightly.

With Sendak, then, we are summoned back into the emotional state of childhood, to experience its joys and pains as participants in every tale. . . . [He] increasingly brings his considerable and constantly deepening graphic gifts to bear upon the subterranean essence of childhood itself.

Selma G. Lanes, in her Down the Rabbit Hole: Adventures and Misadventures in the Realm of Children's Literature *(copyright © 1971 by Selma G. Lanes), Atheneum, 1972, pp. 74-5, 78.*

Sendak is an eclectic artist, much of whose work has been based on traditional models. . . . Sendak's dominance today is indisputable. I agree with the general verdict; indeed, without claiming undue significance for him in art history at large, I am prepared to say that he is the greatest creator of picture books in the hundred-odd years' history of the form. . . . He is also a fine illustrator who never seeks to bludgeon his text into submission. And he is more than competent as a writer; his texts of (especially) the books in the 'Nutshell Library' and *Where the Wild Things Are* make their full contribution to the total impact.

John Rowe Townsend, in his Written for Children: An Outline of English Language Children's Literature, *revised edition (copyright © 1965, 1974 by John Rowe Townsend; reprinted by permission of J.B. Lippincott Company), Lippincott, 1974, p. 310.*

ALLIGATORS ALL AROUND (1962)

[*Alligators All Around* is an] alphabet book in which a family of three ingratiating alligators is shown on each page. . . . The fact that each letter of the alphabet has only two or three words used alliteratively makes the text easy to remember, even if some of the words are unfamiliar when first heard by a child. The illustrations are, of course, repetitive, but the repetition is alleviated by engaging silliness of occupation and facial expression.

Zena Sutherland, in Bulletin of the Center for Children's Books *(copyright 1963 by the University of Chicago; all rights reserved), March, 1963, p. 117.*

CHICKEN SOUP WITH RICE (1962)

[*Chicken Soup with Rice* is a] small read-aloud book with a nonsense verse for each month of the year; the illustrations are delightful, but the text seems to get a bit thin and repetitious. The paramount joys of chicken soup are cited on each page: "In January it's so nice while slipping on the sliding ice to sip hot chicken soup with rice. Sipping once sipping twice sipping chicken soup with rice."

Zena Sutherland, in Bulletin of the Center for Children's Books *(copyright 1963 by the University of Chicago; all rights reserved), February, 1963, p. 100.*

HECTOR PROTECTOR AND AS I WENT OVER THE WATER (1965)

The fun the artist must have had in illustrating these two nursery rhymes will surely carry over to the reader and viewer of this diverting picture book. With originality and imaginativeness and in the playful, childlike vein of his *Where the Wild Things Are* . . . Sendak not only interprets but extends the rhymes in his delightful pictures.

The Booklist and Subscription Books Bulletin *(© 1965 by the American Library Association), December 15, 1965, p. 410.*

Sendak has chosen two of the briefest Mother Goose rhymes to expand with drawings, adding "surprising dimensions." He clearly reveals the roots which, he has acknowledged, go back to Caldecott. But he is also plainly himself, in the vein of *Where the Wild Things Are*. . . . Each rhyme, ingeniously detailed in illustrations, offers something humorous to the small child.

Virginia Haviland, in The Horn Book Magazine *(copyright © 1966, by The Horn Book, Inc., Boston), February, 1966, p. 48.*

Two relatively unfamiliar nursery rhymes provide the pegs on which Maurice Sendak builds two picture stories which seem to show him at his best and worst at the same time. Each is well-planned as a whole and executed with care, the lay-out and colours are most agreeable and the notions of having the Queen in the first look like Victoria and of introducing a monster to swallow and disgorge a ship in the second are both successful. But Hector's tantrum, amusing at first, seems to go on too long and he looks so disagreeable throughout his rather overextended trip to court it is hard to care what happens once he gets there yet is still disappointing to find that really nothing in particular *does* happen. A monosyllabic blackbird helps, a dog like Max's does not. Two blackbirds are in the second and the scene in which their teeth are knocked out provides a sort of climax, while the fact that blackbirds do not *have* teeth, anyway, and the reconciliation between hero, birds and monster should reassure anyone shaken by this sudden violence. It is odd however that anyone as gifted as Mr. Sendak should remain so under the influence of the books he first illustrated with their tiresome insistence on sharing children's moods and silly moments. The elaborate cake Hector is to take to the Queen, his "Bye" to the lion, the second hero's "hee-hee" all diminish the effect of a book conceived in the Caldecott tradition. . . . The book is beautifully made but the result is only fun, not something really marvellous.

The Junior Bookshelf, *February, 1968, p. 30.*

OTHER CITATIONS

Library Journal, *November 15, 1965, p. 5073.*

***HIGGLETY PIGGLETY POP! OR THERE MUST BE MORE TO LIFE* (1967)**

The story of a small dog who runs away to find the "more to life" than having everything and, after failing some tests and passing others, finds herself a star in the Mother Goose theater, may make nonsense to the literal-minded. It takes imagination to see that Mr. Sendak is saying something serious about "having" and "living."

Patience M. Daltry, in The Christian Science Monitor *(reprinted by permission from* The Christian Science Monitor; *© 1967 The Christian Science Publishing Society; all rights reserved), November 2, 1967, p. B6.*

[*Higglety Pigglety Pop!*] has elements of tenderness and humor; it also has those typically macabre Sendak touches that were enjoyed by readers of *Where the Wild Things Are*. . . . The illustrations are beautiful, amusing, and distinctive; the story is freshly imaginative, subtly direct, wryly perceptive.

Zena Sutherland, in Bulletin of the Center for Children's Books *(copyright 1967 by the University of Chicago; all rights reserved), December, 1967, p. 66.*

A daring imagination has woven a simple rhyme into a complex and brilliantly original tale . . . . The fantasy is ordered and controlled, full of allusion, wisdom, and flashes of wit. Forty children sat spellbound one day as the book was read aloud; but for an individual reader the story is enormously extended by the pictures, each one a masterpiece of impeccable drawing, restraint, and emotional depth.

Ethel L. Heins, in The Horn Book Magazine *(copyright © 1968 by The Horn Book Inc., Boston), February, 1968, pp. 61-2.*

Higglety Pigglety Pop! is a work of beauty—in production, in story, and in pictures. Sendak makes his points subtly, and his story is ingeniously constructed. In fact, the book must be read more than once. Its humor has an underlying emotional tug. . . .

Sendak emphasizes the dreamlike quality of the story by drawing the heads [and features] of the characters . . . slightly larger than life, giving them an eerie, distorted look. He uses . . . minute black dots, [and] . . . he has framed his pictures in black. In many ways the pictures bear a striking resemblance to . . . turn-of-the-century photographs. . . .

Arthur Bell, in The Horn Book Magazine *(copyright © 1968 by The Horn Book, Inc., Boston), April, 1968, p. 154.*

Higglety, Pigglety, Pop! or There Must Be More to Life (1967) by Maurice Sendak is funny, mystifying, childlike, and original. . . . It is a book to be read aloud, and more than once. Many children found it hilarious; many adults found it puzzling.

Ruth Hill Viguers, in A Critical History of Children's Literature, *revised edition, by Cornelia Meigs, Anne Thaxter Eaton, Elizabeth Nesbitt, and Ruth Hill Viguers, edited by Cornelia Meigs (copyright © 1969 by The Macmillan Co.), Macmillan, 1969, p. 473.*

OTHER CITATIONS

Publishers' Weekly, *September 18, 1967, p. 67.*

Library Journal, *December 15, 1967, p. 76.*

Constantine Georgiou, in his Children and Their Literature, *Prentice-Hall, 1969, p. 283.*

***IN THE NIGHT KITCHEN* (1970)**

In a highly original dream fantasy a small boy falls through the dark, out of his clothes, and into the bright night kitchen. . . . Every detail of the deliciously playful illustrations—three look-alike bakers, the kitchen open to the starry sky, buildings made from cans, jars, eggbeater, and other kitchen utensils—and the chantable, easily remembered text maintain their dreamlike quality throughout. [*In the Night Kitchen* is pure] delight for young children.

The Booklist *(© by the American Library Association), January 15, 1971, p. 423.*

[*In the Night Kitchen*] tells a simple story of a young child running the gamut of a psychological fantasy until he returns to everyday reality. . . . Accompanying the story in the form of an elaborate obbligato is the vision of a city—obviously New York—transformed by night into an interestingly composed collection of labeled bottles, boxes, and jars . . . looking like the flat backdrop found in old vaudeville performances. . . . The story is carried forward pictorially by a skillful adaptation of the comic-strip format. . . . [Psychologists]—and others—will discover where subconscious elements may appear to impinge on storytelling and picturization. It will not, however, be the first time in the history of mankind that a work of art will have had a disturbing effect.

Paul Heins, in The Horn Book Magazine *(copyright © 1971 by The Horn Book, Inc., Boston), February, 1971, pp. 44-5.*

Whatever the adult reaction, young children will find pure delight in Sendak's dream fantasy. The dreamlike quality of the chantable, easily remembered text and the original, deliciously playful illustrations remains constant in every detail.

Helen E. Kinsey, in Top of the News, *April, 1971, p. 306.*

[It] should be clear that Mr. Sendak is having a very individual way with fantasy [in this book], and the confidence and artistry of his performance is almost completely persuasive. Whether one focuses attention on his painting or his words one finds constantly renewed sources of wonder. His mastery of colour produces beautifully juxtaposed tints of brown, grey and mauve, night-blue and moon-yellow; and his creation of an infinitely detailed dream-townscape out of culinary provisions is carried through with total conviction. Given the idea, any creator of comic-strip pictures might have managed the pepperpot and a couple of detergent bottles, but none would have seen such possibilities in the scene or worked at them with such an absorbed, affectionate sense of detail. . . .

Judged by the highest standards though, and despite the masterly handling of its parts *In the Night Kitchen* does not add up to a satisfying whole. Being a dream-sequence the 'story' is subject to arbitrary laws which make for entertaining improvisations but not in the end for much more—a view substantiated by the artist's lame conclusion to his book 'And that's why, thanks to Mickey, we can have cake every morning'. The play of fancy has here outstripped the unifying energy of imagination; the force that made *Where the Wild Things Are* so complete a book is here allowed to spend itself upon contingencies.

Brian W. Alderson, in Children's Book Review *(© 1971 by Five Owls Press Ltd.), June, 1971, p. 84.*

[In] *The Night Kitchen*, Sendak has moved in a new direction. The book has all the consistency and coherence one has come to expect, but it is in a totally different style—a comic strip, pop art style. Micky, the hero, has much in common with Max [in *Where the Wild Things Are*], both in looks and in his attitude to the adventure he has in his fantasy world. Yet again Sendak uses the dream, as Micky investigates a racket in the middle of the night, falling out of one world into the farcical world of the night kitchen. There are touches of Sendak's poetic skill here in 'and fell through the dark, out of his clothes, past the moon and his mama and papa sleeping tight, into the light of the night kitchen', but the general level of both text and pictures is less pleasing. The comic strip influence which includes the depiction of three bakers as a triplet Oliver Hardy, and also the comic strip typographic convention, is so strong that all Sendak's earlier beauty of illustration is quite obliterated. It is perhaps more obviously 'contemporary'—even to the point of full-frontal nudity—but it is neither as exciting nor as satisfying as earlier work. It is true that Micky survives any danger that threatens, but surely the possibility of being baked in a cake is more disturbing than any wild creature. Strangely enough, this seems much more nightmarish in the real sense, in its inconsequentiality, than any of the monsters in *Wild Things*.

Averil Swanton, "Maurice Sendak's Picture Books," in Children's Literature in Education *(© 1971, APS Publications, Inc.; reprinted by permission of the publisher), No. 6 (November, 1971), p. 48.*

[*Where the Wild Things Are*] was the work not just of a master but of a grandmaster. It was hard to see how Sendak could go on to surpass himself. I do not think he did so in *In the Night Kitchen* . . .; but neither was that book the anti-climax it might well have been. The two are too unlike for detailed comparison, and a crude assertion of personal preference would be pointless; yet at this level the unlikeness is something of an achievement in itself. In *Night Kitchen* Sendak demonstrated the breadth of his visual and verbal imagination: it may not be 'better' than *Wild Things* but it is boldly, splendidly different.

John Rowe Townsend, in his Written for Children: An Outline of English Language Children's Literature, *revised edition (copyright © 1965, 1974 by John Rowe Townsend; reprinted by permission of J.B. Lippincott Company), Lippincott, 1974, p. 314.*

OTHER CITATIONS

Zena Sutherland, in Bulletin of the Center for Children's Books, *January, 1971, p. 80.*

Amy Kellman, in Grade Teacher, *March, 1971, p. 96.*

The Booklist, *April 1, 1971, p. 661.*

Derwent May, in The Listener, *November 11, 1971, p. 665.*

THE JUNIPER TREE, AND OTHER TALES FROM GRIMM (1973)

[*The Juniper Tree*] is the best work Sendak has ever done. The two-volume boxed set is a model of compact, sober design, easily handled by a child. Within the small format, Sendak's drawings are monumental, hypnotic in their stillness, their power to draw us into his world of thick-calved peasants, sturdy princesses and enchanted animals. . . . The wicked Queen in "Snow-White" is like no other artist's—a motherly, middle-aged woman pensively smiling. Only her bright, fixed gaze betrays her obsessive narcissism, her joy when "she thought she had eaten Snow White's lung and liver."

Walter Clemons, in Newsweek *(copyright 1973 by Newsweek, Inc.; all rights reserved; reprinted by permission), December 3, 1973, p. 104.*

[Maurice] Sendak's pen-and-ink drawings [for the Grimm fairy tales in *The Juniper Tree*] measure only 3½ inches by 4½ inches. But like Dürer's *Little Passion of Christ*—an influence Sendak gladly acknowledges—the effect is monumental. Sendak tricks the eye. Rabbits, crows, . . . peasants, princesses loom enormously from the small page.

Menace, ecstasy, mirth and wisdom fill the eyes of the animals [and characters].

There is an authority in Sendak's line detail and composition that permits comparison with such illustrators as John Tenniel and Edward Lear. His Grimm pictures draw on a tradition that encompasses not only the lessons of 15th and 16th century engraving but the lyricism of English illustrators of the 1860s.

> Time *(reprinted by permission from* Time, The Weekly Newsmagazine; *copyright Time Inc.), December 10, 1973, p. 96.*

A milestone, a tour de force, a joy to see, this two-volume edition of some of the stories from the Grimm brothers' collection includes some familiar tales and others that are less well-known. . . . The illustrations are superb: beautiful, imaginative, appropriate, tender and terrible—as though the tales had been waiting for Maurice Sendak to interpret them. For children and adults.

> *Zena Sutherland, in* Bulletin of the Center for Children's Books *(© 1974 by the University of Chicago; all rights reserved), March, 1974, p. 110.*

There is a quiet intensity in each illustration [of *The Juniper Tree, and Other Tales from Grimm*]. . . . [Sendak] freely combines patterns of clothing and architecture derived from the Middle Ages, the Renaissance, and later eras. . . .

Each picture has its own aura—one might say a Blake-like aura about it. . . . [One] observes tactile and symbiotic relationships between the human and animal forms. Yet, the realism of the draftsmanship is subordinated to, but never repressed by, the architectural balance of the composition or the numinous power of each illustration.

> *Paul Heins, in* The Horn Book Magazine *(copyright © 1974 by The Horn Book, Inc., Boston), April, 1974, pp. 136-37.*

Though it's good, in short, to have a celebratory selection like [*The Juniper Tree*] that directs attention to the neglected tales, eschews every element of retelling or timid tailoring and represents the 'Household Tales' fairly (by which I mean, I suppose, darkly), one has perhaps to remember that it's only in degree that the effect of Grimm, however represented, has been less than shuddersome.

All the same, I don't think I'd recommend these volumes for the nursery shelves, just like that. It's true that the worst stories (in respect, that is, of the terror they might cause) have the best endings. The murderous stepmother of 'The Juniper Tree' is duly squashed literally, by a millstone): the dead boy is restored: father, boy and girl sit down happily, at last, to supper. But the fiercer twists of these folk tales—even their more brutal turns of humour—might disturb any child reading them alone.

The translations, freshly done—all but four, which are by the late Randall Jarrell—are the work of Lore Segal. . . . [Compared to] the versions in Josef Scharl's great complete edition . . . the new versions have a more relaxed character. They run quickly, with the quality of a tale told rather than written. . . .

The most splendid things in these admirable volumes, however, are Maurice Sendak's line drawings. Each freezes a moment in a tale: they are, as it were, seen through cracks and keyholes. Eyes are enormous—fixed in cunning, horror, delight. In almost every one there's a distance—a far view of church tower, forest, a dangerous moon. There are obviously other ways of doing it—to some eyes, these drawings may seem altogether too considered—but they do capture, marvellously, the mesmeric quality of the tales.

> *Edward Blishen, in* Books and Bookmen *(© copyright Hansom Books 1974), December, 1974, pp. 74-5.*

***KENNY'S WINDOW* (1956)**

Maurice Sendak's distinctive sketches . . . [and] his own text . . . have created a little boy's unique world blended of the reality inside and outside his window and the make-believe of his dreams. . . . In mood and expression and inner meanings it is all fragile and poetic. The quiet tans and greys of the drawings effectively suggest nightime and dream worlds, while their lines bring out humor in the action.

> *Virginia Haviland, in* The Horn Book Magazine *(copyrighted, 1956, by The Horn Book, Inc., Boston), April, 1956, pp. 108-09.*

[*Kenny's Window* is] as sensitive and distinctive as the drawings for which [Maurice Sendak] is well known. The fragile narrative is concerned with seven questions which Kenny brings back from a dream, questions such as Can you mend a broken promise? . . . Only the most imaginative child is likely to appreciate the mood of this story which moves between the dream world and the world of reality and to sense the inner meanings of the answers which Kenny, in his growing awareness, finds within himself.

> The Booklist and Subscription Books Bulletin *(© 1956 by the American Library Association), May 15, 1956, p. 393.*

[Maurice Sendak] has written an unusual, imaginative story [in *Kenny's Window*]. Distinctive pictures in soft night colors produce an appropriate atmosphere for Kenny's dream of the four-legged rooster who gives him seven questions to answer. . . . Lovely word pictures are interspersed with passages of lesser quality. There are bits of humor, philosophy, and some puzzling bits in the book. . . .

> *Laura E. Cathon, in* Junior Libraries *(reprinted from the September, 1956, issue of* Junior Libraries, *published by R. R. Bowker Co., a Xerox company; copyright © 1956 by Xerox Corporation), September, 1956, p. 52.*

The dream situation has obviously interested Sendak from early on, since in one of his earliest books, *Kenny's Window*, the hero meets in a dream a cockerel who sets him seven questions of the order 'What is a very narrow escape?' with the answer "When someone almost stops loving you'. . . . The story line is both longer and more developed [than *Very Far Away*, 1959] and shows a fascinating understanding of a sensitive child, but the illustrations are disappointing, and that superb synthesis of text and illustration is lacking.

Averil Swanton, "Maurice Sendak's Picture Books," in Children's Literature in Education *(©1971, APS Publications, Inc.; reprinted by permission of the publisher), No. 6 (November, 1971), p. 48.*

OTHER CITATIONS

Kirkus Reviews, *April 1, 1956, p. 242.*

Mildred R. Phipps, in Saturday Review, *June 23, 1956, p. 32.*

***KING GRISLY-BEARD* (1973)**

Sendak transforms the Edgar Taylor translation [of *King Grisly-Beard*] . . . into a play within a tale within a sort of magically animated comic strip. . . . [The] performance . . . constitutes the illustrations, extending and propelling the action much as Sendak's *Hector Protector* pictures enlarged the nursery rhyme. It's an unpretentiously perfect expression of Sendak's (or any child's) feeling for the synergistic layering of fantasy and reality. As for the story, however—let's just say that we'd prefer to give the snooty princess' lesson . . . a socialist rather than a sexist interpretation.

Kirkus Reviews *(copyright © 1973 The Kirkus Service, Inc.), September 15, 1973, pp. 1030-31.*

In a format resembling that of an I Can Read, [this] familiar Grimm tale has been illustrated as though it were a play, a device [Sendak] used with a nursery rhyme in *Higglety Pigglety Pop!*. . . . The cheerful illustrations, done in slightly subdued colors, are close in feeling to Sendak's earlier work; but in their effect, they contrast greatly with the all-stops-pulled-out artistry of his illustrations for *The Juniper Tree and Other Tales from Grimm*. . . .

Sidney D. Long, in The Horn Book Magazine *(copyright © 1974 by The Horn Book, Inc., Boston), February, 1974, p. 46.*

[*King Grisly-Beard* is a] delightful picture book version of the familiar [Grimm] tale. . . . Maurice Sendak does not just add funny (and lovely) pictures, but interprets and expands the story so that it achieves a robust shrew-taming humor, and he uses three devices that should appeal to children: his leads are played by children, briefly introduced in audition pictures that precede the story proper, by one-line balloon captions within the drawings, and by the inclusion of a small, vocal dog in every set of illustrations.

Zena Sutherland, in Bulletin of the Center for Children's Books *© 1974 by the University of Chicago; all rights reserved), February, 1974, p. 95.*

"King Grisly-Beard" is just a piffle of a book, but it's an ingenious, snappy piffle. (Not all piffles are). . . . At the top of every page is the tale, on the bottom is the mock-solemn staging. (There are wonderfully silly, deadpan comments in the balloons.) The pictures kid the quaint 1823 translation, but they don't destroy the story—they give it a second life.

Sendak is still unpredictable. His illustrations for "The Juniper Tree" are elusive and softly grotesque in meaning; here he's more like popular comics, though with his usual witty details.

Sanford Schwartz, in The New York Times Book Review *(© 1974 by The New York Times Company; reprinted by permission), February 17, 1974, p. 10.*

NUTSHELL LIBRARY: *Alligators All Around; Chicken Soup with Rice; One Was Johnny; Pierre*

How delightful these little books are—and what a bargain: four complete books in color for what is usually the price of one! Then there is the fun of taking them in and out of the slipcase and choosing one's favorite. . . . They are all very entertaining, and first-class Sendak. Why hasn't he written more of his own books before?

Alice Dalgliesh, in Saturday Review *(copyright © 1962 by Saturday Review, Inc.; reprinted with permission), November 10, 1962, p. 34.*

["Nutshell Library"] is a box of four delights, tiny enough for a child to hide away and keep. All the stories are both written and illustrated by Sendak, who is the Picasso of children's books, and each of them has a function: one teaches counting, another the alphabet, a third offers a strong moral (you should *care*), and the fourth praises the wonders of chicken soup with rice.

Time *(reprinted by permission from* Time, The Weekly Newsmagazine; *copyright Time Inc.), December 14, 1962, p. 96.*

The story of Pierre is in the tradition of Belloc with Pierre's nonchalant "I don't care!" and the alarming result. In *One Was Johnny*, children will be amused by the details of the pictures. . . . *Chicken Soup and Rice* with its rhyme for each month, seems somewhat forced in its invention. . . . *Alligators All Around* with its dull colours and its too many alligators may fail to appeal to [children], unless the use of alliteration catches their fancy.

The Junior Bookshelf, *December, 1968, p. 360.*

The four irresistible books that make up Maurice Sendak's *Nutshell Library* (1962) are approximately two and one-half by three and three-fourths inches; they are tidily contained in a small box, and the box, the book jackets, and the books are illustrated with Mr. Sendak's impish, round-faced boys. The text of the four little books is as original as the pictures. *One Was Johnny* is a counting book, which winds up and unwinds in fine, cumulative style. *Pierre*, subtitled "a cautionary tale," describes the horrible fate of a boy who keeps saying "I don't care." But the ending is droll. *Alligators All Around* is one of the funniest alphabet books yet, and *Chicken Soup with Rice* is hilarious nonsense about the months of the year. These are "funny books," original and beguiling in miniature form.

May Hill Arbuthnot and Zena Sutherland, in their Children and Books, *4th edition (copyright © 1947, 1957, 1964, 1972 by Scott, Foresman and Co.), Scott, Foresman, 1972, pp. 257-58.*

OTHER CITATIONS

Laurie Dudley, in Library Journal, *February 15, 1963, p. 857.*

ONE WAS JOHNNY: A COUNTING BOOK **(1962)**

[*One Was Johnny: A Counting Book* is a] small book, engagingly illustrated, told in rhyme. . . . The text is one that children can memorize easily—to "read" the book and count to ten: ". . . 5 was a turtle who hit the dog's tail—6 was a monkey who brought in the mail. . . ."

Zena Sutherland, in Bulletin of the Center for Children's Books *(copyright 1963 by the University of Chicago; all rights reserved), February, 1963, p. 100.*

PIERRE: A CAUTIONARY TALE **(1962)**

[*Pierre: A Cautionary Tale* is bland] nonsense, but a bit slow-moving, with not quite enough vitality or humor to compensate for the slightly static quality of the story.

Zena Sutherland, in Bulletin of the Center for Children's Books *(copyright 1963 by the University of Chicago; all rights reserved), March, 1963, p. 117.*

WHERE THE WILD THINGS ARE **(1963)**

[*Where the Wild Things Are* is a] most imaginative and unusual read-aloud picture book, with illustrations that are marvelously detailed; some of the details are humorous, some are beautiful, some are delicately grotesque. . . . The drawings get larger and larger, the creatures [Max] meets are huge and bizarre, and Max is their king and they love him. . . . The text has a lovely lyric quality, and the psychological implications are sound but are not obtrusive in the story—rather, they give it body.

Zena Sutherland, in Bulletin of the Center for Children's Books *(copyright 1963 by the University of Chicago; all rights reserved), December, 1963, p. 65.*

This vibrant picture book in luminous, understated full color has proved utterly engrossing to children with whom it has been shared. As well as the pictorial grotesqueries—both deliciously monstrous and humorous—they love the idea of a small boy, punished by isolation for his naughty "wildness," dreaming up hideous wild things to whom he sails away in a private boat, taming them and then becoming their king. The situation is entirely composed and child-like. . . . [*Where the Wild Things Are* is a] sincere, perceptive contribution which bears repeated examination.

Virginia Haviland, in The Horn Book Magazine *(copyright © 1964, by The Horn Book, Inc., Boston), April, 1964, p. 172.*

One does not need to be a Freudian expert to guess what the Wild Things can be to the young human mind, the forbidden desires, the hidden guilty feelings dredged up from the subconscious. I would respectfully discount Brian Alderson's opinion . . . that "these ludicrous beasts are no more terrible than the sealyham which Max chases with a fork at the beginning of the story". Ultimately there is comfort in the book, and familiar bed and "supper still hot", but for the now they are as the Americans would say "real scarey", and poor things they would be if they were not. As in other books containing naughty children, bad behaviour, wicked beasts, devils, witches or what-have-you, they express the inexpressible, and in doing so give release.

Constance Martin, "Wild Things," in The Junior Bookshelf, *December, 1967, pp. 361-62.*

What's wrong with [*Where the Wild Things Are*] is that the author was obviously captivated by an adult psychological understanding of how to deal with destructive fantasies in the child. What he failed to understand is the incredible fear it evokes in the child to be sent to bed without supper, and this by the first and foremost giver of food and security—his mother.

The basic anxiety of the child is desertion. To be sent to bed alone is one desertion, and without food is the second desertion. The combination is the worst desertion that can threaten a child. . . .

We're never going to get a child to believe that he's really in control of his fantasies if, at the very beginning, the stage is set to show him that if you look clearly at your fantasies and are open about them, you'll be deserted. Once this image is evoked, it rouses tremendous anxiety in a child, so he wants to race through the book to find out how it ends. If the child wants to read it again and again, that proves nothing to me except that the child seeks repeated relief. If I were writing the book, where the child said, "I'll eat you up (Mommy)" maybe I'd first let the mother explain why children want to eat up their mothers and not have her send them to bed without supper.

Dr. Bruno Bettelheim, in Ladies' Home Journal *(© 1969 Downe Publishing, Inc.), March, 1969, p. 48.*

[*Where the Wild Things Are*] is the kind of fantasy that adults will rate highly for its technical, brilliant, and sometimes frightening pictures, but youngsters will claim it as a book written for them.

Through bold, vivid pictures and very few words . . . [this] book offers the momentary escape that most children need. It vicariously provides wild adventure and a refreshed return to a relatively calmer reality. This need for release or escape is common to humankind and to children particularly, on whom so many social limits for conformity are imposed.

Constantine Georgiou, in his Children and Their Literature *(copyright © 1969 by Prentice-Hall, Inc.), Prentice-Hall, 1969, pp. 82-3.*

The psychological implications [in *Where the Wild Things Are*] are sound, and the reassuring note in closing has a touching quality. Those adults who were apprehensive about the possibility of the wild things (they are deliciously hideous) frightening children seem to have been mistaken: the pictures amuse and delight small children, and many Sendak fans have sent him their own pictures of wild things which, he says, outdo his own beasts in ferocity. And children see the reassurance in Max's return home from his fantasy land when he "wanted to be where someone loved him best of all."

May Hill Arbuthnot and Zena Sutherland,

in their Children and Books, *4th edition (copyright © 1947, 1957, 1964, 1972 by Scott, Foresman and Co.), Scott, Foresman, 1972, p. 257.*

Where the Wild Things Are . . . must surely be the best-known picture book of the 1960's. . . . As the story opens out from the confines of Max's home to the fantasy world he is creating for himself, the pictures expand. From postcard-size with broad white surround, they grow to near-page, full-page, page-and-a-bit; then the 'wild rumpus' fills three great wordless double page spreads; and on the return journey everthing gradually closes in again. The text is strong, sounding, and just right for reading aloud; the story sails swiftly along, and although there are psychological implications which may well occur to adults they do not deflect it from its course or slow up the voyage.

John Rowe Townsend, in his Written for Children: An Outline of English Language Children's Literature, *revised edition (copyright © 1965, 1974 by John Rowe Townsend; reprinted by permission of J.B. Lippincott Company), Lippincott, 1974, p. 313.*

OTHER CITATIONS

The Booklist and Subscription Books Bulletin, *December 15, 1963, p. 386.*

Margaret Sherwood Libby, in Book Week, *December 22, 1963, p. 13.*

Patience M. Daltry, in The Christian Science Monitor, *March 12, 1964, p. 14.*

* * *

SINGER, Isaac Bashevis 1904-

A Polish-born American author of numerous books in Yiddish, Isaac Bashevis Singer is known especially for his stories of the *shtetl*, or ghetto. His children's tales include *Zlateh the Goat, and Other Stories* and *A Day of Pleasure*, which won the 1970 National Book Award. (See also *Contemporary Authors*, Vols. 1-4, rev. ed., and *Something About the Author*, Vol. 3.)

GENERAL COMMENTARY

I. B. Singer's uniformly excellent books have opened a remarkable world of Hasidic and old-world legend to Jewish, as well as to Gentile, children.

Eric A. Kimmel, in The Horn Book Magazine *(copyright © 1973 by The Horn Book, Inc., Boston), April, 1973, p. 171.*

ALONE IN THE WILD FOREST (1971)

But for its fairy tale paraphernalia, "Alone in the Wild Forest" could well pass as an apocryphal book of the Old Testament. It is spare, severe, oddly humorless. It celebrates the justice of a very angry and uncompromising God. . . .

Style and tone correspond: subject, verb, object, few subordinate clauses, fewer metaphors, no detailed description. "Alone in the Wild Forest" sounds like the synopsis of some proposed longer work. . . . Certainly there is a sketchiness, a declarative Ten Commandments sound, that Singer and his co-translator Elizabeth Shub have not been able to soften. The narrator has no voice; this is not a book that reads easily aloud.

The illustrations by Margot Zemach are unfortunately apt, mildly vulgar. Even the presumably attractive characters are dowdy, somnolent. They resemble Punch and Judy hand puppets, without enlivening human fingers. The evil characters possess considerably more élan, both in illustration and in text, but that, I suppose, is always the hazard in morality tales.

There is a sufficiency of the marvelous in Singer's tale: magic amulets, talking animals, transformations. It is surely meant to entertain and to cheer, but the cheerfulness is depressingly businesslike. . . . This is a book for dour, older children. For the sort of child who looks forward to Sunday (or Saturday) school. For the sort of child who arranges elaborate funeral services for dead birds and mice.

D. Keith Mano, in The New York Times Book Review *(© 1971 by The New York Times Company; reprinted by permission), October 17, 1971, p. 10.*

Margot Zemach's soft black and white drawings illustrate [*Alone in the Wild Forest*,] a tale that combines magic, adventure, piety, and romance with less effectiveness than Singer's stories usually have. For one thing, the tale shifts away from the hero for a long episode; for another, the beginning (a childless couple consult a saintly man to ask how they can get a son) has little to do with the rest of the story. . . . Too bad: too much.

Zena Sutherland, in Bulletin of the Center for Children's Books *(© 1972 by the University of Chicago; all rights reserved), February, 1972, p. 97.*

OTHER CITATIONS

Publishers' Weekly, *September 6, 1971, p. 50.*

Rebecca Ricky Friesem, in Library Journal, *January 15, 1972, pp. 285-86.*

A DAY OF PLEASURE: STORIES OF A BOY GROWING UP IN WARSAW (1969)

[*A Day of Pleasure* is] a powerful, brilliant children's book. . . . [Isaac Bashevis Singer] lays out a panorama of Jewish life in [Warsaw before the First World War]. . . . But even more, the author reveals himself; and the torments and mysteries that plagued him as a child will make his stories fascinating to other children. Lonely, watchful and imaginative, he stands at the center of each story. . . . In perhaps the most perfect story in the collection, "The Mysteries of the Cabala," the forces in both the internal and the external world of the boy combine, and the result is an experience filled with wonder, terror, and beauty. . . . Reflecting a bygone world, [Roman Vishniac's photographs] add a further note of realism and power to the collection.

Sidney D. Long, in The Horn Book Magazine *(copyright © 1970 by The Horn Book, Inc., Boston), February, 1970, pp. 48-9.*

Singer is basically retelling [in "A Day of Pleasure"] what he wrote about fictionally elsewhere in "The Family Moscat'' etc., and as fictionalized memoir in ''In My Father's Court.'' . . .

In the process of presenting to a different audience the same material about a way of life that was destroyed so painfully for him and others, a certain preachiness, a moralism, a sentimentalism intrudes. . . .

Similarly, when Singer tries to suggest that backwardness may be wisdom and dogmatism the truth through these portraits of his pietistic family and their world, he is either being easily cynical or a sentimentalist or both.

Richard M. Elman, in The New York Times Book Review *(© 1970 by The New York Times Company; reprinted by permission), February 1, 1970, p. 30.*

The narrative skill evinced in [Isaac Bashevis Singer's] fictional tales gives warmth and vitality to 19 autobiographical stories of his childhood in Poland during the first two decades of the twentieth century. These remembrances of people, school and family life, and of a deeply religious father who was a combination rabbi, judge, and spiritual leader recreate with humor and affection a world that no longer exists. . . .

The Booklist *(© by the American Library Association), February 15, 1970, p. 740.*

In [*A Day of Pleasure*], Singer celebrates the eternal verities and life as of infinite value even in the meanest circumstances. His sense of wonder, his ''pleasure'' in all the days of man, are desperately needed by all humanity. Apart from the simple joy of reading the book so poignantly illustrated by Roman Vishniac's photographs of Warsaw's Jews, Singer leaves readers with a renewed sense of the *joy* of knowing—enough to establish the book as required reading for all those jaundiced by learning, whether they are young or old.

Bruce L. MacDuffie, in School Library Journal *(reprinted from the April, 1970, issue of* School Library Journal, *published by R. R. Bowker Co., a Xerox company; copyright © 1970 by Xerox Corporation), April, 1970, pp. 124-25.*

OTHER CITATIONS

Zena Sutherland, in Bulletin of the Center for Children's Books, *April, 1970, p. 134.*

***ELIJAH THE SLAVE* (1970)**

[*Elijah the Slave* is a] Hebrew legend told with simplicity and spirit and illustrated with richly colored paintings reminiscent of medieval art. . . . While the tale may lack general appeal [Antonio Frasconi's] illustrations in the stunning picture book are a feast for the eyes.

The Booklist *(© by the American Library Association), February 1, 1971, p. 453.*

OTHER CITATIONS

Kirkus Reviews, *November 15, 1970, p. 1247.*

Sada Fretz, in Library Journal, *February 15, 1971, p. 718.*

***THE FEARSOME INN* (1967)**

[*The Fearsome Inn* is a] story which lives up to the highest standards of folk literature. . . . [Singer's] writing is taut to the point of understatement yet so perfect for this subtly magnetic story of evil overcome by magic and common sense at the level of universal wisdom. Miss Hogrogian's flawlessly executed illustrations render character and atmosphere with restraint and great beauty. On all counts, a book of uncommon quality.

Margaret A. Dorsey, in School Library Journal *(reprinted from the September, 1967, issue of* School Library Journal, *published by R. R. Bowker Co., a Xerox company; copyright © 1967 by Xerox Corporation), September, 1967, p. 122.*

The characters [in ''The Fearsome Inn''] are only vaguely differentiated. They fail to achieve the heightened significance of great folk lore which Singer has accomplished so magnificently for adults and children in the past. Only the background—the immediately realized scene and the beliefs of Eastern European Jewish civilization—gives the book depth. Here, the author's genius doesn't fail him. We are engulfed by a universe in which absolute good and absolute evil are real and at eternal variance. . . . Yet the book is too sketchy to support its intimated meaning. It remains merely a charming story whose overtones are almost lost.

Hugh Nissenson, in The New York Times Book Review *(© 1967 by The New York Times Company; reprinted by permission), October 8, 1967, p. 38.*

[Isaac Bashevis Singer], one of the great creative writers of our time, has used the pattern of folklore and the devices of Jewish traditional tales to tell [this] original fairy story rich in atmosphere. [Nonny Hogrogian's] wonderful illustrations in full color flow with the story, contributing greatly to the feeling and giving individual personality to each character. Combining romance and fearsomeness the book is beautiful, distinguished, and wholly satisfying.

Ruth Hill Viguers, in The Horn Book Magazine *(copyright © 1967, by The Horn Book, Inc., Boston), December, 1967, p. 752.*

OTHER CITATIONS

Kirkus Service, *August 1, 1967, p. 880.*

Zena Sutherland, in Bulletin of the Center for Children's Books, *December, 1967, p. 67.*

Polly Goodwin, in Book World, *March 3, 1968, p. 21.*

***THE FOOLS OF CHELM AND THEIR HISTORY* (1973)**

Singer's broadside history [*The Fools of Chelm*] reminds us that the population of Chelm consists of no one but fools, and they've known nothing but trouble ever since Gronam Ox, first ruler and Sage of Sages, invented the world crisis. . . . Shulevitz' [illustrations] of all parties . . . [are] as consistently dim as Singer's; the Chelmites' universal uncomeliness in both pictures and action is relieved only by the ludicrous extent of the caricature.

Kirkus Reviews *(copyright © 1973 The Kirkus Service, Inc.), September 15, 1973, p. 1037.*

Drawing loosely—very loosely—on Chelm legendry, [Singer] satirizes government, politics, and human foibles in a story that should have different meanings to readers of different ages but that emerges for all readers as a smooth, humorous narrative—an amusing story, well-told. [Uri Shulevitz's] pen-and-ink illustrations embellish the text, adding droll touches of their own.

Anita Silvey, in The Horn Book Magazine *(copyright © 1973 by The Horn Book, Inc., Boston), December, 1973, p. 594.*

In this whimsical satire, Singer mocks the "advantages"—such as war, crime, and revolution—that civilization brings to Chelm, as the leadership changes but never improves, passing from Gronam Ox to Bunem Pokraka to Feitel Thief and, finally, to the women of the town. The tales [in *The Fools of Chelm and Their History*] are amusing and the message, although blunt, is extremely valid, while any political offense is alleviated by the totally improbable characters created in Singer's best style.

The Booklist *(© American Library Association 1973), December 1, 1973, p. 389.*

This dark comedy is illustrated with [Uri Shulevitz's] black-and-white illustrations that certainly reinforce the mood: they are funny and frightening in their grotesque, skillfully controlled ugliness. Like the travels of Gulliver, the history of Chelm will take readers as far as their understanding permits. Hopefully, children who read [*The Fools of Chelm and Their History*] will appreciate the book for its humorous absurdities without scraping against the bedrock of nihilism and despair.

Marilyn Singer, in School Library Journal *(reprinted from the January, 1974, issue of* School Library Journal, *published by R. R. Bowker Co., a Xerox company; copyright © 1974 by Xerox Corporation), January, 1974, p. 53.*

[Uri Shulevitz's] illustrations are vigorous and funny, [and] the story has the same earthy humor and exaggeration that [have] made other Singer stories so engaging; here there seems almost too much silliness, even for a noodlehead story: elections to be held every forty years, for example, is one of the edicts of Bunem Pokraka; another is promulgated by his successor, "All knives, axes, meat cleavers, forks, as well as penknives and hairpins, are confiscated for the use of the army."

Zena Sutherland, in Bulletin of the Center for Children's Books *(© 1974 by the University of Chicago; all rights reserved), February, 1974, p. 101.*

OTHER CITATIONS

Publishers' Weekly, *September 17, 1973, p. 56.*

Psychology Today, *January, 1974, p. 101.*

Doris Noble, in Childhood Education, *February, 1974, p. 230.*

MAZEL AND SHLIMAZEL: OR THE MILK OF THE LIONESS (1967)

In Yiddish, "mazel" means luck, or good luck, and "shlimazel" means misfortune. In Isaac Singer's latest parable, these are two invisible spirits, the one jauntily dressed, well intentioned and a trifle foolish, the other bent over, evil, prone to drink and looking for all the world like an ancient Polish Joe Bffstkk. . . .

["Mazel and Shlimazel"] is an exceptionally winning tale, gentle, light-hearted, wholesome, and with just the right edge of moral mystery below the surface to hold one's interest and perk one's wonder.

Eliot Fremont-Smith, in The New York Times Book Review *(© 1968 by The New York Times Company; reprinted by permission), January 7, 1968, p. 30.*

This Jewish fairy tale about Mazel, the spirit of good fortune, and Shlimazel, the spirit of bad luck, and their rivalry over the fate of a simple peasant boy should find a wide audience. [Singer's] remarkable storytelling skill . . . is again evident in a rather long but thoroughly engrossing narrative. The large picture-book format is a fitting showcase for [Margot Zemach's] strong, deep-colored illustrations with their Eastern European atmosphere.

The Booklist and Subscription Books Bulletin *(© 1968 by the American Library Association), January 15, 1968, p. 595.*

[Isaac Bashevis Singer] has skillfully retold [*Mazel and Shlimazel*,] an old tale remembered from childhood, one that readers of fairy tales should greatly enjoy. Although the large oblong format suggests a picture book for young children, for whom the narrative would have little appeal, [Margot Zemach's] strong, humorous illustrations in deep, warm colors are in tune with the story.

Ruth Hill Viguers, in The Horn Book Magazine *(copyright © 1968 by The Horn Book, Inc., Boston), February, 1968, p. 62.*

[*Mazel and Shlimazel* is a] tale in the folk tradition, illustrated with [Margot Zemach's] lively, lovely illustrations and told with eloquent simplicity by a master-storyteller. . . . [Singer's] triumph is that the story, really a moral tale, is more enjoyable as a good story than it is uplifting or minatory.

Zena Sutherland, in Bulletin of the Center for Children's Books *(copyright 1968 by The University of Chicago; all rights reserved), March, 1968, p. 116.*

OTHER CITATIONS

Polly Goodwin, in Book World, *March 3, 1968, p. 21.*

THE TOPSY-TURVY EMPEROR OF CHINA (1971)

Singer can't write badly, and the illustrations by William Pène du Bois (black and white) are imaginative to the extent of making ugliness elegant, but the story [*The Topsy-Turvy Emperor of China*] is really an extended description of a situation, with the love affair and succession of the new ruler the only development. The author has a good point, but it so buttressed by iteration that it is overburdened.

Zena Sutherland, in Bulletin of the Center for Children's Books *(© 1971 by the Univer-*

sity of Chicago; all rights reserved), November, 1971, p. 51.

[In *The Topsy-Turvy Emperor of China*, goodness] and beauty win out in spite of an ugly emperor's decree that the bad and ugly be revered.

But this book by the famous Yiddish storyteller Isaac Bashevis Singer must be at the bad end of almost anybody's whimsy scale. It is grotesque. [William Pène Du Bois'] weird black and white drawings and the bizarre story are sure to cause a parent to frown and a child, perhaps, to have nightmares.

June Goodwin, in The Christian Science Monitor *(reprinted by permission from* The Christian Science Monitor; *© 1971 The Christian Science Publishing Society; all rights reserved), November 11, 1971, p. B3.*

OTHER CITATIONS

Publishers' Weekly, *September 6, 1971, p. 50.*

***WHEN SHLEMIEL WENT TO WARSAW AND OTHER STORIES* (1968)**

The title story [in *When Shlemiel Went to Warsaw and Other Stories*] and "Shrewd Todie & Lyzer the Miser" are treasure for storytellers. The others are rich in descriptive language, local atmosphere, and period flavor but lack the dramatic impact that made all of the tales in *Zlateh the Goat* . . . so exciting to read and to tell. . . . Both this collection and the first one, *Zlateh*, need to be introduced to young people; every child should be given the opportunity to enjoy their robust humor, shrewd wit, and perceptive insight into human nature.

Diane Farrell, in The Horn Book Magazine *(copyright © 1969 by The Horn Book, Inc., Boston), February, 1969, p. 50.*

For reading aloud, for storytelling, or for private delight this collection of tales in the folk tradition is a variable joy. [Margot Zemach's] illustrations capture both the tenderness and the sly, wry wit of [Singer's] stories in soft line drawings. . . . Some of the tales are fanciful, but most of them have the nonsensical humor that is the trademark of Chelm.

Zena Sutherland, in Saturday Review *(copyright © 1969 by Saturday Review, Inc.; reprinted with permission), February 22, 1969, p. 47.*

Eight stories, some of them based on traditional Jewish tales, are included in a new collection by one of the great storytellers of our time. . . . [Singer's] writing has a cadence that is especially evident when the tales are read aloud; the length, the style, and the humor make them a happy source for storytelling; the individual reader will have the added pleasure of [Margot Zemach's] illustrations, which are distinctive in their own right.

Zena Sutherland, in Bulletin of the Center for Children's Books *(copyright 1969 by The University of Chicago; all rights reserved), March, 1969, p. 118.*

In his first book for children—the seven Jewish stories collected in *Zlateh the Goat* . . .—[Isaac Bashevis Singer] had the ideal accompaniement of illustrations by Maurice Sendak; now, in a further collection of eight tales, including three original ones, he has the no less ideal support of . . . Margot Zemach. In contrast to Sendak's work, which showed all the detail of a nineteen-century engraving, Miss Zemach provides what at first appear to be little more than sketches. The closer one looks at them, however, the less sketch-like they become and it is possible to discern a marvellous artistry both in the way the drawings catch the atmosphere of these Jewish small-town tales and in the way the drawings are set on the page—the balance of line and space, the gradation in the weight of the pencil so that the emphasis of the drawing falls where it should. . . .

Every one [of the tales]—not excluding the slightly sentimental original stories—is beautifully told. . . . In addition, each is salted with a wit that can be coarse or subtle by turns: 'Shrewd Todie and Lyzer the Miser' is a gorgeous new version of an old practical joke, while the three 'Gothamite' tales of Chelm—which include the title story—show no let-up in the foolishness which was one of the joys of *Zlateh*. Like that book too, the present one is a model of elegant production.

Brian W. Alderson, in Children's Book Review *(© 1974 Five Owls Press Ltd.), Summer, 1974, p. 74.*

***WHY NOAH CHOSE THE DOVE* (1974)**

[Singer's] light retelling of the old story [of Noah] is acceptable but inclined toward monotony as each animal parades by with his snatch of repartee. [Eric Carle's] expansive, full-color pictures play out their amusing message to the edges of each big page, on which stiff, cut-out-style figures gaily romp.

The Booklist *(© American Library Association 1974), March 15, 1974, p. 825.*

[Eric Carle's handsome] collage and paint illustrations show the animals that are, in [Singer's] free interpretation of the Biblical story, quarreling about who is best suited to be chosen for the ark. . . . The story loses pace during the long catalog of bragging statements, and the pacific message of the ending, albeit a noble one, sounds flat when read aloud. The dialogue is interesting in its capsule characterizing, but Singer is not at his best when writing within the limitations of the picture book for young children.

Zena Sutherland, in Bulletin of the Center for Children's Books *(© 1974 by the University of Chicago; all rights reserved), September, 1974, p. 17.*

OTHER CITATIONS

Mary E. Vorwerk, in Library Journal, *May 15, 1974, p. 1469.*

***THE WICKED CITY* (1972)**

[*The Wicked City* is the] cautionary chronicle of Lot, elaborately embroidered. . . . Admittedly, Singer gives a particularizing fictional dimension to the story and the characters. . . . [His] depiction of the city verges on the comic—its *Topsy Turvy* legal system makes no sense otherwise—but [he] also seems to expect us to take the evil and its destruction in dead earnest. . . . Altogether, this is no more outrageous a violation than, say, Hawthorne's *Tanglewood Tales*, but Singer's uneasy blend of the mythic and the colloquial [makes] it hard to swallow whole, even with all those grains of salt.

Kirkus Reviews *(copyright © 1972 The Kirkus Service, Inc.), February 1, 1972, pp. 140-41.*

In [Singer's] forceful retelling, the familiar story of Lot from the Book of Genesis becomes a dramatic narrative with characters and background skillfully expanded. . . . The drama of the story is heightened by the deep-red monotone of [Leonard Everett Fisher's] full-page illustrations. . . . [The text and illustrations] form a remarkably unified whole.

Beryl Robinson, in The Horn Book Magazine *(copyright © 1972 by The Horn Book, Inc., Boston), April, 1972, p. 142.*

[This] story [of Lot] cleaves fairly closely to Genesis, although it does not include everything and it does add some details. The fictionalization is not wholly successful, especially in the dialogue. It's a dramatic story, but the embellished version lacks the stately sonority and impressiveness of the original.

Zena Sutherland, in Bulletin of the Center for Children's Books *(© 1972 by the University of Chicago; all rights reserved), December, 1972, p. 65.*

ZLATEH THE GOAT AND OTHER STORIES (1966)

These clever, tender, bittersweet tales [in *Zlateh the Goat and Other Stories*] may be enjoyed for themselves, for their literary mastery, for their reflection of a strong, strange tradition. They may be read silently or aloud, but they are best shared, with ample [time] to examine the subtleties of [Maurice Sendak's] etched illustrations. (Many of these tableaux have the fixed intensity of hallucination.) The stories vary in interest, some being no more than vignettes, but the first, *Fool's Paradise*, and the last, the title story, are masterpieces: the one is magnificent irony and the other is tender, unashamed love.

Virginia Kirkus' Service *(copyright © 1966 Virginia Kirkus' Service, Inc.), October 1, 1966, pp. 1045-46.*

[The stories in *Zlateh the Goat and Other Stories*] are for the most part thin and perfunctory, the master having chosen to act as the scribe of tradition . . ., and he is content to fill out here and there, fuse items, sharpen a point, enliven a description with the rapidity of his style. Only the moving title story goes beyond this measure and seems to catch up the interest of the author himself. . . .

[Maurice Sendak's] somber stumpy figures solidly posed in their timeless gestures perform a counterpoint to the metamorphoses and apparitions of the stories and, at the same time, underscore the commemorative intention of which Singer speaks in his brief foreword.

Irving Feldman, in Book Week (© The Washington Post), *October 30, 1966 (Part 2), p. 4.*

With the restraint and simplicity of a natural storyteller, Mr. Singer has made a gift of seven stories to all children—seven insights into the world of early twentieth-century middle-European rural Jewish life. These tales will have wide appeal for the excellence of their interpretation: they have the poetic power of folk tales—a quality of timelessness in the wisdom imparted and a feeling for the essense of human nature. . . . Readers [of *Zlateh the Goat and Other Stories*] can say with Mr. Sendak, whose illustrations are in complete harmony with the stories, "I am grateful to Isaac Bashevis Singer."

Helen B. Crawshaw, in The Horn Book Magazine *(copyright © 1966, by The Horn Book, Inc., Boston), December, 1966, p. 712.*

Based on middle-European Jewish folk material, the stories [in *Zlateh the Goat*] are told and illustrated with distinction. The Sendak illustrations are softly charming, with the humor and with just a bit of the grotesquerie of *Where the Wild Things Are*. Mr. Singer achieves the ultimate in the genre—he never gets between the story and the audience.

Zena Sutherland, in Bulletin of the Center for Children's Books *(copyright 1967 by the University of Chicago; all rights reserved), January, 1967, p. 79.*

OTHER CITATIONS

Hugh Nissenson, in The New York Times Book Review, *October 9, 1966, p. 34.*

Lavinia Russ, in Publishers' Weekly, *October 10, 1966, p. 74.*

Zena Sutherland, in Saturday Review, *November 12, 1966, p. 49.*

Margaret Hodges, in Library Journal, *December 15, 1966, p. 6197.*

* * *

STERLING, Dorothy 1913-

Dorothy Sterling is an American author noted for her books on science and Black history. (See also *Contemporary Authors*, Vols. 9-12, rev. ed., and *Something About the Author*, Vol. 2.)

CAPTAIN OF THE PLANTER: THE STORY OF ROBERT SMALLS (1958)

Though the real climax of the story, [Robert Smalls'] escape to freedom, occurs early in the book, making later chapters anticlimactic if informative, there is rich material throughout to dovetail with Civil War study for the serious reader at high school level. Ernest Crichlow's illustrations are black and whites—tenderly charming studies, pleasant in themselves, but depicting women chiefly, in maternal attitudes—which seem not quite right for this book about civil conflict.

Virginia Kirkus' Service, *January 1, 1958, p. 5.*

This outstanding biography of Robert Smalls, born a South Carolina slave, recaptures a people's indomitable will for freedom. . . . Authoritatively documented, vividly illustrated by Ernest Crichlow, the story possesses keen character and social analysis. Catapulted into the re-enactment of a nation's struggle for man's equality, the reader recognizes a similar conflict in our current national life. Highly recommended.

Spencer G. Shaw, in Junior Libraries *(reprinted from the April, 1958, issue of* Junior Libraries, *published by R. R. Bowker Co., a Xerox company; copyright © 1958 by Xerox Corporation), April, 1958, p. 52.*

Dorothy Sterling's story of Robert Smalls, well documented by a list of sources and an extensive bibliography, is dramatic because of its subject matter: Smalls' personal achievement and the events of the years of the Civil War and the Reconstruction. What Sterling has added to the inherent drama of the *Captain of the Planter* (1958) is a powerful picture of the tragedy of the postwar years and a personal portrait of a man whose true greatness lay not in one single courageous act but in the fact that he never compromised his principles for the sake of expediency.

May Hill Arbuthnot and Zena Sutherland, in their Children and Books, *4th edition (copyright © 1947, 1957, 1964, 1972 by Scott, Foresman and Co.), Scott, Foresman, 1972, p. 566.*

OTHER CITATIONS

The Booklist and Subscription Books Bulletin, *March 15, 1958, p. 418.*

Zena Sutherland, in Bulletin of the Center for Children's Books, *June, 1958, p. 114.*

Margaret Warren Brown, in The Horn Book Magazine, *August, 1958, p. 283.*

CATERPILLARS (1961)

All you would want to know about caterpillars has certainly been assessed from the characteristics of a score of varieties to the operation of one's own "caterpillar cafeteria". . . . But like the precise and colorful illustrations conceived by Winifred Lubell and sprinkled in gay profusion everywhere, the text here and there appears somewhat disorganized.

Virginia Kirkus' Service, *March 15, 1961, p. 261.*

This handsome picture book [*Caterpillars*], with many of [Winifred Lubell's] excellent drawings in color, turns the child into a home naturalist with materials usually at hand. . . . Throughout the book, the illustrations are accurate and fascinating, and the text is gay, fresh, and scientific, resulting in a nature presentation of real distinction.

Millicent Taylor, in The Christian Science Monitor *(reprinted by permission from* The Christian Science Monitor; *© 1961, The Christian Science Publishing Society; all rights reserved), May 11, 1961, p. 6B.*

OTHER CITATIONS

Virginia Haviland, in The Horn Book Magazine, *June, 1961, p. 279.*

Gladys Conklin, in Library Journal, *June 15, 1961, p. 2360.*

The Booklist and Subscription Books Bulletin, *July 15, 1961, p. 705.*

FALL IS HERE! (1966)

[This is a] description of some of the phenomena of fall, with handsome and informatively detailed illustrations, most of them in black and white. The writing style is informal, almost garrulous; the organization of material is loose although the material itself is quite accurate and is interesting. The writing has a condescending and, here and there, a coy tone particularly inappropriate in a book giving scientific information. Some of the topics discussed are migration, hibernation, leaf color, and photoperiodism. An index is appended.

Zena Sutherland, in Bulletin of the Center for Children's Books *(copyright 1966 by the University of Chicago; all rights reserved), October, 1966, pp. 32-3.*

OTHER CITATIONS

The Booklist and Subscription Books Bulletin, *October 1, 1966, p. 188.*

Zena Sutherland, in Saturday Review, *October 22, 1966, p. 61.*

FOREVER FREE: THE STORY OF THE EMANCIPATION PROCLAMATION (1963)

Although this book may shock and enrage some readers, it is sure to hold their interest at all times and to tell them a great deal more about American slavery than their history books can provide. An impressive bibliography and a convenient index add to the excellence of the book; [Ernest Crichlow's] illustrations do not.

Michael McWhinney, in The New York Times Book Review *(© 1963 by The New York Times Company; reprinted by permission), May 19, 1963, p. 30.*

A well-researched account, [*Forever Free*] traces the history of slavery in the U.S. from its African beginnings to the signing of the Emancipation Proclamation on January 1, 1863. Using many quotations, the author describes dramatically and with unusual clarity the times, the events which led to the Emancipation Proclamation, and the people—slaves, defenders of the slave system, and abolitionists—who were, in one way or another, deeply involved in the slavery issue. An important and timely record.

The Booklist and Subscription Books Bulletin *(© 1963 by the American Library Association), June 15, 1963, p. 858.*

OTHER CITATIONS

Alice Dalgliesh, in Saturday Review, *January 19, 1963, p. 49.*

***FREEDOM TRAIN: THE STORY OF HARRIET TUBMAN* (1954)**

The picture of slavery given here in Harriet Tubman's childhood and young womanhood in Maryland is as graphic a one as we are likely to have for young people. It provides a full background for the account of her ardor and ingenuity as a conductor in the Underground Railroad. . . . Out of naturally exciting material the author has built a fast-moving story for which her bibliography indicates thorough research (although her use of Quaker speech is confused). Verses from Negro spirituals add to the effectiveness of the story.

Virginia Haviland, in The Horn Book Magazine *(copyrighted, 1954, by The Horn Book, Inc., Boston), April, 1954, pp. 107-08.*

[In *Freedom Train*] Mrs. Sterling has given us an excellent picture of a period in American history which was full of drama and excitement. The historical atmosphere has not been weakened by the substitution of regional vernacular for dialect and the elimination of epithets. Harriet Tubman was a person of great dignity, integrity, and courage and these qualities have been interpreted in this book. It is exciting fare for readers of ten and over.

Augusta Baker, in Saturday Review *(copyright © 1954 by Saturday Review, Inc.; reprinted with permission), April 17, 1954, p. 28.*

OTHER CITATIONS

Virginia Kirkus' Bookshop Service, *December 1, 1953, p. 762.*

The Booklist, *March 15, 1954, p. 283.*

***LIFT EVERY VOICE* (with Benjamin Quarles, 1965)**

[The character of each of the four Black leaders included in *Lift Every Voice*] is fully developed with exceptional sensitivity and warmth. . . . In this volume, [Booker T. Washington, W. E. B. DuBois, and James Weldon Johnson] are refreshingly presented with human frailties which heighten rather than dilute the immensity of their contribution to the history of America and their fellowman. Mrs. [Mary Church] Terrell, less well-known and not heretofore presented in a biography for children, is equally appealing and courageous in her efforts to achieve equality despite handicaps of sex and race. This book is enthusiastically recommended.

Allie Beth Martin, in School Library Journal *(reprinted from the September, 1965, issue of* School Library Journal, *published by R. R. Bowker Co., a Xerox company; copyright © 1965 by Xerox Corporation), September, 1965, p. 152*

In the straightforward, highly readable style familiar in Dorothy Sterling's excellent biographical writing, this volume combines four sketches of great Negro leaders. Tailored to the pattern of a series, Zenith Books, each part here has limiting brevity, but the four become unified by the related contributions of these leaders all working to elevate their people through education, organization, writing, and political participation. [This is an] excellent addition to the growing body of books on Negro history for teen-age readers.

Virginia Haviland, in The Horn Book Magazine *(copyright © 1965, by The Horn Book, Inc., Boston), October, 1965, p. 512.*

The writing [in *Lift Every Voice*] is straightforward, with little fictionalization; balanced in coverage and objective in tone, the book is especially valuable for the integration of material in the separate biographies as the paths of the four subjects cross. An index is appended.

Zena Sutherland, in Bulletin of the Center for Children's Books *(copyright 1966 by the University of Chicago; all rights reserved), February, 1966, p. 106.*

OTHER CITATIONS

Virginia Kirkus' Service, *July 15, 1965, p. 685.*

Zena Sutherland, in Bulletin of the Center for Children's Books, *February, 1966, p. 106.*

The Booklist and Subscription Books Bulletin, *February 1, 1966, p. 533.*

***LUCRETIA MOTT, GENTLE WARRIOR* (1964)**

Dorothy Sterling's book ["Lucretia Mott, Gentle Warrior"] is not so dramatic as were her biographies of Robert Smalls and Harriet Tubman. It is hard to keep in mind all those meetings that Lucretia attended and all the speeches she made—but this biography repays careful reading. It offers a clear portrait of a remarkable woman and it gives insight into two great movements of the 19th century. Large-minded, starchy, witty, Lucretia fought through most of her life for the rights of the Negro and of women, without losing her womanliness, her humor or her feeling for individuals.

Ellen Lewis Buell, in The New York Times Book Review *(© 1965 by The New York Times Company; reprinted by permission), January 31, 1965, p. 26.*

[*Lucretia Mott, Gentle Warrior* is a] well-balanced narrative biography of a nineteenth-century reformer who devoted much of her life to the causes of Negroes and women. Diminutive Lucretia Coffin Mott is ably portrayed not only as an eloquent Quaker preacher and a strong-minded leader in the abolitionist and woman's rights movements but also as a good-natured and loved wife, mother, and grandmother. [This book is timely] and inspiring. A number of Lucretia Mott's contemporaries are identified in an appendix. No index [is provided].

The Booklist and Subscription Books Bulletin *(© 1965 by the American Library Association), April 15, 1965, p. 805.*

OTHER CITATIONS

Houston L. Maples, in Book Week, *January 31, 1965, p. 15.*

Priscilla L. Moulton, in The Horn Book Magazine, *February, 1965, p. 66.*

***THE MAKING OF AN AFRO-AMERICAN: MARTIN ROBISON DELANY, 1812-1885* (1971)**

In "The Making of an Afro-American" . . . we get a substantial portrait [of Martin Robison Delany] along with good narrative. Delaney is one of the major figures among black abolitionists, one of the most prolific, active and certainly gifted men of the period. His triumphs and tragedies are expertly handled minus pathos or propaganda. Miss Sterling gives us what good biographies ought to give: an exhaustive, untampered with, skillful re-telling of a life of consequence.

Toni Morrison, in The New York Times Book Review *(© 1971 by The New York Times Company; reprinted by permission), May 2, 1971 (Part 2), p. 3.*

[This is a biography] of a Negro among the first to teach that Black can be beautiful—and strong, smart, patriotic, and progressive as any white man. . . . The main bibliographic source was another biography written in close collaboration with [Delany], so much information may have a natural bias. Dorothy Sterling attempts to avoid a repetition by using almost two hundred additional pieces of source material. Good historical background of black nationalism.

Mrs. John G. Gray, in Best Sellers *(copyright 1971, by the University of Scranton), June 15, 1971, p. 151.*

Because of the dialogue included, this biography appears to be quite fictionalized in regard to much of Delany's personal life. However, the author does include an impressive 13-page list of her sources. The book is long but reads well enough and should hold the interest of most of its readers.

William M. Forman, in School Library Journal *(reprinted from the September, 1971, issue of* School Library Journal, *published by R. R. Bowker Co., a Xerox company; copyright © 1971 by Xerox Corporation), September, 1971, p. 180.*

[*The Making of an Afro-American* is a] well-researched substantial biography of a nineteenth-century black man whose pride in his blackness led him to spend his life working for black independence. . . . The temper of the times and Delany's relationships with his contemporaries are vividly portrayed in a brisk account recommended for junior high and high school age readers interested in black studies or U.S. history.

The Booklist *(© by the American Library Association), October 1, 1971, pp. 148-49.*

OTHER CITATIONS

American Libraries, *April, 1972, p. 421.*

Paul Heins, in The Horn Book Magazine, *April, 1972, pp. 159-160.*

Zena Sutherland, in Bulletin of the Center for Children's Books, *April, 1972, pp. 128-29.*

***MARY JANE* (1959)**

While the fictional aspects of [*Mary Jane*] are little more than adequate, the real value for the . . . reader is the clear, undeviating challenge to prejudice, the exposé of some of its evils in their active and virulent forms, and a removal of the issue from the academic to the recognizable level.

Virginia Kirkus' Service, *February 1, 1959, p. 94.*

[This is an] honest and moving book. . . . While Mary Jane's integration [into an all-white high school] is successful, the author has carefully avoided either an unrealistic complete capitulation on the part of her fellow citizens or a dramatic event that makes the girl a heroine. Mary Jane is a nice girl, but quite ordinary; she rises to courage in a time of crisis. . . . This distinguished book is written in a straightforward style, and the people and events have a powerful emotional impact on the reader.

Zena Sutherland, in Bulletin of the Center for Children's Books *(published by the University of Chicago), May, 1959, p. 158.*

Dorothy Sterling in *Mary Jane* . . . shows just how it would feel to walk "around and around" in the shoes of a Negro girl at a newly integrated high school. Not that the book depends on the controversial issue to make it an absorbing story—it is mostly the portrayal of Mary Jane that does that. The author has made her a real girl with her own prejudices and with emotions that change from fear to a sense of heroism to loneliness and boredom. The adults, troubled, fearful, are well drawn too.

Pamela Marsh, in The Christian Science Monitor *(reprinted by permission from* The Christian Science Monitor; *© 1959, The Christian Science Publishing Society; all rights reserved), May 14, 1959, p. 9.*

[Dorothy Sterling's] moral is too blatant to be concealed, but she has coated the pill so skilfully that it is sweet to the taste and is the more telling since she has not forgotten those whites in the town who felt helpless and saddened by lawlessness. Perhaps she has cheated just a little to make Mary Jane acceptable to white readers. She is "cinnamon-coloured," not black, her hair is long, her "grampa" used to teach biology at the state college.

The Times Literary Supplement *(© The Times Publishing Company Ltd. 1959), May 29, 1959, p. v.*

Against the background of [Mary Jane's] ordeal is shown an appealing and realistic picture of childhood and the things important to children of all races. Because of Dorothy Sterling's perception and remarkable objectivity, this deceptively simple story has unusual power. Girls between ten and twelve can find here two engaging new friends and will probably be as much concerned over the trouble caused by an ingratiating but obstreperous pet squirrel as over the problems of school integration. They may also, however, gain some insight into the inheritance of young people everywhere today—an inheritance that is demanding of them understanding and great courage.

Ruth Hill Viguers, in The Horn Book Magazine *(copyright, 1959, by the Horn Book, Inc., Boston), June, 1959, p. 216.*

Dorothy Sterling's *Mary Jane* (1959) faces fully the violence that met the first black children to try out school integration in a segregated community. . . . By the year's end, things are better and the future a shade more hopeful. Is this too easy and too quick a conclusion? Who can say? Both black and white children must have courage and hope. Books can help to build both.

May Hill Arbuthnot and Zena Sutherland, in their Children and Books, *4th edition (copyright © 1947, 1957, 1964, 1972 by Scott, Foresman and Co.), Scott, Foresman, 1972, p. 462.*

OTHER CITATIONS

The Booklist and Subscription Books Bulletin, *May 15, 1959, pp. 514-15.*

Aileen O'Brien Murphy, in Saturday Review, *September 19, 1959, p. 38.*

SPEAK OUT IN THUNDER TONES: LETTERS AND OTHER WRITINGS BY BLACK NORTHERNERS, 1787-1865 **(1973)**

[Dorothy] Sterling has done a remarkable job of using these writings to trace the evolution of the aspirations of free blacks. . . . Although prominent leaders such as Paul Cuffe, the Forten family, Frederick Douglass and Martin Delaney . . . account for the bulk of the selections here, the letters of lesser known citizens . . . are often the most enlightening. . . . Sterling has provided transitional notes and contemporary illustrations, but as she draws few explicit conclusions, this collection will still be most rewarding to the student who brings to it preexisting curiosity and some maturity.

Kirkus Reviews *(copyright © 1973 The Kirkus Service, Inc.), October 15, 1973, p. 1175.*

[Dorothy] Sterling presents an excellent history of free blacks living in the North from 1787-1865. The selections, which are arranged chronologically overall, represent a distinctly black point of view, with few excerpts from white sources. The collection is divided into six sections followed by a biographical directory of about 50 men and women mentioned in the book. Also included is a fascinating and extremely revealing chapter on the social and cultural life of ante-bellum Northern blacks. . . . A skillful commentary threads through the material, providing the necessary background for a complete understanding of the contents.

Norman Lederer, in School Library Journal *(reprinted from the November, 1973, issue of* School Library Journal, *published by R. R. Bowker Co., a Xerox company; copyright © 1973 by Xerox Corporation), November, 1973, p. 68.*

[*Speak Out in Thunder Tones* is] the first of a projected three-volume collection of letters, diaries, and other writings delineating the concern of the free blacks who lived in the North before and during the Civil War. Not only do these documents illuminate a long-neglected corner of American history, they also bear witness to the long struggle for respect and recognition which began more than a century ago. . . . [Dorothy Sterling has provided succinct] introductory commentaries . . . to a work which should serve admirably as reference reading for mature students or as source material for junior high school studies programs.

Mary M. Burns, in The Horn Book Magazine *(copyright © 1973 by The Horn Book, Inc., Boston), December, 1973, p. 600.*

OTHER CITATIONS

The Booklist, *January 15, 1974, p. 537.*

Zena Sutherland, in Bulletin of the Center for Children's Books, *March, 1974, p. 118.*

SPRING IS HERE! **(1964)**

This charming book, for the up-to-10's or so, captures the very essence of the emerging life and activity that is spring. . . . The child is carried along with exciting narrative that is accurate and detailed but as poetic as the spring itself. Throughout are delightful and decorative sketches [by Winifred Lubell] adorning every page, many of them in color. This is a book to awaken observation and appreciation, and to read again and again.

The Christian Science Monitor *(reprinted by permission from* The Christian Science Monitor*; © 1964, The Christian Science Publishing Society; all rights reserved), May 7, 1964, p. 9B.*

Growth and reproductive processes set in motion by the light and warmth of spring sunshine are introduced to the primary-grade child [in *Spring Is Here!*]. . . . The text fairly scampers from one busy scene to another, and spring's bright mood is caught in the lilting lines and in the soft colors of [Winifred Lubell's] illustrations.

Priscilla L. Moulton, in The Horn Book Magazine *(copyright © 1964, by The Horn Book, Inc., Boston), June, 1964, p. 301.*

OTHER CITATIONS

Elsie T. Dobbins, in Library Journal, *April 15, 1964, pp. 1852, 1854.*

TEAR DOWN THE WALLS! **(1968)**

[*Tear Down the Walls!*] is replete with dramatic incidents which make it more stirring reading than either Bradford Chambers' *Chronicles of Negro Protest* (. . . 1968) or Robert Goldston's *The Negro Revolution* (. . . 1968), but [Dorothy Sterling's] conclusions frequently lack validity—for example, her emphasis throughout on the activities of the NAACP and her relatively skimpy treatment of more militant organizations and philosophies currently active. While the drama of this book will draw readers into sympathy with the movement, Goldston's title, with its greater objectivity and more extensive historical coverage, is still the preferable book.

Leora Oglesby, in School Library Journal *(reprinted from the December, 1968, issue of* School Library Journal, *published by R. R. Bowker Co., a Xerox company; copyright © 1968 by Xerox Corporation), December, 1968, p. 56.*

[*Tear Down the Walls!* is a] very good history of the Negro people, covering much of the same material as does Goldston's *The Negro Revolution* (. . . 1968) but written in a slightly less formal style. The author describes the African beginnings of black Americans, the slave trade, the abolitionists and the Civil War, such familiar figures in Negro history as Carver, Douglass and DuBois, the Klan, the black stereotype, and the accelerated pressures of recent years. . . . [This book] is comprehensive, objective, and smoothly written.

Zena Sutherland, in Bulletin of the Center for Children's Books *(copyright 1968 by The University of Chicago; all rights reserved) December, 1968, p. 66.*

***WALL STREET: THE STORY OF THE STOCK EXCHANGE* (1955)**

In . . . clear and direct language the history, purpose, and work of the stock exchange are presented. Though written for the nine- to twelve-year-olds, this account will prove useful to anyone desiring an understanding of the way in which the work of the stock exchange is carried on.

Nancy Jane Day, in Saturday Review *(copyright © 1956 by Saturday Review, Inc.; reprinted with permission), March 10, 1956, p. 31.*

[This is a] fascinating introduction not only to Wall Street and its two markets but also to basic economics. . . . Ideas are organized so well and introduced so gradually that the text never becomes confusing. . . . Throughout, Myron Ehrenberg's photographs are interesting and helpful. This is a book which many adults will want to borrow from children.

Heloise P. Mailloux, in The Horn Book Magazine *(copyrighted, 1956, by The Horn Book, Inc., Boston), April, 1956, p. 115.*

OTHER CITATIONS

Kirkus Reviews, *November 15, 1955, p. 838.*

Therese C. Kelly, in Library Journal, *January 15, 1956, p. 244.*

The Booklist, *February 1, 1956, p. 237.*

* * *

SUTCLIFF, Rosemary 1920-

An English author noted for her historical novels for children, Rosemary Sutcliff has received several awards, including the 1959 Carnegie Medal for *The Lantern Bearers* and a 1971 Lewis Carroll Shelf Award for *The Witch's Brat*. (See also *Contemporary Authors*, Vols. 5-8, rev. ed., and *Something About the Author*, Vol. 6.)

GENERAL COMMENTARY

Undoubtedly [Rosemary Sutcliff] has a genius for the recreation of an historical period. She has learned to restrain her early overenthusiasm, which at times was dangerously near to sentimentality, and to tone down the lushness of her descriptive passages. . . . Her style has become vigorous, direct, and mature. . . .

It is perhaps in her reconstruction of religious rites and ceremonies that Rosemary Sutcliff shows her imaginative understanding of her characters and her period most strikingly, for she never dismisses what seem to be savage customs as barbarous and without significance. As a result we are given fascinating pictures of an unfamiliar way of life. . . .

Eileen H. Colwell, "Rosemary Sutcliff—Lantern Bearer" (1960), in Horn Book Reflections: On Children's Books and Reading, *edited by Elinor Whitney Field (copyright © 1969 by The Horn Book, Inc., Boston), The Horn Book, 1969, pp. 123-24.*

Miss Sutcliff's books have an organic unity which sets them apart from the extrovert "good yarn" of historical fiction, and they make no concessions to ideas of what is a suitable book for children. . . .

[Her] theme is the struggle of the Roman ideal, the light, against the dark ignorance of the barbarians. Aquila in *The Lantern Bearers* learns that an ideal persists even when empires totter, and the reader knows that history is the continuity of the past and present; the soil and the people remain. Owain in *Dawn Wind* discovers that a nation grows when warring tribes join in a common cause. These books provide the definition of authentic Sutcliff material: symbolic action, the heroic figure who surmounts his disability, the father figure, the links with the past in the timeless characters of seers and 'little dark people'. There are hosts of other good books for children on the Roman period; these are among the best because the universality of Miss Sutcliff's themes is balanced by detailed description. . . .

The secret of [the] success [of her books about Roman Britain] is the close identification of the author, reader and hero. The books seem to be written from the inside so that the author's imagination is fused with the reader's response. . . . Another point emerges. Adolescents recognize the adult complexity of Miss Sutcliff's themes and respond to it while continuing to read the stories with the total involvement which is the best feature of the reading done by children. . . .

She is fortunate in that she has no self-consciousness when writing about sublimity. Her style rises to a bardic strain and, while some passages are over-written, there is, on the whole, more restraint than excess. Charles Keeping has served Miss Sutcliff well with his stark illustrations. There is no lack of realism.

The Times Literary Supplement *(© The Times Publishing Company Ltd. 1965), June 17, 1965, p. 498.*

Although it is not too difficult to find differences among Rosemary Sutcliff's heroes, they nevertheless seem . . . to be from the same mould. They are brave but not reckless, thoughtful but limited, conscientious, reliable, true to their friends, stiff-upper-lipped. . . .

The fiery girls who make up Miss Sutcliff's little band of feminine characters are thinly sketched, and only just exist as people. Her villains . . . come straight from stock. . . . She rarely practices the novelist's art of building up tension towards a single climax, and she is not above making excessive use of coincidence.

Yet there can be few writers who cope anything like so well

as she does with the passage of time, who can speed or slow up the narrative so effortlessly as it leaves or arrives at its significant points. Miss Sutcliff's writing is highly pictorial. At the same time she has a splendid gift for the stirring account of swift action, and she can combine these qualities most effectively. . . .

There is a great deal of violent action in her books, but it is never meaningless violence, violence for violence's sake. . . . Always one has a sense of what it is all about. At the same time there is little that is abstract, and there are no painstaking and lifeless reconstructions. For Rosemary Sutcliff the past is not something to be taken down from the shelf and dusted. It comes out of her pages alive and breathing and now.

John Rowe Townsend, in his A Sense of Story: Essays on Contemporary Writing for Children *(copyright © 1971 by John Rowe Townsend; reprinted by permission of J. B. Lippincott Company), Lippincott, 1971, pp. 198-99.*

[Rosemary Sutcliff's] books are superior not only because they are authentic records of England's earliest history with its bloody raids and its continuous wars for occupation by Norsemen, Romans, Normans, and Saxons, but also because every one of her memorable books is built around a great theme. Her characters live and die for principles they value and that men today still value. . . .

Rosemary Sutcliff gives children and youth historical fiction that builds courage and faith that life will go on and is well worth the struggle.

May Hill Arbuthnot and Zena Sutherland, in their Children and Books, *4th edition (copyright © 1947, 1957, 1964, 1972 by Scott, Foresman and Co.), Scott, Foresman, 1972, pp. 508-09.*

Rosemary Sutcliff feels the past through her nerves. No other writer for children of any age or country gives so vivid an impression of just how it felt to live in Britain after the departure of the Legions or under the weight of the conquering Normans; these descriptions, one feels, are the work of an eye-witness. . . .

At its best the Sutcliff style is flexible, eloquent and evocative, but it is often dangerously near to taking charge; it has a self-intoxicating quality.

Marcus Crouch, in his The Nesbit Tradition: The Children's Novel in England 1945-1970 *(© Marcus Crouch 1972), Ernest Benn, 1972, pp. 63, 65.*

The themes of historical novels are satisfying in proportion to their permanent relevance; and Miss Sutcliff's major books have had some of the largest themes that are open to fiction: death and rebirth, order and freedom, the long slow making of a people. . . .

Most of Miss Sutcliff's books, including the four just mentioned, are linked together as parts of a larger body of work. From the Bronze Age in *Warrior Scarlet* (1958) to the Norman period of *Knight's Fee* (1960), the story of Britain is being told: the mixing of races, the absorption of conquerors, the endurance through all strife of the little unregarded Dark People. In *The Mark of the Horse Lord* (1965) the hero moves from the Roman world into that of the Gaelic 'horse people'—a contrast more complex and profound than can be conveyed by attaching such labels as 'civilized' and 'barbarian'. Miss Sutcliff has also ventured from historical territory into Arthurian legend with *Sword at Sunset* (1963) and—to my mind more successfully—with *Tristan and Iseult* (1971). Rosemary Sutcliff writes with power and sensitivity and makes no concessions for the sake of easy reading. Her handling of time is especially skilful: a day's events may call for many pages while years may be passed over in a sentence, but proportion is nevertheless maintained, for this is the true and constantly varied tempo both of history and of individual life.

John Rowe Townsend, in his Written for Children: An Outline of English Language Children's Literature, *revised edition (copyright © 1965, 1974 by John Rowe Townsend; reprinted by permission of J.B. Lippincott Company), Lippincott, 1974, pp. 219-21.*

THE ARMOURER'S HOUSE (1952)

Like the author's *The Queen Elizabeth Story* . . . [The Armourer's House] is for the child who enjoys a leisurely paced, richly descriptive story with only a fair amount of dialog. Life within the large family at Dolphin House and in and about London Town at the time of Henry VIII are vividly pictured and the narrative is well sustained.

The Booklist, *September 1, 1952, p. 21.*

The richly detailed atmosphere of Henry VIII's London is the main attraction of ["The Armourer's House"]. For young people this is unlikely to be enough. The author's emphasis upon background deprives the story of full development; there are numerous events but no real plot.

Irene Smith, in The New York Times Book Review *(copyright, 1952, by The New York Times Co.), October 26, 1952, p. 32.*

OTHER CITATIONS

Jennie D. Lindquist, in The Horn Book Magazine, *October, 1952, pp. 326-27.*

Elizabeth Mitchell, in Library Journal, *October 1, 1952, p. 1667.*

BEOWULF (1962)

There is spirit, drama and finely molded language in Rosemary Sutcliff's "Beowulf." Her scholarship covers not only the plot of the epic—and she retells it all, not merely its more famous sections—but also its moment of history and its mood. She conveys the physical harshness of the times, men's dark acceptance of fate, absorption with deeds of super strength and bravery, virile devotion to friendship. The well-read will revel in the generous use of historical detail and in the impressiveness of the language.

Mary Louise Hector, in The New York Times Book Review *(© 1962 by The New York Times Company; reprinted by permission), November 11, 1962, p. 49.*

[Rosemary Sutcliff's *Beowulf* is an] excellent retelling in prose of the classic verse epic, with distinguished illustrations [by Charles Keeping]. . . . Miss Sutcliff has achieved the same authenticity of language and creation of mood [as Ian Serraillier's verse version]; the prose version may appeal to more young readers and the verse to a wider age range, but there can hardly be a preference—only appreciation of both books.

Zena Sutherland, in Bulletin of the Center for Children's Books *(copyright 1962 by the University of Chicago; all rights reserved), December, 1962, p. 66.*

***BROTHER DUSTY-FEET* (1953)**

[Rosemary Sutcliff], so completely at home in the Elizabethan period, has again created a vivid tale of adventure. . . . Entertaining scenes of play-acting in old inn courtyards and market places and the happy feeling of carefree wandering give [*Brother Dusty-Feet*] a greater liveliness than some young readers might expect. Well-illustrated with line drawings [by C. Walter Hodges].

Virginia Haviland, in The Horn Book Magazine *(copyrighted, 1953, by The Horn Book, Inc., Boston), December, 1953, p. 458.*

OTHER CITATIONS

Virginia Kirkus' Bookshop Service, *August 15, 1953, p. 533.*

Elizabeth Johnson, in Library Journal, *October 1, 1953, pp. 1699-1700.*

***THE CAPRICORN BRACELET* (1973)**

[In *The Capricorn Bracelet*] Sutcliff traces the withdrawal of Roman power from Britain through its waning influence on the lives of successive generations of the Calpurnius family. . . . The contrast between the second Lucius . . . and his descendant and namesake . . . is subtly and skillfully developed without stilted dialogue or obtrusive background. The potentially confusing succession of characters with identical names and the episodic framework might present problems for some readers, but Sutcliff's talent for evoking the spirits of loyal Roman soldiers and long-suffering Britons, and even the magic of the seldom seen Little Dark Ones remains unparalleled.

Kirkus Reviews *(copyright © 1973 The Kirkus Service, Inc.), March 15, 1973, p. 324.*

In six episodes that span three centuries, [*The Capricorn Bracelet*] passes on to other members of the family who serve Rome in Britain. The stories are exciting in themselves, and they give a vivid picture of the years of Roman occupation and of the gradual merging of the native peoples and the Legionnaires. The vigor and authenticity of the book are yet another testament to Sutcliff's supremacy in the field of historical fiction. An annotated chronology, divided by chapters, is included.

Zena Sutherland, in Bulletin of the Center for Children's Books *(© 1973 by the University of Chicago; all rights reserved), July-August, 1973, p. 178.*

Like the dolphin ring in Miss Sutcliff's cycle of Romano-British novels, the capricorn bracelet stands as a constant factor in the flux of history. . . .

The six brief episodes in its progress which make up this book were first prepared by Rosemary Sutcliff as scripts for Radio Scotland (and in the 'historical outlines' that are appended to each chapter there still remains a hint of the didacticism inseparable from any series called 'Stories from Scottish History'). The tales are simple enough . . . and their significance lies not so much in the events that they recount as in the changes which they illuminate. Deep in the current of the book—regardless of the intrusive historical summaries—there is Rosemary Sutcliff's extraordinary consciousness of a time and a place, an island standing on the edges of the dark. Her Roman family, passing its heirloom down three centuries, is not just seen as a part of military or political history but is emblematic of the gradual merging of conqueror and conquered. The hero of the book is not any one of the Lucius Calpurnii, but the country that nurtured them, whose wolves and plovers continue to cry after the last seedy emperor has taken his rabble from the Wall.

Brian W. Alderson, in Children's Book Review *(© 1973 Five Owls Press Ltd.), September, 1973, pp. 115-16.*

No one writes more convincing battle scenes than Miss Sutcliff. Her landscapes are alive with movement and color. Yet her heroes are curiously stereotyped, unchanged, whether the power they serve is on the rise or falling apart at the seams. They are all brave, decent young men concerned with the esteem of their peers, never entertaining a doubt about their obligations.

"The Capricorn Bracelet" is not Miss Sutcliff at her best. Still it is very good.

Feenie Ziner, in The New York Times Book Review *(© 1973 by The New York Times Company; reprinted by permission), September 30, 1973, p. 8.*

OTHER CITATIONS

The Booklist, *June 15, 1973, p. 991.*

Ruth Robinson, in Library Journal, *July, 1973, p. 2204.*

Virginia Haviland, in The Horn Book Magazine, *August, 1973, p. 387.*

***DAWN WIND* (1962)**

Set in sixth-century Britain at the time of the Saxon invasion, [*Dawn Wind*] is the story of Owain, a British farmer's son. . . . The adventurous tale, told against a realistic and vividly re-created background, is as perceptively conceived and skillfully written as its author's other historical narratives. For discriminating junior high and high school readers.

The Booklist and Subscription Books Bulletin *(© 1962 by the American Library Association), March 15, 1962, p. 484.*

[The] background [in *Dawn Wind*] is almost flawless. All the details . . . are tightly woven into the fabric. The people and story are so integrated as to be unforgettable in their setting. There are suspense and excitement and, now and then, moving passages. But, in spite of wry, perceptive little gleams, . . . the humor that makes fiction come perfectly to life is missing. . . . However, boys and girls who have been living through the whole long story of ancient Britain in Miss Sutcliff's other books will probably not feel especially the shadow that dominates this one, for it is exciting and rewarding reading. The strong, black, grotesque illustrations do nothing to lighten the mood of the story.

Ruth Hill Viguers, in The Horn Book Magazine *(copyright, 1962, by The Horn Book, Inc., Boston), April, 1962, pp. 181-82.*

In telling of Owain's experiences and his reactions to them, Rosemary Sutcliff provides a fascinating impression of what that [6th century] era of defeat meant to the Britons. In her enthusiasm for her subject she covers too much ground, slowing her pace toward the end, but that very enthusiasm permeates the story and infects the reader.

Margaret MacBean, in The New York Times Book Review *(© 1962 by the New York Times Company; reprinted by permission), April 22, 1962, p. 20.*

Evidence of scholarly research gives the flavor of authenticity throughout [*Dawn Wind*]; this, added to warmth of characterization and a suspenseful narrative, makes the book a worthy successor to the author's previous superb stories, all of which make English history come to life for young readers.

Marion West Stoer, in The Christian Science Monitor *(reprinted by permission from* The Christian Science Monitor; *© 1962, The Christian Science Publishing Society; all rights reserved), May 10, 1962, p. 6B.*

OTHER CITATIONS

Virginia Kirkus' Service, *February 1, 1962, p. 117.*

Zena Sutherland, in Bulletin of the Center for Children's Books, *March, 1962, p. 117.*

I. Elizabeth Stafford, in Library Journal, *May 15, 1962, p. 2036.*

***THE EAGLE OF THE NINTH* (1954)**

[*The Eagle of the Ninth*] is carefully thought out. . . . [Rosemary Sutcliff] has been indefatigable in collecting facts and working up atmosphere. She is particularly good in giving a sense of the dark magic and ritual of primitive peoples.

The drawbacks of the book are over-sweetness of writing and some sentimentality in the personal relationships. Slightly irritating, too, are the many echoes of Kipling, the Roman army in Britain being equivalent to the British army in India. Occasionally also, though less than in former books, one has the impression of shaky grammar under the fine writing.

The Times Literary Supplement, *November 19, 1954, p. vi.*

[*The Eagle of the Ninth*] is one of the few good stories of the Roman occupation of Britain, a period and setting that seem especially difficult to make credible, authentic, and also interesting. This is all three, and after a moderate start winds up with a race south to the protection of the wall ahead of the infuriated wild clansmen that is very exciting.

Ruth M. McEvoy, in Junior Libraries *(reprinted from the January, 1955, issue of* Junior Libraries, *published by R. R. Bowker Co., a Xerox company; copyright © 1955 by Xerox Corporation), January, 1955, p. 33.*

The outcome of [a young centurion's] difficult and dangerous quest is revealed in an unusual blend of stirring action and poetic symbolism. Authentic in background, skillful in plot, and perceptive in characterization, this beautifully conceived and executed re-creation of the past will reward appreciative readers from junior high age up.

The Booklist, *February 1, 1955, p. 251.*

OTHER CITATIONS

Virginia Kirkus' Bookshop Service, *October 15, 1954, pp. 711-12.*

Heloise P. Mailloux, in The Horn Book Magazine, *April, 1955, p. 119.*

***HEATHER, OAK, AND OLIVE: THREE STORIES* (1972)**

[*Heather, Oak and Olive* presents three] of Rosemary Sutcliff's carefully crafted recreations of ancient times, generally less compelling than her full-length works though they exemplify the same seemingly effortless blend of story and setting. . . . Each offers a sharp if fleeting glimpse of a different culture, but it is the reality of the settings and not the unremarkable plots that must sustain Ms. Sutcliff's considerable reputation.

Kirkus Reviews *(copyright © 1972 The Kirkus Service, Inc.), June 1, 1972, pp. 623-24.*

Three tales of ancient times, each different in setting and all compelling, are told by a master storyteller who is also an excellent historian. The period details are vivid but do not overburden the stories, the structure is deft and sturdy, the characters strong. . . . [Victor Ambrus'] black and white illustrations, handsome in themselves, echo the dignity and the romanticism of Rosemary Sutcliff's writing.

Zena Sutherland, in Bulletin of the Center for Children's Books *(© 1972 by the University of Chicago; all rights reserved), September, 1972, p. 19.*

[Sutcliff's] unifying theme [in *Heather, Oak, and Olive*] is not the individual acts of heroism themselves but the acceptance of what those acts will bring. . . . Examining not only the measures by which heroism is judged but also the nature of friendship, the author has skillfully woven three separate pieces into whole cloth. They are steeped in the atmosphere of ages past, but their intensity will attract young readers today.

Sheryl B. Andrews, in The Horn Book Magazine *(copyright © 1972 by The Horn Book, Inc., Boston), October, 1972, pp. 470-71.*

OTHER CITATIONS

The Booklist, *October 15, 1972, p. 206.*

HEROES AND HISTORY (1966)

By way of a writing style admirably suited to the fresh, brash actions of the heroes, the reader [of "Heroes and History"] careens along a racecourse of English history, now pausing to lay siege to a Welsh castle, or to participate in the mood and tempo of a medieval battlefield, now skimming a decade of intrigue via an adroit sentence. Missing, however, is insight that would press the stamp of individual personality upon the hero mold.

Polly Longsworth, in The New York Times Book Review *(© 1966 by The New York Times Company; reprinted by permission), January 30, 1966, p. 22.*

Both legends and historical evidence are cited [in *Heroes and History*] to show how fact and fiction merge to produce the hero tale. Though the author frequently mentions various scholarly historical sources, she does not include a bibliography, an unfortunate omission for the serious history reader. Sketches are heavy with detail, including many long battle descriptions and involved historical relationships which will make stiff reading for anyone other than an English history enthusiast.

Emma H. Kirby, in School Library Journal *(reprinted from the March, 1966, issue of* School Library Journal, *published by R. R. Bowker Co., a Xerox company; copyright © 1966 by Xerox Corporation), March, 1966, pp. 256-57.*

[*Heroes and History* presents ten] dramatic figures, ten vividly written descriptions of their exploits; these are not full or balanced biographies—they are not meant to be—but detailed accounts of the years and deeds of glory. . . . There are more names and placenames than the young reader in this country can easily absorb, but they lend color even if they remain unidentified. The illustrations are Keeping's usual bold style, but they prove quite distracting when they fill a page almost completely and face a page of solid (and small) print.

Zena Sutherland, in Bulletin of the Center for Children's Books *(copyright 1966 by the University of Chicago; all rights reserved), May, 1966, p. 155.*

OTHER CITATIONS

The Times Literary Supplement, *December 9, 1965, p. 1145.*

The Booklist and Subscription Books Bulletin, *March 15, 1966, p. 720.*

THE HIGH DEEDS OF FINN MacCOOL (1967)

[*The High Deeds of Finn MacCool*] is pure pleasure. [Sutcliff's] style is flowingly beautiful, poetical and humorous in an Irish vein, and totally suitable to its fairy and folk-tale material. The stories are releasing in their use of unexpected magic event, within tales courageously comic and starkly tragic.

The Times Literary Supplement *(© Times Newspapers Ltd., 1967), May 25, 1967, p. 450.*

In this retelling [Rosemary Sutcliff] builds up the legend of this famous captain of the Fianna, with all the elements of adventure, action and romance that come from Ireland. With the decline of storytelling this volume will be a fine addition to the reading audience that has missed out on the spoken tales of Irish tradition.

Best Sellers *(copyright 1967, by the University of Scranton), November 1, 1967, p. 315.*

Rosemary Sutcliff has retold with great style 15 tales of magic and heroism from the old, old story cycle [of Finn MacCool]. Her prose is fluid, bright with imagery and so vivid that you can almost smell the peat fires. Yet her writing never overburdens either the action or the characters. . . . [The characters] are all alive, and a little larger than life, striding through the mists of an Ireland in which there once were giants.

Ellen Lewis Buell, in Book World *(©* The Washington Post*), November 5, 1967 (Part 2), p. 12.*

A worthy successor to *The Hound of Ulster* by the same author, the stories of Finn MacCool are told with a lilt and a cadence that fairly cry out for listeners. . . . Wonder and adventure go hand in hand in these stories. . . . Especially fine are the tellings of how Finn saved the young hero's children from a giant and of how the lovers, Dearmid and Grania, outwitted Finn MacCool himself. But most wonderful of all is the account of the latter-day return of Oisin, Finn's son, who told his story to Saint Patrick.

Paul Heins, in The Horn Book Magazine *(copyright © 1968 by The Horn Book, Inc., Boston), February, 1968, pp. 62-3.*

OTHER CITATIONS

Kirkus' Service, *August 15, 1967, p. 978.*

The Booklist and Subscription Books Bulletin, *January 15, 1968, p. 595.*

THE HOUND OF ULSTER (1963)

In *The Hound of Ulster* . . . Rosemary Sutcliff starts a little uncertainly, hampering herself with too richly ornamented a style. But gradually the reader begins to lose awareness of stylistic effects, and—Miss Sutcliff's great triumph—of the intervention of the modern storyteller at all. Only the stories come through—*sing* through.

The Times Literary Supplement *(© The Times Publishing Company Ltd. 1963), June 14, 1963, p. 425.*

Rosemary Sutcliff . . . challenges the masters in telling the story of Cuchulain, the Champion of Ulster. Arming herself with various weapons, she interprets rather than echoes the old sagas with terseness and economy. She achieves an astounding depth of feeling and a sense of mounting excitement. . . . Rarely are young readers confronted with such exultant joy, such fierce hatred and such stark tragedy as in the account of the winning of the beautiful Emer as a bride, the wild forays, and the final catastrophe brought on by Deirdre and Maeve.

Margaret Sherwood Libby, in Book Week *(© The Washington Post), March 15, 1964, p. 12.*

In a magnificent retelling of the early Irish story of Cuchulain, [Rosemary Sutcliff's] style, which occasionally makes use of words and expressions found in Irish dialect, is vivid, straightforward, and forceful. . . . The episodes of the hero's life range from the heroic and the humorous to the supernatural and the tragic. . . . [This] rich and powerful version of the Gaelic epic reveals the probable source of such characters as Queen Mab, the witches in *Macbeth*, and the challenger in *Sir Gawain and the Green Knight*.

Paul Heins, in The Horn Book Magazine *(copyright © 1964, by The Horn Book, Inc., Boston), June, 1964, p. 273.*

OTHER CITATIONS

Zena Sutherland, in Bulletin of the Center for Children's Books, *May, 1964, p. 147.*

Padraic Colum, in The New York Times Book Review, *May 3, 1964, p. 26.*

KNIGHT'S FEE (1960)

This story of England at the end of the eleventh century is, as are all of Miss Sutcliff's historical novels, written with infinite craftsmanship and perceptiveness. As an adventure, as a picture of feudal life, and as a moving story of two friends, *Knight's Fee* is absorbing reading.

Zena Sutherland, in Bulletin of the Center for Children's Books *(published by the University of Chicago), November, 1960, p. 49.*

Interesting characterizations, intricate political backgrounds, and skillfully introduced details about everyday life mark this variation on Horatio Alger's theme as the work of a historian and a craftsman. [*Knight's Fee* is a] fascinating supplement to textbooks and term papers.

Saturday Review *(copyright © 1960 by Saturday Review, Inc.; reprinted with permission), November 12, 1960, p. 96.*

While there is little obvious humor [in *Knight's Fee*] there is a sure balance that keeps a serious story from becoming weighty, and the characters in their vividness command deep concern. Few stories of the Middle Ages bring the whole ritual of knighthood and the life of the feudal manor within the realm of the reader as does this one. Anyone who has lived with these people within this world will not forget it soon.

Ruth Hill Viguers, in The Horn Book Magazine *(copyright, 1961, by the Horn Book, Inc., Boston), February, 1961, p. 59.*

OTHER CITATIONS

Virginia Kirkus' Service, *September 15, 1960, p. 820.*

The Booklist and Subscription Books Bulletin, *December 1, 1960, p. 214.*

Sister Mary Hugh, in Library Journal, *December 15, 1960, p. 4578.*

THE LANTERN BEARERS (1959)

Here is a creator of historical fiction who does not pander to her readers, but expects they can take in their strides a thoroughly mature, researched-background story. Even her characters are not set in the mold. . . . [*The Lantern Bearers*] is not always an easy book, with its unfamiliar names and locales, but a book that rewards careful reading and that tells a good story.

Virginia Kirkus Service, *September 1, 1959, p. 657.*

To read a new book by Rosemary Sutcliff is an enriching experience. In all her stories she evinces the rare power of transporting her readers straight into her chosen period, and in this story of the last of the Romans in Britain she weaves once again this magic spell; and yet it is, of course, much more than magic which produces such a story as *The Lantern Bearers*. It is surely a combination of a great many things—patient attention to detail so that the historical facts are correct, a brilliant prose style, and a penetrating insight into human character. . . .

No significant fact of costume or of the manners of the day escapes Miss Sutcliff, while her use of words seems to grow more splendid with every book she writes; her occasional use of alliteration—"A flamed and feathered sunset was fading behind the Great Forest," "the faint and farmost fringe of the lantern glow"—is skilfully introduced. Then there are the perfect character studies of the humble, God-fearing and gentle Brother Ninnias, . . .or of Eugenius. . . .

Miss Sutcliff does not overload her stories with dialogue so that they may be easier to read, but for the children who are not afraid of a superbly written descriptive passage, this is history unveiled as it must have been.

The Junior Bookshelf, *November, 1959, pp. 297-98.*

There is much of Kipling in *The Lantern Bearers*, in the idea, in the sweep of the story, in—it must be confessed—certain stylistic mannerisms which from time to time stick out their uncomfortable spikes. . . . [Miss Sutcliff] handles her narrative with superb skill, particularly in scenes of violent action, but holds up the movement too often with passages of mannered prose. . . .

Miss Sutcliff is at her best in the invention of vividly seen, memorable episodes, in the management of colour and of sharp contrasts of light and dark.

The Times Literary Supplement *(© The Times Publishing Company Ltd. 1959), December 4, 1959, p. vii.*

Rosemary Sutcliff brings extraordinary scholarship to every one of her books and complete integration of setting and story, but it is the recreation of life—her penetration into the human heart no matter how distant the time—that makes each period live and gives continuity to history. . . . [*The Lantern Bearers*] is a book which educates the heart while it opens doors for the mind.

Ruth Hill Viguers, in The Horn Book Magazine *(copyright, 1960, by the Horn Book, Inc., Boston), February, 1960, p. 42.*

The best of Rosemary Sutcliff's stories have a tremendous power, an overwhelming sense of atmosphere and the kind of 'otherness' which vitalizes and accentuates the difference and distance of a past age—and yet makes it personal and immediate to the reader. The scene is set with the skill of sure knowledge and understanding, by a mind that has digested its history and archaeology and feels it instinctively rather than calling for it consciously. Few scenes remain more completely in the mind than that of the Roman villa in the first chapters of *The Lantern Bearers*, with each member of the family stepping straight into life as if at the touch of a magic wand. But the magic is hidden. The writing is a trifle over-decorated and the emotions played down—both characteristics of today's storytellers—but the picture remains behind and also the sensations and experiences of the chief characters. The resultant feeling is that of a remembered experience: we know what it was like to be a boy in England in the last red twilight of Roman rule—we feel the conflict of loyalties between Britain and Rome, the knowledge that the Rutupiae Light will shine out no more hurts us as it hurts Aquila—suddenly it is there, like a reawakened memory. The plot itself may be slight, the ultimate fortunes of the characters cease to be a matter of much moment—but the sense of an experience is an abiding treasure, and this is the gift which Rosemary Sutcliff can give at least to those readers who are fortunate enough to find themselves in tune with her own particular powers of evocation.

Roger Lancelyn Green, in his Tellers of Tales: British Authors of Children's Books from 1800 to 1964, *revised edition (copyright 1946, © 1965 by Edmund Ward, Publishers, Ltd.), Kaye & Ward Ltd., 1965, pp. 267-68.*

This is a book of unequal quality, but its basic idea is deeply characteristic of the writer. . . .

Among other things *The Lantern Bearers* is a story about Arthur . . . In a fine passage at the end of the book . . . Aquila wonders whether the people beyond the darkness will remember them. His friend looks across to Arthur, a 'tall man . . . flushed and laughing, with a great hound against his knee', and says, '"You and I and all our kind they will forget utterly, though they live and die in our debt . . . but he is the kind that men make songs about to sing for a thousand years".' The episode is one that only Rosemary Sutcliff could invent, and the language, with its incantatory lilt, is hers alone. At its best the Sutcliff style is flexible, eloquent and evocative, but is is often dangerously near to taking charge; it has a self-intoxicating quality.

Marcus Crouch, in his The Nesbit Tradition: The Children's Novel in England 1945-1970 *(© Marcus Crouch 1972), Ernest Benn, 1972, p. 65.*

OTHER CITATIONS

Zena Sutherland, in Bulletin of the Center for Children's Books, *January, 1960, p. 90.*

Shirley C. Belden, in English Journal, *May, 1965, p. 458.*

***THE MARK OF THE HORSE LORD* (1965)**

In action and tone [*The Mark of the Horse Lord*] is the most truly epic of the novels and, so far as readers are concerned, the most adult. It shows how far Miss Sutcliff has come from the wounded Marcus in *The Eagle of the Ninth*. . . .[The] awareness that public excellence is the extension of private integrity links this novel with *The Lantern Bearers, Warrior Scarlet,* and *Knight's Fee*. The familiar elements recur: the dark patch of history, the tribal feud, the hunts, the battles. The plot is slight, apart from the central action, so that each scene is described in detail to carry the intensity of the feud. The reader needs more experience than can generally be assumed of eleven-year-olds. For the first time in her novels for the young Miss Sutcliff may have outstripped her readers.

Unlike the other Roman stories, this book has a Gaelic rather than a British background: the hero goes into the darkness of the land beyond the Wall and stays there. Phaedrus stands alone: the old man of the tribe and the faithful friend are left behind.

The Horse Lord becomes larger than life until he becomes Arthur, Cuchulain, and Beowulf in one. There is enough artistry and complexity to extend an adolescent's experience. Undoubtedly the book is another success for Miss Sutcliff. The battle scenes are as grand as ever, but even in the descriptive passages there is a sharper edge on the prose which makes the style more taut. . . .

The Mark of the Horse Lord shows the coming-of-age of Miss Sutcliff's hero and the total assurance of the writing indicates an author fully in command of her power.

"The Search for Selfhood: The Historical Novels of Rosemary Sutcliff," in The Times Literary Supplement *(© The Times Publishing Co. Ltd. 1965), June 17, 1965 (reprinted in* Only Connect: Readings on Children's Literature, *edited by Sheila Egoff, G. T. Stubbs, and L. F. Ashley, Oxford University Press, 1969, pp. 252, 253, 254.*

From the start to the finish of this book, [Rosemary Sutcliff] maintains a steady thread of excitement spurred by imminent tragedy which allows the reader to forget the plot owes much to [Anthony Hope's] *The Prisoner of Zenda*. . . . [This] master storyteller once again proves that she can write a better historical novel than anybody currently on the bestseller list at the adult level. The battle scenes are terrific, the love story tastefully handled and the sense of how-it-must-have-been is just as strong as it was in *The Shield Ring* and *Warrior Scarlet*.

Virginia Kirkus' Service *(copyright © 1965 Virginia Kirkus' Service, Inc.), October 15, 1965, pp. 1084-85.*

Miss Sutcliff's story and characters are splendidly credible [in "The Mark of the Horse Lord"]. Her mastery of the period enables her to choose the exact detail of dress, speech, customs, and the wild land itself to make the background vivid. This gift, along with her richness of language, is so skillfully used that the rush of events is never impeded: savage battles, great danger, and the interplay of opposing forces keep the reader enthralled throughout a story showing the power of the human spirit to rise from slavery to great heights. Fine reading for the discriminating older boy or girl.

Elizabeth Hodges, in The New York Times Book Review *(© 1965 by The New York Times Company; reprinted by permission), November 7, 1965 (Part 2), p. 20.*

In full mastery of plot, characters and background, [Rosemary Sutcliff] has written a tightly woven, convincing historical novel that will be read eagerly for the good story, and remembered and reread because of the development of Phaedrus' character and the intriguing question posed—whether the playing of a part is enough to "change a slave gladiator, in truth and not mere seeming, into a prince of the Dalriadan."

Margaret Sherwood Libby, in Book Week *(©* The Washington Post*), November 21, 1965, p. 28.*

[*The Mark of the Horse Lord*] is an exciting adventure, a novel of historical interest, and a literary jewel. Set in Scotland during the second century, the book gives an amazing impression of spontaneity and immediacy. The Romans, the Picts, the Scots are real people: beautifully individualized, universally motivated. . . . Deftly constructed, fast paced, and colorful; there is no slackening of suspense up to the last stunning episode.

Zena Sutherland, in Bulletin of the Center for Children's Books *(copyright 1966 by the University of Chicago; all rights reserved), January, 1966, p. 91.*

[Rosemary Sutcliff] feels very strongly the gulf between civilized man who draws strength from the tradition of his family and his legion and primitive man whose strength comes from the earth. . . . [The contrast] is the essence of . . . *The Mark of the Horse Lord*. . . . In this formidably difficult book the hero is a Roman, or rather a gladiator-slave belonging involuntarily to the Roman tradition, who becomes, first, the lord of a barbarous kingdom, then the willing sacrifice, the king who dies for his people. In his fatal dilemma Phaedrus listens to voices from a deeper past than that of Rome, and his solution belongs to the oldest of all traditions. This is a dark story, powerful and compelling for all that it is grossly over-written. In it Rosemary Sutcliff seems to be writing compulsively, as if for once she has surrendered to an external, or perhaps a deep internal, force over which she lacks control. It is her grimmest book —and Charles Keeping provided it with illustrations as grim and compelling—and it is potentially her finest. So stern a theme called for a disciplined approach, and the writer weakened the impact of the story by stylistic extravagance. If only she had matched its starkness with words equally bare!

Marcus Crouch, in his The Nesbit Tradition: The Children's Novel in England 1945-1970 *(© Marcus Crouch 1972), Ernest Benn, 1972, pp. 65-6.*

OTHER CITATIONS

Julia Losinski, in Library Journal, *March 15, 1966, pp. 1722-23.*

OUTCAST (1955)

[*Outcast*] is distinguished for sensitive character development and easily handled background and incident that make early Rome and Roman Britain real for the reader. . . . How [Beric] survived horror after horror and lost all faith in man, but finally came out whole in body and mind and ready for the legion is not incredible but gripping, convincing fiction. It will delight those who have found reading about early times fascinating and will be memorable for anyone.

Virginia Haviland, in The Horn Book Magazine *(copyrighted, 1956, by The Horn Book, Inc., Boston), February, 1956, p. 40.*

OTHER CITATIONS

The Booklist, *February 1, 1956, p. 235.*

THE QUEEN ELIZABETH STORY (1950)

[*The Queen Elizabeth Story* is for] those who are still fairy- and once-upon-a-time-minded. . . . There's lots of detail here, of customs, clothing, houses, speech, education, etc., and the story is unhurried in its progress. Not for the action-minded child but for the more serious reader, rather.

Virginia Kirkus' Bookshop Service, *August 1, 1950, pp. 417-18.*

Country and family life in a quiet Devonshire village early in the reign of Queen Elizabeth [are] delightfully detailed in [*The Queen Elizabeth Story*]. There is little dialog, the pace is leisurely, and the tone just a bit precious; children not entirely beyond fairy tales who can savor long descriptive passages and are unhurried in their reading will find much enjoyment in the scene, the changing seasons, and the big and little events in Perdita's eighth year.

The Booklist, *September 15, 1950, p. 48.*

OTHER CITATIONS

Jennie D. Lindquist and Siri M. Andrews, in The Horn Book Magazine, *September, 1950, p. 376.*

Carolyn W. Field, in Library Journal, *September 15, 1950, p. 1515.*

THE SHIELD RING (1972)

American children's lack of knowledge of English history and the author's use of unfamiliar words . . . make [*The Shield Ring*] a difficult book. Good readers who don't mind skipping over a few such obstacles will read it and love it. . . . But less-good readers should have it, too, for it is an unusually vivid picture of medieval life in the Great Hall of the Norsemen and among the lakes and fells. Parents and teachers who share it with boys and girls will give them a rich and long-to-be-remembered experience.

Jennie D. Lindquist, in The Horn Book

Magazine *(copyrighted, 1957, by The Horn Book, Inc., Boston), April, 1957, p. 141.*

Because of the remote, unfamiliar period and the many Old Norse and English words [in *The Shield Ring*], it is probably only the exceptional child who will read the richly rewarding tale in which all characters are convincingly portrayed, period and scene vividly reconstructed, the heroic and indomitable spirit of the Vikings revealed, and the stirring action thrillingly recounted.

The Booklist and Subscription Books Bulletin *(© 1957 by the American Library Association), April 1, 1957, p. 412.*

OTHER CITATIONS

Virginia Kirkus' Service, *March 1, 1957, p. 183.*

Sarah Jones, in Saturday Review, *May 11, 1957, p. 57.*

Laura E. Cathon, in Library Journal, *May 15, 1957, p. 1364.*

Bulletin of the Center for Children's Books, *October, 1957, p. 28.*

***THE SILVER BRANCH* (1958)**

Those who have enjoyed and been richly rewarded by the author's earlier novel, *The Eagle of the Ninth*, will be equally held by the reading of [*The Silver Branch*, a] further picture of political and military moves in Roman Britain. . . . [Rosemary Sutcliff gives superb] treatment of scene and character, as always, and of the underlying theme of the future of the Province of Britain. Enthusiastically recommended for young people on the way to becoming discriminating readers of adult historical fiction.

Virginia Haviland, in The Horn Book Magazine *(copyright, 1958, by the Horn Book, Inc., Boston), June, 1958, pp. 209-10.*

OTHER CITATIONS

The Booklist and Subscription Books Bulletin, *March 15, 1958, p. 418.*

Zena Sutherland, in Bulletin of the Center for Children's Books, *June, 1958, p. 114.*

Therese C. Kelly, in Library Journal, *June 15, 1958, p. 1952.*

***SIMON* (1953)**

Rosemary Sutcliff's earlier stories, for all their charm of writing, have been marred by excessive sweetness. Too many of the characters are too often unbearably nice. The past, too, has glowed for her with a mellow, tender light such as never was on land or sea. In *Simon*, however, she comes to sudden and unexpected maturity. This is a story of the Civil War, but Miss Sutcliff abandons the time-worn formula (Roundheads—right but repulsive; Cavaliers—wrong but romantic) in favour of portraying individual soldiers on either side as human beings. . . . The story gains conviction from this method more than from an Olympian detachment; here is history in the making.

The Times Literary Supplement, *November 27, 1953, p. xii.*

[*Simon*] is a well-written and thrilling tale. There is nothing labored about it; it flows along swiftly and naturally out of the author's thorough knowledge of and love for England; but its appeal may be limited to young people who have some background in English history. Simon's sister, Mouse, and Susanna, in whose mother's house Simon is cared for after he has been wounded, give the book a touch of romance. All the characters are well drawn.

Jennie D. Lindquist, in The Horn Book Magazine *(copyrighted, 1954, by The Horn Book, Inc., Boston), August, 1954, p. 252.*

OTHER CITATIONS

Virginia Kirkus' Bookshop Service, *February 15, 1954, p. 119.*

Elizabeth Malone, in Library Journal, *March 15, 1954, p. 566.*

***TRISTAN AND ISEULT* (1971)**

The Arthurian cycle is a defining element in our culture, as the Trojan war was in the ancient Greek, and the Tristan story is one of its loveliest strands. Miss Sutcliff tells it with her admirable mastery of that difficult thing, an epic style—never incongruously modern, never fusty or obscure, believable even in dialogue. The pace and shape of the narrative are superbly managed.

The Times Literary Supplement *(© Times Newspapers Ltd., 1971), July 2, 1971, p. 764.*

Traditionally associated with the narratives clustering around King Arthur . . . [*Tristan and Iseult*] has been successfully recast in a number of ways. First, it has been brought back to its obvious origins in Celtic legendry. . . . Also, the famous love potion has been omitted. . . . [Rosemary Sutcliff's] storytelling is superb. Direct and forceful, it moves along with epic cadence and grandeur. . . . Passion and action are held in perfect balance, and both are set in motion by the purity and dignity of the style. . . . In so strong a retelling, one only wishes that the last paragraph of the story, smacking of late Gothic sentimentality, had been omitted.

Paul Heins, in The Horn Book Magazine *(copyright © 1971 by The Horn Book, Inc., Boston), December, 1971, p. 621.*

The famous love story of Tristan and Iseult is beautifully retold in poetic prose by [Rosemary Sutcliff]. . . . [The] omission [of the love potion] may bother purists, but it adds to the strongly human characterization of Tristan and Iseult without detracting from the heroic, larger-than-life qualities of the story.

The Booklist *(© by the American Library Association), January 15, 1972, p. 435.*

To one of the great love stories of all time, Rosemary Sutcliff brings the felicity of historical detail and the lyric, flowing style of a master storyteller. . . . The quality that emerges most clearly from Sutcliff's retelling is the bittersweet urgency of the love between the Queen and Tristan.

Zena Sutherland, in Bulletin of the Center

for Children's Books *(© 1972 by the University of Chicago; all rights reserved), April, 1972, p. 129.*

OTHER CITATIONS

Publishers' Weekly, *November 1, 1971, p. 55.*

WARRIOR SCARLET (1958)

It is one of the mysteries of the creative spirit that a slight and elegant stylist should have become, quite suddenly, a writer of genius. *Warrior Scarlet* is mature writing; it is, too, mature in its historical thought and in its wisdom. . . . The story of Drem . . . is finely told, moving and exciting. In its use of setting and apparatus it is a convincing piece of historical reconstruction. Only in characterisation does it seem less than excellent, and the writing is sometimes a little self-consciously "fine". Perhaps that is unfair; what I mean is that the writer's beautiful prose is not always disciplined to the duty of furthering the story. It is perhaps the one hint of immaturity in a splendid and powerful book. When Miss Sutcliff has a tighter hold on the language which she uses so vigorously she will fulfil the promise she so abundantly offers. In the meantime we must be deeply grateful for so compelling a glimpse of life in Sussex a hundred years "before wild Latin herdsmen pitched their tents . . . and founded Rome."

The Junior Bookshelf, *November, 1958, pp. 281-82.*

[This is a] stark and beautifully written story. . . . Rosemary Sutcliff is pastmistress in the re-creation of period. In "Warrior Scarlet" she surpasses herself. Her research is so skilfully assimilated that the reader shares Drem's harsh life, savors his satisfactions and his griefs, becomes—in short—thoroughly identified with the fierce, brave youth.

Aileen O'Brien Murphy, in Saturday Review *(copyright © 1958 by Saturday Review, Inc.; reprinted with permission), November 1, 1958, p. 55.*

Since [*Warrior Scarlet*] is a story for young people, all ends happily. But even the adult reader, who knows how the plot must work out, is continuously interested by the vigour and scope of the author's invention. Every aspect of the life of these people has been completely realized. . . .

In short, *Warrior Scarlet* deserves unqualified praise. It is a well-imagined story which teaches sound doctrine, and at the same time a fascinating picture of a strange way of life. Rosemary Sutcliff goes from strength to strength.

The Times Literary Supplement, *November 21, 1958, p. iv.*

[*Warrior Scarlet* is a] story of the Bronze Age in England, fast-paced and with a sustained excitement. . . . The details of ritual training and rites make convincing the picture of an ancient culture. Such details mean that the story cannot be read superficially, but the very real and timeless people and the drama of the action create an absorbing book.

Zena Sutherland, in Bulletin of the Center for Children's Books *(published by the University of Chicago), December, 1958, p. 75.*

[*Warrior Scarlet* is a] dramatic and moving historical story in which Miss Sutcliff again offers a real experience of entering another era. Even the younger reader . . . should appreciate the rich detailing of life pattern here in the late Bronze Age as he becomes interested in the flesh-and-blood figures. . . . With dexterity there is injected the feeling of imminent change from Bronze Age to Iron Age. Many young people will need leading into this book, but they will inevitably be impelled onward and rewarded by much that becomes a lingering picture. The writing carries grace of expression, as well as meticulous research.

Virginia Haviland, in The Horn Book Magazine *(copyright, 1959, by the Horn Book, Inc., Boston), February, 1959, pp. 56-7.*

In [*Warrior Scarlet*] many strands come together—awareness of historical continuity, the significance of the countryside, tribal rituals—to explore the theme of initiation into manhood. Drem with his withered arm is so determined to conquer his disability that he ignores the fact that to be a Warrior is to be more than strong and skilful. It is to be magnanimous and humble, to accept a disability, to lose the self-regard of the child. *Warrior Scarlet*, with its flashing bronze and gold colouring, its archetypal issues and conflicts, is the strongest emotional experience Miss Sutcliff provides and is outstanding among children's books of any kind.

"The Search for Selfhood: The Historical Novels of Rosemary Sutcliff," in The Times Literary Supplement *(© The Times Publishing Co. Ltd. 1965), June 17, 1965 (reprinted in* Only Connect: Readings on Children's Literature, *edited by Sheila Egoff, G. T. Stubbs, and L. F. Ashley, Oxford University Press [Canadian Branch], 1969, p. 251).*

OTHER CITATIONS

The Booklist and Subscription Books Bulletin, *December 1, 1958, p. 189.*

Constantine Georgiou, in his Children and Their Literature, *Prentice-Hall, 1969, pp. 346-47.*

THE WITCH'S BRAT (1970)

[*The Witch's Brat* presents a] slow serene accounting of a life lived in twelfth-century England that gives glimpses into the various strata of feudal society: the harsh law of the manor, the orderly, disciplined regimen of the monastery, the teeming city with its hopeless poor, the craftsmen and builders with their own complex structure of skills and rewards. The writing is vivid and the characters alive. Shorter and less involved than the author's other books.

Diane Farrell, in The Horn Book Magazine *(copyright © 1970 by The Horn Book, Inc., Boston), December, 1970, p. 621.*

[*The Witch's Brat* is an] evocative story of Norman England, based on the actual founding of St. Bartholomew's Hospital. . . . The story has strong, taut structure and good characterization, but is most distinguished by the colorful and consistent picture of a historical period.

Zena Sutherland, in Bulletin of the Center for Children's Books *(© 1971 by the University of Chicago; all rights reserved), April, 1971, p. 130.*

OTHER CITATIONS

Kirkus Reviews, *November 1, 1970, p. 1201.*

The Booklist, *February 1, 1971, p. 454.*

WHITE, E(lwyn) B(rooks) 1899-

E. B. White is an American essayist, editor, and author who received the 1970 Laura Ingalls Wilder Award for "a lasting contribution to children's literature." Best known of his children's books is *Charlotte's Web*. (See also *Contemporary Authors*, Vols. 13-14 and *Something About the Author*, Vol. 2.)

GENERAL COMMENTARY

Waiting and working are in some forms familiar to children but the rarity of birth in their literature is related to a deeper omission which corresponds to a limitation in their lives—the dimension of time. Just because children's temporal span is so short and their experience of relationships necessarily one sided, it is difficult to convey gradual transition; the pattern of changes which make up the full compass of a life. . . .

White transcends these limitations. His solid evocation of shifting seasons, the perpetually changing landscape, the ceaseless mobility of 'here and now' is the foundation of his achievement in making us believe in his characters and care about the events which affect them. Risk and pleasure combine in the unifying imagery of height and flight which symbolizes the launching of new life—the children swinging from the barn roof, the spider-balloonists sailing off into the unknown, Henry and Fern on the Ferris wheel. 'They've got to grow up some time,' said Mr Arable, 'and a fair is a good place to start, I guess.' (p. 7)

White's books are rich in skills and strategems, solid with feasts, tools, gear. . . . Actuality is a brand name; even *things* have a history, a past and a future. There is a lot of twentieth century junk around the garbage that entraps Stuart on the East River, the stormblown newspapers and candy wrappers in the Philadelphia Zoo. But the trash dump raided by Templeton is the repository of the media, food for fantasy, and speaks the twentieth century message. 'Bring me back a word,' Charlotte called after him. The rat tears out ads and labels—'Crunchy' 'Pre-shrunk' 'With New Radiant Action'. 'Actually,' said Wilbur, 'I *feel* radiant.' (p. 9)

In the witty handling of serious themes [in stories for children] . . . White found the exact mode of expression for his gifts. . . .

Thurber repeatedly used the word 'perfection' of White's work. White himself is fascinated by images of natural perfection. The artifacts of instinctive skill, the spider's web, the swan's nest—'Nobody ever taught her'—are set beside the processes of teaching and learning, the effort and frustration involved in mastering human skills, writing and making music. (p. 11)

Marion Glastonbury, "E. B. White's Unexpected Items of Enchantment," in Children's Literature in Education *(© 1973, APS Publications, Inc.; reprinted by permission of the publisher), No. 11 (May, 1973), pp. 3-12.*

CHARLOTTE'S WEB (1952)

[*Charlotte's Web* is] an engrossing and amusing story that will appeal to young readers for its realism and humor in both characterizations and situations, and that also has a more sophisticated humor and meaning that will appeal to adults. Garth Williams' illustrations help bring all the characters to life.

Bulletin of the Center for Children's Books *(published by the University of Chicago), December, 1952, p. 36.*

Entirely different from *Stuart Little* but just as original is this story of Wilbur, the Pig, and his friends—Fern, a little girl of eight, and Charlotte, the spider, whose remarkable spinning astonished the countryside and saved his life. To write a nonsense story around this situation might not be too difficult, but it took an E. B. White to get beauty and wisdom into the story along with the humor. And only a real farmer could have pictured so convincingly the folk of the farmyard!

Jennie D. Lindquist, in The Horn Book Magazine *(copyrighted, 1952, by The Horn Book, Inc., Boston), December, 1952, p. 407.*

[*Charlotte's Web*] got off to a fine state. Fern was as living a girl as one could wish when she rescued the runt pig from her father's ax, but no such country child would have spent day after day beside the manure pile to which the pig was consigned and repeated afterward to as dumb a mother as a parent's page ever invoked what the animals told her in their language. Fern, the real center of the book, is never developed. The animals never talk. They speculate. As to Charlotte, her magic and mystery require a different technique to create that lasting interest in spiders which controls childish impulse to do away with them.

Anne Carroll Moore, in The Horn Book Magazine *(copyrighted, 1952, by The Horn Book, Inc., Boston), December, 1952, p. 394.*

Mr. White's wit and grace—the hallmarks of his style—are exemplified in his delightful fantasy about a young girl, a little pig, and a spider. . . .

The profound themes of selfless love and acceptance of death are found in this story, and are significantly although delicately explored. On a superficial level, the scenes of barnyard life are explicit and yet charmingly drawn. A child's instinctive love of nature and animals is recreated through the eyes and ears of the heroine.

John Gillespie and Diana Lembo, in their Juniorplots: A Book Talk Manual for Teachers and Librarians *(© 1967 by the R. R. Bowker Co.), Bowker, 1967, pp. 199-202.*

E. B. White's *Charlotte's Web* is funny to children for many reasons, but probably the principal one is its character mix-ups. Wilbur the Pig's given name contrasts with his barnyard environment, and his piggish form is delightfully out of keeping with his gentle, lonely personality; Charlotte's loyal, cooperative, domestic personality makes a funny contrast with our normal picture of a spider. And they are set off by selfish, scheming Templeton the rat.

James Steel Smith, in his A Critical Approach to Children's Literature *(copyright © 1967 by McGraw-Hill Inc.), McGraw-Hill, 1967, p. 216.*

Restrained in its use of "magic" or "miracles," the story [*Charlotte's Web*] makes the reader conscious of the irrational that underlies events of everyday farm life, and it does this while still keeping the animal and human characters real. . . .

E. B. White's particular contribution to a fantastic, rural adventure is the way he describes certain of his characters—man and beast—with such succinctness and variety that he brings the whole account in direct line with actuality. And mirrored in the personalities of the barnyard population are human characteristics that always override whatever bizarre intimations there may be.

Constantine Georgiou, in his Children and Their Literature *(copyright © 1969 by Prentice-Hall, Inc.), Prentice-Hall, 1969, pp. 256-57.*

The situation [in *Charlotte's Web*], congenial to the commonplace earthiness of the setting, is imaginative, but it is nonsense and a fragile fabric to burden with so much emotion. But Mr. White triumphed. The style and wit of his writing, his wisdom, and his remembrance of a child's rapt concern with the things he loves strengthened the slender thread of story.

Ruth Hill Viguers, in A Critical History of Children's Literature, *revised edition, by Cornelia Meigs, Anne Thaxter Eaton, Elizabeth Nesbitt, and Ruth Hill Viguers, edited by Cornelia Meigs (copyright © 1969 by The Macmillan Co.), Macmillan, 1969, p. 470.*

E. B. White tells the story of Wilbur's escape within a context that embraces the natural world, the process of growth and change. . . . Allied to the rescue story is the plot implicit in Charlotte's methods, the advertising slogans in her web ("SOME PIG!"), a comment on the gullibility of man, a kind of self-delusion which in this book at least is life-giving. . . . [*Charlotte's Web*] holds to the idea of death as a fact of life, but the last chapter brings new spiders, new lambs, new goslings, another spring. The book is not about the charmed life of Wilbur, but about real life and all that implies.

Gerald Weales, "The Designs of E. B. White" (1970), in Authors and Illustrators of Children's Books: Writings on Their Lives and Works, *edited by Miriam Hoffman and Eva Samuels (copyright © 1972 by Xerox Corp.), Bowker, 1972, pp. 409-10.*

[In *Charlotte's Web*] E. B. White has not only given us a revelation of farm life as much from the point of view of his animals as from that of his human beings, but has also created his protagonists with absolute truthfulness, each to his kind. . . .

It is the burden of feeling and meaning in *Charlotte's Web* which makes it memorable, which will speak to all times and not just to our own time.

Eleanor Cameron, in The Horn Book Magazine *(copyright © 1972 by The Horn Book, Inc., Boston), December, 1972, pp. 575-76.*

The story [of *Charlotte's Web*] . . . is far-stretched; but like the web it is cleverly spun, and stronger than it looks. And it is something more than simple fantasy. The point about loyal, intelligent Charlotte is that she is our kin, one of us. So is poor fat unheroic Wilbur, gulping and slurping in the warm slops or wallowing in the manure-heap; so are the gobble-obble-obbling geese and the greedy self-seeking rat Templeton. The death of Charlotte is the death of a person, made bearable by the continuance of life through her offspring. The barn and farmyard are a world. The passage of seasons, the round of nature, are unobtrusively indicated.

Outside the life of the farmyard there is another world, not perhaps more real but on a different plane, which is that of commonplace human life; and perhaps the most poignant thing in the book is the passage of small girl Fern from involvement with the animals as people to a perfectly normal, but imaginatively regressive, preoccupation with the glittering actualities of the fairground. Fern has begun the saving of Wilbur, but by the end she has forgotten him; that is life, too. Childhood passes. *Charlotte's Web*, though a short and apparently straightforward story, is astonishingly full and rich.

John Rowe Townsend, in his Written for Children: An Outline of English Language Children's Literature, *revised edition (copyright © 1965, 1974 by John Rowe Townsend; reprinted by permission of J.B. Lippincott Company), Lippincott, 1974, pp. 241-42.*

The buildup in barnyard details, such as manure piles and board fences and spider webs, sets the stage for a fantasy which ends in a rather adult irony: Wilbur gets all the credit from people for being "Terrific" and "Some pig" while the remarkable Charlotte dies an unsung death. . . . E. B. White builds his characters somewhat on animal stereotypes—the stuttering goose, the sometimes proud, sometimes insecure pig, the sneaking, self-serving rat—but he uses these stereotypes as a point of departure for creating totally unique and unforgettable characters.

Juliet Kellogg Markowsky, in Elementary English *(copyright © 1975 by the National Council of Teachers of English), April, 1975, p. 462.*

OTHER CITATIONS

The Booklist, *September 1, 1952, p. 2.*

Mary Gould Davis, in Saturday Review, *November 15, 1952, p. 50.*

Elizabeth Hodges, in Library Journal, *December 15, 1952, pp. 2185-86.*

***STUART LITTLE* (1945)**

One of the major pitfalls in writing books in which animals are personified is a tendency to sentimentalize. E. B. White successfully avoids this [in *Stuart Little*] and instead has created a lively and, at times, tender book that is a delight to both the imagination and the emotions. The rather inconclusive ending has somewhat marred its appeal for a few readers. . . . Garth Williams' illustrations—there are eighty-seven of them—complement the text beautifully.

John Gillespie and Diana Lembo, in their Introducing Books: A Guide for the Middle Grades *(copyright © 1970 by Xerox Corp.), Bowker, 1970, p. 259.*

In E. B. White's fairy tale *Stuart Little* (1945), his first book for children, the mouse-child hero, Stuart, is the second son of an otherwise perfectly ordinary American family. . . . [It] is possible to read into Stuart's unexpected arrival an unconscious metaphor for the scaling down of grandiose American hopes and expectations, for ourselves and our children, that began to occur in American life at that time.

Selma G. Lanes, in her Down the Rabbit Hole: Adventures and Misadventures in the Realm of Children's Literature *(copyright © 1971 by Selma G. Lanes), Atheneum, 1972, pp. 104-05.*

Stuart is a model hero, cool in a crisis, dauntless in a quest, unflinching in the defence of principle—but he is a mouse. Endlessly resourceful, Stuart is the converse of White's Mittyesque depiction of himself 'at the mercy of inanimate objects which deliberately plot to destroy a man'. The son of Mr and Mrs Little of New York masters the intricacies and hazards of the apartment and the city by pioneering zeal and technical ingenuity, adjusting piano keys from inside and boarding trams in trouser turn-ups. His triumphs of self-help are contrasted with the unproductive brain-waves of his brother George, who litters the bathroom floor with tools. White is particularly good at rendering boisterous boys and sorely-tried parents, and this realism sets off the paragon of American family life which Stuart embodies, with his adventurous spirit, courtesy, early rising and well-exercised stomach muscles. . . .

For the young, Stuart provides a chance to identify simultaneously with underdog and topdog. His mastery of the world is achieved through the universal paraphernalia of miniature boats and cars with which children rehearse their own adult performances; his feats complement their fantasy. . . .

The mock heroics of Stuart Little depend on your consciousness of incongruity; the difference between the hero's picture of the figure he is cutting and our own.

Marion Glastonbury, "E. B. White's Unexpected Items of Enchantment," in Children's Literature in Education *(©1973, APS Publications, Inc.; reprinted by permission of the publisher), No. 11 (May, 1973), pp. 4-5, 6.*

Stuart Little . . . takes the idea of animals-as-people to its logical conclusion. Stuart is not only a mouse; he is also the child of a human family. The book is a funny one with serious undertones. The comedy is partly Lilliputian, as when Stuart takes the helm of a model yacht in a race on the pond; partly derived from a straightforward acceptance of the absurd. . . . But the story ends in what appears to be midstream, with Stuart searching for the vanished bird Margalo whom he loves. Perhaps the ending is right; Stuart's is a quest for freedom and beauty, and such a quest is never completed.

John Rowe Townsend, in his Written for Children: An Outline of English Language Children's Literature, *revised edition (copyright © 1965, 1974 by John Rowe Townsend; reprinted by permission of J.B. Lippincott Company), Lippincott, 1974, pp. 242-43.*

***THE TRUMPET OF THE SWAN* (1970)**

The start [of *The Trumpet of the Swan*] is a jolt, and subsequently there are breaks (Louis has had no prior exposure to the written word) and some big accidents—especially Serena's abrupt reappearance. However, when Louis raises his trumpet—to serenade the skeptical hotel clerk, for instance—or Mr. White pinions human foibles—"Kookooskoos" because "a boy's camp should have a peculiar name"—reservations have a way of evaporating.

Kirkus Reviews *(copyright © 1970 The Kirkus Service, Inc.), April 15, 1970, p. 455.*

The plot is diverting, and the half-tone illustrations [by Edward Frascino] reflect its humor, but it is the style that makes [*The Trumpet of the Swan*] a masterpiece. The father swan, orotund in the Micawber tradition, intones at the first cygnet's birth: "Oh, blessed little son of mine, how good it is to see your face peering through the protecting feathers of your mother's breast, under these fair skies. . . ."

Zena Sutherland, in Saturday Review *(copyright © 1970 by Saturday Review, Inc.; reprinted with permission), June 27, 1970, p. 39.*

While not quite so sprightly as "Stuart Little," and less

rich in personalities and incident than "Charlotte's Web" . . . "The Trumpet of the Swan" has superior qualities of its own; it is the most spacious and serene of the three, the one most imbued with the author's sense of the precious instinctual heritage represented by wild nature. Its story most persuasively offers itself to children as a parable of growing, yet does not lack the inimitable tone of the two earlier works—the simplicity that never condescends, the straight and earnest telling that happens upon, rather than veers into, comedy. . . .

John Updike, in The New York Times Book Review *(© 1970 by The New York Times Company; reprinted by permission), June 28, 1970, p. 4.*

[The] unexpected events which follow the discovery that Louis is "'defective'" are carried along by [White's] characteristically understated style, which extracts the essential humor from the most unprepossessing of situations and often spills over into uproariously ludicrous episodes. Like the author's earlier works, [*The Trumpet of the Swan*] lends itself to reading aloud. It is not, however, the equal of *Charlotte's Web*—but, then, *Charlotte's Web* is a tightly woven fabric involving life and death. [Edward Frascino's] black-and-white drawings effectively point up the poetic as well as the humorous elements of the story.

Paul Heins, in The Horn Book Magazine *(copyright © 1970 by The Horn Book, Inc., Boston), August, 1970, p. 391.*

The account of Louis's education, his practice sessions, his relationships with human beings in the course of a varied and distinguished musical career are hilarious, told with the distinctive blend of calm acceptance and the patently ridiculous that have made [E. B. White's] *Stuart Little* and *Charlotte's Web* classics in their own time.

Zena Sutherland, in Bulletin of the Center for Children's Books *(© 1970 by the University of Chicago; all rights reserved), October, 1970, p. 35.*

[*The Trumpet of the Swan*] is a disconcerting mixture of fact and fantasy, beginning as a story of wildlife and soon developing into a fantastic tale of a swan who learns to read, to play a trumpet and to earn money.

There is more than a fertile imagination behind the story for it also has compassion and wisdom and a real feeling for the joy of the free life of the wild. Its final sentence is an indication of the spirit behind it: "As Louis relaxed and prepared for sleep, all his thoughts were of how lucky he was to inhabit such a beautiful earth, how lucky he had been to solve his problems with music, and how pleasant it was to look forward to another night of sleep and another day tomorrow and the fresh morning, and the light that returns with the day".

The Junior Bookshelf, *April, 1971, p. 125.*

[Louis'] real search [in *The Trumpet of the Swan*] is not for money but the heart of a beautiful swan named Serena. Women's libbers will find her a vain, stereotyped, empty-headed female, but she's what Louis wants. . . . White's writing [is] effortless and always right. . . .

Judith Higgins, in Teacher *(excerpted with permission of the publisher; © 1974 by Macmillan Professional Magazines, Inc.; all rights reserved), May-June, 1974, pp. 81-2.*

The Trumpet of the Swan is not 'flat' comedy; there is a third dimension in which fantasy blends with the real life of the wild, and our kinship with the creatures is . . . evident. It is a loving book as well as a funny one.

John Rowe Townsend, in his Written for Children: An Outline of English Language Children's Literature, *revised edition (copyright © 1965, 1974 by John Rowe Townsend; reprinted by permission of J.B. Lippincott Company), Lippincott, 1974, p. 243.*

OTHER CITATIONS

Margaret A. Dorsey, in Library Journal, *July, 1970, p. 2537.*

The Booklist, *September 1, 1970, p. 59.*

* * *

WOJCIECHOWSKA, Maia 1927-

A Polish-born American writer of poetry, articles, and books for adults and young people, Maia Wojciechowska received the Newbery Medal in 1965 for *Shadow of a Bull*. (See also *Contemporary Authors*, Vols. 9-12, rev. ed., and *Something About the Author*, Vol. 1.)

"DON'T PLAY DEAD BEFORE YOU HAVE TO" (1970)

[This is strong] stuff, and valid for today's young, but it loses much of its impact because the entire book is a monologue—over the years—by Byron, so that although there is change, there is no relief from the emotional intensity that seems always at a peak.

Zena Sutherland, in Bulletin of the Center for Children's Books *(© 1971 by the University of Chicago; all rights reserved), January, 1971, p. 83.*

"Don't Play Dead Before You Have To" (1970) explores the sense of commitment and the values of young people in a time of protest. The literary form is unusual, the book being a long monologue by teen-ager Byron. . . . Byron changes through the course of the book, and—although the form becomes monotonous—there is great impact in his growing concern for others and in his intense yearning for a better world. It is this belief that our only hope is in young people which distinguishes Maia Wojciechowska's writing.

May Hill Arbuthnot and Zena Sutherland, in their Children and Books, *4th edition (copyright © 1947, 1957, 1964, 1972 by Scott, Foresman and Co.), Scott, Foresman, 1972, p. 466.*

OTHER CITATIONS

Kirkus Reviews, *May 15, 1970, p. 560.*

John W. Conner, in English Journal, *February, 1971, p. 278.*

"HEY, WHAT'S WRONG WITH THIS ONE?" (1969)

[*"Hey, What's Wrong with This One?"* is] a charming happy story, told with good humor and, though it lacks the resonance of this fine author's books for older children, it is fun, like a good situation comedy, and penetrating enough to withstand many, many readings.

Laura Polla Scanlon, in Commonweal *(copyright © 1969 Commonweal Publishing Co., Inc.), May 23, 1969, p. 298.*

OTHER CITATIONS

Polly Goodwin, in Book World, *May 11, 1969, p. 15.*

***THE HOLLYWOOD KID* (1966)**

Maia Wojciechowska writes about boys with parent problems; [*The Hollywood Kid*] hasn't got the stature of *Shadow of a Bull*, but it certainly avoids the sentimental sludge of *A Kingdom in a Horse*. . . . The strength of the book is in the fact that it doesn't touch up the basic problem of any youngster's accommodation to adults who are what they are and who will stay that way, and it reads with the greatest of ease. This one will probably arouse argument (where's Mom?) but then you usually land on a safety when you play parchesi in Hollywood.

Virginia Kirkus' Service *(copyright © 1966 Virginia Kirkus' Service, Inc.), August 1, 1966, pp. 757-58.*

[*The Hollywood Kid*] is a blatant failure mainly because it is a pseudo-adult rather than a juvenile novel. . . . Bryan's search for help somehow strikes the wrong note and the solution to his problems does not ring true. In many scenes, Bryan seems to be an adult masquerading as a teen-ager, in other scenes he is realistic and appealing. The conversations between Bryan and Martha, his 12-year-old friend, and Paula Wing, an ex-movie star, are stilted and embarrassingly false. The style of writing is contrived and there is a basic flaw in the use of point of view.

School Library Journal *(reprinted from the November, 1966, issue of* School Library Journal, *published by R. R. Bowker Co., a Xerox company; copyright © 1966 by Xerox Corporation), November, 1966, p. 105.*

Maia Wojciechowska again illustrates, through "The Hollywood Kid," her sensitive insight into the enigma of a genuinely troubled juvenile born to the purple of picture royalty. . . .

[The author's adults] come off as commonplace, one-dimensional characters—unlike the fully developed, tenderly understood 15-year-old Bryan Wilson, the lonely and perplexed son of Jody Blake, an overpossessive movie-queen mother. Bryan's anxieties and confusion are not contrivances for plot purposes. Miss Wojciechowska's taut, precise prose makes it plain that she knows the heart and mind of an unusual lad struggling to free himself from a tinseled world he never made or wanted.

A. H. Weiler, in The New York Times Book Review *(© 1966 by The New York Times Company; reprinted by permission), November 6, 1966 (Part 2), p. 8.*

[In *The Hollywood Kid*] Bryan must choose between psychic independence or a relationship in which he is his mother's prop. This is a problem faced by many adolescents, a problem not always recognized by the parental instigator; for this reason, the book has value. It is weakened rather than strengthened by the extravagant Hollywood milieu which puts a common situation into so exotic a frame that it seems uncommon.

Zena Sutherland, in Bulletin of the Center for Children's Books *(copyright 1967 by the University of Chicago; all rights reserved), March, 1967, p. 116.*

OTHER CITATIONS

Lavinia Russ, in Publishers' Weekly, *September 26, 1966, p. 133.*

Zena Sutherland, in Saturday Review, *November 12, 1966, p. 52.*

Best Sellers, *December 1, 1966, p. 343.*

***A KINGDOM IN A HORSE* (1965)**

[In *A Kingdom in a Horse*, one] is carried along and persuaded, because Miss Wojciechowska . . . is a skillful writer; a suspicion lingers, however, that her interest in David declines as the story proceeds. Horse-story fans will relish the vivid portrait of a beautiful animal, probably without worrying about the significance of the horse. More thoughtful readers may be disappointed in the baldly convenient happy ending, which undermines the integrity of the whole.

Houston L. Maples, in Book Week *(©* The Washington Post*), October 31, 1965 (Part 2), p. 41.*

A Kingdom in a Horse . . . at first seems to aim . . . at exploring the thoughts of a boy on the threshold of growing up, but soon the focus becomes too blurred to be effective. The point of view shifts back and forth confusedly from 13-year-old David to elderly Sarah Tierney, and from them to Gypsy, the mare they both love. At times, the story-line practically disappears, and the book seems to assume the nature of a manual on how to take care of a horse.

Marion West Stoer, in The Christian Science Monitor *(reprinted by permission from* The Christian Science Monitor*; © 1965 The Christian Science Publishing Society; all rights reserved), November 4, 1965, p. B11.*

[It] is distressing to read of a 64-year-old woman as enamored of her first horse as any teen-age heroine. It is also hard to believe that Sarah, a Vermont farm woman, though newly widowed and lonely, would spend most of her waking and some of her sleeping hours with her mare. . . .

[Maia Wojciechowska] can convey the doubts and fears of a young boy. . . . David, in his hurt and natural self-centeredness, is the real thing but Sarah is an awkward invention. It follows that ["A Kingdom in a Horse"] is fantasy, rather than the moving study of friendship between youth and age it might have been.

Ellen Lewis Buell, in The New York Times Book Review *(© 1965 by The New York*

Times Company; reprinted by permission), November 7, 1965 (Part 2), p. 20.

This is a book with some good characterization and some very good writing. Much of the story, however, is devoted to minute details of the acquisition and care of the horse and the training of Mrs. Tierney. . . . Fine for readers who love horses, but sentimental and a little heavy for others. Much of the plot about David is dependent on the fact that his father has incurred resentment; it is not until the end of the story that his father gives the boy a real explanation, although this would seem a natural thing to have done at the time of the decision to move.

Zena Sutherland, in Bulletin of the Center for Children's Books *(copyright 1966 by the University of Chicago; all rights reserved), April, 1966, p. 140.*

OTHER CITATIONS

Virginia Kirkus' Service, *October 1, 1965, p. 1046.*

Grace Wohlsen, in Library Journal, *December 15, 1965, pp. 5533-34.*

***THE LIFE AND DEATH OF A BRAVE BULL* (1972)**

Magnificent, and at the same time pathetic, the brave bull laconically celebrated [in *The Life and Death of a Brave Bull*] is the culmination of generations of breeding. . . . His death (honored by three trips around the ring) is unlikely to change anyone's opinion of bullfighting. The psychology of the proud bull is beyond reproach, but there's some doubt whether the predominant human emotion here is courage or self-indulgence—in either case "a sight to make good men cry."

Kirkus Reviews *(copyright © 1972 The Kirkus Service, Inc.), March 15, 1972, p. 326.*

Maia Wojciechowska's "The Life and Death of a Brave Bull" . . . [is] a prosy defense of bullfighting . . . that is unnecessary because she has done this better and more poetically in "Shadow of a Bull" and unconvincing because she tries to take the point of view of the bull.

Jean Fritz, in The New York Times Book Review *(© 1972 by The New York Times Company; reprinted by permission), April 23, 1972, p. 8.*

To those who appreciate the art of bull fighting, the lyric writing that details the breeding and training of the bull destined for death may be meaningful. . . . Written with grace, illustrated with verve, [*The Life and Death of a Brave Bull* is] a story that will probably find no middle ground of reaction, but be appreciated by aficionados and resented by those who consider killing for sport a cruelty.

Zena Sutherland, in Bulletin of the Center for Children's Books *(© 1972 by the University of Chicago; all rights reserved), July-August, 1972, p. 179.*

***ODYSSEY OF COURAGE: THE STORY OF ALVAR NUÑEZ CABEZA DE VACA* (1965)**

[*Odyssey of Courage* is a] vividly written description of the dramatic story of Cabeza de Vaca's two long visits to the New World in the sixteenth century. . . . The writing is authoritatively detailed, a bit weak in dialogue—not because it seems overly fictionalized but because it occasionally has phraseology that seems too modern. A bibliography is appended.

Zena Sutherland, in Bulletin of the Center for Children's Books *(copyright 1965 by the University of Chicago; all rights reserved), May, 1965, p. 139.*

Maia Wojciechowska . . . faces the facts [about the Spanish conquistadors] squarely in her brief, vigorous biography of the man who first explored much of the area that became the southern United States and who later served as Spanish Governor of Paraguay. . . .

Miss Wojciechowska has based most of her book on Cabeza de Vaca's own "Relation," from which she quotes often and effectively. She employs imaginary dialogue skillfully if sometimes fancifully. "Odyssey of Courage," part fact, part plausible fiction, makes a fascinating, often shocking story of one man's courage in the face of appalling physical hardships and human opposition.

Alden T. Vaughan, in The New York Times Book Review *(© 1965 by The New York Times Company; reprinted by permission), June 13, 1965, p. 29.*

OTHER CITATIONS

Mary Silva Cosgrave, in Book Week, *May 9, 1965 (Part 2), p. 35.*

***THE ROTTEN YEARS* (1971)**

Despite her obvious attempt to speak for contemporary young people in [*The Rotten Years*], Maia Wojciechowska succeeds only in tediously preaching at them. The barest essentials of characterization and plot are summarily disposed of in the first two chapters which introduce the protagonists. . . . Elsie Jones is clearly the vehicle for the author's beliefs and very obtrusive biases, and the rest—a militant mother who wants only black studies taught; foster parents whose charges "[mean] no more than a monthly check"; etc.—are clay pigeons set up to be shot down.

Pamela D. Pollack, in School Library Journal *(reprinted from the November, 1971, issue of* School Library Journal, *published by R. R. Bowker Co., a Xerox company; copyright © 1971 by Xerox Corporation), November, 1971, p. 127.*

Elsie Jones, age fifty-four, is a teacher who is the channel for the author's ideas on relationships, responsibilities, ethical values, etc. . . . [*The Rotten Years*] has some cohesive narrative at the beginning and the end, but is otherwise a long homily (showing deep concern for young people) punctuated by minimal action.

Zena Sutherland, in Bulletin of the Center for Children's Books *(© 1972 by the University of Chicago; all rights reserved), January, 1972, p. 83.*

***SHADOW OF A BULL* (1964)**

Miss Wojciechowska knows bullfighting and, more important, she is a magnificent writer. In spare, economical prose she makes one feel, see, smell the heat, endure the hot Andalusian sun and shows one the sand and glare of the bullring. Above all, she lifts the veil and gives glimpses of the terrible loneliness in the soul of a boy.

Perhaps the ending was ever so slightly contrived. But the whole is so good it does not detract from an eloquent, moving book, superbly illustrated by Alvin Smith, who surely knows the people of Spain.

John R. Tunis, in The New York Times Book Review *(© 1964 by The New York Times Company; reprinted by permission), March 22, 1964, p. 22.*

[*Shadow of a Bull* is a] story about bullfighting, written with a unity of scope and construction that is as unusual as is the subject. . . . The writing style is starkly simple, the prose having the flow of spoken Spanish with no obtrusive use of the bilingual. The book gives a great deal of information about bullfighting; the story has good characterization and a convincing detailed analysis of the boy's motivation and his conflict. A glossary of bullfighting terms is appended.

Zena Sutherland, in Bulletin of the Center for Children's Books *(copyright 1964 by the University of Chicago; all rights reserved), May, 1964, p. 148.*

No manifesto for or against bullfighting, [*Shadow of a Bull*] is a perceptive story, with a perfectly realized setting, of a boy torn between loyalty and the need to be himself. Rarely in a book for any age does one find such understanding of bullfighting background and the symbolic role of the *torero* (the "killer of death"), of the agonies of an adolescent boy longing to be understood and recognized for himself, and of the phenomenon of the oneness of viewpoint of all the people of a village.

Ruth Hill Viguers, in The Horn Book Magazine *(copyright © 1964, by The Horn Book, Inc.), June, 1964, pp. 293-94.*

In this somber tale, the author captures the rhythm of the Spanish people and the personal conflict of a young boy. Miss Wojciechowska's style reflects the austere grandeur of the Andalusian countryside. It is reminiscent of Hemingway, both in the knowledge of bullfighting and in the deceptively spare construction.

John Gillespie and Diana Lembo, in their Juniorplots: A Book Talk Manual for Teachers and Librarians *(© 1967 by the R. R. Bowker Co.), Bowker, 1967, p. 54.*

OTHER CITATIONS

Clayton E. Kilpatrick, in Library Journal, *March 15, 1964, p. 1470.*

Margaret Sherwood Libby, in Book Week, *May 10, 1964 (Part 2), pp. 4, 16.*

***A SINGLE LIGHT* (1968)**

Roughly the first half [of *A Single Light*] is the girl's story, and it has the undeniable heart-tug of a Jane Wyman movie at a more measured pace. With the advent of Larry Katchen, the American, the somber absorption is blasted into facetious fragments; although he has a chance to recover his humanity, the book never recovers even a sympathetic conviction. It becomes a crypto-parable that masticates love and morality into pulp.

Kirkus Service *(copyright © 1968 Virginia Kirkus' Service, Inc.), March 15, 1968, pp. 344-45.*

[*A Single Light*] is a legend imbued with the desperation of the human need for love. Its vivid setting is the harsh, gnarled landscape of Spanish Andalucia. . . . It concludes with a miracle of understanding and regeneration which some readers may find a little too pat.

Maia Wojciechowska's message of love and understanding is somewhat impaired by didacticism and over-simplification. And yet, although her new book is not entirely successful, it is a far better one than most, which are less ambitious and do succeed.

Edward Fenton, in Book World *(©* The Washington Post*), May 5, 1968 (Part 2), p. 22.*

Basically a parable, "A Single Light" is a message of love and need, hung round a deaf-and-dumb girl. . . . The unnamed girl's story is told in the simplest terms. As it moves to its climax, we see how her presence changes the lives of those around her. . . .

But the overtones in Maia Wojciechowska's book defy synopsis. The finale, in the hands of a less skillful craftsman, could have seemed overdone, even spurious. Here, it is both austere and moving. The whole tale moves and flows, like life. Hope for the future of man is its essence.

John R. Tunis, in The New York Times Book Review *(© 1968 by The New York Times Company; reprinted by permission), May 5, 1968 (Part 2), p. 3.*

The old theme of a handicapped child bringing about the regeneration of an embittered people is given original form and treatment [in *A Single Light*]. The direct and occasionally understated writing makes the story all the more poignant.

Ruth Hill Viguers, in The Horn Book Magazine *(copyright © 1968 by The Horn Book, Inc., Boston), June, 1968, p. 332.*

Told with controlled pathos, [*A Single Light* reveals] the plight of a young deaf and dumb girl. . . . The themes are the overwhelming human need for love and the possibility for even the meanest persons to change. Because of the appeal which these universal themes have for young people and the smooth and unobtrusive quality of the writing, the book should have a wide readership.

Bernice Levine, in School Library Journal *(reprinted from the September, 1968, issue of* School Library Journal, *published by R. R. Bowker Co., a Xerox company; copyright © 1968 by Xerox Corporation), September, 1968, p. 202.*

OTHER CITATIONS

Zena Sutherland, in Bulletin of the Center for Children's Books, *July-August, 1968, p. 183.*

***THROUGH THE BROKEN MIRROR WITH ALICE* (1972)**

A black Alice, kicked out of her twelfth foster home and with a "bee" buzzing inside her head (the result of witnessing the murders of her father and grandfather), steps through the looking glass and finds herself being fought over by the Black and White Queens. . . . Lest anyone miss the point, we are assured that "what Alice was actually doing was trying to survive a very difficult day by escaping into fantasy." A very difficult day indeed, and the pretentiously allegorical parade of stereotypes doesn't make it any easier.

Kirkus Reviews *(copyright © 1972 The Kirkus Service, Inc.), April 15, 1972, pp. 486-87.*

The theme [in "Through the Broken Mirror with Alice"] is Man Against Man; nature has already been eliminated and, as far as one can see, all good men, including fathers and grandfathers, have been killed off. . . . [This is a] bitter and clever book with the air of a "West Side Story."

Jean Fritz, in The New York Times Book Review *(© 1972 by The New York Times Company; reprinted by permission), April 23, 1972, p. 8.*

***TILL THE BREAK OF DAY* (1972)**

In reviewing her childhood and early adolescent years as a refugee from Poland during World War II, Maia Wojciechowska avoids the pious solemnity that might be expected and concentrates on the small personal encounters and responses that absorbed her at the time. . . . Though her reminiscences are not large enough to illuminate a people's experience of the war . . . or probing enough to break through her own fierce childhood defiance, they offer an individual view of how it was for one displaced child, determined to be herself even when that self is negatively defined.

Kirkus Reviews *(copyright © 1972 The Kirkus Service, Inc.), October 15, 1972, p. 1210.*

[Maia Wojciechowska's] reminiscences of the three turbulent years [in France during World War II] are intense and personal, emphasizing her own fears, ploys, loves and hatreds, so that [*Till the Break of Day*] is less a history of war and displacement than it is a journal of an emotional adolescent.

Zena Sutherland, in Bulletin of the Center for Children's Books *(© 1973 by the University of Chicago; all rights reserved), March, 1973, p. 116.*

Many of Maia's escapades and lucky breaks [in *Till the Break of Day*] will make the reader gasp. In describing herself Maia gives a true picture of the adolescent. Her obsession with ideals, death, love, self-hatred will strike a responsive chord. This is a book for everyone.

Shirley Weinstein, in Best Sellers *(copyright 1973, by the University of Scranton), April 15, 1973, p. 47.*

OTHER CITATIONS

The Booklist, *December 15, 1972, p. 407.*

***TUNED OUT* (1968)**

Tuned Out . . . is a tough, troubling book, in its terror for adults as well as children heightened by Miss Wojciechowska's considerable skill. To witness, as readers of this book must do, a boy struggling with a beloved older brother in the throes of a "trip" so bad he loses his mind, is horribly unforgettable.

The author is equally skillful in showing exactly the state of thought that might lead a youngster to drug experimentation.

Pamela Marsh, in The Christian Science Monitor *(reprinted by permission from* The Christian Science Monitor; *© 1968 The Christian Science Publishing Society; all rights reserved), November 7, 1968, p. B12.*

[*Tuned Out* is] a story of intensity and bleak honesty. . . . At times the writing slows, but this seems curiously appropriate in a story in which the stunned protagonist is fighting against time. [The book is candid], with no melodrama except the terrible melodrama of what is happening, and with a lack of didacticism that makes the message all the more effective.

Zena Sutherland, in Bulletin of the Center for Children's Books *(copyright 1969 by The University of Chicago; all rights reserved), February, 1969, p. 104.*

OTHER CITATIONS

Zena Sutherland, in Saturday Review, *November 9, 1968, p. 70.*

Jane Manthorne, in The Horn Book Magazine, *December, 1968, pp. 714-15.*

***WINTER TALES FROM POLAND* (1973)**

There is no overall tone or mood to unify the ten brief folk tales included [in *Winter Tales from Poland*], and it's hard to know what to make of the unfolksy opener, with its pointed putdown of people who are greedy or who distrust what is different, about a Polish poet-angel with clipped wings. . . . The flimsiest tale concerns an incompetent witch who falls in love; the one about a tailor so skinny he can only eat spaghetti is both funnier and more fully treated in Haviland's *Favorite Fairy Tales Told In Poland* (1964). Peripheral.

Kirkus Reviews *(copyright © 1972 The Kirkus Service, Inc.), December 1, 1972, p. 1358.*

These freely adapted and embellished Polish folk tales contain all of the elements familiar to folklore: the mixture of mysticism and common sense; the presence of angels and death in human guise; and, the testing of wits or virtue by riddles and dilemmas. . . . The vigor and humor of Borski and Miller's *The Jolly Tailor and Other Fairy Tales* (. . . 1957) are less evident here, where the balance falls to more somber themes. However, Wojciechowska effectively carries the cadence of folk telling, and this book is pleasant in style and content.

Gertrude B. Herman, in School Library Journal *(reprinted from the September, 1973, issue of* School Library Journal, *published by R. R. Bowker Co., a Xerox company; copyright © 1973 by Xerox Corporation), September, 1973, p. 136.*

Eight tales of mixed origins are included in a collection that is uneven in fidelity to the genre, although the stories are adequately told [by Maia Wojciechowska]. Some, like "How a Tailor Became a King," and "Seven Black Crows," have a folk quality; others, like "The Time of the Ugly" and "The Angel," have none.

Zena Sutherland, in Bulletin of the Center for Children's Books *(© 1973 by the University of Chicago; all rights reserved), October, 1973, p. 36.*

OTHER CITATIONS

Publishers' Weekly, *February 12, 1973, p. 68.*

CUMULATIVE INDEX TO AUTHORS

CUMULATIVE INDEX TO TITLES

CUMULATIVE INDEX TO CRITICS